Philosophical Approaches to Communication

Claude Mangion

intellect Bristol, UK / Chicago, USA

First published in the UK in 2011 by
Intellect, The Mill, Parnall Road, Fishponds, Bristol, BS16 3JG, UK

First published in the USA in 2011 by
Intellect, The University of Chicago Press, 1427 E. 60th Street,
Chicago, IL 60637, USA

Cover designer: Holly Rose
Copy-editor: Integra Software Services
Typesetting: Mac Style, Beverley, E. Yorkshire

ISBN 978-1-84150-429-2

Printed and bound by Gutenberg Press, Malta.

Contents

Introduction

The current interest in communication studies is understandable given the proliferation of communication technologies that are part and parcel of today's world. However, while this interest tends to focus on the media applications of communication technologies, the concept of communication that underlies these technologies remains unexamined. The purpose of this text is to provide an overview of the different aspects that are entailed by the concept of communication.

The early theories of communication adopted a relatively simple model to explain the process of communication. Known as the process or linear model of communication, it assumed a sender who transmitted a message to a receiver. In a slightly more complex version of this model, the sender encoded a message that was transmitted to the receiver who in turn decoded it to understand the message. Understanding the message entailed that the receiver would be able to understand what the speaker intended to mean when he/she communicated his/her message. Although popular, this model of communication is too simple as it fails to take into account the situation in which communication takes place. Communication is not an abstract activity dissociated from a context of conventions, rules or a way of life.

The goal of this book is to highlight the role of the context in the process of communication. Although the study of communication includes the domain of non-verbal communication (kinesics, paralanguage, proxemics, chronemics and haptics), I am focusing mainly on linguistic communication. However, in the case of C.S. Peirce and Umberto Eco, I will outline their accounts of perception insofar as these provide the basis for understanding their semiological theories.

The concept of communication has a number of characteristics: it always takes place within a context of production (Chapters 1–3), reception (Chapters 4–6) and action (Chapters 7–12). Although the writers I am focusing on tend to prioritize one characteristic over another, this is not to say that they ignore the other features. It is merely for the purpose of analysis that I have placed each writer in the category where I consider his work to be particularly influential. Some of the themes dealt with by these writers could be better placed within other categories. A general theory of communication would necessarily include all these characteristics in a comprehensive account.

Chapters 1 and 2 tackle the founding fathers of structuralism and semiology, these being F. de Saussure and C.S. Peirce, respectively. Saussure has tended to be the source of inspiration for Continental theorists, while Peirce has provided the intellectual background for American theorists. Nowadays, however, theorists of communication and philosophy cannot afford to ignore either of them, and in some ways they can be said to complement each other. One major difference between the two is that while Saussure focused exclusively on language as a system of signs, leaving the application of his insights to others, Peirce widened his theoretical enterprise and attempted to explain the nature of all signs, starting from the non-linguistic and culminating in the linguistic.

With Saussure's writings I examine the two basic principles for the study of language: the principle of the arbitrary nature of the sign and the principle of difference. The consequence of these principles is that language is no longer considered as representational, that is, as a mirror of the world, but as a system that constructs the world. The world does not come to us already neatly parcelled out, with language 'picturing' or representing it, but it is rather the network of differences that make up a language that in effect constitutes the world. To argue for his case on what the appropriate study of language should entail, Saussure introduces a number of conceptual distinctions, such as the distinction between *langue* and *parole*, value and signification, the synchronic and diachronic, and the syntagmatic and paradigmatic aspects of language. I end the chapter by showing the influence of Saussure's thought upon cultural studies, notably through the work of Roland Barthes.

The writings of Peirce examine the nature of signs from a different perspective. Whereas the background to Saussure's study of signs was that of linguistics, the background to Peirce is that of mathematics. From these he became convinced that the only way to understand a sign was by applying a triadic conception of Firstness, Secondness and Thirdness. A sign establishes a connection or what he calls an interpretant (Thirdness) between a quality (Firstness) and a thing (Secondness). In this chapter, I continue to develop Peirce's theory of signs together with the way in which basic signs can be combined into more complex ones. The chapter proceeds with an overview of Peirce's pragmatism that connects the meaning of a concept to its consequences and the method of dialogue in the production of knowledge. In the final section, I examine the possible relation between Peirce and journalism, media and communication studies.

In Chapter 3 I outline the views of Michel Foucault. Although not typically associated with communication studies, some of his views contribute interesting insights to the philosophy of communication. The first part of the chapter provides an in-depth description of the theory of discourse with the next sections describing Foucault's archaeological readings of the history of madness and knowledge. In these archaeological studies, emphasis is placed on discourse and epistemes. The next sections are marked by the shift from archaeology to the genealogical readings of incarceration and sexuality in Foucault's writings. In the genealogical writings Foucault moves away from an analysis of discourse to the relation between discourse and institutional sites. The context of discourse becomes important since it enables him to highlight the relationship between power and knowledge. I conclude this chapter by examining the way Foucault's ideas have been taken up within surveillance theory.

In Chapter 4 I turn my attention to Umberto Eco. I start with his generalized account of signs and codes as the foundation for the study of culture, and its development into a set of overlapping concepts, namely communication and signification. On Eco's account, while communication describes the transfer of information between machines, signification entails the insertion of humans into the process of communication. In the following sections I examine the concepts of abduction, the role of labour in the production of signs, and Eco's distinction between the dictionary and the encyclopaedia. After discussing this generalized theory of signs, I examine Eco's contribution to semiology and literary interpretation through the twin distinction between Model Authors and Model Readers, and Open and Closed texts. The last section of the chapter is an application of Eco's semiological theory to the James Bond novels.

In Chapter 5, I turn to the philosophy of Jacques Derrida and the philosophy of deconstruction. I first examine Derrida's critique of two popular accounts that consider language as either representing the world or expressing mental states. This is followed by a discussion of Derrida's deconstruction of the spoken–written contrast in the writings of Plato and Saussure. With these readings in mind, I then return to Derrida's analysis of language, where he develops the concept of meaning in terms of *différance* and his generalized notion of writing as arche-writing or grammatology. In the nest section, I examine both Derrida's engagement with speech act theory and the subsequent discussion with John Searle. The last section describes the possible contribution of deconstruction to film studies.

The hermeneutics of H.G. Gadamer is the topic of Chapter 6. As with deconstruction, hermeneutics is also concerned with the processes of interpretation. The first section of the chapter offers an account of Gadamer's interpretation of the history of hermeneutics in an attempt to show the historical displacement of hermeneutics by science. This is followed by Gadamer's critique of natural science as being the sole repository of truth that justifies its claims on the strength of the use of a specific method. Gadamer proposes an alternative account where prejudice and authority – tradition – are revived to counter the hegemony of science and its claim to truth. In the subsequent sections, I develop Gadamer's account of the understanding of the processes of interpretation in terms of what he calls the 'fusion of horizons'. The following two more sections deal first with interpretation as a form of dialogue that follows the model of question and answer, and the second with language as the very foundation of human existence. I end this section with an account of the way in which hermeneutics might be useful in intercultural communication.

In Chapters 7–12, I examine communication from the point of view of the things done or performed by participants in the act of communication. The point of departure is L. Wittgenstein, whose writings on language have had a profound influence on the developments in the philosophy of language. In his early writings Wittgenstein starts with a model of language that is restricted to the function of describing the world. Known as the Picture Theory of Language, Wittgenstein uses this model of language to distinguish between what can be said about the world and what cannot be said but shown. He eventually came to reject this distinction in his later work and replaces it with the distinction between describing and explaining. The new phase in Wittgenstein's thinking about language also leads to the introduction of the concept of language games and the critique of the Private Language Argument. The last section of this chapter offers an account of the way Wittgenstein can be utilized within film theory.

I start Chapter 8 with a discussion of J.L. Austin's theory of speech acts. Austin starts by drawing a sharp contrast between 'constative' and 'performative' utterances, that is, between statements that describe things or events and those whose utterance (in the right circumstances) is also a doing. He then comes to the realization that formulated in this way, the opposition is untenable. He therefore reconfigures performative and descriptive statements within the broader theory of speech acts. It should be pointed out that although it is customary to use the label 'speech act', this generic term subsumes all forms of communication, including writing and gestures. This chapter ends with an examination of the way speech act theory has been applied to discourse analysis.

In Chapter 9 I turn to P. Grice, whose work focuses on the study of language from the point of view of the speaker's intentions in the communication of meaning. After analysing both the role of the speaker's intention to mean something and the recognition of that intention in the act of communication, I go on to look at Grice's account of those contexts within which an utterance can be true, although misleading. This account anticipates Grice's later theory of the maxims of conversation and his reflections on conversation. In the following section of the chapter, I examine Grice's stance on the relation between logic and conversation, concluding the chapter with an account of the way Gricean ideas contribute to the understanding of humour.

In Chapter 10, I examine John Searle's elaboration of speech act theory, where he focuses on the intentions speakers have in communicating together with the rules that make the communication of such intentions possible. This elaboration of speech act theory takes as its point of departure an analysis of speech acts in terms of their reference and predication. Searle identifies the conditions that make speech acts possible as well as formulate a taxonomy that shows the difference between the various speech acts. This makes it possible to both classify speech acts and examine the more complex types. The next section describes Searle's discussion of the context – as a network and as a background – of speech acts followed by an account of the way language functions in the construction of social reality. In the final section I examine Searle's account of computer communication.

In Chapter 11 I focus on the writings of Jurgen Habermas, who places communication at the heart of his attempts to explain the way social order is maintained and society reproduced. I open the chapter with a detailed investigation of the processes involved in acts of communication and follow this up with an account of the way breakdowns in communication are repaired in discourse. The next sections examine the relation between communication and social theory with Habermas distinguishing between the different types of action (communicative, strategic and instrumental) as well as the lifeworld and the system. In the following section, I outline Habermas's analysis of communication within the narrower sphere of ethical discussion and conclude the chapter with a description of Habermas's account of political communication and the media.

The final chapter is an overview of M.A.K. Halliday's theorizing of language as a form of action within a context. I start by outlining the background influences of Malinowski and Firth, whose writings on the concept of context are central to Halliday. This is followed by an account of language that is utilized functionally within society. In the next section, I introduce the conceptual framework that Halliday considers necessary of a sociolinguistic theory of language. In the final section, I describe one of the ways Halliday's social semiotics has been further developed.

Chapter 1

Saussure on the Structure of Communication

Ferdinand de Saussure (1857–1913) is quite rightly considered to be the founder of structural linguistics, and his posthumously published work, *Course in General Linguistics* (1983), formulated the general principles for the scientific study of language. His goal was to establish the scientific credentials for the study of language so that linguistics would no longer be judged as 'speculative', and instead acquire a certain degree of prestige as a discipline.

In general, it could be said that Saussure revolutionized linguistics by proposing a new method for the study of language. This method focused on explaining the way language as a system functions to generate meanings that are subsequently communicated; it was the system used for communication – rather than the actual things communicated – that was prioritized. This insight into the workings of language led to the further realization that the model of language could also be used to understand the way non-linguistic systems function.

The influence of Saussure upon a number of key thinkers cannot be underestimated and his model was adopted by different generations of thinkers from a spectrum of disciplines such as structural philosophy (Foucault), structural literary theory (Barthes) and structural anthropology (Levi-Strauss). It is no exaggeration to claim that the structural revolution of the 1960s traces its origins to the *Course in General Linguistics*.

In this chapter, I shall outline (1) the innovations that distinguish Saussure's approach to the study of language from the historical and comparative approaches of his predecessors. In the next section, I shall introduce (2) Saussure's founding concepts on the arbitrary nature of the sign, followed by (3) the principle of difference. The final sections examine (4) the conceptual innovations that justify the status of linguistics as a science and (5) the applicability of Saussure's concepts to cultural studies.

Historical background

The context within which Saussure's study of language unfolded was dominated by two main ways of studying language: the first phase was that of comparative philology or comparative grammar that took as its starting point the work of Franz Bopp on Sanskrit in 1816; the second phase occurred around 1870 when questions concerning both the historical origin of words and methodology were raised.

Culler (1985: 53–70) points out that these developments in the study of language were themselves reactions to the theories proposed by the seventeenth-century Port Royal

Grammarians and the theorists of the eighteenth century. Both – for different reasons – justified the study of language on the grounds that by studying language it would be possible to understand human thought and consequently acquire a deeper understanding of the human mind. The Port Royal Grammarians considered language to be a picture or a mirror of thought, so that by studying language one would in fact be studying the laws of reason – laws that are common to all humans, and therefore universal. The underlying assumption was that speech and grammar had a rational foundation. Commenting on the Port Royal Grammarians, Saussure acknowledged their contribution to the study of language in their emphasis on the synchronic dimension of language (1983: 82).

The eighteenth-century theorists (e.g. Condillac) found the emphasis of the Port Royal Grammarians on the synchronic study of language unsatisfactory. They felt that the study of thought or reason first required knowing how ideas originated out of sensation. The search for origins informs the pattern of thinking of Western civilization in the eighteenth and nineteenth centuries; it was argued that to understand the nature of something – linguistic, political or psychological – one must discover its origins. In the case of language, the eighteenth century attempted to explain linguistic signs and abstract concepts by reducing them to their non-linguistic origins in gestures, actions and sensations. By understanding the origins of language it was believed that one could understand the nature of language, and therefore the nature of thought.

The nineteenth-century theorists of language rejected the concerns with language and mind. The word was no longer considered a sign that represented something, and linguistics turned to comparative studies. With Franz Bopp the object of study became the form of words, and by comparing forms in different languages a pattern was identified that would explain its historical evolution. The interest in comparing forms pertaining to different languages arose from the discovery of Sanskrit by European linguists who noticed a number of similarities among Sanskrit, Greek, Germanic and Latin. Instead of trying to find an original primitive meaning that would be the basis or foundation of different expressions, the goal of linguists became that of finding similarities across different languages. The identification of these similarities led to the realization that each language followed its own internal laws. Although Saussure appreciated the work of the comparative grammarians, he clearly states that they did not succeed in establishing linguistics on a scientific basis, since they failed to identify what it was they were studying and to recognize the implications of their own work (1983: 3).

There were two other major influences on Saussure. The first was the work of the Neo-Grammarians, who at around 1870 began to lay the foundations for the proper study of language.[1] The Neo-Grammarians argued that the laws that governed changes in sounds functioned without any exceptions. Culler explains

> [...] the principle at stake – of change without exceptions – is crucial, for reasons which perhaps none but Saussure understood. The absolute nature of sound change is a consequence of the arbitrary nature of the sign. Since the sign is arbitrary, there is no reason for a change in sound not to apply to all instances of that sound; whereas if sounds

were motivated ('naturally' expressive, like *bow-wow*) then there would be resistance, depending on the degree of motivation, and exceptions. There are no exceptions because, given the arbitrary nature of the sound and its phonetic realizations, change does not apply directly to signs themselves but to sounds, or rather, to a single sound in a particular environment. (1985: 65)

The second influence upon Saussure were the developments that took place after 1870 when the Neo-Grammarians attempted to establish the historical evolution of languages using the results of their comparative accounts. Their goal was therefore the historical reconstruction of a language, which although important did not satisfy Saussure, for it confused the synchronic with the diachronic aspect of language. By focusing excessively on historical reconstruction, the Neo-Grammarians did not understand the nature of what they were studying: in effect, they had forgotten to ask the question of how language functions. Saussure realized that by returning to the notion of the sign as representational, the crucial elements that would transform linguistics into a scientific study could be identified. However, his use of the concept of representation differed from that of the earlier eighteenth-century linguists, since it involved the sign as representing a particular meaning that differed from another meaning within the linguistic system.

Although comparative studies were the intellectual context within which Saussure was working, his work returned – with modifications – to the work of the eighteenth-century linguists (Culler 1985: 69–70). He reintroduced the study of language in terms of the study of signs, but instead of studying signs in isolation from each other he argued that signs can only be studied in relation to each other. Furthermore, his focus on the methodology needed for the study of language also reveals an indirect answer to the question concerning the connection between language and mind: the operating principle for the functioning of language as a system that generates meaning is its power to differentiate. And this process is not only an aspect of language, but is in fact a description of the way the mind operates so as to understand meaning.

The nature of language

Linguists, according to Saussure, had failed to establish what it was that they were trying to study (1983: 3). As a result of this failure, linguistics could never aspire to the status of a science and could therefore not achieve the respectability that it deserved. Saussure was determined to change this but he first needed to identify those features that are essential for the functioning of a language. The difference between a language and noise is that noise does not communicate anything whereas a language communicates meanings. In order to communicate meanings there must be a system to which the meanings belong, and since there is a system, there are a number of conventions that govern the way signs are used to communicate meanings. Language is therefore a system of signs.

To argue for the thesis of language as a system of signs – as opposed to language as a mirror or as representing the world – Saussure gives importance to rejecting the nomenclaturist theory of language. According to this view, the meaning of a word is the object that it names, so that the relationship between a word and an object is one of naming or labelling. The biblical narrative of Genesis which portrays Adam as naming the objects of the world shows how deeply ingrained within our cultural psyche this view of language is. This view presupposes that there is a radical separation between language and the world: objects – whether material (table, dog) or abstract (love, happiness) – exist independently of language and are named by it.

There are several difficulties with this theory. For a start, the most obvious one is that if this theory were true, then translating from one language to another would be a relatively easy task: all one would have to do is change the words from one language to another. But anyone who remembers his/her translation exercises at school will remember that it was a difficult task because each language had a different way of talking about the world. For example, if one had to translate the French word *aimer* into English, one would have to see the sense in which it is being used, for *aimer* can mean either 'to love' or 'to like' in English. Another difficulty with nomenclatures is the way they ignore the passage of time: according to this view, the name or label changes over time but the meaning or concept remains the same. The concepts, as language-independent entities, would be immune to historical evolution. But in actual fact the history of language is full of both concepts changing their meanings and words changing their form. The word *silly* used to refer to a happy and blessed person, but with time the meaning changed and in the sixteenth century it referred to an innocent and helpless person. Today the word *silly* is used to refer to a foolish person. And just as the concept changed its meaning, the name also changed with its central vowel modified (Culler 1985: 22).

The sign

What Saussure's criticism of language as naming shows is that the relationship between words and meaning is not as clear-cut as one might have presupposed. It is in this light that we can perhaps understand the introduction of the terminology of 'signs' by Saussure to the study of language. His use of the term is narrower than the way it is used in everyday life, as when, for example, we say that the dark clouds are a sign of the approaching rain. Saussure uses the term *sign* to mean the combination of a sound (a spoken word) or graphic inscription (a written word) together with a concept or a meaning. Although Saussure uses the terminology *signification* and *signal*, contemporary writers have replaced these terms with *signified* and *signifier*, respectively. I am following this practice.

Although for the purpose of analysis these two components can be differentiated, it should be pointed out that they can never be found to be independent of each other. Within a language, a sound or graphic inscription always has a concept or meaning attached to it.

Saussure pointed out that for the linguist it was the psychological aspect of communication that should be given absolute priority, that is, the meaning that speakers want to communicate rather than the sounds produced. By analogy, Saussure argued that the instrument used to transmit the Morse code was secondary to what was communicated. Despite the emphasis on language as a tool for communication in general, Saussure goes on to privilege the spoken medium over the written one. This is odd because, given his claim that the medium is not important, then both the spoken and the written word should be on an equal footing. Derrida (Chapter 5) will later seize upon this inconsistency.

Saussure's fundamental contribution to the study of language is the principle of the arbitrary nature of the sign. By 'arbitrary', Saussure claims that there is no intrinsic or necessary reason as to why a particular sound is connected to a particular concept. This is why the connection is described as 'arbitrary': the signifier *long* has nothing long about it, just as there is nothing dog-like about the signifier *dog*; and just as *cactus* means a particular type of vegetation, there is no reason why this vegetation could not have been called anything else. There is nothing in the vegetation, no essential property that obliges a person to call it with a particular signifier; it could be equally called 'toots' or 'plat' so long as communication between members of the community is successful. This latter point is important, for despite the arbitrary connection between signifier and signified, Saussure insists that there is no question of a person changing the meaning of a sign at-will happening (as Humpty Dumpty does in *Alice in Wonderland*). It is the linguistic community, not the person, that has the power to change the meaning of signs; arbitrary does not mean an individualistic free for all.

The only possible exceptions to the principle of the arbitrary constitution of the sign are those of (1) onomatopoeic words, where the sound is similar to the meaning, so that the signifier *cookoo* means or represents the bird because the bird produces the sound; (2) interjections: when, as a result of some injury, a person says 'ouch', the sound is a natural production. Saussure rejects both: in the case of onomatopoeic words, there are too few to even remotely make up a language (and even the naturally produced sound is an approximation); and the fact that there are so few reinforces the arbitrary thesis. Interjections are dismissed outright without consideration.

By arguing for the arbitrary nature of language, Saussure realizes that he has placed the study of language on a non-rational foundation. To counter the tendency of equating the arbitrary with individual, Saussure reiterates the fact that languages are a historically constituted social institution. It is therefore up to him to explain both how changes occur and why languages are relatively stable. Saussure offers four reasons that account for the stability of language:

1. Since the sign is arbitrary and therefore non-rational, there can be no (rational) discussion about whether to change it or not:

   One can, for example, argue about whether monogamy is better than polygamy, and adduce reasons for and against [...] But for a language, as a system of arbitrary signs, any such basis is lacking, and consequently there is not firm ground for discussion. No reason can be given for preferring *soeur* to *sister*, *Ochs* to *boeuf*, etc. (1983: 73)

2. The sheer number of signs within the linguistic system makes it difficult to change:

> A system of writing, comprising between 20 and 40 letters, might conceivably be replaced in its entirety by an alternative system. The same would be true of a language if it comprised only a limited number of elements. But the inventory of signs in any language is countless. (1983: 73)

3. The fact that the system can only be understood by 'experts' means that the masses are unaware of it and cannot therefore change it:

> Any such change would require the intervention of specialists, grammarians, logicians, and others. But history shows that interference by experts is of no avail in linguistic matters. (1983: 73)

4. As an institution language differs from all others: while institutions require the involvement of a certain number of people, language is used by everybody. It is hard to get everybody to change a language, but it is even harder to get an individual to change an aspect of it:

> Legal procedures, religious rites, ships' flags, etc. are systems used only by a certain number of individuals acting together and for a limited time. A language, on the contrary, is something in which everyone participates all the time, and that is why it is constantly open to the influence of all. This key fact is by itself sufficient to explain why a linguist revolution is impossible. Of all social institutions, a language affords the least scope for such enterprise. It is part and parcel of the life of the whole community, and the community's natural inertia exercises a conservative influence upon it. (1983: 74)

However, given that the reasons for the stability of language are so compelling, explaining change turns out to be a rather difficult task, and in this respect Saussure's reasons are quite weak. It is again the arbitrary nature of the sign that accounts for change:

> A language is a system which is intrinsically defenseless against the factors which constantly tend to shift relationships between signal [signifier] and signification [signified]. This is one of the consequences of the arbitrary nature of the linguistic sign. (1983: 76)

Saussure does introduce a limitation upon the principle of the arbitrariness of the sign, because without any limitation there would be chaos rather than a functioning linguistic system. Arbitrariness in language is limited by the fact that as a system, language is a complex and sophisticated phenomenon, and this cannot be the result of complete arbitrariness. Holdcroft argues that this justification is weak, for the fact that a sign is constructed systematically does not make it any less arbitrary (Holdcroft 1991: 93–94).

Although Saussure was aware of the radical implications of his view on the arbitrary nature of signs, it was only in the 1950s that these implications became central tenets to a number of different disciplines. One could say that Saussure is the precursor of the movement broadly known as constructivism, for, on his account, language constructs or organizes reality rather than reflect or name what is already articulated or categorized. This is why, for example, the English word *river* means a large moving body of water, whereas the French word *fleuve* means both a moving body of water and the entry of the water into the sea. The point is that each language constructs or organizes the world differently.

Identity and difference

Given Saussure's argument on the arbitrary connection between the signifier and the signified, how does language function as a medium for communication? How is it that both the signifier and the signified can be identified as the same despite variations in, for example, tone of voice? A word or sentence might be uttered with a different tone of voice and yet be identified as the same word or sentence. The innovative solution that Saussure offers is that the identity of the sound (signifier) or the meaning (signified) is established relationally or negatively by a process of difference.

In the case of signifiers, the phoneme – or the basic unit of sound – is recognized because it differs from other sounds within the linguistic system. The letter /b/ can be pronounced in a number of ways and would still be identified as /b/ as long as the different pronunciation does not overlap into the letter /p/. The extent to which a signifier is considered identical depends on its not being confused with another signifier; in other words, a sound can be considered functionally significant in a language only to the extent that it can be contrasted with other sounds from the spectrum of sounds within that same language.

The argument from difference also holds for signifieds: the meaning of a signified depends on its being different from other signifieds within the linguistic system. A signified has an identity constructed out of its relations to other signifieds, so that the meaning of 'man' is 'not woman', 'not boy', 'not lady', 'not youth' and so on. What is important in understanding the signified *man* is not to find some essential property or characteristic that belongs to all men, but to know that 'man' is the product of a system of distinctions. The linguistic system that Saussure proposes constitutes a flexible grid between signs, but one where the borders are precisely established by their negations. Saussure is helpful in elaborating this crucial point by using the game of chess as an analogy. How do we know the significance of each piece? We know the significance of the king neither because it is made of wood or of plastic nor because it is bigger than the other pieces. Rather, the identity of the king is established because we know the value of the king within the game of chess. This value is that of being able to move one square in any direction (and being defeated only by being checkmated) as opposed to, for example, the queen, who can move in any direction and for any distance (and who can be killed without the game being lost). And just as the king has an identity in relation to the queen, the meaning of the king is also established in relation to the other pieces.

Holdcroft (1991: 125) clarifies that the differences between terms in a relation are different in respect of something, but it must be emphasized that not all differences necessarily give rise to an opposition. The terms *dog* and *table* are different but not opposed to each other. The emphasis is on belonging to the same domain: if one says 'x is a male', then clearly 'x is not a female'. These terms exhaust the gender domain but not all terms within domains are necessarily exhausted: if one says 'x is not Monday', it could imply any other day of the week. The point is that not all differences give rise to opposites, but those differences that do are significant, for otherwise there would be an endless number of differences without significance. To have differences that are opposed to each other, the binary set must have some underlying similarity. Thus, while 'man' and 'woman' are opposed, they are similar in that they are both human.

So far, most of the examples used to describe the relational aspects of signs have involved words, and this might lead one into thinking that Saussure's theory applies solely to vocabulary. However, he points out that the relational aspect also applies to the grammar of language, so that the difference between a word in the singular and a word in the plural is precisely a relational distinction: the singular *night* assumes its identity in opposition to the plural *nights* (1983: 120).

In sum, the identity of a sign is the product of its differential relations within a linguistic system. This is why Saussure claims that 'in a language there are only differences, with *no positive terms*' (1983: 118). On this account, language is a system of signs that refer to each other; these are locked in a (relatively) stable network of contrasts that give them their vocal and conceptual identity. And while all differences are relational, it is not necessarily the case that all relations are differential. Saussure had used the example of a train timetable to argue for the differential nature of the sign. Just as a train has a place in a timetable that opposes it to another train (the 8: 15 train to Zurich as opposed to the 8: 30 train to Zurich), a sign has a place in the linguistic system that opposes it to other signs (1983: 107).[2]

Key concepts

Langue and *parole*

Although it is common to think that speech is natural to humans, Saussure argues that it is not the spoken word that is natural to humans, but rather the 'faculty' of language, for it is this faculty that explains the possibility of learning a language at all. Clearly, Saussure distinguishes between natural language (the faculty of language), a particular language (*langue*) and speech (*parole*). The latter two are subsumed within the category of natural language:

> [l]inguistic structure [langue] is only one part of language, even though it is an essential part. The structure of a language is a social product of our language faculty. At the same time, it is also a body of necessary conventions adopted by society to enable members of society to use their language faculty. (1983: 9–10)

Langue is the system of rules that the individual absorbs as he/she learns a language; it is the inherited body of linguistic knowledge that enables the continued existence of the community. *Parole*, on the other hand, is the externalization of this internalized system: it is the expression of the individual's thoughts through a physical medium, that is, the larynx. The importance of the *langue–parole* distinction lies in the fact that it provides Saussure with the possibility of identifying the proper object of the scientific study of language. The analysis of *parole* cannot constitute a science, for it is not about what one should know so as to claim that one knows a language. Rather, knowledge of a language involves knowing the rules that enable a speaker to combine words in the language. Again, the analogy taken from the game of chess is fruitful. To learn how to play chess it is not necessary to observe and study every move that was played in the history of chess, but, more importantly, one must learn the rules that enable each piece to move in the game.

However, although *langue* constitutes the primary object of linguistic study, the importance of *parole* should not be underestimated. There are three reasons for this importance: (1) *parole* as face-to-face communication enables language to get consolidated into a social system; (2) *parole* describes the free choice with regard to the word selection that the speaker is permitted from within the available system; (3) *parole* shows how changes can take place within *langue*, in effect performing the 'double' function of providing an explanation for the relative stability of the linguistic system, but also of its openness and possibility of change.

The utility of distinguishing between *langue* and *parole* can be seen in the way each has developed into a separate branch of the linguistic study of sound. *Langue* has developed into the discipline of phonology, while *parole* has developed into the discipline of phonetics. In the case of the latter, it is the actual physical event that is considered important, while in the case of the former, what is studied is the functional difference among signifiers within the linguistic system. The same point can be applied to 'meaning': a sentence establishes its meaning in relation to other sentences (*langue*), but two utterances (*parole*) of the same sentence might have a different meaning on account of their tone and context.

Synchronic and *diachronic*

It is obvious that language is continually in evolution and is subject to historical and contingent forces. These changes make it difficult to pinpoint what it is we are supposed to study in language, and yet Saussure argues that such a study is both possible and necessary. To explain the effect of time and history upon a language he introduces a distinction between synchronic and diachronic linguistics.

The situation with the study of language is paradoxical: if signs are historical – the product of a community at a particular time – then how is it possible to study language as a (relatively) stable system that enables communication to take place? To put this another way, if a language is evolving and changing, how is its functioning to be studied? The solution is to conduct an ahistorical analysis; in other words, to transform language into an object of study one must 'step outside' language and then observe it. Despite the element of change that a language undergoes, it must be 'frozen' in time so that the relations between signs within the system can be studied. The synchronic study of language focuses precisely on the interrelationship between signs at a particular moment within the linguistic system. In effect, this is another result of the arbitrary nature of the sign. Since there is no essential or necessary meaning that is inherent in a sign, and since the meaning is derived from its relationships to other signs, then it is the way signs function within the total system at a given moment that enables them to be studied: 'a language is a system of pure values, determined by nothing else apart from the temporary state of its constituent elements' (1983: 80).

Saussure describes the difference between synchronic and diachronic linguistics:

Synchronic linguistics will be concerned with logical and psychological connections between coexisting items constituting a system, as perceived by the same collective consciousness.

Diachronic linguistics on the other hand will be concerned with connections between sequences of items not perceived by the same collective consciousness, which replace one another without themselves constituting a system. (1983: 98)

The two domains are mutually exclusive, and for Saussure it was synchronic linguistics that had absolute priority. Synchronic linguistics constituted the scientific study of language, since it entailed the study of the psychologically real units of the linguistic system as opposed to diachronic linguistics, which studied the successive relations or evolutionary development of linguistic units. The latter is irrelevant to the study of language, so much so that it is from synchronic statements that diachronic statements can be derived. It is not changes in sounds that lead to changes in the system, but rather the other way round. When a signifier acquires a new phonetic association, the old form and the new form differ but are used interchangeably by speakers. From a phonological point of view, they retain the same functional identity within the synchronic system, but over time one of the forms is dropped even though the synchronic system that supports that form remains the same. Diachronic changes can only be explained with in relation to a series of successive synchronic systems.

When it comes to explaining the origins of change, Saussure realizes that changes take place in *parole*, in the actual performance of language. The linguistic system reacts and adjusts to these changes. Clearly it is not the system that causes the changes, but in order to understand change one needs to know the synchronic system. The point that Saussure vehemently opposes is the idea that there is an intrinsic goal towards which change in language is directed, that is, a teleological movement of language. When a language changes from one state to another it is not the result of some goal, but the result of a reaction to changes that happen outside language. It cannot be claimed that language changes from one state to another in progressive evolutionary steps.

While Saussure uses morphological and grammatical examples to explain the way the linguistic system adjusts to changes, he admits that it is much harder to explain semantic changes. Culler (1985) offers an explanation:

> Suppose one were studying the change in the meaning of Kunst in Middle High German between roughly 1200 and 1300. What would be synchronic and what diachronic here? To define change of meaning one needs two meanings and these can only be determined by considering synchronic facts: the relations between signifieds in a given state of the language which define the semantic area of 'kunst'. At an early state it was a higher, courtly knowledge or competence, as opposed to lower, more technical skills ('list'), and a partial accomplishment as opposed to the synoptic wisdom of 'wisheit'. In a later stage the two major oppositions which defined it were different: mundane versus spiritual ('Wisheit') and technical ('wizzen') versus non-technical. What we have are two different organizations of a semantic field. A diachronic statement would be based on this synchronic information, but if it were to explain what happened to 'kunst' it would have to refer to non-linguistic factors or causes (social changes, psychological processes, etc.) whose effects happened to have repercussions for the semantic system. For the analysis of language the relevant facts are the synchronic oppositions. The diachronic perspective treats individual filiations which are identifiable only from the results of synchronic analysis. (p. 44)

However, it should be mentioned that although Saussure favoured the synchronic approach to the study of language, it would be inaccurate to say that he dismissed nineteenth-century historical linguistics entirely, because he also attempted to develop a methodology for both historical and comparative linguistics.

Syntagmatic and *paradigmatic*

While we have spoken so far about the relational aspect of signs within the synchronic linguistic system, this relational aspect is developed by Saussure into a further set of concepts: the syntagmatic and the paradigmatic (or associative). The difference between the two is that syntagmatic relations involve a 'horizontal' axis of meaning whereas the paradigmatic involves a 'vertical' axis of meaning.

> Syntagmatic relations hold *in praesentia*. They hold between two or more terms co-present in a sequence. Associative relations, on the contrary, hold *in absentia*. They hold between terms constituting a mnemonic group. (1983: 122)

Syntagmatic relations occur when elements can be combined sequentially. Saussure uses *re-read* and *God is good* as examples (1983: 121); in the case of the first utterance both items are syntagmatically related to each other, while in the case of the second, *is* is related to both *God* and *good*. On the other hand, paradigmatic relations occur when there are similarities of form and meaning, of which Saussure outlines three instances (1983: 124).

1. The sign *teaching* is associated with 'to teach' and 'we teach', so there is a common or similar element between the idea or concept and the signifier.
2. The sign might be associated with a series such as verbs with the *-ing* ending (gerunds), such as *singing, laughing*, etc.
3. The sign might be associated with a series that has a similar meaning, such as *lecturing, educating* and *teaching*.

It is clear that the way the series is constructed differs according to what is being compared. Series (2) is constructed according to the grammatical structure of the sign, while series (3) is constructed according to the contrast between the similarities of meaning.

The problem with Saussure's views on paradigmatic and syntagmatic relations is that while he is clear on the paradigmatic relations' belonging to the domain of *langue*, he is unclear about the position of syntagmatic relations. But if we recall Saussure's claim that paradigmatic and syntagmatic relations are mutually interdependent, then the conclusion would be that they both belong to *langue*. The interdependence of the syntagms and the paradigms within the field of *langue* is further highlighted by Saussure's example of the syntagm *un-do*, which is a combination of *un-* and *do*, but is also paradigmatic in its contrastive relation to other possibilities such as *unpick*. These processes can be described in the following way: in the case of syntagms there is a relation of combination where one combines elements together; in the case of paradigms there is a relation of selection where one chooses one element instead of another.

While the analysis of syntagmatic and paradigmatic associations has so far concentrated on words, it would be a mistake to think that Saussure restricted his analysis to phonemes and morphology. These relations were also applied at the syntactic level. While the uttering of a sentence would clearly belong to the domain of *parole*, it was also clear that the analysis of sentences belonged to the domain of langue. The same relations of combination and selection take place within sentences; in a syntagmatic relation, words can be combined to produce a sentence and the meaning is not evident until the final word has been uttered. To know the meaning of the sentence *the cat sat on the [...]* we must wait until we hear or read the last word, *mat*; with this word the sentence is complete and its meaning is generated. Syntagmatic relations are spatial ones with one word following the other. But it is also important to note that not all possibilities can be realized: it is not possible to say 'the cat sat on the sea' or 'the cat grumbled'. Knowing the syntagmatic possibilities influences our paradigmatic choices. Paradigmatic relations differ from syntagmatic ones in that each individual word in a sentence is selected by the speaker out of a series of potential words. In the sentence *the cat sat on the mat*, the speaker might select *rat* or *dog* instead of *cat*, or *table* instead of *mat*. The sentence context conditions the choices that are possible for the speaker, and – depending on what is selected – a different meaning is generated. The paradigmatic relations of sentences show that the meaning of a sign is constituted by what is absent. The sign *cat* is present while the other signs that could replace it are absent from the sentence and yet are part of the linguistic system that makes the sign *cat* possible.

Value and *signification*

Another set of concepts that Saussure introduces are those of value and signification: while the value of a sign is determined by its place within the linguistic system, 'signification' does not refer to the functioning of the linguistic system, but to the way it connects to the world. The difference between value and signification is derived from the distinction between *langue* and *parole*: values are the elements that acquire an identity within langue, while signification describes the relationship between the utterance and the world. In the case of signification, it is the 'extra' linguistic element that comes into play.[3]

Saussure explains the difference between meaning and value when he describes the difference between the English sentence *I saw a sheep* and the French sentence *J'ai vu un mouton*. The two sentences are the same in terms of their signification, in the way that they both refer to a particular animal in the world. Signification describes the speaker's relation to a state of affairs in the world. But the value of the terms *sheep* and *mouton* differs within the English and French languages: in the case of English, when sheep are eaten the meat is called mutton, while in the case of French, *mouton* means two things – the meat itself and the animal (1983: 114).

Saussure and cultural studies

One of the clearest examples of the way Saussure's ideas on semiology were utilized can be seen in *Mythologies* (1993) by Roland Barthes (1915–80). This text is one of the founding texts of cultural studies and it consists of a number of articles published under the title of 'Mythology of the month' for the journal *Les Lettres Nouvelles* together with a theoretical piece called 'Myth Today'. While the articles are readings of many different facets of contemporary culture the latter theoretical piece is an elaboration of the method employed for these readings. Although Barthes situates the methodological explanation in the second half of the text, I am reversing the sequence to show his appropriation and elaboration of Saussurean methodology.

Saussure had argued that a sign is composed of a signifier and a signified so that the sign 'Coca Cola' is composed of a signifier 'Coca Cola' and a signified 'fuzzy brown drink'. This level of signification constitutes a first level system in so far as it utilizes the basic resources to generate the meaning. Barthes introduces a second level of meaning so as to account for the production of mythology: this second level is 'parasitic' on the first and functions by transforming the sign of the first-order system into a new signifier so as to carry a new meaning: 'myth is a peculiar system, in that it is constructed from a semiological chain which existed before it: it is a *second-order semiological system*. That which is a sign (namely the associative total of a concept and an image) in the first system becomes a mere signifier in the second' (1993: 114). In some advertisements the signifier Coca Cola is associated with a new signified such as freedom or youth.

In 'Myth Today' Barthes offers a number of examples of the way the transformation from the first level to the second level takes place. The first of these is taken from Paul Valéry and it describes (1993: 115–16) a schoolboy who reads the phrase *quia ego nominor leo* from his Latin grammar book. The Latin phrase means 'because my name is lion', but while the phrase itself tells the reader nothing about lions it does provide him/her with information about the grammatical rule concerning predicates. This is the second-order meaning that Barthes calls 'signification' and it functions by utilizing the first-order meaning to communicate its information. In the second example, Barthes describes the image of a black French soldier on the cover of the magazine *Paris-Match*. The first-order meaning is that of a soldier saluting the French flag; it is what can be literally described, that is, the colours, location, uniform and regiment that make up the photo. But another meaning or signification is being generated by the image: this is the idea of France as a gentle colonizing power that is beloved by the people it is colonizing to such an extent that they are willing to serve under the French flag; in effect, the image is justifying French colonial policies. This is the ideological meaning of the image: it is transforming a historical situation (colonization) into a natural one, making it seem only natural (and right) for France to colonize other countries.

The interesting point is that while a myth functions at a second-order level, the first-order level of meanings is still there to be read. If one points to the ideological effect of myth (patriotism), the answer might be that there is only an image of an individual soldier; if one goes on to ask for information about that particular soldier then the answer would be that the details of that soldier's life (origin, biography) are not the point of the image but rather what it signifies. There is an inherent doubleness in all myth, and while this might make a critique of ideology difficult, the promise of semiology was that such a critique is possible.

However, Barthes is also aware of the power of recuperation of bourgeois ideology. It was not the first time that cultural formations (e.g. the avant-garde) that attempted to destabilize bourgeois culture are accommodated within it. The only available strategy for Barthes in the years following *Mythologies* was that of adopting a guerrilla-like practice that was constantly on the move, resisting those attempts at 'taming' semiology by constantly revising his terminology so as to pre-empt any attempt at fixing his thought.

I have already pointed out that in the first part of *Mythologies* Barthes uses his semiological method to read a number of cultural phenomena that were in vogue in the 1950s. His target remains, as it was in *Writing Degree Zero*, bourgeois culture which had presented objects and values that were the product of human history, that is, situated at a certain moment in time, as though they were natural.

> The starting point of these reflections was usually a feeling of impatience at the sight of the 'naturalness' with which newspaper, art and commonsense constantly dress up a reality which, even though it is the one we live in, is undoubtedly determined by history. (1993: 11)

This process of transforming history or culture into nature is one way that the concept of ideology is defined. And by saying that things or values are natural, one is attributing a certain 'power' to them in that others can be obliged to do as one wants because the 'natural' is equated with the 'good'. This is Barthes's exposure of bourgeois culture in that it imposed the values that it claimed were natural (its own) onto other classes of society.

Myths are ideological and the several readings Barthes offers reveal the different ways in which these ideological processes play out. In 'The Romans in Film' (1993: 26–28), Barthes describes how in the film *Julius Caesar* there is a fringe in the hairstyles of the actors that was not a Roman feature but was added to create an illusion of 'Romanness'. In 'Soap-Powders and Detergents' (1993: 36–38), Barthes shows how certain substances are imbued with certain ideological meanings within a culture. The soap-powder Persil and the detergent Omo are both produced by the same company that has created an elaborate system of classification of the differences between them. The powder of Persil, functioning like a policing agent, liberates clothes from stains, while Omo penetrates clothes to wage its war on dirt. And in 'Wine and Milk' (1993: 58–61), Barthes illustrates the way wine is equated with being French, functioning as a marker of French identity. This entails showing how drinking wine is considered natural in France, which further entails showing that in France it is never associated with the desire to get drunk or with crime. Interestingly Barthes further goes on to argue that the mythology of wine in France succeeds at the expense of others: in Algeria, Muslims use their land to produce wine that they are in turn not allowed to drink. That they continue to produce wine is a sign of the colonization that Barthes frequently highlights. Finally, in 'The Poor and the Proletariat' (1993: 39–41) Barthes turns to a Franciscan monk, Abbé Pierre, who had been a media celebrity in Paris for his work among the poor and the homeless. However, instead of analysing the good works of Abbé Pierre, Barthes concentrates on his haircut, which he argues enables the Abbé to be associated with sainthood. What Barthes objects to is not the Abbé, but to the way the reality of poverty and homelessness has been replaced by the iconography of the Abbé. Instead of challenging the capitalist-bourgeois system that led to these social conditions, the media have been content to 'substitute with impunity the signs of charity for the reality of justice' (1993: 49).

Critical remarks

The work of Saussure has not passed without critical examination and a number of objections have been raised with regard to his work. One particular objection concerns the connection between the linguistic system on the one hand and the non-linguistic world on the other. Saussure provides no account of the way these two different realms are connected together. Fiske (1990: 44) points out that Saussure neglected this aspect, concentrating more on the intralinguistic relationship between terms, while the semiology of C.S. Pierce (Chapter 2) explained this connection. In addition, Culler (1985: 33) defends Saussure on this point, arguing that the distinction between signification and value was intended to show that there were two kinds of meaning, a relational one where the meaning or value of a term is defined by its place in the linguistic system, and a meaning that is the result of signification where the meaning depends upon the context of actualization of utterances.

There are also problems with Saussure's 'internal' account of language. Peter Serracino Inglott (1995: 72–75) argues that explaining the nature of language as a self-enclosed system of signs does not necessarily entail excluding reference to the world and that the Saussurean model leads to the more serious difficulty of explaining the way language is learnt. Strinati (1995: 94–95) also points out that the Saussurean distinction between *langue* and *parole* is inadequate, for it assumes that *langue* represents the social dimension of language while *parole* represents the individual use of language. The problem is that Saussure places speech and writing on the side of *parole* and it is obvious that these are also social and not individual phenomena; it was also Saussure who recognized that the only way to learn about the rules of *langue* was indirectly through *parole*. As Strinati points out, it is not possible to understand *langue* independently of *parole*, that is, of its particular uses.

Others such as the Marxist critic Volosinov lament the total lack of recognition of the role of ideology in Saussure's theory of language, particularly his concept of *langue*. In opposition to Saussure's view of *langue* as a stable system, that is, the condition of the possibility of meaning, Volosinov argues that meaning is produced in the process of ideological struggle: meaning is the site of a contestation among groups, differing in class, race, profession, gender and so on. There is no homogenous structure of language that produces the same meanings within a society, but rather a number of different groups that read different meanings into signifiers. And this has important consequences, for the meaning associated with a signifier can have a significant effect on the actions and behaviour of these groups (in Schirato and Yell 2000: 26).

Despite these criticisms, Saussure's theory of signs rightly highlights the centrality of context in the production of meaning. In the process of understanding the way meaning is generated, Saussure's analysis of language highlighted the social dimension of language: insofar as the members of a community use units of meaning to communicate between each other, then this community has constructed a system of signs, each of which has a distinct meaning precisely for this purpose.

In this chapter, I have outlined (1) the historical background within which Saussure develops his linguistics, and followed this with (2) an examination of the nature of the sign and (3) the underlying principles that account for the generation of meaning. The rest of the chapter is taken up with (4) the conceptual distinctions introduced by Saussure and with the way (5) his innovative ideas have become central to the semiological analysis of the cultural domain.

Notes

1. The Neo-Grammarians Hermann Osthoff and Karl Brugman wrote, 'every sound change, in as much as it occurs mechanically, takes place according to laws that admit no exception. That is, the direction of the sound shift is always the same for all members of the linguistic community except where a split into dialects occurs; and all the words in which the sound subjected to the change appears in the same relationship are affected by the change without exception (in Culler 1985: 65).
2. Holdcroft (1991: 97) uses this analogy to argue that if a train needs to connect with another train to reach its destination, this is clearly a case of a relationship that is not differential but rather a positive one, precisely the opposite of what Saussure claims.
3. Using an economic model, Saussure makes two claims about the way something is given a value: first, if two dissimilar things have an equal value they can be exchanged so that, for example, one can buy a magazine or a sandwich for 2 Euro; secondly, if two things have an equal value then they can be compared, so that ten Euro can be exchanged for 16 US dollars (1983: 113). In the case of language, a word can also be exchanged with another word or idea, or it can be compared to other words. But to know the value of the word, one must be able to relate it to other words within the linguistic system. The possibility of exchanging a word with another word can only be realized if one can compare and contrast it to other words. It is clear that the value of a sign is the result of the syntagmatic and paradigmatic relations between signs within langue.

Chapter 2

Peirce on the Life of Signs

Charles Sanders Peirce (1839–1914) was a philosopher and logician whose writings range across a number of different areas of philosophy – from perception to science, metaphysics and religious experience. However, the questions that really interested him were those concerning meaning and reference, and his theory of signs or semiotics offered a framework that accounted for them. The centrality of semiotics to his philosophical writings cannot be understated, and Peirce claimed that the only way he could approach these philosophical subjects was through semiotics. Unlike Saussure, who focused solely on linguistic signs and their binary relations, Peirce's theory of signs and its triads were applied to both linguistic and natural realms.

Peirce's general theory of signs grew over the years – from the basic triads into a classification of ten signs, and ultimately into a complex one of 66 kinds of signs, which through various combinations led to 59,049 types of signs. The latter system is highly sophisticated and it is not the point of this chapter to delve into the details of that typology. The domain of Peirce's theory of signs is composed of 'speculative grammar', 'critical logic' and 'speculative rhetoric'. Speculative grammar deals with the formal conditions of signs; while critical logic concerns the relations of signs to objects, raising the question of truth, speculative rhetoric studies the necessary conditions for the transmission of meaning from the sign to its interpretants. This chapter focuses on speculative grammar with its emphasis on the necessary conditions for the production of signs, and on speculative rhetoric with its emphasis on meaning situated within a pragmatic context.

Throughout his lifetime, Peirce produced a prodigious amount of material, which is available in *The Collected Papers of Charles Sanders Peirce* (1931–58). The main source that I am using is the shorter *The Essential Peirce* Vol. 1 and Vol. 2 (Houser and Kloesel 1992–98), where one finds two of his crucial essays: 'On a New List of Categories' (1867) and 'A Guess at the Riddle' (1887–88). Currently there is an ongoing project to reorganize his writings in a more chronological order that should culminate in a 30-volume set – some of which have already been published – called *The Writings of C. S. Peirce*.

Although Peirce's semiology is not restricted to linguistic communication, but to the broader field of interpretation, his influence upon theorists of textual interpretation is such that an account of his philosophy deserves examination. In this chapter I first outline (1) the categories that are fundamental to his thought; this is followed by (2) an account of his theory of signs. The following section develops (3) an account of signs showing their possibilities of combination, while the final sections examine (4) the role of pragmatism as a tool for the examination of meaning and (5) the method that should be used for the acquisition of knowledge. The film section (6) offers an account of the way Peircean ideas can be used within the fields of journalism, media and communication studies.

The categories of mathematics: Firstness, Secondness and Thirdness

One of the most enduring influences upon Peirce was the philosopher Immanuel Kant, who had attempted to unify philosophy into a system of categories that had a logical foundation.[1] Peirce admired this systematic attempt and likewise attempted to organize philosophy into a systematic order that would reflect the whole structure of knowledge. His categories were an alternative to the Kantian categories, and he continually refined them throughout his life. His point of departure was the need to revise logic itself since he considered the way it was formulated as inadequate. Unlike Frege and Russell, Peirce believed that logic was derived from mathematics and that mathematics was the foundation of any philosophical system: in effect, logic was applied mathematics. Today Peirce is considered to be one of the founders of modern mathematical logic.

The difference between logic and mathematics is that the goal of the latter is to establish the necessary relations of hypothetical constructions together with their conclusions, independently of whether these apply to anything real or ideal. According to Peirce's account, it is this concern with everything that situates mathematics at the pinnacle of knowledge: 'Mathematics [...] is the only one of the sciences which does not concern itself to inquire what the actual facts are, but studies hypotheses exclusively' (1992–98b: 35). Mathematicians are indifferent as to whether the objects of their study are real as can be seen by the study of imaginary numbers, such as the square root of −1, an 'impossible number'.

On the other hand, the goal of logic is that of right reasoning, and since it is concerned with the rightness or wrongness of reasoning, it should be considered a normative science, that is, with how one should reason. Given the equation of logic with rightness, Peirce considered logic to be a branch of ethics:

A logical reasoner is a reasoner who exercises great self-control in his intellectual operations; and therefore the logically good is simply a particular species of the morally good. (1992–98b: 200–01)

Since mathematics focuses on working out the necessary consequences of propositions, all other disciplines depend upon it.[2] Just as Kant had devised twelve categories that could explain how it is possible for us to experience objects, Peirce attempted a similar strategy, but reduced the twelve to three more basic ones. The three categories were derived mathematically and the whole point was to show that these categories could be applied to any and all objects and topics, irrespective of whether they actually existed or whether they were just a possibility. If it is possible to think about something, then the categories must be applicable to it. It is in this specific sense that the categories should be considered universal.

The universality of these mathematically derived categories shows that they apply equally to cars, aeroplanes, Achilles and centaurs. The inclusiveness of mathematical thinking demonstrates why it is foundational.

Pierce derived the categories from the study of graphs proposed by J. J. Sylvester. If you place a dot or point on a white piece of paper you have a first, but since the dot or point is contrasted with the paper you have a second (the black dot and the white paper), and the connection between them is a third (the black dot relates to the white background) to someone. The use of graphs to exemplify the categories is better illustrated with more dots: when you have two dots on a paper, the mind supplies the connection between them. Peirce's use of graphs demonstrated some of the basic points of his categories: no matter how many dots and lines are added, these can always be reduced to the basic two dots and one line schema (. – . – . = .-.). To show that the three categories cannot be reduced to two, Peirce uses the example of the relation of giving: A gives B to C. If A gives B to C, this action cannot be reduced to three sets of dual relations ((1) A connecting to C; (2) A connecting to B; (3) B connecting to C) since all these would show would be three disconnected events rather than a single act of giving. Similarly, when it is a relation among four, these can be reduced to two sets of three.

> Take *giving* for example. The mere transfer of an object which A sets down and C takes up does not constitute giving. There must be a transfer of *ownership* and ownership is a matter of Law, an intellectual fact. You now begin to see how the conception of representation is so peculiarly fit to typify the category of Thirdness. (1992–98b: 171)

Peirce's argument is that this reduction or 'derivation' is neither psychological nor linguistic, but mathematical. His categories are interconnected: the First produces a Second that entails a Third; he called these the 'cenopythagorean' categories (*ceno* is Greek meaning 'new') because his thinking was similar to that of the Pythagoreans who believed that mathematics was concerned with the structure of reality, unlike the contemporary view of number as concerned with quantities.

After mathematics, Peirce considered philosophy to be a fundamental study, but unlike mathematics it was concerned with what is real. On the other hand, the difference between philosophy and the other sciences is that unlike the other sciences, philosophy does not require any special equipment or laboratories, but can be practised by anyone: 'the kind of philosophy which interests me and must, I think, interest everybody is that philosophy which uses the most rational methods it can devise' (in de Waal 2001: 15).

Phenomenology (or, as called by Pierce, 'phaenoscopy') is the first branch of philosophy: it is concerned with whatever appears before consciousness, from perception to imagination to conception. Since its domain is fairly broad – anything that appears before consciousness – it also includes aspects that would not usually be analysed (hallucinations and illusions). The truth of what appears is, so to speak, put on hold and is therefore not an issue. Peirce describes the task of phenomenology vividly:

the initial great department of philosophy is phenomenology whose task it is to make out what are the elements of appearance that present themselves to us every hour and every minute whether we are pursuing earnest investigations, or are undergoing the strangest vicissitudes of experience, or are dreamily listening to the tales of Scheherazade. (1992–98b: 147)

Peirce's fundamental categories are those of Firstness, Secondness and Thirdness: since they were the basis for his new philosophical system, he had to show that these categories were universal, irreducible and complete.

First is the beginning, that which is fresh, original, spontaneous, free. Second is that which is determined, terminated, ended, correlative, object, necessitated, reacting. Third is the medium, becoming, developing, bring about. (1992–98a: 280)

Whether existing or not, it is always some 'thing' that is being considered, and in this respect is independent of anything else. This is the idea of Firstness. When we think of something, we can oppose it or think about it as different from something else. Secondness is this otherness, this negation of Firstness. The category of Thirdness connects the two distinguishable objects: it mediates between them. De Waal writes,

The relation of a first to a second, however, brings with it the notion of mediation; that is, of setting two objects in relation to one another. This introduces the third category, which is that mode of being that derives its identity entirely from it relating two objects to one another. For example, when a fox chases a rabbit, the relation of chasing can be distinguished from both the fox and the rabbit. Moreover, this relation is what it is purely by virtue of the relation between the fox and the rabbit. (de Waal 2001: 10)

It is useful to think of the categories of Firstness, Secondness and Thirdness as roughly the domains of possibility (what might be), actuality (what is), and potentiality, probability and necessity (what could be, would be or should be). This triad is analytically broken down for methodological purposes, as in fact the three are found together. While Firstness is the abstract possibility of a sensation, feeling or quality in an agent, it is experienced as Secondness in a particular object, existing in the world as a token or particular instantiation of a type; it is the other of the agent. Thirdness connects the first (sensation, vague feeling) to the second (the object) to generate a meaning. Thirdness is the category of classes of types; a particular object (Second) belongs to a type or class of objects that have a function within a society.

The Firstness of perception is not that of something that we are immediately conscious of: it is chaotic, formless, pre-conscious and elusive:

Stop to think of it, and it has flown! What the world was to Adam on the day he opened his eyes to it, before he had drawn any distinctions, or had become conscious of his own existence [...] (1992–98a: 248)

It is the realm of the possible. Secondness is the domain of 'facts', of 'brute actuality'. It is 'eminently hard and tangible. It is very familiar too; it is forced upon us daily: it is the main lesson of life' (1992–98a: 249). In the course of walking in the street, the pavement remains a sensation that we are hardly aware of. The moment we slip, it becomes a Second: we are now aware of it as other, as something hard. We should remember that Peirce's Firstness is always about possibilities that can be actualized into Secondness, rather than Secondness replacing Firstness as though one were superior to the other. Thirdness takes place when we pick ourselves up: we have realized what has happened and act upon it. It is 'the representation mediating between these two that is preeminently third' (1992–98a: 250).

The condition that makes Firstness possible is that of 'nothingness', which is to be differentiated from negation. Peirce writes,

We start [...] with nothing, pure zero. But this is not the nothing of negation. For *not* means *other than*, and *other* is merely a synonym of the ordinary numeral *second*. As such it implies a first; while the present pure zero is prior to every first [...] it is the germinal nothing, in which the whole universe is involved and foreshadowed. As such, it is absolutely undefined and unlimited possibility – boundless possibility. There is no compulsion and no law. It is boundless freedom. (in Merrell 1995: 69)

It is evident that phenomenology is devoted to the universal features that can be found in all phenomena. Since the categories are derived from mathematics and these categories are universal, then they must also apply to phenomenological objects. However, instead of applying the categories that are fundamental to mathematics, Peirce opts to show that the same categories can be derived from phenomenology. The Firstness of phenomenology is the fact that it is there, present without reference to anything else: it would be consciousness of 'just an odour, say, the smell of attar' (1992–98b: 150). The second feature of phenomenology is that a First is opposed, contrasted or connected to something else. The category of Secondness describes the singularity of the object, its otherness. The category of Thirdness connects the First and the Second: the smell with the flower we call 'rose'. Although each category is distinct, whatever appears before consciousness includes all three categories.

Abduction is Peirce's novel contribution to logic and his theory of signs. While deduction and induction have been given much attention, Peirce introduces this third mode of reasoning that takes place prior to deduction and induction.

Deduction is defined as an argument, such that 'in the long run of experience the greater part of those whose premises are true will have true conclusions' (1992–98b: 298). On the other hand, although with induction it is not necessarily the case that true premises will always lead to true conclusions, 'it will in the long run yield the truth, or an indefinite approximation to the truth, in regard to every question' (1992–98b: 298). Abduction is defined as

> a method of forming a general prediction without any positive assurance that it will succeed either in the special case or usually, its justification being that it is the only possible hope of regulating our future conduct rationally [...] (1992–98b: 299)

Abduction is the process of grouping together a number of facts that impress the person. The facts are combined with others until an explanation can be offered. At this stage, a hypothesis is proposed, and if the hypothesis is true, then the facts have been explained. Deduction involves examining the necessary consequences of a hypothesis: if one is proposing a certain hypothesis, then within the framework of that hypothesis we should be able to ascertain what must follow. A trivial example of a hypothesis is that if it has been raining, then the street must necessarily be wet. Induction is that process of checking whether the way things are corresponds to the way it has been hypothetically proposed. Again, the actual wet road confirms the hypothesis that it has been raining. At this stage, the 'theory' conforms to the facts. Peirce writes that an abductive inference suggests that something may be, deduction shows that something must be and induction shows that something is (1992–98b: 216).

Abduction falls within the category of Firstness and it can be described as a 'creative guess'. It is the preliminary hypothesis that is subsequently confirmed or rejected: slipping on the wet pavement, we – for an instant – do not know what is happening until we realize that we have slipped. The initial hypothesis is confirmed as we look around sitting on the pavement. Abduction, like Firstness, concerns the domain of the possible; these possibilities are not only unusual events (like slipping on the pavement) but a part of our everyday life. They constitute the process that takes place from the vague sensation of Firstness to the actuality of Secondness, from the vague sensation of hardness to the actuality of the pavement.

The nature of the sign

Peirce uses Locke as his point of departure and develops a highly sophisticated account of signs (the term *semeiotic* is derived from *semeion*, the Greek word for *sign*, although nowadays the 'e' is dropped and an 's' is added to produce *semiotics*). Given Saussure's background in linguistics, his account of signs focuses on their arbitrary and conventional nature; on the other hand, Peirce's background in the natural sciences directs his attention towards 'natural' signs and subsumes conventional signs within the category of natural signs. The branch of semiotics that studies the conditions that transform something into a sign – in other words into their formal character – is called 'speculative grammar'.

A sign is defined as

Anything which stands *for* something *to* something. What the sign stands *for* is its object, what it stands *to* is the interpretant. The sign relation is *fundamentally* triadic: eliminate either the object or the interpretant and you annihilate the sign. (1992–98a: xxxvi)

This definition highlights three fundamental and interrelated features of a sign:

1. a representamen (that is itself sometimes confusingly called a sign);
2. an object that the representamen is related to; and
3. the interpretant (not to be confused with the interpreter) as the activation of the meaning of a sign.

The process of semiological activity moves along this triad: a representamen is associated with an object that is connected by or through the interpretant. In turn, the object and the interpretant have the possibility of being transformed into another sign for other objects and interpretants. Corresponding to the representamen-object-interpretant triad is the Firstness-Secondness-Thirdness triad: while the First is independent of everything else, the Second is related to something else and the Third connects the First and Second. The category of Thirdness is important in that it generates the interpretation of the sign: the sign–object relation requires an interpretant to have a meaning or significance. To say 'the sun is shining' requires an interpretation that could focus on the sentence as an explanation of what the words mean, or on my suggestion that we go swimming, or on my pleasure that summer is approaching. Unless a sign can generate these further interpretations it will have no significance. One might say that the significance of a sign depends upon its effects, upon the interpretants it produces.

An important feature of Peirce's account of signs is that they are always embodied; in other words, there is always some 'vehicle' that he calls the 'ground' or 'representamen' that function as a sign. The material in which signs are embodied range from mental states (dreams), to metal (road-signs) or wood (chairs), to the entire universe (as a sign of God). However, this embodiment has its constraints as not every feature functions as a signifying one. The material of a signpost is not important, but that the representamen is clearly indicated as a tunnel and not a one-way road is important.

In the relationship between the representamen and its object, the sign is passive since it is the object that determines the representamen without the representamen having any effect on the object (the quality of redness is the result of the apple, not the other way round). On the other hand, in the relationship between the representamen and the interpretant, the representamen plays an active role since it determines the interpretant (the quality of redness 'imposes' itself upon the interpretant).

An important and fundamental characteristic of Peirce's theory of signs is the notion that it is the nature of signs to continually generate new signs. The interpretant can enter into a new sign-relation, thereby becoming an object that will function as a sign for another interpretant. Eco has labelled this process 'unlimited semiosis' (1976: 69), and it refers to the way a sign is associated with a certain meaning that in turn activates other meanings.

Peirce does not allow for the ultimate meaning of a sign, since a sign can always be 'translated' into another sign. The process of semiosis is ongoing, and to talk of a final meaning or of a grand sign would be to talk about something outside human life. This is why it is fruitful to say that when a person interacts with a situation, the person – as a thinking, feeling being woven into the web of semiosis – responds by producing more signs. The aeroplane flying overhead might mean an inconvenience to the person living in the flight path, summer holidays to the student and pollution to the environmentalist. The same sign can produce different interpretants.

In Peirce's view, the universe is an endless process of signs generating more signs. But for signs to generate meanings it is necessary to have interpreters – a sign must be a sign of something for someone. There are many things that are signs, but for them to function as signs there must be interpreters to generate the interpretant:

> Mayan hieroglyphs are signs, no doubt, and we can assume they once enjoyed a set of relatively developed interpretants. But remaining to this point in time largely undeciphered and undecipherable by present-day archaeologists, they have not produced a massive body of interpretants *for* some group of interpreters *in* our cultural milieu. They are a set of signs in search of their fulfillment. (Merrell 1995: 93)

It is the interpretant that accounts for the dynamism of signs, for once a sign has an interpretant, then it has the potential for transformation into another sign. Semiosis is a process that is always on the way to something else, and in this process the sign is transformed into something other, something different from what it was before.

Peirce's definition of signs is broad precisely because it is intended to include within it almost everything, since almost everything can function as a sign. His account entails the entire universe being 'perfused with signs, if it is not composed exclusively of signs' (1992–98b: 394). Given the breadth of his definition, Peirce's understanding of the world differs greatly from that of, say, Aristotle, for whom the world can be understood by reference to substances, essences and purposes. Aristotle's world was fundamentally a static one, while Peirce on the other hand offers a dynamic vision of the world that can be explained in terms of events, processes and happenings.

In the case of the representamen, the sign can be a quality, an individual object or a general type.

1. The representamen as qualisign is a feeling, sensation or the vagueness of something that we cannot identify as something existing. The First of a perceptual object is the 'qualisign': the 'quali' is a quality such as redness or sourness. Since redness and sourness do not exist on their own, for them to function as a sign they must be embodied in objects. Despite being embodied, the quality itself as a sign is not affected by the object (1992–98b: 291).

2. The representamen as sinsign. When the representamen is a Second, it is a sinsign or a token: it is singular so that it functions as a sign by being 'an actual existent thing or event' (1992–98b: 291). A sinsign is the sign of a thing or event that exists now in isolation from other signs: it is a sign of something or an event that we are conscious of.
3. The representamen as legisign. Legisigns usually signify as a result of conventions, habits or laws (e.g., traffic lights) and they include classes or types. They become legisigns as a result of their being repeated. It is language that best exemplifies legisigns because language entails the use of general terms such as *dog* or *car*. A general term or type applies to all particular instantiations or tokens, such as *this dog* and *this car*. The word *dog* is a general type or legisign, but each time the word is uttered, the utterance is a token of the type, an instantiation of it. In addition, the event of uttering the word *dog* does not influence the type 'dog'. Peirce writes that a legisign is

> not a single object, but a general type [...] thus the word 'the' will usually occur from fifteen to twenty-five times on a page. It is in all these occurrences one and the same word, the same legisign. Each single instance of it is a replica. The replica is a sinsign. (1992–98b: 291)

In the case of objects, the sign can be an icon, index or symbol.

1. Objects as icons. The iconic sign functions as a sign by virtue of resembling or being a likeness to an object. Icons 'serve to convey ideas of the things they represent simply by imitating them' (1992–98b: 5). Included among these are photography, paintings, maps and caricatures. Other icons include resemblances even to objects that do not necessarily exist, such as a picture of a unicorn. However, Peirce does point out that the terminology or 'likeness' or 'resemblance' is too restrictive if it is used to mean only a correspondence between a physical likeness and its object. Iconic signs include:

   a. images where the image resembles the object to such an extent that they can be considered as one: the image is like the object without any difference from it;
   b. diagrams which resemble their object but are different from them. The resemblance could be of parts, or of the structure of the object (e.g. the diagram of a house and the house);
   c. metaphors: when signs that are not usually found together are combined in a sentence, the relation between them generates a metaphor. It is not usual to associate a human being with a lion, but in the sentence *Charles Borg is a lion*, a man is said to possess the qualities that are associated with lions.

An icon functions as a sign irrespective of whether the object exists or not, and irrespective of whether it is interpreted or not. The road sign of a tunnel functions as a likeness of a tunnel, even if there is no tunnel or anyone to interpret it. A sign that functions as a warning

– *do not enter* – still signifies a warning, whether it is at the entrance of a field or lying in a heap of scrap. There is no way of knowing whether there is anything more than just the sign functioning.

Can there be such a thing as a 'pure' icon? If icons belong to the category of Firstness, and if this category is independent of everything else, then a pure icon would be a qualisign, a pure sensation or feeling without any connection to a consciousness (since consciousness would transform it into a sinsign). The notion of a pure icon is therefore only hypothetical and Peirce called them 'hypo-icons' since he believed that there was always a conventional element involved. Take for example maps: although maps are supposed to be 'just' a resemblance or likeness of the terrain that they are maps of, they too have a conventional element in that there are rules that tell us how to use the map as an icon. In the same way, when icons are defined as 'resemblances', this labelling does not carry with it the negative connotation of being without value. On the contrary, icons are valuable insofar as they enable us to learn, since by studying features of the icon it is possible to learn more about the object. By observing a map, we can learn more about the terrain; by examining a photograph, we can learn more about a building.

2. Object as index. A sign is indexical if there is a natural or causal relation between the sign and the object. Such a relation or connection is existential since it involves actual existing objects or events. Indices direct our attention to the object as when the weathercock directs our attention to the wind blowing. They function like pronouns since they point to something, and their 'force' is such that they connect an object to our senses and to our memory (since we remember having experienced such a connection). So, for example, when we hear thunder we know – because we remember our past experiences of thunder – that lightening is the cause of it.

> I see a man with a rolling gait. This is a probable indication that he is a sailor. I see a bowlegged man in corduroys, gaiters, and a jacket. These are probable indicators that he is a jockey or something of the sort. A weathercock *indicates* the direction of the wind. A sun-dial or a clock *indicates* the time of day. Geometricians mark letters against the different parts of their diagrams and then use those letters to indicate those parts. Letters are similarly used by lawyers and others. Thus, we may say: if A and B are married to one another and C is their child while D is brother of A, then D is uncle of C. Here A, B, C, and D fulfill the office of relative pronouns, but are more convenient since they require no special collocation of words. A rap on the door is an indication. Anything which focuses the attention is an indication. Anything which startles us is an indication, in so far as it marks the junction between two portions of experience. Thus a tremendous thunderbolt indicates that *something* considerable happened, though we may not know precisely what the event was. But it may be expected to connect itself with some other experience. (1992–98b: 8)

Peirce describes the indexical sign as something 'which it could not have if its object did not exist, but which it will continue to have just the same whether it be interpreted as a representamen or not' (in Merrell 1995: 84). The weathercock is a sign of the direction of the wind: it 'depends' upon the wind and will point somewhere independently of whether the person is looking at it or not. As with icons, indices still signify irrespective of whether there are interpreters – a can with a bullet hole still functions as a sign of a bullet shot irrespective of whether there is anybody to interpret it. While indices refer to actual things or events, these do not necessarily occur in the external world, as they could just as easily be occurrences that that take place within our minds (as in dreams or mathematical constructions).

There are two kinds of indexical signs: genuine indices (or 'reagents') point to actual existing objects or events and these indexical signs have a natural connection between them. On the other hand, degenerate indices do not point to actual existing objects but are mental or artificial. A prime example of a degenerate sign is a symbol since there is no natural connection between the sign and the object, even though it still points to the object.

The question once again is whether there is such a thing as a pure index; and clearly, since a genuine index describes the relation between a sign and an actual object, then a pure indexical relation would be one without any human involvement in it. This – Peirce acknowledges – is 'impossible', for it is impossible to know the world as it is independently of humans. Furthermore, even if it were a case of genuine indices, there is always an element of human psychology since the human mind associates one event with another (association by contiguity). Pointing with our fingers to an object seems to be a prime example of a pure index, but the rule which tells us that a finger points to an object does not tell us which object it is pointing to. Peirce calls these 'sub-index'.

3. Object as symbol. A symbol has a meaning by virtue of its habitual associations: symbolic signs 'or general signs […] have become associated with their meanings by usage. Such are most words, and phrases, and speeches, and books and libraries' (1992–98b: 5). Symbols are signs that are conventionally and habitually related to their object. For example, a flag is conventionally associated with a country, and words are conventional agreements to use them in a certain way: the word *dog* and the animal dog. The best examples of symbols are natural languages (English, Maltese), formal languages (mathematics, logic) and artificial languages (the Morse Code, Braille).

Linguistic signs are prime examples of symbols:

any ordinary word, as 'give', 'bird', 'marriage', is an example of a symbol. It is applicable to whatever may be found to realize the idea connected with the word; it does not, in itself, identify those things. It does not show us a bird, nor enact before our eyes a giving or a marriage, but supposes that we are able to imagine those things, and have associated the word with them. (1992–98b: 9)

The relation between symbolic signs and objects is the product of human minds: the symbol has nothing in common with what it refers to. While an icon might resemble something real or fictional and an index points to something independently of semiotic agents, symbolic signs depend entirely on minds. It is humans who agree to use a symbol in a certain way, to use the sign *dog* to refer to particular dogs or to the category or class of dogs. Symbols are conventional through and through. The difference between the symbol and icons or indices is that symbols depend upon the interpretant – since anything can function as a symbol, the symbol needs an interpretant, a meaning to function as a sign. Symbolic signs as interpretants or meanings can generate other interpretants or meanings.

> Symbols grow. They come into being by development out of other signs, and particularly from likenesses or from mixed signs partaking of the nature of likenesses and symbols. We think only in signs. These mental signs are of a mixed nature; the symbol-parts of them are called concepts. If a man makes a new symbol, it is by thoughts involving concepts. So it is only out of symbols that a new symbol can grow. *Omne symbolum de symbolo.* A symbol, once in being, spreads among the peoples. In use and in experience, its meaning grows. Such words as *force, law, wealth, marriage* bear for us very different meanings from those they bore to our barbarous ancestors. (1992–98b: 10)

Although a sign is symbolic, this does not mean that there are no traces of iconicity and indexicality in them. The iconic aspect involves the similarity or resemblance evoked in the agent by other uses of the sign, and the indexical aspect involves what the sign points to (for the agent). The sign *dog* functions iconically because it resembles other times that the person used the sign, and it functions indexically when it points to any associations – real or imagined (when a real dog 'causes' us to say 'dog' or when we remember our dog and start talking about it) – that we have of it.

The use of symbols carries a background, a form of life alongside them. Symbols communicate – directly or indirectly – the values and beliefs of a community. Given this implicit background knowledge, an utterance will never be able to express a complete context: it is always possible for more to be communicated. Peirce's account helps to explain the way signs proliferate and multiply – from icons, to indices, to symbols, to icons again and so on. When a symbol is a term, it has the potential to generate other symbols: the term *Shakespeare* is not just about a particular person but carries with it a network of cultural associations. Additionally, just as a term can generate a profusion of signs, a sentence can generate texts. The sentence *the war on terror must be won* generated a multitude of discourses – economic, political, military – that together make up the intertextual world.

The sign as interpretant can be a word, proposition or argument. The final classification concerns the way signs relate to the interpreter: the interpreter can 'read' the sign in terms of its qualities, existence or generality. Peirce considers this classification similar to the division in logic between terms, propositions and argument.

1. Firstness: the interpretant as term or word (a rheme). The word functions as a possibility, 'such and such a kind of possible Object. Any rheme, perhaps, will afford some information; but it is not interpreted as doing so' (1992–98b: 292). A term represents the possibility of a type of object and as a term (e.g. dog) it cannot be true or false.
2. Secondness: the interpretant as a dicent sign (a sentence or proposition). The interpretant is the 'dicent' and propositions are the best models of dicents, since it is of a proposition that one can say that it is true or false. A proposition combines 'rhemes' into a whole, such as *the dog is sleeping*, and this proposition describes whether something exists or not. A sentence is composed of a number of symbols strung together. In *the sun is shining* the 'sun' here functions chiefly in an indexical way – it is about the sun; the verb functions in an iconic way since it resembles other instances of when the sun did shine.
3. Thirdness: The interpretant as arguments. The function of this sign is to arrive at a conclusion as a result of dialogue and argumentation. Here language – as the most developed of signs – is used as a tool to further communicative exchanges in the form of reasoned arguments.

A word on its own – the first of Thirdness – is a word that has the possibility of being combined with other words. At this stage we could say that the word still needs to be realized, its potential as yet unfulfilled. This fulfillment begins when it is placed within the context of a sentence since solitary words are useless for communication. The sentence is the second of Thirdness: in *the sun is shining*, the sun is seen as shining – a quality is attributed to a subject. The third of Thirdness is the condition of possibility for dialogue and communication: our utterance, *the sun is shining*, might lead to a discussion of the depletion of the ozone layer and the resulting increase in skin-related problems.

The combinations of signs

Given the three different classes of signs, each with their own types, Peirce thought it was possible to combine them to account for all possible signs. In principle, this should have amounted to 27 possible signs, but given certain rules of combination these are reduced to ten classes. The two rules for the classification of the signs is that (1) there is one from each of the tables – one from the representamen, from the object and from the interpretant; and (2) a 'lower' level sign cannot be combined with one from a level above it. So, for example, a qualisign, icon or rheme cannot combine with any entity above them, and a sinsign, index or dicent cannot combine with one from the list above.

1. Rhematic iconic qualisign. This is the most basic and fundamental level of signs; it is the minimum of information processed by the human body in terms of its biological structure from the pre-First 'world'. The formlessness of the 'world' is the condition that makes any sensation and experience for humans possible.

2. Rhematic iconic sinsigns. This sign includes qualisigns within it, and since it is as yet unrelated, it is chiefly iconic. Peirce's example of a 'self-contained diagram' (in Merrell 1995: 132) is an individual copy of a map that is not related in the agent's mind to other maps (since it is one replica among others); neither is it related to the territory that it is a map of. The map is a self-contained entity. Merrell gives an example of rhematic iconic sinsigns:

> Some unintelligible squiggles on a subway wall in some unknown language can contain the possibility of symbolic signs, but as such they are *for* us related to nothing, they are no more than meaningless marks. At this juncture they enjoy interaction with no semiotic agent conscious *of* them *as* signs *of* something *that* have such-and-such characteristics, hence they are devoid of a well-wrought symbolic interpretant. If they vaguely resemble, say, a bow-tie, they can make up an ironic sinsign. But they do so only insofar as the squiggles-tie connection has not (yet) been established, for the icon is at this point no more than self-contained, without relation to anything else. (1995: 132)

3. Rhematical indexical signs. These signs are pointers that direct the attention of the interpreter. A scream – or as Peirce calls it 'a spontaneous cry' – directs the interpreter to the person screaming without knowing why he or she is screaming. Given certain contextual cues, the interpreter can probably figure out why the person is screaming since the context conditions our expectations of what might be about to happen ('look out!' as we are walking past a building site). At this stage the reaction to the sign is spontaneous; therefore, there is no full-blown conscious awareness of the sign as a sign.

4. Dicent indexical signs. The indexical character of this sign is that of causality, where there exists a natural connection between the two events. The direction of the weathercock is the effect caused by the wind: when we look at it, we learn about the wind. As the nature of a sign is to incorporate – and not eliminate – other signs, this indexical sign retains the iconic aspect in that the direction of the weathercock is like the direction of the wind. Merrell elucidates,

> a photograph, when related to that of which it is a photograph, functions in indexical fashion. But it cannot so function without its iconic quality that endows it with the wherewithal for its indexicality. An image of Madonna on the cover of a magazine at the news-stand can be at a glance tacitly acknowledged as Madonna, without any explicit relation consciously and conscientiously established between sign and object. But the image, to be seen *as* a photograph, involves indexicality – without there (yet) being any words (symbolicity), either evolved in the mind or expressed, regarding the image. (1995: 132–33)

5. Rhematic iconic legisigns. These are signs that establish a relation between a sign and an aspect of the object: the image of cutlery displayed on a door is a sign of a place to eat, a restaurant or diner. The cutlery is like the cutlery found in any kitchen but they represent food. Other signs of this class include onomatopoeic words that are like the object. The sound of 'cuckoo' resembles the sound of the cuckoo bird (it is different in the case of the written *cuckoo*, since the written sign does not resemble the cuckoo bird).

6. Rhematic indexical legisign. Although this sign points to something else, there is a sense of absence, of deferral. The pointing does not have to be immediate as when the weathercock points to the direction of the wind. This class of signs includes demonstrative pronouns (this, that) and other place markers (here, there). Using these signs also enables one to talk about something implicitly, to talk about absences ('I didn't do that'). Signs of this type are legisigns because they involve a degree of generalization – they are a type as opposed to a token of a thing. 'The shout of "Hullo!" is an example of the ordinary variety – meaning, not an individual shout, but this shout, "Hullo!" in general – this type of shout' (1992–98b: 297)

7. Dicent indexical legisign. This sign can be of two kinds: linguistic and non-linguistic. Both the linguistic and the non-linguistic are general or routine but not necessarily conventional. In the case of linguistic signs, the generality of a legisign is displayed in everyday expressions ('how are you doing?', 'OK?'). The indexical element of these signs can be seen in the way they are used as greetings or acknowledgements to connect with other people we are familiar with. The iconic aspect is the resemblance or likeness of these expressions to other similar expressions. In the case of non-linguistic signs, communication in the animal world displays these generalized patterns of behaviour that are innate: bees perform the waggle dance not because they have learnt it from other bees, but because nature has programmed them to communicate in this way (by instinct).

8. Rhematic symbolic legisigns. These signs are words or general terms, usually nouns (*table* or *television*). They are generated by the interpretant by virtue of the semiotic agent's previous experience of them: having in the past used the sign *chair* to refer to a chair, this association is memorized and upon future experiences of a chair one is able to retrieve the sign *chair* from his/her memory. Since these signs are the exclusive domain of humans, there is something in the person's memory bank that predisposes him/her towards using these signs. The activation of these signs requires both an interpretant and objects that are particular instantiations of the general term; thus, for example, the general term *chair* can be applied to an infinite number of particular chairs of all shapes, sizes and colours.

9. Dicent symbolic legisigns are sentences or propositions. From a single sign a series of responses are enacted that combine signs into a whole. This stage can be considered as a preliminary conversation. Propositions in formal language (2 + 2 = 4) belong to this category, and while a proposition might seem context-free it is always embedded within a linguistic context.

10. Delome symbolic legisigns are arguments whereby one moves from premises to conclusions:

> an Argument is a sign whose Interpretant represents its Object as being an ulterior sign through a law, namely, the law that the passage from all such premises to such conclusions tend to the truth. (1992–98b: 296)

Pragmatism, knowledge and dialogue

Peirce's ideas on pragmatism (renamed pragmaticism in 1905) are chiefly discussed in *The Fixation of Belief* (1877) and *How to Make Our Ideas Clear* (1878). Although the term *pragmatism* was coined by Peirce as a way of testing the content of concepts, propositions and hypothesis within science, its range of application was broadened to include both logic and philosophy. The idea behind pragmatism was that the investigator of concepts would adopt an experimentalist approach similar to one used by scientists in laboratories.

Pragmaticism forged a link between the understanding of a concept and the consequences of that concept. To understand a concept, or to know what it means, entails that it has some observable effect:

> Consider what effects, which might conceivably have practical bearings, we conceive the object of our conception to have. Then, our conception of these effects is the whole of our conception of the object. (1992–98a: 132)

This formulation of the pragmatic maxim suggests that if a person can provide all the conditional propositions (if one did A, then one can observe B) related to the concept, then if one applies them to the object, one can predict the results or consequences: 'To say that a body is heavy simply means that, in the absence of opposing force, it will fall [...] what we mean by the force itself is completely involved in its effects' (1992–98a: 133). For Peirce, the meaning of a concept is nothing but the sum total of possible effects.[3]

Since the observable effects of a concept constituted the criterion of concept meaningfulness, this also implied what counted as meaninglessness: if a concept has no observable consequences, then it is empty or useless. Peirce's hope was that by adopting the pragmatic maxim, several questions that had seemed irresolvable could now be eliminated. In one of his examples, Peirce dismissed the religious concept of transubstantiation as meaningless since it could have no conceivable practical effect. According to the doctrine of transubstantiation, during Mass the bread and wine literally change into the body and blood of Christ. Since we know what bread and wine are through their qualities (their taste, texture or colour), and since these remain the same after transubstantiation, then how can we say that they are now the body and blood of Christ? In other words, the same qualities are now supposed to belong to a different substance. If, according to the pragmatic criterion, we understand the meaning of a concept according to its conceivable effects, then the concept of transubstantiation has no meaning:

> We can consequently mean nothing by wine but what has certain effects, direct or indirect, upon our senses; and to talk of something as having all the sensible characters of wine, yet being in reality blood, is senseless jargon. (1992–98a: 131)

One might disagree with this view by arguing that the doctrine of transubstantiation makes a difference or has an effect upon a person. Such a view is not Pierce's, as the pragmatic maxim is not a psychological tool but a conceptual one. It is not a question of what the doctrine of transubstantiation might have for you or me, but a question of whether the doctrine is conceptually tenable or not. And this is why Peirce proposes experience as the counterweight to all those theorists that have relied exclusively on reason: while we might be led to a conclusion through our reason, experience is the 'test' for whether these conclusions are valid or not.

> In all the works on pedagogy that ever I read [...] I don't remember that any one has advocated a system of teaching by practical jokes, mostly cruel. That, however, describes the method of our great teacher, Experience. (1992–98b: 154)

Pragmatism is closely connected with truth, for it enables us to differentiate those propositions that are true (since the effects support them) from those that are false (since they run counter to the effects). Talisse and Aiken provide an example:

> [...] understanding the truth of the proposition *the cat is on the mat* is constituted by an understanding of the practical consequences of the cat being on the mat – a bowl of milk next to the mat will likely be drunk, mice will avoid the mat, one should expect howls of protest if one wipes one's feet on the mat. Truths have consequences, and to understand those truths, we must grasp the differences they make for our experience. (2008: 61)

Aside from the question of how to sort out those concepts that are tenable from those that should be discarded, Peirce was also greatly interested in the method that should be used for the attainment of knowledge about ourselves and about the world.[4] As a point of departure, Peirce clarifies the difference between being in the condition of doubt and being in the condition of belief. While the characteristic of belief is that a person is serene, in the condition of doubt a person is dissatisfied. A person in the condition of dissatisfaction attempts to return to the condition of belief[5] (1992–98a: 114). The reason for thinking about something or conducting an inquiry is precisely to remove that doubt. Once a belief is achieved – whether true or not – then the thinking or inquiring ceases. Peirce's approach differs from the Cartesian proposal to doubt everything before one can proceed to a state of belief. Rather, the opposite is the case, as one always starts with some belief; but should that belief be challenged by the evidence, then the belief should be abandoned or modified accordingly. There are four ways to settle an opinion:

1. The method of tenacity is the one where a person adamantly holds on to and defends his/her ideas. It is the method of 'stubbornness', where one clings to one's belief despite evidence of the contrary. Anybody has the right to believe what one wants, but an idea must hold favour with the rest of the community for it to be accepted. Without the latter's approval or agreement it would always be difficult to establish whether the belief deserves being listened to be heard out or whether it should be dismissed as something personal. This method fails because it is not very useful in solving disputes since one ignores the views of others or the facts; and if they are listened to, one is disturbed to hear contrary views:

> The man who adopts it will find that other men think differently from him, and it will be apt to occur to him, in some saner moment, that their opinions are quite as good as his own and this will shake his confidence in his belief. (1992–98a: 116)

2. The method of authority is similar to the method of 'tenacity', but rather than being individually centred, it is upheld by an institution such as the state or the Church:

> Let an institution be created which shall have for its object to keep correct doctrines before the attention of the people, to reiterate them perpetually, and to teach them to the young; having at the same time power to prevent contrary doctrines from being taught, advocated, or expressed. (1992–98a: 117)

Something is believed because the authorities say so, and whoever disagrees with this belief or idea is plainly mistaken. The problem with this method is that it assumes that knowledge is completely in the hands of the institutional authorities who monitor the evidence, eliminating anything that threatens the belief. As a result, any individual who comes up with new ideas is seen as threatening to the order of things. This method eventually fails, as an institution cannot control everything at all times.

3. The 'a priori' method was utilized by Descartes to eliminate all doubt and which, as a result, would guarantee certainty. Descartes's account claims that the search for knowledge is the work of the solitary individual using his/her reason. Any conflict of opinion is settled by supporting those beliefs that we find agreeable – in other words, those that conform to our reason. If the belief fits into our network of beliefs then we tend to agree with it. This method fails because

> [i]t makes of inquiry something similar to the development of taste; but taste, unfortunately, is always more or less a matter of fashion, and accordingly metaphysicians

have never come to any fixed agreement, but the pendulum has swung backward and forward between a more material and a more spiritual philosophy, from the earliest times to the latest. (1992–98a: 119)

As a result, beliefs change according to the times. According to Peirce, this method overlaps with the previous two: the solitary person promotes what he/she considers knowledge, that is, the 'method of tenacity', and if these beliefs are accepted as founding truths, these truths become 'eternal' because of the respect gained by the person who founded them, that is, 'the method of authority'.

However, despite the overlap Peirce noticed a big difference between the a priori method and the methods of authority and tenacity. Since the a priori method is influenced by what is agreeable to reason, the 'what' or the content of the beliefs is determined by what is agreeable at the time. In the case of the methods of tenacity and authority, the content is determined according to the strength or power of the individual or the institution. Strictly speaking, since there is no discussion of the content but a mere exercise of force, the methods of tenacity and authority should not be considered to be legitimate methods of inquiry.

The problem that is common to the three methods is that none seem able to offer a way of providing secure belief, because in all three it is we who determine what is to be believed or not. As a result, Peirce thought that a better way would be one where our beliefs were fixed by something independent, or larger than us. If our beliefs were not affected by what we thought about them, then it would be more likely that they would provide security.

4. The dialogical method is the method proposed by Peirce, where knowledge is achieved by members of the scientific community in dialogue with each other.

> Thus, the very origin of the conception of reality shows that this conception essentially involves the notion of a COMMUNITY, without definite limits and capable of an indefinite increase of knowledge. (1992–98a: 52)

The advantage of Peirce's method is that it eliminates the following unpleasant situations of perseverance of foolish ideas (tenacity), the pretensions of grandiose persons (authority) or the solitary discovery of truth (the Cartesian method).

Within the context of a dialogue, the movement of ideas between participants who might agree, challenge or defend an idea is essential to its justification and subsequent acceptance. While the method of dialogue ensures that an idea or belief is always open to succeeding developments, at that point in time – by virtue of its being shared by members of the community – it remains true.

This is not to say that knowledge is constructed by the members or the community irrespective of reality. On the contrary, reality operates independently of anything that a person or a group might think about it:

There are real things, whose characters are entirely independent of our opinions about them; those realities affect our senses according to regular laws, and though our sensations are as different as are our relations to the objects, yet, by taking advantage of the laws of perception, we can ascertain by reasoning how things really are; and any man, if he have sufficient experience and reason enough about it will be led to the one true conclusion. (1992–98a: 120)

The interesting thing about Peirce's view on reality is that a number of people thinking about it on their own will – over time – have a convergence of their thinking. Reality as a zone of experience 'co-ordinates' the reasoning of these persons into a shared belief. It would seem that eventually a final opinion, a true conclusion, would be arrived at. Since the pragmatic maxim applies to 'conceivable' practical effects, and since anything can be rationally examined, at some point in time there would be nothing left to examine. In addition, the communal aspect of inquiry also plays a part in ensuring that the 'true conclusion' is achieved. A group of investigators each contributing their opinions will – in the process of discussion and debate – eventually overcome any mistakes made. Peirce's example of the blind and deaf man highlights this communal process: 'One hears a man declare he means to kill another, hears the report of the pistol, and hears the victim cry; the other sees the murder done' (1992–98a: 89). Eventually, the two men with their different perceptions of what happened will arrive at one conclusion. The scientific method works by following a process where errors are eliminated and the conclusion is reached.

While the differences of opinion might delay arriving at the final opinion, ultimately, and independently of the persons, the final opinion 'imposes' itself:

the arbitrary will or other individual peculiarities of a sufficiently large number of minds may postpone the general agreement in that opinion indefinitely; but it cannot affect what the character of that opinion shall be when it is reached. (1992–98a: 89)

The innovative aspect of Peirce's view is the idea that it is the 'community of inquirers' dialogically engaged that acquires knowledge. Unlike the model offered by Descartes of the solitary man who searches for knowledge, the Peircean model for the acquisition of knowledge involves communication between members of the community. Knowledge acquisition is a collaborative process. This final opinion can be considered to be the truth.

It should be pointed out that by 'final opinion' Peirce is not suggesting that we are unable to pass a judgement on whether something is true or false until the final opinion is reached. Rather, the search for a final opinion functions as a regulative ideal: it is an ideal because were the discussion to be continued, eventually the final opinion would be achieved. But in practice this does not mean that we must suspend judgement until it is reached, for if this were the case then it would be unlikely that anyone would question anything, since it would seem that they could never get an answer.

On Peirce's view, then, all advanced thinking depends on one's participation in a linguistic or semiotic *community*. Peirce's stress on the importance of community was a common theme throughout his work, and it increased as he came to understand more fully the importance of convention for semiosis. Peirce appealed to a community of inquirers for his theory of truth, and he regarded the *identification with community* as fundamental for the advancement of knowledge (the end of the highest semiosis) and, also, for the advancement of human relations. (1991–98a: xl)

Peirce and journalism, media and communication studies

In 'Cultural pragmatism and *The Life of the Sign*' (2008: 155–65), Gary Richmond outlines the way Peirce's semiology can be used for journalism, media and communication studies. He does this by following through with the ideas that Arnold Shepperson developed in 'Realism, Logic, and Social Communication: C.S. Peirce's classification of science in communication studies and journalism' (2008: 242–94).

Richmond claims that Shepperson realized the potential of Peirce's pragmatism when applied to the interdisciplinary aspects of cultural studies. The triadic nature of Peirce's theory of signs necessary leads to a theory of inquiry that can fruitfully resolve obstacles to interdisciplinary studies. (2008: 156–57) The starting point of Peirce's pragmatism is the idea that signs or the process of semiosis is dynamic; this dynamism can be seen in the signs of growth ranging from biological evolution to the growth of organizations and institutions. Pragmaticism, on this account, is a form of inquiry that is focussed on the 'reality of changing relations' (2008: 158).

Shepperson argues that journalism, media and communication studies are concerned with issues of social conduct. But to inquire into such conduct journalists, media and communication scholars must already have some notion of what is 'right' or 'true' or 'fair', however vague they might be. This is where Peirce's pragmatism is especially relevant: since its highest goal is that of modifying conduct it might be possible through inquiry into one's own ethical assumptions to find more agreeable ways of communal living. It is the nature of journalism, media and communication studies to be 'always experimental, always experiential and in flux' so that Shepperson claims that journalism, media and communication studies are in the favourable position of helping with the ethical development of a community. Richmond writes,

> Shepperson imagined that journalism, the media, and communication studies generally had an important role to play in bringing to critical awareness 'how human society ought to work', especially should these disciplines be able to shed the nearly pervasive nominalism and relativism which up until now have prevented such self-awareness and self-criticism occurring at the levels and in the ways needed. (2008: 159)

The question that still needs to be examined concerns the way Peirce's pragmatic method can be applied within journalism, media and communication studies. Shepperson argues that Peirce's system of classification of the sciences provides an invaluable approach to the classification of journalism and media studies that would serve to bring 'the practices of JMC [journalism, media and communication studies] to bear on the global dimension of the human condition' (2008: 271). Just as Peirce had argued that there is a triadic relationship between the sign, object and interpretant, Shepperson argues that there is a triadic relationship between the media, the producer and the consumer of messages. The media are not to be confused with what they convey: they are 'not *what they transport*, but the techniques that *make such transport possible*' (2008: 257).

Shepperson answers the question of how journalism, media and communication studies can become involved in ameliorating the human condition by arguing that there is a kind of sampling that is appropriate to these areas of study. Instead of the usual reliance on statistical probabilities, he suggests that journalism, media and communication studies should concentrate on future or potential populations. Statistical sampling, whether of the present (e.g. a consensus) or a partial one (e.g. a generation within a society), can only give a distorted picture of a social realm that is constantly changing. This is not to say that statistical sampling is never useful but it is to suggest that considerations of the future of the social realm can never be determined. Instead, the only option is to 'continually test our hypotheses against experience, correcting as we learn from the errors that this experience reveals' (2008: 265).

While Richmond points out that Shepperson's work provides an excellent starting point for what might be called 'cultural pragmatism', he acknowledges that Shepperson has only provided an outline that needs further elaboration. His article is, in effect, a call to potential future researchers to continue developing Shepperson's unfinished work.

Critical remarks

The impact of Peirce cannot be underestimated and his ideas have influenced a wide range of contemporary thinkers – Sebeok, Eco, Derrida, Davidson, Habermas, Kuhn and Popper to name just a few. Although he has contributed to several fields such as ethics and religion, his legacy is ensured in the now established field of semiotics, where he is regarded as one of the founding fathers. The value of semiotics also lies in its range of application so that it contributes to a better understanding of the more traditional disciplines of epistemology, anthropology, literary theory and linguistics. Furthermore, and in relation to semiotics, Peirce will be remembered for introducing pragmatism or – as he preferred to call it – pragmaticism, as a method for the clarification of concepts.

Peirce has also been a major influence on Habermas, who adopted his ideas to buttress his social and political philosophy. In particular, Habermas transformed Peirce's concept of the community of inquirers from that of a regulative ideal that legitimizes knowledge to a ground that functions within actual communities, enabling free and open debate within democratic societies (in Edgar 2006: 119–21). However, in his paper 'Peirce and Communication' (in Ketner Laine, Kenneth 1995: 243–66), Habermas comments that Peirce neglects the importance of communication between persons because he focuses on the representative function of the sign. Peirce is more interested in the relation between the sign and the world, and as a result, Habermas claims that the interpretant replaces the interpreter – who has in a sense become invisible, with serious consequences for semiotics and ethics. In 'A Response to Habermas' (in Ketner Laine, Kenneth 1995: 267–71) Oehler defends Peirce, arguing that Habermas's critique is formulated along the lines of his theory of communicative rationality, whereby reason is manifested in intersubjective communication. But Peirce did not think that language was an adequate medium for the expression of rationality, as is evidenced by his preference for diagrams and graphs to enable understanding.

Peirce's concept of 'unlimited semiosis' has led some to argue that given that everything is a sign and signs in the process of interpretation produce more signs, then signs contain within them the possibility of unlimited interpretations. Eco (1995: 205–22) rejects this interpretation of Peirce arguing that while there is this potential in signs, these signs do not float freely and endlessly but are situated within a context of relevance. This context of relevance or the 'given universe of discourse' sets the limit on what counts as a legitimate interpretation at a given moment: in other words, it is not a question of anything goes since what is being interpreted always takes place within a framework. Eco argues that both interpretations in general and textual interpretation in particular are subject to 'habit': according to Peirce's pragmaticism, habit lies outside the sphere of interpretation since it is a disposition to behave in a certain way towards something. Habit is closely connected to communities that both regulate and are the source of interpretations. So too, textual interpretations are subject to the habits of the community that 'decides' which further interpretations of the text are possible.

Finally, Sebeok's essay on Peirce titled 'Indexicality' (in Ketner Laine, Kenneth 1995: 222–42) demonstrates why Peirce rightly considered the index as the most important type of sign. It is the sign that is used in a large number of disciplines not usually associated with semiology, such as biology and ornithology. However, the more important point is that the indexical sign always reminds us of a specific and relevant context. As Sebeok points out, these contexts include the features that identify a person as a member of a group, a region, a social situation or an occupation; they can point to a person's personality, psychology or physiology.

In this chapter, I have given a broad overview of Peirce's writings, focusing chiefly on his theory of signs. The first section (1) has shown the mathematical and phenomenological basis of his theory of signs, and was (2) followed by a detailed account of the nature of signs. The third section (3) has developed Peirce's account of combinations of signs while the final section was concerned with (4) examining his views on pragmatism and knowledge.

Notes

1. In the early paper 'On a New List of Categories' (1867), Peirce shows the influence of Kant when he introduces the ideas of Firstness, Secondness and Thirdness. Although he reformulated this early theory, he still retained the underlying argument that understanding involves a triadic relationship between a sign (or as he sometimes calls it representamen or ground) and object and an interpretant. In 'A Guess at the Riddle' (1887–88), he detected the triad at work in logic, semiotics, metaphysics, psychology, physiology, biology, physics and theology.

2. In 'How to Reason', Peirce wrote, '[e]very science has its mathematical part. As soon as propositions are proposed for acceptance, even before they are yet adopted, the mathematician has to be called in to declare what consequences they would involve' (in de Waal, 2001: 8).

3. Peirce writes, 'If one can identify accurately all the conceivable phenomena which the affirmation or denial of a concept could imply, one will have therein a complete definition of the concept, and there is absolutely nothing more in it' (in Talisse and Aiken 2008: 10).

4. The analysis of the different methods is taken up in 'The Fixation of Belief' (1877) and 'How to Make Our Ideas Clear' (1878).

5. Peirce writes, 'Doubt is an uneasy and dissatisfied state from which we struggle to free ourselves and pass into the state of belief; while the latter is a calm and satisfactory state which we do not wish to avoid, or change to a belief in anything else. On the contrary, we cling tenaciously, not merely to believing, but to believing just what we do believe' (Vol. 1, 1992–98: 114).

Chapter 3

Foucault on Discourse and Power

M ichel Foucault's (1926–84) writings present a challenge to the way Western civilization has constructed its own identity – an identity that is heir to the values of the Enlightenment. The values of reason, progress and knowledge have been accepted unquestioningly as signs of the maturity of the West, so it is no surprise that Foucault's challenging of these foundational values has disturbed many.

Foucault's writings are divided into three phases: the first is commonly known as the archaeological period, and the texts include *The Order of Things* (1970) and *Madness and Civilisation* (1993). These are philosophical-historical analyses of the conditions that can account for the emergence of knowledge and madness in Western civilization. *The Archaeology of Knowledge* (1972) also belongs to the early Foucault, but unlike his other texts it is not an analysis of any historical phenomena, but a methodological text explaining the concepts that he used in his early writings. The genealogical phase reveals a change of emphasis in Foucault's writings with an increasing awareness of the relationship between power and knowledge in the formation of carceral institutions and in the study of sexuality. The texts included in this phase are *Discipline and Punish* (1991) and *The History of Sexuality Vol. 1.* (1978). In the later writings, Foucault once again shifts the direction of his thinking towards the subject or agency and the texts here include *The History of Sexuality Vol. 2* and *Vol. 3*.

It should be pointed out that when Foucault discusses the historical emergence of discourse in the archaeological and the genealogical writings, the time frames he adopts for historical periodization differ from those customarily used within the English-speaking world. The historical periods or epistemes that constitute the object of Foucault's attention are those of the Renaissance (1450–1660), the classical world (1660–1800) and the modern world (1800–1950).

While his writings have produced a number of theses on the interconnectedness between subjectivity, knowledge and power in modern society, my interest is that of showing the way power communicates through discourse. In this chapter I shall begin by elaborating (1) the concept of discourse, followed by (2) an overview of Foucault's archaeology of madness and knowledge and (3) his genealogical analysis of prisons and sexuality; I will finally (4) show the way Foucault's theses on discipline and surveillance are being utilized as a platform for the critique of contemporary social practices.

A theory of discourse

In *The Archaeology of Knowledge*, Foucault presents a theoretical account of his earlier writings such as *Madness and Civilisation* and *The Order of Things*, offering an explanation of the conceptual tools – discourse, episteme and archive – that he had employed in these analyses. In this text, Foucault both explains what his archaeological method involves and provides a detailed analysis of the concept of discourse. However, the concept of the episteme – that had been central to his earlier writings – is sidelined.

Discourse is defined as 'the general domain of all statements, sometimes as an individualizable group of statements, and sometimes as a regulated practice that accounts for a number of statements […]' (1972: 80). What this definition highlights is the idea that statements are produced within institutions and that these institutions operate according to certain rules that permit some statements and forbid others. These are transcendental in the sense that they are the conditions that make knowledge possible. Clearly a discourse should not be confused either with a way of using language or as an analysis of conversations; it is used by Foucault to define an area of social knowledge constituted by a regulated body of statements. This is why within a particular historical period it is possible to think and communicate in a certain way about an area of knowledge (madness or punishment). Given that statements are essential to the concept of discourse, Foucault describes the nature of the statement by contrasting it with

1. propositions: a proposition is the basic unit of analysis that logicians focus upon. In the study of propositions, the content of a proposition is considered as remaining the same throughout different usages; in addition, a proposition depends on truth conditions independently of other propositions. A statement on the other hand is dependent upon the context of realization. As Foucault points out, the same utterance can belong to an author, a character in a novel, or be part of a monologue (1972: 81). While a proposition as a declarative utterance represents or describes states of affairs as true or false, a statement does things, producing certain effects. Statements are analysed from the point of view of its functioning. So as to highlight their function or effect in the world he introduces the term *statement-event*.
2. sentences: a sentence is typically analysed by linguists from the point of view of its syntax, of the ordering of units with the sentence. A statement can also have an order or sequence to it but need not be a sentence: it is possible to order words into a certain sequence such that, although it would not count as a sentence, it would still count as a statement, as in, for example, the verbs in present tense in Latin. So too, statements are not necessarily linguistic: they can include graphs, tables of classification, genealogies and so on (1972: 82). Foucault's analysis of the statements takes place in terms of their functions both at a semiological level and at the level of the relations between statements within a discourse.

3. speech acts: although there is an overlap between the statement and speech act, since they both produce effects, they are not identical. Speech Act theory as proposed by Austin (Chapter 8) and Searle (Chapter 10) offers an analysis of the speech acts of everyday life (promising, commanding) in terms of their success. However, while a successful speech act usually consists of a number of statements, for Foucault a statement can be analysed individually in terms of its effects and is situated within a certain historical period. McHoul and Grace offer an excellent example to highlight the difference between speech acts and statements:

> Can we say, for instance, that there is equivalence between 'I promise' (when it is said as a proposal of marriage within the *discourse* of medieval romance) and 'I promise' (when it is said as an agreement to meet for lunch)? Perhaps these are equivalent speech acts (strictly, they are both 'commissives'), but each is a different statement. The two statements occur in totally different social 'technologies' and historically formed discursive practices. Each if successful produces distinct individual human subjects: lovers and lunchers; each, again if successful, (re)creates and maintains political institutions as different as love and lunch! (1993: 38)

In sum, the statement is not a stable entity since it depends upon the (varying) conditions of its production within a discourse and can be put to various uses (from statistics to literature). McHoul and Grace sum up Foucault's description of the statement as (1) a functional unit; (2) belonging to the domain of knowledge and (3) one of the techniques that institutions use to produce subjects (1995: 37–38).

Given the centrality of discourse in the acquisition of knowledge, the question that Foucault must examine concerns the origin or cause of a discourse. A popular view in the 'history of ideas' is that a particular person, a genius (Darwin or Einstein), is the originator of a discourse. The assumption underlying the 'history of ideas' is that there is a continuity between the great minds of the past who have communicated their ideas successively to each other and culminated in the present. This view implies that the present period – as the culmination of ideas – is superior to the past. Studies in the 'history of ideas' focus on the causes of these ideas, on what led to the originality or creativity of the author. But paradoxically, as Foucault points out, by focussing on the background causes that conditioned the author, the value and the centrality of the author as the original creator is displaced. Foucault's analysis is critical of the assumptions underlying the history of ideas, and this critique is directed at a cluster of concepts that serve to bolster the assumptions of continuity:

1. The concepts of tradition, influence, development and evolution, and spirit: The concept of tradition ensures that the continuity in history can be traced back to certain origins – the founding genius – so that what is new and different now leads back to this origin, in effect revealing it to be more of the same (1972: 21). The concept of influence also explains discourse as a repetition of something previously said, where by virtue of causal

processes an author is influenced by another across time; the concepts of development and evolution serve to give unity to a number of discourses by connecting concepts with their origins (1972: 21–22). Likewise, the concept of 'spirit' enables a number of discourses to be gathered under a 'collective consciousness' and offers the possibility of explaining a discourse (1972: 22).

2. The concept of the genre: genres – of philosophy, science and literature – are constructed within a certain historical period, but can they be applied to past discourses? As Foucault points out, the discourses of literature or politics are recent inventions that do not apply to medieval culture. It is only from our present point in time that such categories are applied (1972: 22).

3. The book and the oeuvre: The problem with the book is that it is a false unity: would we consider the text of a trial, a novel, a work within the collected writings of an author in the same way? And what is the relationship between two books by different authors and two books by the same author but constituting a series? Foucault's account claims that a book belongs to a network of books that are interrelated to each other. The category of the book as an independent entity is an effect of a particular discourse (1972: 23). In the case of the oeuvre or the complete works of the author, the problem is accentuated in that it is difficult to justify what to place and what to exclude in the oeuvre. Are the private letters of the author part of the oeuvre? The unpublished notes? Those works published under a pseudonym? And what about the works that the author himself/herself rejects (1972: 24)?

4. Marxist or hermeneutic explanations of discourse: These explanations posit an underlying origin that is the cause of the discourse: for Marxists, it is the material conditions of the sub-structure that explain the surface or apparent statements of the discourse; for hermeneutic theorists, the text has a secret meaning that needs to be decoded. The problem with the search for origins is that the origins can always be displaced to another further origin. The archaeologist is not interested in either psychological or sociological explanations of ideas. For Foucault, the statements of a discourse are what they are – material manifestations that do not necessitate looking 'behind' them or an act of interpretation. 'Discourse must not be referred to the distant presence of the origin, but treated as and when it occurs' (1972: 25).

The analysis of discourse that Foucault proposes is radical in that it does not focus on what the writers – scientists, historians, philosophers – are saying, but on the rules that make their discourse possible. In *The Archaeology of Knowledge,* Foucault offers a detailed theoretical elaboration of the rules that govern the production of statements and the role they play in the formation of discourse.

In his early descriptions of discourse Foucault adheres to the constructivist view, where discourses create or construct their objects rather than mirror a pre-existing reality. His goal is to substitute for the enigmatic treasure of 'things' anterior to discourse, the regular formation of objects that emerge only in discourse. To define these *objects* without reference to the *ground*, the *foundation of things*, but by relating them to the body of rules that enable them to form as objects of a discourse and thus constitute the conditions of their historical appearance. (1972: 47–48)

This construction takes place at a particular moment and the analysis of their rules describes the conditions of their historical importance. It is not a question of who is saying something, but a question of what it is possible to say in accordance with certain rules. These rules concern:

1. the formation of objects: the question Foucault tackles concerns the way an object such as madness comes into being. Its emergence is the result of:

   a. mapping out of the '*surfaces* of their *emergence*': different criteria of rationality and various theories establish the individual identity of (for example) alienation, dementia or psychosis and so on (1972: 41).[1]
   b. a practice of 'delimitation': the authorities regulate and determine which objects belong to which discipline (1972: 42).
   c. an analysis of the '*grids of specification*': objects are classified according to properties or symptoms (1972: 42).

2. the modalities of enunciation: Foucault describes the process whereby statements are not produced by subjects or persons working independently. Rather, the subject is immersed in a network of discourses.[2] These are:

   a. the right to speak: what is it that gives certain persons the right to speak and have their discourse legitimized, so that (for example) a doctor achieves his/her authority through a network of institutional practices (1972: 50)?
   b. the institution: the location or space from which statements are produced such as (for example) the hospital, laboratory or library (1972: 51).
   c. the relation between the subject and the object: the subject can occupy various positions in relation to different objects and domains ranging from the re-arrangement of the perceptual field, new techniques of registration, new forms of teaching and so on (1972: 52–53).

3. the production of concepts: In his analysis of the way concepts are developed within a discursive field, Foucault's interest is directed at:

   a. the 'forms of *succession*': Foucault includes two ways in which concepts are organized – '*the orderings of enunciative series*' and the '*types of dependence* of the statements'.

The former establishes both the rules between statements – so that inferences, implications and demonstrative reasonings are established in a certain way – and the latter the way statements are described sequentially (1972: 56–57).

b. the forms of 'coexistence': these forms include the *'field of presence'*, the *'field of concomitance'* and the *'field of memory'*.

The field of presence describes the way some statements belong, are present within a discourse or are excluded from it (1972: 58). The field of concomitance describes those statements that are not part of a discourse but are active so that (for example) the discourse of Linnaeus was influenced by the discourse of philosophy, theology, cosmology and so on (1972: 58). The field of memory concerns those statements that are no longer part of the accepted discourse, but that still have a connection through 'filiation', 'geneis', 'transformation', 'continuity' and 'historical discontinuity' with a particular discourse. As a result, some fields of memory might be richer than others (1972: 58).

c. the *'procedures of intervention'*: these procedures are not the same for all discursive formations. It is possible identify specific formations through the links and unities established between them. Foucault (1972: 58–59) specifies these interventions:

- the *'techniques of rewriting'*: there is a procedure that allows for the rewriting of data from one period (lists and groups) to another in another form (tables of classification);
- the *'methods of transcribing'*: here statements of a natural language are transcribed into a more formal one;
- 'the *modes of translating'*: here quantitative statements are translated into qualitative formulations (and vice-versa) so that, for example, statements of perceptual data can be translated into descriptive accounts;
- 'the means used to increase the *approximation* of statements and to refine their exactitude': by using form, number, arrangement and size of the elements, it became possible to produce a degree of constancy in descriptive statements;
- 'the way in which one *delimits* once again': one intervenes in a discourse either by extending or by restricting the domain of what counts as the validity of statements;
- 'the way in which one *transfers* a type of statement from one field of application to another': in this case, for example, the characteristics used to describe vegetal life are transferred to the animal world;
- 'the methods of *systemising* propositions': Foucault writes that this procedure has two possibilities – the first includes those propositions that already exist in a separate state but are utilized in a new way, and the second consists of those statements that are already part of a discursive formation but have been re-arranged to form a new whole;

4. the formation of strategies: the way a theory or a theme emerges within a discourse. This depends upon

   a. the *'points of diffraction'*: these follow a certain sequence. First, as *'points of incompatibility'*, opposite objects, concepts or utterances that do not belong to the same discursive formation appear within the same discourse. Then they are established *'as points of equivalence'*, as alternatives to the either/or opposition despite being chronologically different or of unequal importance. Finally, they are organized into *'link points of systemisation'* so that they come to constitute 'discursive sub-groups' within the total discourse (1972: 66).
   b. the *'economy of the discursive constellation'*: out of the several possibilities that are available, not all have materialized. For certain objects or concepts to become prominent, a number of choices by the relevant authorities need to be made, and this entails seeing other contemporary or relevant discourses (1972: 67).
   c. the role of the authorities: first, when a discourse is being studied, what is taken into consideration by the authorities is its function in relation to *'a field of non-discursive practices'*. Thus, for example, General Grammar played an important role in pedagogy, as did politics in the Analysis of Wealth. There is also what Foucault calls *'rules and processes of application'*, where choices can only be taken by certain individuals or groups with the right to speak. *'The possible positions of desire in relation to discourse'* describes the relationship between desire and authority, a relationship that is mistakenly associated only with fiction or poetry.

The corpus of texts or other materials that the archaeologist works with is found in what is customarily called the archive. Usually the value of the archive is that of providing the texts and materials that enable historians to examine their content, to see what they have to say. This is not Foucault's concept of the archive; rather, he considers it to be the repository of those conditions that made it possible for something to be said. From an archaeological analysis of the statements found in the archive, it is possible to uncover the rules that make knowledge within a period possible: 'The archive is first the law of what can be said, the system that governs the appearance of statements as unique events' (1972: 128–129).

The consequence of Foucault's analysis of the archive is that it reveals both the transitory and (relatively) unstable way in which the statements that constitute knowledge at a particular point in time are produced, and, furthermore, the way these statements are transformed into new ones (1972: 130). The archive situates what can be known between the continuum of the momentary and the enduring: it does not change every other day, but neither does it last forever.

While Foucault had explained in detail the way the rules functioned to produce the statements within a discourse, he still had to explain the way a discourse was controlled and regulated. An analysis of the relationship between discourse and power still needed to be undertaken, and in *'L'ordre du discours'*, somehow translated as 'The Discourse on Language',

Foucault writes '[i]n every society the production of discourse is at once controlled, selected, organised and redistributed according to a certain number of procedures [...]' (1972: 216). There are both external and internal procedures for the control of discourse. The external procedures involve:

1. an exclusion that is topically oriented: certain discourses are permitted while others are forbidden. At the time of writing, Foucault claimed that the areas in which freedom of discourse was prohibited were those of politics and sexuality.
2. an exclusion based on 'division and rejection': a discourse is classified according to the criteria of rationality, so that statements are judged according to whether they are reasonable or unreasonable. Foucault demonstrated this in the *History of Madness and Civilisation*, where discourses were structured according to the division of the sane and the insane. As a result, the utterances of the insane were immediately disqualified.
3. an exclusion based on the exclusion of the false: Foucault characterizes contemporary discourse as dominated by the will to truth. The will to truth – as propositional – is the acknowledged mode of cognition and is supported by institutional mechanisms such as libraries, publishing houses, and laboratories and so on (1972: 219). The function of the institutions in modern society is that of perpetuating and circulating true statements while eliminating false ones.

The internal procedures for the control of discourse are:

1. those of the commentary: a commentary is a series of statements about the statements of other texts. According to Foucault, they bring out what is already in the text but that has not yet been said (1972: 221). The importance of the commentary is not only that by commenting on a text it remains in circulation, but that the author of the commentary acquires a privileged position since he/she is able to say what the author struggled to say, or said unclearly.
2. those of the author: the function of the author is to provide a principle of organization over disparate texts so that a unity is established. In this way, if a number of texts are produced by the same author over a period of time, and if these texts are very different from each other, their diversity is nullified and subsumed under the name of the author. In contemporary society, the author is a privileged figure on account of the legal status and rights endowed upon him/her; but these rights have been historically acquired, coinciding with the emergence of capitalism. In the Middle Ages, for example, literature was enjoyed without the need to establish the identity of the author.[3]
3. those established by the discipline: each discipline or subject places boundaries or limits as to what counts as knowledge within that discipline; and each subject has certain rules and procedures that allow for the production of new statements. The difference between linguistics and philosophy can be described as the difference between what practitioners of each consider as belonging to their discipline. One of the goals of academic journals

and magazines is that of policing their domains. As a result of policing what counts as the knowledge of the subject, other 'threatening' knowledge is excluded (1972: 224).

There is a further cluster of rules forming the third mechanism for the control of discourse:

1. the 'rarefaction among speaking subjects': not everybody is entitled to speak on every subject and only those speakers who are qualified can participate in a discourse. Only those who have been vested with the authority to speak are entitled to do so: this is the domain of specialists. It is the educational system that transforms persons into professionals, giving them the 'right' to talk about certain things.
2. rituals: participating in a discourse entails adhering to conventions. Rituals dictate the qualifications that the person must hold in order to be part of the discourse, the behaviour that is appropriate and the language used within the discourse (1972: 225).
3. the 'fellowship of discourse': this refers to those communities that tightly control the preservation and reproduction of discourse, ensuring that the possession of the discourse remains within the community. Within a fellowship, the role of the speaker and the listener are not on a par.
4. 'doctrinal groups': a doctrinal group differs from a fellowship of discourse in that a doctrine is a sign that its holders belong to a particular class, status (social or racial), national identity and so on.
5. 'social appropriation': persons acquire a discourse through the education system. But while in principle the educational system is open to all, it still operates within a social-political framework and is therefore a site of social conflict (1972: 227).

There are some far-reaching and interesting implications of Foucault's analysis of discourse. Mills (2003: 71–72) describes the way nineteenth-century European botanists travelled to non-European countries with the classification of plant life that was devised by Linnaeus. When they discovered new plants, they fitted their discoveries into the Linnaeus classification, which they were familiar with. It was not considered important that the local people classified plants differently (in terms of their medicinal use, food value or ritualistic value). It could be said that the local knowledge was colonized by the European botanists, who renamed the plants according to the Latin names of the Linnaeus system, coupled with the name of the person who discovered them. This supports the argument that the European quest for knowledge has never been a neutral project, but tainted by political expediency. The discursive formations constructed by Western botanists had far-reaching political effects for they furthered the cause of colonization.

Archaeological analysis 1: The discourse of madness

In his early writings, Foucault focussed his attention on the way knowledge is produced during different stages of Western civilization. The concepts of episteme and discourse were utilized as the theoretical tools with which he conducted his analysis. I have already described in detail his concept of discourse, and in this section I will describe his concept of episteme as it is applied in *Madness and Civilisation* and *The Order of Things*.

In *The Archaeology of Knowledge*, Foucault describes an episteme as

> the total set of relations that unite, at a given period, the discursive practices that give rise to epistemological figures, sciences, and possible formalised systems [...] The episteme is not a form of knowledge or type of rationality which, crossing the boundaries of the most varied sciences, manifests the sovereign unity of a subject, a spirit, or a period; it is the totality of relations that can be discovered for a given period, between the sciences when one analyses them at the level of discursive regularities. (1972: 191)

Within an episteme, a various number of discourses circulate and achieve the status of knowledge on account of their adherence to the underlying rules of a particular episteme; they constitute what counts as knowledge as well as the limits of that knowledge.

However, what Foucault's analysis strikingly shows us is that although disciplines within a specific period might be different, at the level of the rules there is a striking similarity. Different discourses are conditioned by the same underlying rules operating 'behind' the backs of their authors, and each episteme has its own specific rules for the formation of discourses. In *The Order of Things*, Foucault brings out these similarities between natural history, economics and linguistics:

> [W]hat was common to the natural history, the economics and the grammar of the Classical Period was certainly not present to the consciousness of the scientist; or that part of it that was conscious was superficial, limited and almost fanciful (Adanson, for example, wished to draw up an artificial denomination for plants; Turgot compared coinage with language); [...] but unknown to themselves, the naturalists, economists and grammarians employed the same rules to define the objects proper to their own study, to form their concepts, to build their theories. (1970: xi)

What the analysis of the Classical Period shows is that scientists from different disciplines shared certain assumptions about the world (that it existed out there 'waiting' to be mapped) and about what counted as knowledge of the world. These operational assumptions conditioned the scientists without them being aware of it; as a result, we find knowledge in the Classical Period consisting of tables and lists of classifications. By way of contrast, in today's world, to know the nature of something does not require the search for large quantities of data that are then organized into lists and grids.

In *Madness and Civilisation,* Foucault examined the way Western culture came to terms with the experience of madness. In this early text, he still used the terminology of *experience,* which he replaced with the much less subjective *episteme* in his other writings. The analysis of madness focusses on the Renaissance, the Classical Age and the Modern Age so as to trace the different ways that madness was understood and spoken about. The result of this analysis reveals (1) the emergence of two different categories of thought: the Renaissance distinction between reason and unreason and the classical distinction between reason and madness, the latter distinction giving rise to the disciplines of psychiatry and psychology. It also makes apparent (2) the demise of the houses of confinement and the birth of the asylum in the eighteenth century.

The Renaissance understood madness as a particular kind of wisdom, and strictly speaking it was not called madness but 'unreason'. It was still conceptualized in relation to reason, thus constituting an interrelationship rather than an opposition. However, the Renaissance also displayed an ambivalent relation to madness, as depicted by the ship of fools with the mad sailing across the canals of Europe (1993: 8). On the one hand the ship of fools symbolized madness expelled from the cities, from reason; but on the other hand the mad – as unreason – were still free to navigate from city to city. No attempt was made to either confine or eliminate them, and at times they were even allowed to enter different towns. The dialogue between reason and unreason was maintained but kept at a distance. Within the framework of Renaissance thinking, the mad were considered as having certain insights into life, into the truths of human existence that were unattainable from a rational perspective. The mad were privileged in that they had access to a different world of meaning, a world that revealed the absurdity of reason. With this mindset, madness was not considered a disease or an illness, and at this stage Foucault argued that reason and unreason were still in dialogue, a dialogue that would end with the opposition of reason to madness.

The break occurred in the Classical Age, which 'was to reduce to silence the madness whose voices the Renaissance had just liberated, but whose violence it had already tamed' (1993: 38). During the seventeenth century, an assorted number of people – the poor, the sick, the mad, the promiscuous, rebellious children, irresponsible parents – were locked up in the empty leper houses that dotted the countryside of Europe. These houses had originally been built in the Middle Ages, when leprosy had posed a problem for public health. Once leprosy had been contained, the leper houses became disused and remained empty; however – and crucially – the way of thinking that excluded those who posed a danger remained (1993: 3). This exclusivist way of thinking resurged with the creation of the houses of confinement from 1656 onwards, where the aforementioned individuals were obliged to work. Although there was a strong economic incentive for the practice of confinement – since it prevented these people from committing crimes in times of unemployment, while at the same time providing a cheap source of labour in times of employment – Foucault argued that the underlying motive was a moral one (1993: 57). Through the discipline of labour, the moral reform of these individuals would take place since forced labour induced a sense of responsibility. The problem was that the mad were unable to follow the work routines;

they disrupted the patterns of work within the houses of confinement and this eventually led to special routines being devised for them. The mad were beginning to be identified as a different category from the rest on account of the spectacle they offered through their madness.

Foucault rejects the view that the mad were confined on scientific grounds. Their confinement was justified morally according to this pattern: (1) madness belonged to the category of unreason; (2) it was therefore opposed to reason; (3) it involved a moral choice of unreason over reason; (4) it needed control and administration, which meant that it could not go unchecked and (5) it was a form of 'animality', a space beyond reason and humanity (1993: 71–78). Given their animal nature, human methods could not work upon the mad, so the only solution left was that of disciplining them. The mad could not be treated by medicine nor guided by morality.

Apart from the exclusion of the mad on moral grounds, Foucault's study of madness also takes into consideration the cognitive understanding of madness in the Classical Age. It is not only from the perspective of the practices enacted – as specified in the manuals and records of the period – that Foucault's reading operates, but also from the perspective of the theorization of madness as conducted by philosophers and scientists. The latter argued that since madness was a deviation from the norm of reason, it was therefore something that reason and science could know. It was recognized as a negative form of knowledge, as unreason. The important point is that for the Classical Age, as an illness madness still constituted a form of knowledge, and attempts were made to identify its varieties with the tables and charts common to this period. The problem the thinkers of this age had to contend with was that, on the one hand, the acquisition of knowledge related to positive things – to know meant that one could identify and rationally tabulate the object of one's knowledge; but on the other hand madness constituted a negation of reason, a knowledge that was beyond knowledge. This problem was never resolved by classical thinkers.

Despite their differences, both the moral assessment and the cognitive considerations of madness shared a common underlying basis that justified the exclusion of the mad. They negated the very reason that the Classical Age upheld. There was therefore no place for madness within the structures of classical thinking, so that the only remaining solution was to exclude them. As a result the mad remained alone in the houses of confinement.

Despite being segregated from the rest of society, the houses of confinement created a new social problem. The inhabitants living close to them complained to the authorities that they were at risk of illness (1993: 202). The inhabitants remembered that lepers used to be confined in these houses and this generated a fear of contamination. The mad were slowly being identified with illness, and it was at this stage that the doctor entered the scene, not to help the mad, but to protect the local inhabitants. In effect, madness became medicalized.

In 1793, Pinel liberated the mad from the chains of their confinement and instead created the asylum as the space for the humane treatment of the mad (1993: 243). Pinel in France and Tuke in York are considered to be the forerunners of Modern Age psychology and psychiatry, for they replaced the system of physical restraint with a system of controls, routines, rewards and punishments: 'Tuke created an asylum where he substituted for the free terror of madness the stifling anguish of responsibility [...]' (1993: 247). Tuke and Pinel considered their practices scientific, for the mad were placed in a system of observation where their actions were constantly observed and scrutinized.[4]

The space of the asylum created a relation between the guards and the patients; this would later develop into the relation between the psychiatrist and the patient. Through the practice of assessing and writing reports on the patients, the asylum was transformed into a medical space. But, Foucault points out, while the entry of the doctor seems to have marked the entry of science into the asylum, the ability to cure was not grounded in medical knowledge, but on the moral authority of the doctor who ruled the asylum as a miniature bourgeois society. The asylum was the space

> in which were symbolized the massive structure of bourgeois society and its values: Family-Child relations, centred on the theme of paternal authority; Transgression-Punishment relations, centred on the theme of immediate justice; Madness-Disorder relations, centred on the theme of social and moral order. It is from these that the physician derived his power to cure [...] (1993: 274)

It was the doctor who imposed a regime on the mad using the standard of bourgeois morality which the mad deviated from and had to return to. Ironically, the fathers of modern psychiatry admitted that their work was morally inspired: in their respective practices – Tuke used farm work and Pinel used the new asylum – they deployed systems that would ensure the internalization of fear and guilt. The valorization of science was merely a mask for their moral activities:

> [W]hat we call psychiatric practice is a certain moral tactic contemporary with the end of the eighteenth century, preserved in the rites of asylum life, and overlaid with the myths of positivism. (1993: 276)

Foucault is critical of the commonplace view that the Modern Age brought about an improvement in the lives of the mad. The difference between the Modern Age and the Classical Age is that although the mad were physically imprisoned in the Classical Age, they were free to think whatever they liked. The new 'advanced' techniques of the Modern Age placed the mind of the insane under observation. They were not free to think whatever they liked because it was their consciousness and their thoughts that were subjected to therapy.

In *Madness and Civilisation*, Foucault traces the emergence of madness from the earlier distinction between reason and unreason to its subsequent transformation into a science that is concerned with individual pathology. It is a central part of his argument that the emergence of this specific view of the mad could only take place within the modern episteme in the interplay of both discursive and non-discursive practices.

Archaeological analysis 2: The discourses of the sciences

In *The Order of Things*, Foucault shifts his attention to the historical conditions that enabled man to be both the object (the known) and subject of knowledge (the knower). The concepts of the episteme and of discourse continue to play an important role and his analysis is broadened to cover three discourses within an episteme. While the discourses have changed, the epistemes that frame these discourses have remained the same: the Renaissance, the classical and the modern.

Towards the beginning of *The Order of Things*, Foucault quotes a short story by Borges which tells of a 'Chinese encyclopaedia' where the

> animals are divided into: (a) belonging to the Emperor, (b) embalmed, (c) tame, (d) tame, (d) suckling pits, (e) sirens, (f) fabulous, (g) stray dogs (included in the present classification, (i) frenzied, (j) innumerable, (k) drawn with a very fine camel-hair brush, (l) et cetera, (m) having just broken the water pitcher, (n) that from a long way off look like flies. (1970: xv)

The point that this system of classification brings home is that there are different ways of ordering the world, and of including and excluding data. Given the above observation on world classification, what does this say about the way Western civilization has ordered the world, about the assumptions used in its system of classification? In *The Order of Things* Foucault answers this question by offering a historical account of the way these systems of classification developed.

While Western science has favoured the disciplines that deal with necessary truths – such as mathematics and physics, it has tended to look down on the 'messy' subjects of languages, living things or economics. Foucault's archaeological thinking is intended to redress the balance: according to the classical episteme the general categories of life, labour and language will offer an analysis of man as a living, productive or speaking animal; under a different episteme – the modern one – man will be studied as a biological, economic or philological animal. The innovative point is that while there are dissimilarities between the epistemes, within the same episteme there is a similarity of thinking, a similarity in the conceptual structure that organizes the classifications.

The epistemes are not only different from each other, but from the point of view of one episteme it is impossible to think with the mindset of the other episteme. They are incommensurable, which explains why Buffoon in the eighteenth century (the Classical Age) was completely baffled by the Renaissance thinker Aldrovandi's classification of dragons and serpents. The problem is not that Buffoon is superior to Aldrovandi but that the way each saw the world was completely different, conditioned as it was by a completely different episteme.

The epistemes under analysis are the pre-classical, spanning from the Renaissance to the mid-seventeenth century; the Classical Age that lasts until the end of the eighteenth century and the Modern Age that ends in the 1950. Foucault's analysis focusses on the characteristic features of the epistemes without offering an explanation of why the changes between them took place.

The Renaissance episteme is characterized by resemblances between words and things: a word is like its object. There are four types of resemblances (1970: 18–25):

1. the resemblances of things that are close to each other (*convientia*) such as animals and places, the earth and the sea, the body and the soul;
2. the resemblance of things based on distance (*aemulatio*), so that the sky resembles the face because it has two eyes (the sun and the moon);
3. the resemblances constructed out of analogies, where the relations between things are important;
4. the resemblances of sympathy, which in effect meant that everything could be seen to resemble everything else since all of reality was interconnected. The problem with sympathy was that it had the potential to transform everything into the same; this problem was thwarted by antipathy that counteracted the force of sympathy by setting into motion all of the resemblances.

The underlying assumption of the Renaissance episteme was the world as a text written by God: things resembled each other because God 'signed' them to show their interconnectedness.

> *Convenientia, aemulatio, analogy*, and *sympathy* tell us how the world must fold in upon itself, reflect itself, or form a chain with itself so that things can resemble one another [...] [but] [t]here are no resemblances without signatures. (1970: 26)

The problem was that it was not easy to know the signature of God, and this led to an endless series of interpretations. Knowledge was more a question of guessing rather than proving, since the relation between words and things was God-given. Renaissance writers sought to find the original ground of meanings, the primal natural and universal language before its break-up into many languages.

In his discussion of the Renaissance, Foucault adopts the much criticized strategy of using relatively minor figures as sources of information. Thus, while a study of the Renaissance would not usually fail to mention the leading figures of the times, such as Leonardo or Erasmus (among others), in Foucault they barely get a mention, and are replaced by lesser-known figures such as Aldrovani or Ramus.

With the Classical Age, a new form of knowledge or episteme suddenly appears. The language of analogy is replaced with that of analysis:

> the activity of the mind [...] will no longer consist *in drawing things together*, in setting out on a quest for everything that might reveal some sort of kinship, attraction, or secretly

shared nature within them, but on the contrary, in *discriminating*, that is, in establishing their identities. (1970: 55)

The goal of the classical episteme was that of representing the world through the method of analysis. Representation took two forms: mathesis, where objects were measured, and taxonomia, where objects were ordered and classified (1970: 71–77). The discourse of general grammar studied the representation of words, the discourse of natural history studied the representation of nature and the discourse of wealth studied the representation of needs. The classical strategy had the benefit of eliminating the infinite resemblances (typical of the Renaissance episteme) with finite differences. Tables of varying degrees of complexity were constructed so as to represent and give order to the world; these representations were enacted through a system of signs, where the orderings took place according to those signs that were identical to each other and those that were different from each other. Signs were therefore related to each other in such a way that there 'is a bond established inside knowledge, between the *idea of one thing* and the *idea of another*' (1970: 63.) In this way, it was believed that definitive knowledge could be acquired with the endless guessing and the prolific interpretations of the Renaissance, no longer considered as forms of knowledge. The problem with the classical episteme was that by emphasizing the differences between things and organizing these differences accordingly, no value was attributed to the origin of things; in other words, the historical background was ignored.

The interesting feature of Foucault's claim is that while the knowledge these discourses revealed was important to humanity, humanity was left out of the picture; it was not represented within the classifications. It was only when the classical episteme dissolved that the possibility of a science of human – the human sciences – arose.

With the Modern Age the lack of historical interest shown in the classical episteme was compensated for with a renewed interest in the origin of things. In their analysis of nature, classical theorists were unaware that historical considerations were slipping into the tables that they were formulating. It was as though life sneaked in from behind to reassert its importance. The transition from one episteme to another could be detected in the way the early writers attempted to re-insert history into their studies of life, labour and language even though they still employed concepts from the Classical Age. It was from about 1795 onwards that the Modern Age came completely into being with Curvier in biology, Ricardo in economics and Bopp in philology.

Within the category of life, the classical discipline of natural history was replaced by the discipline of biology so that function, not structure, became important. In the realm of economics, the classical study of wealth and exchange was replaced by the study of production and of who controlled the forces of production. Within the domain of language, the classical discipline of grammar was replaced by philology so that emphasis lay on the origins of language. However, while biology, labour and language were domains of empirical analysis, and therefore sciences, they were not human sciences since the latter were interested in what these subjects meant or represented to humans themselves.

In the attempt to acquire their own identity, the human sciences adopted the methods and models used within the sciences. First they adopted the biological model that used functions for their explanations; then they adopted the economic model that explained phenomena in relation to conflict and finally they adopted the philological model that sought hidden meanings and interpretations. In addition to this, the human sciences shifted their emphasis from processes that are accessible to consciousness to those unconscious structures that influence consciousness – structures of 'norms, rules and systems' (1970: 361).

In the mentality of the modern theoretician, the study of phenomena needed to include the historical forces that affected and constituted these phenomena. Deeper forces affected these surface phenomena and needed to be accounted for. The important point for Foucault is that these new domains were not just developments of earlier ones, but new domains with new concerns:

> Philology, biology, and political economy were established, not in the places occupied by *general grammar, natural history* and the *analysis of wealth*, but in an area where those forms of knowledge did not exist, in the space they left blank, in the deep gaps that separated their broad theoretical segments and that were filled with the murmur of the ontological continuum. (1970: 207)

The conclusion Foucault arrives at from his analysis of the Modern Age is that it was the age that 'invented' the category of humankind as an object of knowledge. This was the period when a number of disciplines – the human sciences – came into being and directed their attention towards humans. The dilemma of the human sciences is that humans were both the subject doing the studying and the object of that study. Humans are the condition of possibility for the study of humanity; they represent themselves within the various human sciences and are the beings that make these representations possible. It is perhaps the label 'sciences' that is misleading. And Foucault's point is that the categories used in these sciences to understand humans were created by the sciences themselves in the first place. The scientific credentials of these disciplines turned out to be human creations. This is why Foucault claims that the time has arrived for us to realize that we must awake from our 'anthropological slumber'.

Genealogical analysis 1: The discourse of punishment

With both *Discipline and Punish* and *The History of Sexuality Vol. 1*, Foucault turned his attention to the way changes occurred between epistemes. In his archaeological writings, he had failed to take into account the influence of institutions in the transition from one episteme to another. In the genealogical approach, Foucault broadens his analysis to show that non-discursive forces, whether economic, political, social, juridical or pedagogical, contribute to the formation of epistemes. One concern that receives sustained attention is the interaction between power and knowledge, with the aforementioned texts providing specific applications of the relationship between power and knowledge in the domains of criminality and sexuality.

The starting point of Foucault's reconfiguration of power is the critique of what he calls the 'juridical' view of power. Society is divided into those who dominate and have the power, and those who are dominated and want the power. The juridical view of power is common to both the left and the right of the political spectrum, with the former thinking of it as something that should be seized, and the latter considering it as something to hold on to. According to this view, power is defined in the negative as a force that says 'no' to everything. For Foucault, this view fails to take into account the positive dimension of power:

> We must cease once and for all to describe the effects of power in negative terms: it 'excludes', it 'represses', it 'censors', it 'abstracts', it 'masks', it 'conceals'. In fact, power produces; it produces reality; it produces domains of objects and rituals of truth. The individual and the knowledge that may be gained of him belong to this production. (1991: 194)

Foucault's reconfiguration of power is conducted at the micro-level: relations of power permeate society so that power is not a monolithic overbearing structure, but is localized and diffused throughout the social network. Foucault's analytic of power introduces two key characteristics: power is both productive and relational. It is productive because it produces new social categories (the criminal, the homosexual) that in turn constitute new objects of knowledge. It is relational because it is generated by the differences between persons, organizations and institutions: the differences between teachers and students, parents and children, the priest and the confessant, the psychoanalyst and the patient. While it is the interaction between them that leads to the production of knowledge, these power relations are characterized by an imbalance of power: some dominate and others are dominated:

> Power is not something that is acquired, seized, or shared, something that one holds on to or allows to slip away; power is exercised from innumerable points, in the interplay of non-egalitarian and mobile relations. (1978: 94)

It is those in the dominant position of power that produce knowledge, so that you find many more studies about the marginalized – deviants, immigrants – than you do about those considered 'normal'. It is the uneven distribution of power that transforms an object into an object of knowledge.

The dynamics involved in the acquisition of knowledge lead Foucault into conceptualizing the knowledge–power relation as symbiotic. Knowledge and power feed on and into each other:

[P]ower and knowledge directly imply one another [...] [such] that there is no power relation without the correlative constitution of a field of knowledge, nor any knowledge that does not presuppose and constitute at the same time power relations. (1991: 27)

This is a controversial claim because the prominent status of science within Western culture has always been justified on the basis of its objectivity, its freedom from the interests of its practitioners. Foucault claims that power produces knowledge, and knowledge empowers.

The interrelationship between power and knowledge is highlighted in his account of the will-to-knowledge that characterized the modern episteme in the nineteenth century. In order to obtain information, procedures were developed to identify, classify, measure and calculate objects. During the age of imperialism, colonists, travellers and missionaries contributed to the compilation of knowledge about the countries they visited. This will-to-knowledge was not impartial but served the interests of the Western colonizing states. It was a type of knowledge that was tied to a particular historical moment in Western civilization – a moment when Western civilization considered itself superior to other cultures; and in so doing, it was judging other cultural systems as superstitious and therefore not worthy of being considered as knowledge (Mills: 71).

In *Discipline and Punish* and the *History of Sexuality Vol. 1*, Foucault, evidently more influenced by Nietzsche, understands discourses as the result of power relations and forces. The influence of Nietzsche brings out the fundamental difference in the goals of the genealogist and the archaeologist: while the archaeologist is interested in describing discourses and their production, the genealogist is interested in their historical-institutional emergence. As a result, a critical engagement with institutional discourses is possible, together with the realization that things do not have to be as they are but can always be otherwise. Unlike the traditional historian who considers the goal of historiography as the objective writing of the past, the genealogist is involved in the writing of the past.

The opening lines of *Discipline and Punish* offer a striking illustration of the way punishment was handed down in the Classical Age:

On 2 March 1757 Damiens the regicide was condemned 'to make the *amende honorable* before the main door of the Church of Paris', where he was to be 'taken and conveyed in a cart, wearing nothing but a shirt, holding a torch of burning wax weighing two pounds'; then, 'in the said cart, to the Place de Greve, where, on a scaffold that will be erected there, the flesh will be torn from his breasts, arms, thighs and calves with red-hot pincers, his right hand, holding the knife with which he committed the said parricide, burnt with sulphur, and, on those places where the flesh will be torn away, poured molten lead, boiling oil, burning resin, wax and sulphur melted together and then his body drawn and quartered by four horses and his limbs and body consumed by fire, reduced to ashes and his ashes thrown to the winds. (1991: 3)

Eighty years later, punishment was no longer physical, but took the form of rules and timetables regulating the entire day of the criminal – from what time to get up to when to eat, pray, work and rest. How did such a change in punishment take place within such a short space of time?

Punishment in the Classical Age necessarily involved brutality and visibility: criminals were punished violently in front of a public since this would serve to reassert the authority of the law. Punishment was read as revenge upon the transgressors for their actions and it always involved torture to a lesser (flogging, branding, etc.) or greater degree (public execution). Capital punishment was considered the appropriate punishment for potential regicides, since it involved breaking the law by both attempting to commit murder and attempting to kill the king whose very person represented the law. The savage revenge by the king was justified on the grounds that it was an attack on the law itself. But despite the barbaric spectacle that was intended to highlight the seriousness of the law, Foucault notes that public executions were frequently transformed into support for the criminal, and that the occasion was used as a springboard for rioting. It became increasingly evident that public execution was not a certain way of re-asserting the sovereignty of the law.

With the Enlightenment it was realized that punishment as brutal force was failing to prevent crime, in addition to being inhuman. There was a shift in the way punishment was conceptualized: it was no longer considered an attack upon the sovereign, but upon society as a whole. Rather than enacting the revenge of the sovereign, punishment came to be considered as something that should strive to re-insert the person into society. The criminal had to be made to understand the nature of his crime: it was the mind, not the body, that had to be punished. To teach prisoners the rationality of their punishment, the Modern Age theorists devised a system of connections between the crime and the punishment. It was important that the punishment did not seem to be capricious, for otherwise social re-integration would be harder to achieve. Punishment was undertaken by a moral impulse, an impulse toward the re-habitation of the criminal.

The prison system as re-habitation replaced the concept of punishment as a spectacle of physical brutality. This involved the maintenance of numerous prisons and a large number of rules that structured and disciplined a prisoner's daily life. The modern penitentiary adopted a whole strategy of techniques for the implementation of its policies, ranging from dossiers that noted in detail all the observations made of the prisoner to the establishment of the right of the penal authorities to punish. Central to Foucault's argument is the model of the Panopticon: it was designed as a structure for the complete and constant surveillance of the prisoner (1991: 200–09). The panopticon was an architectural blueprint created by Jeremy Bentham for the construction of a new prison system. In this new prison the behaviour of prisoners would be monitored through a system of windows. The crucial and important feature was that the prisoners would never know when they were being watched by the wardens. As a result, they would learn how to control their own behaviour; in effect, the prisoners were their own correctional officers, and the penal authorities hoped that their self-controlling behaviour would become the norm. Although the Panopticon was an architectural blueprint, it represented the model for an emerging type of society and the discipline needed to control it.

Modern disciplinary practices made great use of observational techniques with the prisoner unaware that he/she was being observed. The filtering of the data collected necessitated a hierarchical system to ensure that it arrived at those at the summit of the hierarchy. The analysis of these observations led, in turn, to a system of evaluations grounded in the normal: the prisoner was judged to be normal or abnormal with the notion of deviancy as a falling away from the norm. For Foucault, the Modern Age establishes the normal as the basis of judgement in a number of different fields, so that those who failed to adhere to the norm could be corrected. The difference between premodern punishment and modern punishment is that whereas in the Classical Age a person was punished for his/her actions in relation to the law, in the Modern Age actions were judged in terms of how behaviour related to the norm.

Foucault's critical analysis is directed at the values of the Modern Age. The bourgeois and their disciplinary drive introduce a specific value system and practices such as fair trials, the assumption of innocence and a rational system for the examination of evidence. But while these worked well for an educated, upper middle class, that is, the class that used them, another system of values was adopted for the working class, a system that reflected the fear of the bourgeois – social instability. The maintenance of social order was achieved through surveillance, repression and punishment. For Foucault, the success of the prison system could be found not in the unattainable dream of reducing, let alone eliminating, crime, but in its ability to offer a system for the classification of all crimes that in turn justified the intervention and infiltration of power within every sphere of society.

From the violence of the Classical Age to the prison of the Modern Age, the change in the implementation of punishment was not the result of an enlightened view of humaneness (at least this was not its primary objective), but the result of a changing society that made it necessary to think of punishment in terms of control. Foucault is also critical of the liberal-humanist concept of prison that seeks to reform the 'criminal' so as to re-integrate him/her into society. He argues that prison itself functioned as a model of the way society should be: a disciplined body. This can be seen from the way spatial locations and timetables were organized not only in prison but in society as a whole: from schools, to factories, to army barracks, students, workers and soldiers were subjected to a disciplinary routine that had the goal of transforming them into disciplined bodies.

But how are disciplined bodies created? The vision of a disciplined society could be enacted (1) through the organization of physical space with persons segregated in cells, barracks, dormitories and factories. These spaces were organized functionally and placed under supervision; (2) through the regulation of activities: from timetables for workers, prisoners, soldiers and schoolchildren to specific rules prescribing how to write, how to hold a gun and how to salute; (3) through the use of exercise, especially in the army and the schools, with a view to the maximum efficiency of time; (4) the use of tactics where the co-ordination of individuals working together as a disciplined body became essential.

Foucault's analysis of the transition to a disciplined society highlights an important point: discipline and power had been broadened from a state of prevention – of preventing things from happening – to that of production. The point of these disciplinary techniques, for example in the army and the factory, was that of increasing efficiency, productivity and skill. In addition, for these disciplinary techniques to succeed, supervision was necessary. A hierarchy of supervisors, each reporting to his/her respective supervisors, was required for the complete surveillance of the individual (1991: 135–70).

From his analysis, Foucault concludes that since the Modern Age, there has been a collusion between the social sciences and the state. In order to function, the social sciences require the techniques of the state to gather information and create the relevant documentation, while the power of the state in turn needs the social sciences to develop the data into knowledge that can be used to justify the exercise of power. The human sciences were born with 'the modern play of coercion over bodies, gestures and behaviour […]' (1991: 191). The importance of the social sciences – criminology, psychiatry, social work and pedagogy – lies in the fact that they determine the norm, so that anyone who does not follow the norm is labelled as deviant.

In the contemporary world, membership within society entails behaving normally; this normality is ensured by a legion of social workers, teachers, doctors and judges. In what Foucault calls the carceral system, all society is a prison, with the actual prison as the most tangible structure of the disciplinary society. 'Normalisation' is now so ingrained within Western culture that a whole series of tests, questionnaires and programmes have been established to ensure that citizens are dutiful, children are healthy and so on. The combination of observation and evaluation culminates in the examination: throughout a person's life, examinations – whether for school, for health or for employment – are held. These examinations are crucial to the functioning of modern societies, for they oblige the person to reveal the truths about what he/she knows and about his/her health or ambitions. In effect, this knowledge is then used to control the person: it might reveal that a student is not apt for a particular course of studies or that a person needs some kind of therapy. The information derived from these examinations is then documented: one could describe this system as an early version of contemporary databases, where information is collected and used to construct a profile or identity of the person. A person in fact is transformed into a case study and this suggests that he/she is an object of knowledge. Social workers, for example, are agents that monitor the norm. Everyday life in modern society is subject to what Foucault calls the 'normalising gaze'.

Interestingly the norm functions as a continuum, so that whether one is a rapist or a petty thief, one's actions are judged relative to the standard of normal behaviour. Unlike the Classical Age, when the category of the outlaw lived on the fringes or outside society, in the Modern Age there is the category of deviancy, with the deviant as the permanent danger inserted within society. This danger justifies the necessity of constantly surveilling society in the search for potential deviants. For Foucault, we today live in an age of surveillance that has its origins in the Modern Age.

Genealogical analysis 2: The discourse of sexuality

Both *Discipline and Punish* and the *History of Sexuality Vol. 1* are genealogical analyses of power and knowledge, with each text focussing on a specific object of knowledge, namely crime and sexuality. However, while *Discipline and Punish* focussed on the control of others and had a fixed institutional space (the prison) to enact this control, sexuality did not have a fixed space, making it more pliable and conducive to the strategies of power and knowledge. The important aspect of Foucault's study on sexuality is that, rather than studying the development of different sexual practices, it places emphasis upon the actual discourses of sexuality

The question Foucault asks is why did sexuality become the focus of intense scientific investigation in Western civilization? Why is it that Western civilization developed a science of sexuality, a '*scienza sexualis*', whereas in other cultures sexuality developed the erotic arts, an '*ars erotica*'? The erotic arts are directed towards the intensification of the sexual experience under the guidance of a master; eroticism emphasizes the maximization of sexual pleasure. Sexuality in Western civilization was transformed into a science. It did not focus on the subjective quality of the sexual experience, but on its objectivity. The goal of this science was to collect information about a person's sexuality so as to discover the truth about sexuality.

Foucault's central claim is that the modern concern with the sexuality of the person has a premodern origin in medieval confessional practices framed within the discourse of sin and salvation. The interiorization of sexuality has its origins in medieval confession, where the penitent expressed the truths about himself/herself. Confession was established as the system for the production of truth about the self. Penitents were encouraged not only to confess their external sexual actions, but to also voice what went on internally – their thoughts, desires and inclinations that accompanied or were 'behind' their sexual actions. At the beginning, confession was relatively infrequent since the public was expected to confess only once a year, so that the monitoring of sexuality could not have been thorough. However by 1550 this changed, and with it a new concept of identity emerged. Whereas previously the identity of a person took the form of an avowal, with one's identity guaranteed by those whom he/she knew, identity then became formulated in relation to the truths 'lying' within the person:

> [F]or a long time, the individual was vouched for by the reference of others and the demonstration of his ties to the commonweal (family, allegiance, protection); then he was authenticated by the discourse of truth he was able or obliged to pronounce concerning himself. (1978: 58)

Truth, although hidden, was now located within the person. The importance of the medieval confessional system was that it transformed desire into discourse.

From the Middle Ages to the modern world, a shift in context framed the discourse of sexuality differently. While the discourse of the Middle Ages was framed within the religious context of sin and salvation, the discourse of the Modern Age was framed within a scientific context concerned with health and illness. The Modern Age transformed the religiously grounded discourse of sexuality into a science of sexuality, a science that aimed to discover the truth about sex. Despite the different frameworks, the dynamics of power in both religious and secular confessional practices operated along the same binary of questioner and questioned,

> the agency of domination does not reside in the one who speaks (for it is he who is constrained), but in the one who listens and says nothing; not in the one who knows and answers, but in the one who questions and is not supposed to know. And this discourse of truth finally takes effect, not in the one who receives it, but in the one from whom it is wrested. (1978: 62)

By the eighteenth century, sexuality became a target for the authorities, since a link was established between what a person did with his/her sexuality and the administration of society. This connection can be seen in the studies concerning the population, prostitution and the spread of disease. Knowing the sexuality of its citizens provided the information for the development of a politics of the body (anatomopolitics) and for the planning of the population (biopolitics). The sexualized body became the locus of the study of medicine, psychology and demography, studies that in turn fed into the concerns of the state. By managing sexuality, the state was in effect managing life.

The question that faced the scientist of the nineteenth century was that of transforming the pleasures that the individual confessed into a science, into a systematic account rather than just a collection of random experiences. This transformation took place by following a number of procedures (1978: 65–67):

1. *'Through a clinical codification of the inducement to speak'*: by using interrogations and questionnaires, the confession was transformed into an acceptable scientific document.
2. *'Through the postulate of a general and diffuse causality'*: by introducing the principle of sex as the causal origin for all ailments, any illness of a child, adult, old person and even an entire race could be reduced to a sexual origin.
3. *'Through the principle of a latency intrinsic to sexuality'*: by considering sex as something that wanted to remain hidden but could only be extracted through scientific examination.
4. *'Through the method of interpretation'*: by establishing sexuality as a system of signs that could be interpreted, and whose results contributed to the truth.
5. *'Through the medicalization of the effects of confession'*: by replacing the categories of sin with the categories of the normal and the pathological, with sex understood as an unstable pathological field, medical intervention was justified.

The irony of history is that while the Modern Age showed a great interest in questions of sexuality, the period is usually depicted as an age of Victorian Puritanism, where any talk of sex was forbidden. Popular opinion has it that the Victorian Age was one that repressed all sexuality to the extent that the use of the word *sex* was taboo. Foucault calls this alleged denial of sexuality the 'repressive hypothesis', and his strategy is that of re-inserting the discourse of sexuality from the narrow period of the Victorian Age to the broader developments that took place within Western civilization from the twelfth century onwards. What one realizes is that rather than a repression of sexuality, the Victorian Age reveals a large number of discourses on sexuality, discourses that radiated from a number of institutions. While at the level of everyday life talking about sex was forbidden, Foucault shows that at the institutional level – medical, legal, pedagogic, social and psychiatric – rather than censorship one can observe a multiplication of discourses related to sexuality.

Until the end of the eighteenth century, the married couple were the object of observation, and at this stage there was no qualitative difference between violating the rules of marriage and other violations such as incest, sodomy or homosexuality. These infringements were considered as belonging to the same class of violations. The major change occurred in the nineteenth century when discourses on sexuality assumed that since the family unit was the standard of normality, other sexualities did not belong to the same class as that of the family, but something qualitatively different. In other words, a shift of emphasis took place where other sexualities were noticed, observed and studied. The privileged sites for the investigation of sexuality became (1978: 104–05):

1. the hysterical woman whose hysteria was the result of sexual problems and who, as a potential future bearer of children, necessitated investigation;
2. the problem of masturbation for the child who should be protected from its dangers;
3. the question of reproduction which was vital for the growth of the population and
4. the sexuality of adults, which under investigation revealed an increasing number of 'non-normal' sexual activities, leading to the creation of a new category of sexual beings, the pervert.

The creation of new sexual identities is famously described by Foucault in his elaboration of the category of homosexuality. Strange as it might sound, before the nineteenth century the homosexual did not exist. This does not mean that before the nineteenth century there were no same-sex relations, but that same-sex relations were considered to be something one did, an unquestioned action. The idea that there is a class of humans whose identity belonged to that of the homosexual is a product of the nineteenth century. What this means is that the homosexual became a type of being, a being who exists in reality and whose homosexuality is the result of something internal (psychological or physiological). In the nineteenth century the homosexual became a type, a class of being with a particular sexual identity:

The nineteenth century homosexual became a personage, a past, a case history, and a childhood, in addition to being a type of life, a life form, and a morphology, with an indiscreet anatomy and possibly a mysterious physiology. Nothing that went into his total composition was unaffected by his sexuality [...] The sodomite had been a temporary aberration; the homosexual was now a species. (1978: 43)

As with *Discipline and Punish*, while it might seem that the interest in 'deviant' forms of sexuality had the goal of eliminating them, the impossibility of actually achieving these goals suggests that something else was at stake. The intensity with which campaigns were organized to eradicate masturbation in children – campaigns that could never in fact succeed – indicated that, rather than eradication, what was intended was control. The various discourses on sexuality were in effect ways of penetrating society to control and monitor the behaviour of the population. By internalizing the values and norms of society, an individual becomes his/her own keeper – not only an object of sexual knowledge but also a sexual subject monitoring himself/herself according to the norms established within society.

Foucault's criticism of bourgeois sexual values is similar to his criticism of bourgeois justice in *Discipline and Punish*. The bourgeois concern with sexuality was primarily a concern with the preservation of their own class:

[I]t was in the "bourgeois" or "aristocratic" family that the sexuality of children and adolescents was first problematised, and feminine sexuality medicalised…the bourgeoisie began by considering that its own sex was something important, a fragile treasure, a secret that had to be discovered at all costs. (1978: 120–21)

The bourgeois had an interest in safeguarding and promoting themselves by advocating the heterosexual, monogamous couple as the basis of society and morality. They were not interested in the sexuality of the working class, and changes in working class sexuality were enacted only by the end of the nineteenth century.

Foucault's analysis of the functioning of power reveals that power uses communication to control and monitor others. The way power operates makes it seem like a monolithic and inescapable force from which there is no possibility of escape. However, Foucault offers a glimmer of hope. If discourse plays an important role in the communication and transmission of power – since genealogy specifically connects the discursive to the non-discursive, institutional domains – discourse itself becomes the site of contestation or resistance. It is therefore possible to resist the normalizing forces of society. Foucault claims that while power-knowledge has the possibility of its own transmission, there is also the possibility of resisting it: 'discourse transmits and produces power; it reinforces it, but also undermines and exposes it, renders it fragile and makes it possible to thwart it' (1978: 101).

Foucault and surveillance theory

Towards the end of *Discipline and Punish* Foucault wrote,

> Our society is one not of spectacle, but of surveillance; under the surface of images, one invests bodies in depth; behind the great abstraction of exchange, there continues the meticulous, concrete training of useful forces; the circuits of communication are the supports of an accumulation and a centralisation of knowledge;.... (1978: 217)

Although Foucault recognized the emergence of surveillance as a phenomenon in the late twentieth century, he did not perhaps realize the extent to which the technologies used would become such a common feature of daily life that they would themselves be transformed into the perfect tool for surveillance. In *The Mode of Information* (1990), Poster describes the development of communicative technologies in the contemporary world, a development which sees Foucault's Panopticon transformed into what he calls a 'Superpanopticon'.

One of the keys to understanding the changing face of contemporary society is the 'database'. Poster's central thesis is that the role and function of the database constitute a new way of dominating subjects. The database is not a neutral tool; it is not just a new system for gathering information about a person, but rather a system that makes it possible to monitor large numbers of individuals. The use of databases has been increasing at a rapid pace since the 1980s, and it is so widespread that it is considered as part of the modern world. When we watch a crime show on television we expect the investigators to check the fingerprints found at the crime scene against their database to see if there is a 'match'. What we do not realize is that collecting information about individuals is not solely a matter of police work but also a commercial enterprise. Private companies – insurances, hospitals, banks and so on – also collect information that is stored on databases. This has raised a number of worries in the United States and an attempt was made to regulate database information and control those who could have access to it. Unfortunately, this attempt was inadequate as the Privacy Act did not apply to a number of institutions (banks and states), and it also failed to create structures to enforce infringements.

In part the widespread development of databases is connected to the pervasive influence of the capitalist system that dominates economic life in advanced modern societies. It might be thought that the new technologies of information would have eliminated the control that capitalism had over the objects it produced. Whereas in the past it was necessary to buy the books or clothes or furniture that one needed, with the new technologies the consumer could reproduce the data himself/herself (e.g. video and DVD recorders, downloading music or films from the net). But while this may be the case, the search for profit took a different form as the Internet itself is today a major source of any type of business transaction.

This in turn has produced an unintended consequence: when one searches for something on an online catalogue on the Internet, one is accessing the database of that company; but as the person conducts the search, he/she is being transformed into a bit of information for another database. Poster writes:

> In the home networking information loop, one database (product information) generates another database (consumer information) which generates another database (demand information) which feeds the production process. In this context, the commodification of information creates its own system of expanded reproduction: producers have databases about consumers which are the commodities that may be sold to other producers. (1990: 75)

Poster argues that the technology used in the database constitutes a new form of domination because of its specific form of electronic writing (digital encoding). His argument hinges on the distinction between speech, writing and electronic writing; such a distinction is necessary because while speech and writing are frequently described in oppositional terms, electronic writing is usually considered an extension of writing, and not as something with its own identifying features. This, Poster contends, is mistaken. The identifying features of speech are presence, face-to-face communication, and small-scale social organization. The identifying features of writing are distance (or absence, as the sender is not immediately in contact with the receiver) and a solitary mode, as a text can be read on its own (and critically thought about) in a linear and causal manner.

Electronic writing is different from speech and writing because the framework of electronic language undermines the very foundations of speech and writing. Both of these forms of communication are structured in terms of the spatio-temporal presence or absence of the sender and receiver. Electronic language on the other hand undermines the distance that underlies presence and absence, because it is everywhere and nowhere at the same time. Electronic language collapses or undermines the space–time distinction. The database, like the virtual world of computers, can be accessed from anywhere in the world and yet it is nowhere in the world.

The use of the database in contemporary society is a qualitative improvement on the Panopticon that Foucault had analysed in *Discipline and Punish*. The function of the Panopticon was that of 'forcing' prisoners to constantly monitor their own behaviour, since the building was designed in such a way that the inmates would not know when the wardens were watching them. As a result (and coupled with the collection of information on the inmate into a filing system), by repeatedly behaving normally they would become normal and be eventually returned to society and 'rehabilitated'. Despite the improvement of the Panopticon in terms of inmate–warden proportions, since only a few wardens were needed to monitor several prisoners, the Panopticon was still limited since it relied on a physical structure – the location, the equipment – and a centralized administration for the organization of the warden supervision, the filing and the processing of the information. With the database, the physical limitations of the panopticon have been superseded, and Poster suggests that we now live in an era of the Superpanopticon.

In the world of the Superpanopticon, not only are citizens constantly under surveillance, but they actively contribute to their own surveillance. Information is collected from a number of sources such as identity cards, credit cards and driver's licences. However, credit cards are probably the most widespread source of data collection: information is collected about the kinds of restaurants we go to, the magazines and books we read, the clothes we wear and so on, and stored into a database. This information is actively sought by marketing companies as it enables them to construct a profile of the person, which can be used for commercial reasons. And there are companies that pool the data from various databases into a super-database for marketing purposes. It is in this sense that Poster argues that databases constitute individuals, creating a new kind of subjectivity:

> The discourse of databases, the Superpanopticon, is a means of controlling the masses in the postmodern, post-industrial mode of information. Foucault taught us to read a new form of power by deciphering discourse/practice formations instead of intentions of a subject of instrumental actions. Such a discourse analysis when applied to the mode of information yields the uncomfortable discovery that the population participates in its own self-constitution as subjects of the normalizing gaze of the Superpanopticon. We see databases not as an invasion of privacy, as a threat to a centred individual, but as the multiplication of the individual, the constitution of an additional self, one that my be acted upon to the detriment of the "real" self without that "real" self every being aware of what is happening. The figural component of databases consists in such a self-constitution. The innocuous spread of credit card transactions, today into supermarkets, tomorrow perhaps into classrooms and homes, feeds the databases at ever increasing rates, stuffing ubiquitous computers with a language of surveillance and control. (1990: 97–98)

From a political perspective, the database is extensively used to store information and create profiles of those who are involved in any activity that goes against the dominant social order. The information is stored in a database through a list of grids such as age, gender, address, identity card number, social security number, driving licence, phone number and so on.

Since Poster's book was published, the mode of information has made further rapid strides in its application of communication technologies. Some aspects that were only hinted at in his book (such as home networking) have now become commonplace. Commercial shopping with the use of credit cards is now a common fact of business transactions, so that data are collected by the company one purchases from and by the credit card companies. On the personal level, communication possibilities have been further developed with online or virtual communities, online instant communication (chat groups) and online companies ready to provide any service your money can buy (a partner, a friend). There is the further and more insidious intrusion of the technologies of surveillance into the lives of citizens that is given a veneer of justification by claiming that intrusion is necessary to protect their lives (even though they might not have asked for this protection). Indeed, since the attacks of 11 September 2001, the search for potential terrorists has sanctioned the widespread use of information collection and storage. State administrators have been given a free hand into reading emails and listening in on telephone conversations; the technology that was supposed to make the world a better place turned it into a global Big Brother.

Critical remarks

The concept of discourse plays a crucial role throughout Foucault's writings, with varying degrees of emphasis. After 1971 he virtually abandons the concept until he re-utilizes it in *The History of Sexuality Vol. 1*. The problem, however, is that within the span of time during which he utilized it, the concept of discourse had a different meaning, and this therefore causes considerable difficulty in interpretation. On the one hand, Foucault argues that discourse actively constructs or produces reality (1971: 47–48; also, 1981: 67). This is Foucault at his most constructivist moment, and on this account, our perception of the world is constructed by the discourse within which we find ourselves. This raises the serious question of whether there is no reality other than discourse. If this were the case then how would he explain hunger or pain? On the other hand, Foucault also offers a different version of discourse, a version that suggests the existence of a non-discursive realm. In *The Order of Things* he seems to suggest that there could be practices independent of discourse that affect discourse; in order to explain the transition from one episteme to another, Foucault realizes that certain forces outside discourse need to be taken into account (1970: 50). It is evident that in his later writings, Foucault connects institutional practices and interests with the promotion of a particular discourse. In defence of Foucault, Mills (2003: 56) suggests that the early concept of discourse does not describe a sort of discursive idealism. It is not that there is no non-discursive realm, but rather that such a realm – reality – is mediated by language. Language is thus seen as the 'filter' or 'grid' by which and through which we understand reality.

Foucault's shift towards genealogy with *Discipline and Punish* was intended to show the change from one episteme to another, but in this transition the concept of episteme seems to have got lost. Gutting (2001: 281–82) points out that in *Discipline and Punish* the concept of episteme is mentioned only once. In addition there seems to be a difference between the episteme of *Discipline and Punish* and that of *The Order of Things*. Whereas *The Order of Things* is concerned with the epistemological question of the subject and the object, it is not the same subject that is being considered in *Discipline and Punish*. The subject under examination is the criminal subject.

Best and Kellner (1991) are generally supportive of Foucault's goals, although they point to a number of limitations in his thought. Best and Kellner (1991: 44) defend Foucault against the mistaken view attributed to him about the 'discontinuities' in history. Some have thought that by discontinuity Foucault is suggesting complete and radical breaks between historical periods, such that there is no connection between them. However, Foucault argues that each episteme feeds off the previous one. The connection between them is not a causal one, where one is the cause of the other; rather, the connection is one where one episteme is the 'soil' out of which the new one comes about. The point Foucault is trying to emphasize is that there is no teleology of history, no ultimate goal that can be explained in progressive and rational terms. On the other hand, Best and Kellner (1991: 70) argue that Foucault's analysis of power, with its focus on the way power operates, is interesting as it brings out the way struggles of domination occur in relations between individuals and groups. However, this analytic emphasis on the impersonal mechanisms of power fails to take into consideration or ignores those who are in positions of power, such as bankers, the mass media, land developers and so on. And as Ruiz-Miguel[5] points out, the concept of power in Foucault is so broad that it becomes useless for analytic purposes. While it is trivially true that power can be read into every social situation, such a claim prevents one from achieving any depth or complexity of understanding of the concept.

The purpose of this chapter has been to show the way Foucault's writings can be read within the context of communication studies. In this chapter I have shown the way (1) Foucault analyses the relationship between epistemes and discourse in the production and transmission of knowledge. Additionally it has been shown that (2) he supplements this relationship by grounding it within the context of institutions so that (3) the localization of discourse within institutional contexts necessitates a reconfiguration of the power mechanisms operating within them. (4) The final section shows the application of Foucault's ideas within surveillance theory.

Notes

1. Foucault develops this theme: 'These surfaces of emergence are not the same for different societies, at different periods, and in different forms of discourse. In the case of nineteenth-century psychopathology, they were probably constituted by the family, the immediate social group, the work situation, the religious community…although organised according to a specific mode, these surfaces of emergence were not new in the nineteenth century' (1972: 42).
2. On the immersion of the subject in a discourse, Foucault writes, 'Thus conceived, discourse is not the majestically unfolding manifestation of a thinking, knowing, speaking subject, but, on the contrary, a totality, in which the dispersion of the subject and his discontinuity with himself may be determined. It is a space of exteriority in which a network of distinct sites is deployed' (1972: 55).
3. Summarising the role of the commentary and of the author Foucault writes: '[c]ommentary limited the hazards of discourse through the action of an identity taking the form of *repetition* and *sameness*. The author principle limits this same chance element through the action of an *identity* whose form is that of *individuality* and the *I*' (1972: 222).
4. Foucault describes the introduction of science in the asylum: 'The proximity instituted by the asylum, an intimacy neither chains nor bars would ever violate again, does not allow reciprocity: only the nearness of observation that watches, that spies, that comes closer in order to see better… The science of mental disease as it would develop in the asylum would always be only of the order of observation and classification' (1993: 250).
5. See Merquoir 1985: 116.

Chapter 4

Eco on Culture and Communication

Umberto Eco (1932–) is probably a brand name for Italian culture and is well known among the general public for his literary writings, such as *The Name of the Rose* (1983), *Foucault's Pendulum* (1989) and *The Island of the Day Before* (1994). However, it is his writings on semiology – *A Theory of Semiotics* (1976), *Semiotics and the Philosophy of Language* (1984) and *The Role of the Reader* (1979), among others – that have positioned him as one of the leading intellectuals in the world today.

Eco was one of the first Italian academics who undertook a serious analysis of popular culture at a time when other intellectuals of both the right and the left considered the association of 'popular' and 'culture' as a contradiction in terms. Culture in their view could not be 'popular' (defined roughly as appealing to ordinary people), but rather the preserve of those who understood and appreciated it. This elitist view of culture considered popular culture as having nothing intrinsically valuable to communicate. Although Eco could be loosely aligned with the cultural left, he did not accept this thesis, arguing that popular culture had a contribution to make in the analysis of society.

In this chapter I shall start by outlining (1) Eco's theory of signs and codes, followed by (2) the crucial distinction between communication and signification. The next section describes (3) the process of abduction as an integral part of (4) the production of signs. This leads to (5) Eco's elaboration of the encyclopaedia. The last sections of this chapter focus on the narrower domain of textual interpretation, starting with (6) the distinction between Model Authors and Model Readers and (7) open and closed texts. The chapter closes with an analysis of the James Bond novels carried out by Eco.

The study of signs

Eco's 'pre-semiotic' career was grounded in the then fashionable structuralism as the method for the analysis of human culture. The central tenet of structuralism was that by using the models of linguistics and communication, it was possible to understand human culture in terms of coded and decoded messages between the sender and the receiver. Semiotics is also grounded in the interrelation between codes and messages, but unlike structuralism it does not seek to find an ultimate code – an Ur-code – that would explain all the other codes. Since the structuralist Ur-code is ahistorical, transcending space and time, it has always remained indifferent to political and social values and could easily be described as conservative. On the other hand, the codes that semiologists are interested in are historical, the products of a culture at a particular point in time. It therefore makes social critique possible.

In *A Theory of Semiotics* (1976) Eco outlined the domain of semiology. Eco's central argument was that semiology is the discipline that makes studying culture as a system of communication possible, since

> the laws of signification are the laws of culture. For this reason culture allows a continuous process of communicative exchanges, insofar as it subsists as a system of systems of signification. *Culture can be studied completely under a semiotic profile.* (1976: 28)

Since the communication that takes place within a culture is the communication of signs, Eco spends a considerable amount of effort explaining both the ways signs are produced and the codes that make the communication of signs possible.

There are a number of influences upon Eco, but the primary ones are those of the founding fathers of both branches of semiological theory – Saussure and Peirce. Saussure had already realized that semiology had the potential for becoming a general science of signs – a science that studied the life of signs within society, with linguistics as the most important branch of this general study. From Saussure, Eco learns that although the connection between the signifier and the signified is arbitrary, once it becomes common usage within a society the relation could be described as 'necessary'. This 'necessary' relation is imposed by the code that regulates the language. Saussure's concept of a sign 'is implicitly regarded as a communicative device taking place between two human beings intentionally aiming to communicate or express something' (1976: 15).

From Peirce, Eco learns that a sign has a meaning even if there is no interpreter: it is the concept of the interpretant that gives a sign its validity. Eco develops the concept of interpretant, defining it as a process of 'unlimited semiosis'. In the process of defining the interpretant one must use other signs, and these in turn require further interpretation, and so on. Unlimited semiosis describes the endless possibility of generating meaning. While Eco takes into account Saussure's contribution, he considers Peirce's contribution to be of broader application (to non-humans) and therefore more fruitful to semiology. Peirce's concept of the sign 'does not demand, as part of a sign's definition, the qualities of being intentionally emitted and artificially produced' (1976: 15).

Apart from these influences, Eco has also adopted insights derived from information theory to formulate his theory of semiotics.

> The term /information/ has two basic senses: (a) it means a statistical property of the source, in other words, it designates the amount of information that *can be transmitted*; (b) it means a precise amount of selected information which *has actually been transmitted and received.* (1976: 40)

The justification for the use of information theory is twofold: (1) it is increasingly evident that concepts derived from information theory have infiltrated and benefited a number of other disciplines with interesting results, and Eco hopes that information theory can likewise be fruitful for semiological theory; (2) basic communication involves the transmission of information between machines and so this offers, at the very least, a starting point for a model for understanding the processes of communication that involve the use of signals (Caesar 1999: 55).

Non-human communication is the starting point of Eco's semiological theory. An elementary form of communication of information is that of a petrol gauge in a car marking empty: when the buoy in the petrol tank reaches a certain level, a signal is communicated to the petrol gauge. At this stage, Eco is interested in the communication that takes place *before* a person reads the petrol gauge as standing for empty or half-full. The relationship between the buoy and the gauge is said to be one where the former '*stimulates, provokes, causes, gives rise to* the movement of the pointer' (1976: 33).

To explain the processes of communication prior to human intervention, Eco uses the model of a water catchment that he calls the 'Watergate Model', with the water catchment functioning as the source of information. This model shows the way codes develop from basic to more complex ones. When the water level rises to a certain point it reaches the danger level of 0. If this level is reached, an apparatus transmits a signal through a channel to a receiver; this in turn responds to the signal by sending another signal to the machine that operates the water catchment (to decrease water in the catchment). A system is created to warn the receiver about the danger. The system consists of a bulb that, when lit, signals that the danger level 0 has been reached; when unlit, the water catchment is then safe. In this case there is a correspondence between the signifier (lit) and the signified (danger) (or signifier (unlit) and signified (safe)). This sequence can be described as a basic code. Problems occur when 'noise' (such as a power cut) disrupts the communication possibilities of this code, since the bulb would remain unlit even if the danger level was reached. Safeguards are therefore introduced and this involves a more complex code: another bulb is added so that when bulb A is lit it means safety, and when bulb B is lit this means danger. If there is a power cut then both bulbs would remain unlit so one would suspect that there are problems with the power supply.

But what if the disruptive power supply caused one bulb to light up and not the other, so that the 'danger' bulb would light up instead of the 'safe' one? This would necessitate improving the lighting system by adding more bulbs not only to improve security but also to make more messages possible. The introduction of a code helps organize the various messages that the bulbs can communicate. This leads Eco (1976: 36–37) to postulate different kinds of codes (1) syntactical codes, where what is important is the way the signals are combined; (2) semantic codes, where it is the content or what the signals are about that is at issue; (3) behavioural codes, where it is the response of the addressee that is important and (4) rules that couple the previous codes. Eco offers some examples of these different codes: for (1) we have the 'phonological code'; for (2) we have the code of kinship (when considered as 'a system of pertinent parenthood'); for (3) we have the genetic code and for (4) the Morse code. As a result of the possible confusion that arises out of using the word *code* for these different domains, Eco distinguishes between the s-codes, or the code as system (codes as syntax, semantic and behaviour as (1), (2) and (3)), from (4) where a rule couples (1) with (2) or (3) as code.

Communication and signification

A crucial distinction developed in *A Theory of Semiotics* is that between communication and signification and their relation to the code. Although there is an overlap between the domains of communication and signification, there is an important difference between them: communication is the process whereby a signal is transferred from a source to a destination. As such, this process can take place either between machines, machines and humans, or only humans. If the source and destination are machines, then what we have is the communication of information. But if the destination is human, then what we have is a process of signification. The difference between humans and machines is that when the human is the receiver of the message, he/she knows that 0 means danger, unlike the machine that responds without knowing. As a result other elements come into play, such as the fear that might affect the receiver upon reading the message. The introduction of the human element into the model involves a change from the communication of messages as signals to the communication of messages as signification. This is because there are different possibilities of response: interpretation, rather than conditioned reflex, is the characteristic of signification. Communication between humans presupposes the existence of a system of signification, and it is this system that makes human communication possible.

The function of the code is to organize the process of signification: 'A code is a system of signification, insofar as it couples present entities with absent units. When – on the basis of an underlying rule – something actually presented to the perception of the addressee *stands for* something else, there is *signification*' (1976: 8). Having clarified the concept of codes, Eco starts to examine codes in relation to the process of signification. Crucial to his view of semiology as a method for understanding human culture is the strategy of breaking free from the tendency to equate the sign with the linguistic sign. Eco now adopts Hjelmslev's model of the sign that distinguishes between content and expression: '[…] a sign is always an element of an *expression plane* conventionally correlated to one (or several) elements of a *content plane*' (1976: 48).

While the code establishes the relation between content and expression at the conventional level, Eco points out that 'conventional' is not necessarily 'arbitrary' since a sign might be an icon (and therefore motivated). But how does the sign relate to the code? And what about its referent? Eco's proposed solution leads to the introduction of another of Hjelmslev's concepts, namely the sign as function or sign-production. A sign-function occurs when the expression and content are correlated, and when these become correlated to something else, then a new sign-function is born. This sign-function allows for a shift in the understanding of codes: codes do not organize signs but are the rules that enable new signs to be produced. The interaction between codes and sign-function is described in the following way:

> (a) a code establishes the correlation of an expression plane (in its purely formal and systematic aspect) with a content plane (in its purely formal and systematic aspect); (b) a sign-function establishes the correlation of an abstract element of the expression system with an abstract element of the content system; (c) in this way a code establishes general *types*, therefore producing the rule which generates concrete *tokens*, i.e., signs such as usually occur in communicative processes. (1976: 50)

However, having established that the sharing of codes between the sender and the receiver enables communication, Eco adds that contextual cues or circumstances or even different codes can generate the reception of a different message despite the sharing of fundamental code. Everybody knows that a skull on a bottle means poison, but if the bottle is found in a drinking cabinet, a different message is being communicated.

On the question of the referent, Eco followed the practice of semiology to ignore from its considerations the domain of objects and things to which signs refer. In his discussion of the concept of meaning, Eco is concerned to show that 'meaning' and 'referent' are not the same, since it is possible to use a symbol or word that has no referent, such as (for example) *unicorn*. So too, we can have different symbols that express different thoughts (referents) but that refer to the same thing (referent). Semiology is therefore concerned with the cultural conventions used in acts of communication. To return to the example of the water catchment, while the signifier AB denotes the level 0, to the person reading the sign the signifier connotes danger. The connotation is the meaning added to the signifier; from within the parameters of a code, a new signified is generated. Eco's theory of codes is not concerned with meaning and truth but only with meaning (or signification). His reasoning is that whether the sender will be telling the truth or lying, a coded system of signification is always being used. It is on this ground that Eco excludes any consideration of the referent when explaining his theory of codes. For '[…] there exist sign-vehicles which refer to non-existent entities such as "unicorn" or "mermaid"' (1976: 61).

Meaning is therefore a socio-cultural production that organizes the world. A statement such as '/There are two natures in Christ, the human and the divine and one Person/' (1976: 68) has a meaningful content despite not having a referent and irrespective of the beliefs of the community. That the statement itself has generated a number of other messages to explain it points to the fruitfulness of accepting Peirce's notion of interpretant together with that of 'unlimited semiosis'.

In *Semiotics and the Philosophy of Language* (1984), Eco clarifies a notion that is mistakenly attributed to signs; this clarification involves the distinction between the sign as equivalence and the sign as inferential. Frequently, the sign is understood in terms of equivalence so that, for example, Aristotle's definition of man is that /man/ is equal to <rational animal>

(1984: 34). Eco suggests that the inferential model better explains the dynamism of semiosis. Knowing the meaning of a sign requires an act of interpretation since we infer its meaning in order to understand it: 'A sign is not only something which stands for something else; it is also something that can and must be interpreted' (1984: 46).

Abduction

In *A Theory of Semiotics* Eco adopts the concept of abduction from Peirce, distinguishing between 'abduction', 'overcoded abduction' and 'undercoded abduction'.

1. Abduction: Peirce had distinguished between logical deduction, logical induction and abduction (1976: 131). Logical deduction takes place when one passes from a general rule to a specific case and infers a result. Logical induction is the move from a result to a case so as to infer a rule. Logical abduction differs in that from the rule and the result it invents or guesses what the case might be.

Abductive inferences play an important part in our everyday lives, and Peirce describes an experience of his to demonstrate its everyday use. Upon landing at a Turkish port he came across a man travelling on horseback, surrounded by four other men holding a canopy over him. Peirce could only guess that this man was the governor of the province since he was being treated with such honour (1976: 131). Abduction plays a crucial role in Eco's semiological theory because it represents the possibility of new codes – possibilities that were not foreseen, but having been performed become 'a customary social reflex' (1976: 132).

However, Eco points out that Peirce's discussion of abduction involves two further aspects:

2. Overcoding: Using Peirce's example, Eco points out that Peirce could infer that the person was the governor because there already was a convention that established that a canopy over a person's head functioned as a sign of honour. What Peirce did was 'complicate' the code by using other available evidence, such as being in a province, surrounded by four men and so on. Overcoding also takes place with the use of rhetorical and stylistic devices: when a person says /how are you/ or we see the sign /closed on Sundays/ what we have is the basic code of language that is being complicated by the certain circumstances coupled with certain stylistic devices (1976: 133).
3. Undercoding takes place when one lacks the rules but assumes them to be parts of a code. As an example Eco uses the familiar situation of a person going to live in a country in which he does not know the language. After some time the person infers from his experience in the country that a number of expressions /I love you/ or /Hi, man!/ or /How are you?/ can be translated as <<friendship>>. Eco's point is that the above expressions (and his list is longer) do not necessarily mean the same in English, but this code should

prove sufficient to interact in the new country. This is a case of undercoded abduction where, despite the lack of a precise code, one tentatively posits a code.

At times both codes can be mixed together, and Eco calls this process 'extra-*coding*': 'The movements of extra-coding are the subject matter of both a theory of codes and a theory of sign production' (1976: 136).

In *Semiotics and the Philosophy of Language*, Eco elaborates upon the concepts of overcoded and undercoded abduction, but also introduces the concept of creative abduction.

1. 'Overcoded abduction' occurs when the rule is given to us such that we do not realize we are following the rule; the interpretation of a sign takes place 'automatically or quasi-automatically' (1984: 41).
2. 'Undercoded abduction' involves selecting the rule out of a number of equivalent alternatives from within a shared body of knowledge. The point is to choose the most plausible one so that 'when one utters/this is a man/, we have to decide whether one says that this is a rational animal, a mortal creature, or a good example of virility' (1984: 42).
3. 'Creative abduction' necessitates the invention of a rule to make the interpretation of a sign possible. The interpretation of detective novels and the work of scientists provide the best examples of this rule.

> We implement creative abduction when dealing with poetic texts, as well as when solving criminal cases. Many interpretive decisions concerning symbols (see Chapter 4 of this book) involve creative abductions. (1984: 43)

The production of signs

The importance of Eco's theory of codes lies in its ability to explain the production of signs. He defines a sign as '*everything* that, on the grounds of a previously established social convention, can be taken as *something standing for something else*' (1976: 16). Eco attempts to reconcile pragmatics with semantics since his theory of codes explains the way signs and their meaning are generated through usage.

The starting point of Eco's theory of sign-production is the involvement of labour, work: there is labour involved in the production of signals, in choosing from a number of signals, in co-ordinating signals into an acceptable sign-function and in interpreting these signals. This is the labour involved in the production of signs (1976: 153–56). Radford (49–50) summarises the different forms this labour entails:

> The labor required to physically produce signals (sounds, marks on paper, an author typing at a keyboard)

the labor required to articulate expression units (choosing one term instead of another, choosing one style, etc)

the labor required by both the sender and the addressee to interpret messages observing an appropriate code (for example, understanding that my utterance /How are you today?/ is an act of phatic communication and not a request to learn of the state of your health)

the time needed to produce the message

the energy expended in comparing signs to actual events

the labor required to keep the addressee's attention on the sender's message

the labor required b the sender to focus the addressee on her attitudes and intentions

the labor required to elicit behaviorial responses in other people

By replacing the traditional typology of signs with a typology of sign-production, Eco re-iterates his criticism of traditional semiology that overemphasizes the linguistic model. While language is one of the most sophisticated sign-systems available for study, it is not the only one.

Interestingly, Eco applies his theory of sign-production to aesthetic messages, that is, to the use of language for aesthetics. His hope is that by doing so, traditional problems in philosophical aesthetics might be resolved using semiotic analysis. The relation between semiology and aesthetics can be seen because aesthetic texts involve the manipulation of expressions which, as a result, create a new content that in turn initiates a change of codes, producing a new understanding or knowledge of the world. In Eco's analysis of aesthetic texts, both the sender and the reader focus on the material that has been produced and that has been transformed into 'interesting' material through the process of semiology. The material transformed into aesthetics is different from the material used for the communication of signals by information theorists (1976: 266).

In aesthetic texts, both at the level of expression and at the level of content, the codes are 'transcended'; at the level of expression, the material used is semiologized. It is the code that produces the new expressions rather than the individual. At the level of content, aesthetic texts communicate an abundance of meaning that might give the impression that no communication is taking place at all. It is by answering the question of how new works of art are produced that one can see how communication still takes place. Because works of art stimulate an interrogation regarding their own status as works of art, this could lead to the production of a new code that seems connected to a personal style or movement. Once the unique style becomes recognized it tends to become the norm. Despite standardization, the uniqueness of a work of art is still retained because imitations emphasize those aspects that they are imitating. Aesthetic texts have a communicative value in that they involve a process of changing a denotation into a connotation. They communicate a meaning that – as Eco points out – is a form of knowledge. If aesthetics also concerns knowledge we can acquire of the world, then, he suggests, it can likewise contribute to semiology (1976: 275).

The communication between the sender and the receiver in an aesthetic text involves an interplay between the intention of the author and the freedom of interpretation of the receiver. This explains why the meaning of the text is not always or completely predictable. An aesthetic text is a multiple source of *unpredictable "speech acts"* whose real author remains undetermined, sometimes being the sender of the message, at others the addressee who collaborates in its development. (1976: 276)

Following *A Theory of Semiotics*, Eco's research focussed on two overlapping areas: the use of semiology in more general social concerns, where interpretation and inference are part of cognitive activity, and the application of his general semiological insights to texts. However, in *Semiotics and the Philosophy of Language* he elaborates upon the domain of semiotics as a discipline by distinguishing between three different types of semiotics:

1. a 'specific semiotics' that is concerned with particular sign systems and the rules of signification that allow communication. These fields range from the grammars of sign language for the deaf, to traffic signals, to poker. The crucial point for Eco is that the study of these systems leads to a 'scientific' kind of knowledge that entails prediction and the possibility of social engineering:

   [N]otwithstanding, a specific semiotics can aspire to a 'scientific' status. Specific semiotics study phenomena that are reasonably independent of their observations. Their objects are usually 'stable' – even though the duration of a code for traffic signals has a shorter range than the duration of a phonological system, whereas lexical systems are in a continuous process of transformation. Being scientific, a specific semiotics can have a predictive power: it can tell which expressions, produced according to the rules of a given system of signification, are acceptable or 'grammatical' and which ones a user of the system would presumably produce in a given situation. (1984: 5)

2. an 'applied' semiotics that Eco describes as a 'twilight zone', whereby semiological concepts are applied to

   literary criticism, the analysis of political discourses, perhaps a great part of the so-called linguistic philosophy [...] Frequently, the semiotic practices rely on the set of knowledge provided by specific semiotics, sometimes they contribute to enriching them, and, in many other cases, they borrow their fundamental ideas from a general semiotics. (1984: 6)

3. a 'general semiotics' differs from the other two types of semiotics in that it focusses on general categories. This is more of a philosophical enterprise than a scientific one. In this case, semiology posits the category of the 'sign' in much the same way as the philosopher posits the 'good' or the 'true':

To walk, to make love, to sleep, to refrain from doing something, to give food to someone else, to eat roast beef on Friday – each is either a physical event or the absence of a physical event, or a relation between two or more physical events. However, each becomes an instance of good, bad, or neutral behaviour *within a given philosophical framework*. Outside such a framework, to eat roast beef is radically different from making love, and making love is always the same sort of activity independently of the legal status of the partners. From a given philosophical point of view, both to eat roast beef on Friday and to make love to x can become instances of 'sin', whereas both to give food to someone and to make love to y can become instances of virtuous action. (1984: 10)

Since philosophical and 'general' semiotics attempt to make sense of the world by giving it a coherent form, 'general semiotics' has the benefit of explanatory power since it can put together data that seem disconnected, and it is also a 'practical power' since it can change the world. For example, Marxism explained the relations between classes as ones of conflict, suggesting ways in which to transform society; however, while it has this practical potential, unlike science or 'specific semiotics', philosophical or 'general semiotics' does not have predictive power. In other words, it cannot say how things will turn out. The importance of general semiotics is that its objects are all the domain of human-signifying practices. Language in particular is the fundamental semiotic activity of humans: the paradox is that we can only understand language by using language, and as a result 'a general semiotics transforms, for the very fact of its theoretical claim, its own object' (1984: 12).

Dictionaries and encyclopaedias

Linguists have argued that meanings can only be analysed linguistically, and therefore 'belong' to the dictionary. From within this conceptual framework they oppose the intensional constructs of the dictionary to the extensional material of the encyclopaedia. Eco collapses this distinction, arguing that when defining a term, the meaning of the term points to or depends on an external context. It is not possible to have a 'pure' dictionary, uncontaminated by the external world. Consequently, he concludes that the encyclopaedia remains the most fruitful concept of human knowledge, both for that which is true and for that which has been imagined. It is potentially an open-ended field, given that it includes the knowledge of all cultures. Social competence relies on the encyclopaedia.

In *A Theory of Semiotics*, Eco discusses the model proposed by Fodor and Katz (1963), which he dubbed 'the KF model' (1976: 97).

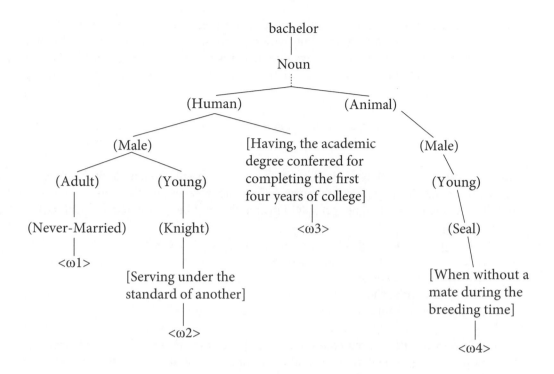

Eco points out a number of weaknesses within this model:

1. Dictionary and encyclopaedia. This model, while supposed to explain the ideal competence of an ideal speaker, turns out to be very similar to a dictionary: it fails to explain the social competence of the speaker (1976: 98). Eco points out that such competence is a requirement for a semiotic theory of communication and signification. Fodor (1972) is very much concerned with leaving the world out of his semantic model, but Eco argues that as long as a term is coded and recognized by society, then one need not worry about whether what the term refers to exists or not (1976: 99).
2. Connotations. Another problem with the KF Model is that it fails to take into consideration the connotations that can be associated with a term. The model 'might be useful for tourists who wanted to order lunch, but would be of little help if they really wanted 'to speak' a given language' (1976: 100).
3. Distinguishers. In the KF Model, the weakness of markers is supplemented by the use of distinguishers, but this in turn leads the Model out of a purely intensional domain (as originally intended) into an extensional one. Thus, for example, the intensional description of an Animal Male Young Seal leads to the external world of seals without a mate during the breeding season, and as a result one cannot distinguish between a seal with a mate from a seal without a mate (1976: 102). There is a further problem in that

while the Human Male Adult Never-Married is considered a marker, the Animal Male Adult, without a mate during breeding season, is considered a distinguisher. It might seem that an unmarried man is always unmarried while the unmated seal is unmated only during the breeding season. However, this is mistaken since both are situational and can therefore change.

In *Semiotics and the Philosophy of Language*, Eco develops the concept of the encyclopaedia using the metaphor of the labyrinth. He describes three different kinds of labyrinths.

1. The classical labyrinth: the labyrinth of Crete is the prototypical example of the classical labyrinth. It was linear and its only purpose was that of reaching the centre and return out of it. As such, one could not get lost in it, and it cannot be considered a model for the encyclopaedia.
2. The maze: this is a 'true' labyrinth, for within it one can get lost. A number of alternatives are available, and out of all the alternatives it is a question of finding the right one in order to be able to get out of it.
3. The net: the labyrinth as a net is one where every point is connected to every other point, leaving open the possibility of establishing new connections:

> The territory of the United States does not oblige anyone to reach Dallas from New York by passing through St. Louis, Missouri; one can also pass through New Orleans. (1984: 81)

Eco lists the fundamental characteristics of the encyclopaedia as a net (1984: 83–85): (1) it is 'structured according to *a network of interpretants*'; (2) it is 'virtually *infinite*', since it takes into account all the interpretations generated by different cultures; (3) it includes what has been believed as true, false, imagined or legendary, 'provided that a given culture had elaborated some discourse about some subject matter'; (4) it is a '*regulative idea*', since it allows for the isolation of a portion of the social encyclopaedia to enable the interpretation of texts and discourse; (5) it provides 'structured knowledge', as long as it is realized that this knowledge is local and not global. The attempt to think of one's local, encyclopaedic knowledge as the only worthwhile knowledge – thus regarding it as global – is in effect an ideological gesture.

Eco's developing ideas on the encyclopaedia as the embodiment of both linguistic and factual knowledge (since the encyclopaedia represents the cultural knowledge generated by the interpretant) is indicative of his thinking moving away from codes as rules to codes as making inferences possible.

Model Authors and Model Readers

A considerable amount of Eco's work is oriented towards the specific application of semiology to the narrower domain of textual interpretation, where the object of interpretation is the complete text rather than simple sentences. These two areas are not mutually exclusive since interpretation is central to both perception and texts. The sign could be the text as a whole, whereby the reader chooses from alternative interpretations. In *The Role of the Reader* (1979), Eco conducts an analysis of the status of the reader as an important pole in the actualizing of texts. The reader must be assumed both as a necessary condition for communication and for the attribution of meaning: it is the reader that makes both communication and signification possible.[1]

Using concepts derived from his semiological theory, Eco's starting point is the words of the text that he had described as the level of expression. This level needs a reader to actualize them, for without the reader, the text (and any message) remains empty. The reader correlates a meaning with an expression in accordance with a code. At the very minimum, it is assumed that the reader has a certain grammatical competence, so that he/she knows how to combine each word to generate a meaning. In the case of written texts the situation is even more complex, since what the reader has to actualize is more than he/she finds on the page at the level of expression.

But while the text assumes that there is a reader who will actualize it, this does not necessarily entail that the message the sender communicates will be the same as that which is interpreted. Eco had already discussed this in the theory of semiotics (1979: 139), where he criticized the sender-message-receiver model of communication because it assumed that the message arrived in 'pure' form from sender to receiver. A number of elements come into play in the interpretation of a message. It is subject to the different codes of the sender and the receiver, and the code itself is complex, structured by a number of rules. Moreover, to understand a linguistic message it is not enough to merely know the linguistic code, since other elements that can hinder or help the reception of the linguistic message come into play. These range from the circumstances, idiosyncrasies and assumptions involved in the production and reception of the message (1979: 5).

In his analysis of textual interpretation, Eco distinguishes between two sets of concepts: the empirical author and the empirical reader are opposed to the Model Author and the Model Reader. Perhaps the best way to start is by examining the role of the empirical author, and many consider the empirical author as essential to the interpretation of a text. Is he/she the empirical, flesh and blood person? Or is the author the subject who intends to mean something by the text? In literary theory the empirical author is considered a problem insofar as the life of the author is unimportant to the meaning of the text.

However, although the empirical author is unimportant for the interpretation of a text, the author is important in another way:

To organize a text, its author has to rely upon a series of codes that assign given contents to the expressions he uses. To make his text communicative, the author has to assume that the ensemble of codes he relies upon is the same as that shared by his possible readers. The author has thus to foresee a model of the possible reader (hereafter Model Reader) supposedly able to deal interpretatively with the expressions in the same way as the author deals generatively with them. (1979: 7)

Through the text itself the Model Reader is constructed as one who is competent enough to co-operate with it:

it seems that a well-organized text on the one hand presupposes a model of competence coming, so to speak, from outside the text, but on the other hand works to build up, by merely textual means, such a competence. (1979: 8)

Eco lists the way texts posit every possible reader through a series of choices: the choice involved in the use of a shared linguistic code; the choice in the use of a specific literary style and the choice in the use of specific markers of specialized subjects. There are also instances where the text is directed at a particular reader (e.g. children's stories), and texts that seek their Model Readers by activating their encyclopaedic knowledge. Using the historical novel *Waverley* (1815), written by Sir Walter Scott, as an example, Eco claims that the competent reader understands certain assumptions concerning chivalry that are inherent within the text (1979: 7).

The text generates its possible interpretations and its possible readers. It postulates a series of competences that the Model Reader is capable of. It is the difference between the competence shared by the author and the reader and the actual knowledge of the addressee that opens the way for different interpretations. The textual clues that point to the Model Readers are

signalled by a number of different means: language, the choice of a particular kind of encyclopaedia or ensemble of cultural references, particular vocabulary or style, or genre. (Caesar 1999: 122–23)

In turn, the Model Reader postulates the Model Author: a process of reciprocal co-operation takes place, where the Model Reader activates the textual strategies of the Model Author. It is the Model Reader who postulates the Model Author through the text. The intentions of the empirical author and reader are irrelevant. It does not matter what the empirical reader thinks the empirical author might have wanted to say; rather, what matters is the text out of which one infers or postulates the author. This is why the empirical author and the empirical reader are considered by Eco as 'textual strategies'. The use of the grammatical markers such as *I* or *you* in a text do not refer to actual persons, but function to actualize a text (1979: 10).

Another key element in the analysis of texts is that of 'Inferences *by intertextual frames*', where '[n]o text is read independently of the reader's experience of other texts' (1979: 21). Eco argues that a text is understood when the appropriate frame is used (just as the use of the wrong frame leads to misinterpretation). Eco (for example) cites a line from *Un drame bien parisien* by Alphonse Allais, where a quarrel takes place between Raoul and Marguerite. When a person reads 'Hands raised to strike, with a remorseless gaze, and a moustache bristling like that of a rabid cat, Raoul bore down on Marguerite, who quickly stopped showing off' (1979: 264), it is evident that the passage belongs to the frame 'violent quarrel'. The reader knows that Raoul's raising of his hand is not a situation of him voting for some issues or person. While these 'frames' govern our reading expectations, it must be added that each reader brings other 'frames' with his/her reading of other texts. The notion of intertextuality refers to this – texts 'carrying' in their wake other texts, and these different 'frames' belong to the mindset of the reader.

Eco distinguishes further between the 'common' frames that members of a culture share as part of their encyclopaedic competence and intertextual frames that are narrower in scope and recognized by a restricted audience:

> Common frames come to the reader from his storage of encyclopaedic knowledge and are mainly rules for practical life (Charniak 1975). Intertextual frames, on the contrary, are already literary 'topoi', narrative schemes (see Riffaterre 1973; 1976). (1979: 21)

These intertextual frames differentiate readers who are informed about what is taking place in the text, who recognize the 'tricks' or 'twists' in the text, from those readers who 'simply' follow the text without a degree of competence.

Open and closed texts

Related to the concepts of the Model Reader and Model Author are those of open and closed texts. The closed text aims for a particular type of Model Reader: he/she is the average person who, for example in the case of detective novels, is merely interested in the way the text ends.

> Those texts that obsessively aim at arousing a precise response on the part of more or less precise empirical readers (be they children, soap-opera addicts, doctors, law-abiding citizens, swingers, Presbyterians, farmers, middle-class women, scuba divers, effete snobs, or any other imaginable sociopsychological category) are in fact open to any possible 'aberrant' decoding. A text so immoderately 'open' to every possible interpretation will be called a *closed* one. (1979: 8)

This is the paradoxical feature of closed texts: because they are supposed to produce a determinate response, it might – and frequently does – lead readers to produce 'aberrant' interpretations. The text as a closed 'entity' produces interpretations that were not intended by the text; they are interpretations that are external to the text. In this situation, what one is doing is not interpreting the closed text but using it, since the interpretation is taking place without any consideration of the textual strategies inherent to the text. As examples of closed texts Eco refers to Superman comics, Eugene Sue, and Ian Fleming's James Bond novels. And in support of this claim, Eco argues that while the closed texts of the Bond novels are aimed at a specific reader, he himself has produced a semiological interpretation of them. The problem with closed texts is that they 'seem to be structured according to an inflexible project. Unfortunately, the only one not to have been 'inflexibly' planned is the reader' (1979: 8).

While closed texts suggest the construction of a certain Model Reader, open texts suggest another kind of 'sophisticated' reader. The construction of this reader depends entirely on the text itself: 'You cannot use the text as you want, but only as the text wants you to use it. An open text, however 'open' it be, cannot afford whatever interpretation' (1979: 9). The text posits in a reader a certain competence; this would entail a reader who, given the appropriate competence, would be considered a 'good' reader of that text. If he/she fails in that competence then he/she has not satisfied the 'felicity' conditions of that text. The kind of good reader expected from *Ulysses* can be discerned from the text itself

> because the pragmatic process of interpretation is not an empirical accident independent of the text qua *text*, but is a structural element of its generative process […] the text is nothing else but the semantic-pragmatic production of its own Model Reader. (1979: 9–10)

Eco argues that the good reader of *Finnegans Wake* couldn't be Greek from the second century BC or an illiterate man of Aran because they would not have the required syntactical and lexical competence. Without the necessary competence to understand the text, Bondella describes the situation as 'a missed opportunity for the actual empirical reader to transform himself or herself into the model reader envisioned by the model author' (1997: 167)

The underlying assumption of this distinction between readers is that some readers carry a larger encyclopaedia with them so that their reading of a text is better informed, therefore allowing for an appreciation of insights that the naïve reader would fail to notice. In *The Limits of Interpretation* (1990), Eco reiterates this point:

> Once again we must remember that every text presupposes and constructs always a double Model reader – a naïve and a 'smart' one, a semantic reader and semiotic or critical reader. The former uses the work as semantic machinery and is the victim of the strategies of the author who will lead him little by little along a series of previsions and expectations. The latter evaluates the work as an aesthetic product and enjoys the strategies implemented in order to produce a Model Reader of the first level. (1990: 92)

While the naïve reader cooperates with the author at the minimum level of generating a narrative from the text, the sophisticated reader goes through the same motions as the naïve one but takes a step back, whereby he/she appreciates the textual strategies inherent to the text.

> In order to know how a story ends, it is usually enough to read it once. In contrast, to identify the model author the text has to be read many times, and certain stories endlessly. (1995: 27)

So too it is possible that some texts posit through their textual strategies both the 'naïve' and the 'critical' reader. Eco refers to Alphonse Allais' *Un drame bien parisien* to point out that there is a big difference in the responses of these readers: 'The naïve reader will be unable to enjoy the story (he will suffer a final uneasiness), but the critical reader will succeed only by enjoying the defeat of the former' (1979: 10).

A question that has always interested Eco concerns the limits of interpretation, and he has long argued against the idea that interpretation is infinitely open ended:

> [Y]ou may infer from texts things they don't explicitly say – and the collaboration of the reader is based on this principle – but you can't make them say the contrary of what they have said. (1995: 92)

To counter the claim – popular with some American practitioners of deconstruction – that every interpretation is equally acceptable, Eco argues that there is something external to the text, something that acts as a boundary or limit to what constitutes an acceptable interpretation. The limits of possible interpretations are established by what he calls the 'consensus of the community' (1992: 144) of interpreters. This community establishes the rules of interpretation and produces a standard for judging its value, and while acceptable interpretations will continue to generate other interpretations, unacceptable interpretations will eventually be forgotten. This is because they are 'unable to produce new interpretations or cannot be confronted with the traditions of the previous interpretations' (1992: 150). The limits that Eco proposes are flexible enough to permit different interpretations, but also provide the framework for those that are unacceptable. Caesar elaborates:

> The reader, we are told, cannot make a text say anything that she or he wants it to say. *The Name of the Rose* contains abundant information on medieval herbalism as well as much useful advice on how to poison people, but it cannot be read as a treatise on botany, pharmacology or toxicology. (1999: 149)

An illuminating example of the limits of interpretation is offered by Eco himself, who shows how the interpretations of Dante's *The Divine Comedy* by Gabriele Rossetti, Eugene Aroux and Luigi Valli in the nineteenth century were fundamentally flawed. These writers whom Eco labels 'Followers of the Veil' were convinced that Dante's poetic work was really a 'veil' hiding secret messages, secret societies and conspiracies. The point is that their interpretations have no historical evidence to support their claims, so it is the text itself that sets the limit to the way it is interpreted in its interaction with the community of interpreters. When a misinterpretation occurs, it is the result of the commentaries about the text rather than the text. This is not to say that commentaries have no contribution to make; on the contrary a commentary, despite being open to potentially endless interpretation, folds upon the text to show its autonomy.

The community of interpreters consists of those who establish the boundaries of what counts as a good or bad interpretation. Authority and interpretation go hand in hand, since judging a reading as bad or unacceptable is in practice an exercise of power. It might be claimed that the author of the text has the 'authority' or 'power' to decide on questions of interpretations. This is a claim Eco rejects – the empirical author has no authority over the text. Rather, authority lies in the hands of the Model Reader.

Eco and popular culture

Eco has always been a defender of the texts produced within the category of popular culture, arguing that such texts should not be dismissed so easily as 'escapist', but are worthy of serious analysis. Popular culture has often been viewed as inferior by cultural theorists of both the left and the right, who maintained the elitist position where only certain works of art deserved to be considered for study.

In 'Narrative Structures in Fleming' (1979) Eco reads the series of James Bond novels written by Ian Fleming. His goal is to explain the success of these novels to both the everyday person in the street and the sophisticated or cultured reader. What is it that makes these texts appealing? How do they function to attract such different kinds of readers? The answer to these questions is that these texts are based on two fundamental sets of relations: the paradigmatic and the syntagmatic.

Paradigmatic relations consist of the rules that are combined to generate the novels. These rules constitute a 'narrative machine' that taps into the values and desires of different kinds of audiences. While these basic rules are common to all of Fleming's novels, it is the ways in which they are combined and re-combined that make each of the novels different. The paradigmatic rules involve both a series of oppositional terms and a relationship between the terms, such as Bond versus M, or the Free World versus the Soviet Union, and so on (1979: 147).

A number of relationships are entailed by this list: relations between characters, between ideologies and between values. The novels constitute the way these different relationships are played out, and Eco examines the different combinations that are used in the respective novels.

Syntagmatic relations explain the sequence of events that takes place in the novels. These sequences are likened to a game where one move by one player is followed by another move by another player; in a similar manner, a Bond novel follows a certain number of moves that are 'prearranged' and 'invariable', such as 'M giving a task to Bond' or 'Villain captures Bond' and so on(1979: 156).

Eco's detailed analyses of Fleming's novels show that while the syntagmatic relations may change, the paradigmatic ones remain the same. It is this possibility of variation upon a structure, coupled with a number of incidental features, that makes the novels a pleasure for the audience. In *From Russia with Love* (1957), the Soviet secret agency called SMERSH plans to assassinate James Bond. But since Bond is no ordinary person, his assassination must not be ordinary but rather an embarrassment both to him and to the British secret service. A trap is laid where Bond must go to Istanbul to get hold of a code-breaking machine, and where his contact there is a 24-year-old Russian woman. M, Bond's chief, tells him that the girl is apparently in love with him after having read all about him. Bond is suspicious of the whole story but is persuaded by M that it is a plausible scenario. Bond agrees, and finally says '[t]here's no reason why a Russian girl shouldn't be just as silly as an English one' (in Radford 2003: 37).

The narrative continues and readers know he will get captured, but the suspense lies in how he will turn the tables on his captors. Captain Nash is the agent of SMERSH who has been entrusted with the task of killing Bond. His professionalism is shown by the accuracy with which he has shot Bond's wristwatch. Evidently, there is no escape for Bond this time. His execution is timed to coincide with the train passing through a tunnel so as to mask any possible sounds that Bond might utter as he dies. But as it turns out, Captain Nash's shooting ability is turned against him. Bond – recalling that Captain Nash had mentioned wanting to shoot him through the heart – places a copy of *War and Peace* in front of his heart.

> It had all depended on the man's accuracy. Nash had said that Bond would get one bullet through the heart. Bond had taken a gamble that Nash's aim was good as he said it was. And it had been. (in Radford 2003: 180)

As readers we know that Bond will survive, and yet we still enjoy reading Fleming's novels. However, Eco distinguishes between two kinds of readers or audience: the 'passive' and the 'cultured' types. With the passive audience pleasure is generated in

> the repetition of a habitual scheme in which the reader can recognise something he has already seen and of which he has grown fond […] [He] finds himself immersed in a game of which he knows the pieces and the rules – and perhaps the outcome – and draws pleasure simply from following the minimal variations by which the victor realizes his objective. (1979: 160)

The passive reader is the one who enjoys going through the motions that structure the novel. Evidently this type of reader contributes little to the reception of the text, and Eco argues that Fleming's use of cold war ideology is drawn from the context that readers were familiar with at the time. By deploying the ideology of the cold war, Fleming made sure that the reader could identify with the novel passively since no contribution was needed on his/her part.

The popularity of the novels among the general public was the result of a reworking of theme of good versus evil. This opposition is, on Eco's account, a 'universal' theme, and Fleming's novels replay in modern form what was traditionally characteristic of the fairy tale. In the fairy tale a certain pattern is followed: the knight (Bond) is sent by the King (M) on a mission to destroy some evil being (the Villain) and rescue the Lady (the Woman) (1979: 161). The universal opposition of good versus evil belongs to the collective consciousness of humankind that has viewed them as forces in eternal conflict. Without knowing it, the passive audience recognizes this conflict since it constitutes the human condition.

What is yet to be provided is an explanation as to why the Bond novels also appeal to the 'cultured' or 'sophisticated' reader. The appeal is grounded in a number of features found in the novels that a person with a cultured background would appreciate. For example, the 'evil characters' in the Bond novels recall Marino's Satan, who through the poet Milton influenced the Romantics; Satan is depicted as 'fascinating and cruel, sensual and ruthless' (1979: 171), features that are also found in the Villain and in Bond. The physical characteristics of James Bond, 'the ruthless smile, the cruel, handsome face, the scar on his cheek, the lock of hair that falls rebelliously over his brow, the taste for display' (1979: 171) would remind the reader of the Byronic hero.

In his analysis of the Bond texts, Eco notices the contrast in Fleming's style between lengthy descriptions of the 'obvious and the banal' and short descriptions of key actions and events. This is because Fleming wants the reader to identify with what he/she is already familiar with such as cars, aeroplanes, restaurant menus and so on (1979: 167).

The point of these long descriptions and digressions is, according to Eco, that Fleming believes that the reader considers these to be the mark of high literature. But Eco's assessment of Fleming is that while the Bond novels succeed in pleasing the public in the way they attract the reader, they are 'only a more subtle, but not less mystifying, example of soap opera' (1979: 172).

In a later work Eco revises his criticism of Fleming, arguing that his own critique was ideologically biased, and that Fleming's technique of shifting from long passages of inessential descriptions to short descriptions of eventful ones was a technique also used by Alessandro Manzoni (1995: 68). In his revision of Fleming, Eco now considers him as a Model Author from whom other aspiring authors might learn something of value.

Critical remarks

Eco is a prolific writer who has raised a lot of interesting points which in turn have been commented upon and challenged. For a start, regarding the distinction between open and closed texts, Lévi-Strauss disagrees with Eco's claim that what defines a work of art is its being 'closed'. Lévi-Strauss argues that there are intrinsic properties within the work that justify its status as a work of art: [2] in other words he shifts the question of establishing the status of something as art onto the search for objective qualities.

Caesar's (1999: 155–57) detailed study of Eco questions the distinction between the naïve and the sophisticated reader, claiming that it does not seem to be a tenable distinction to maintain. He gives the following reasons:

1. in both cases the reader is passive, but with the sophisticated reader, the sophistication lies in his/her admiration of the author's 'cleverness';
2. the relation between the Model Reader and the Model Author is reduced to an appreciation of the skills and techniques in the text and this goes against the reading experience of many who feel that texts highlight their own personal experiences. In addition, the pleasure of reading consists of immersing oneself in the character and the situation, rather than admiring the author's skills;
3. the strict disjunction between the naïve and sophisticated/critical reader is weak since reading can be both: it is not impossible to conceptualize a reader who is naïve but develops a critical attitude, or vice versa. The distinction between the 'sophisticated' and the 'naïve' reader has led Caesar to comment that the concept of the Model Reader is being 'tainted' with empirical (psychological, sociological) considerations.

In the analysis of popular culture, Strinati's (1995: 106–07) discussion of Eco's semiological reading of the Bond novels points to a tension in his theoretical position. On the one hand, Eco claims that it is impossible to know what readers will make of Fleming's texts, with the implication that the reception of these texts depends upon the readers. On the other hand, Eco's own analysis is directed at the universal structures that produce the text independently of readers. In addition Strinati (107–08) refers to the work of Bennett and Woolacott, who argue that there are no universal codes that lie outside history, but rather contexts with specific codes. Readers approach these texts with a certain cultural knowledge and their reading codes are informed through this. Many readers would have had knowledge of British spy thrillers as they read the Bond novels.

In this chapter, I have started by offering a detailed account of Eco's semiological theory. This account has covered (1) the study of signs; followed by (2) the distinction between signification and communication; (3) the concept of abduction; (4) the theory of the production of signs and (5) dictionaries and encyclopaedias. I then focussed on the narrower domain of textual semiotics, (6) starting with the distinction between Model Authors and Model Readers; and (7) open and closed texts. This was followed by (8) Eco's semiological analysis of the James Bond novels.

Notes

1. In *Six Walks in the Fictional Woods*, Eco writes, 'The main business of interpretation is to figure out the nature of this reader, in spite of its ghostly existence' (1995: 15–16).
2. Cited in Bondella (2005: 25): 'what makes a work of art a work is not its being open but its being closed. A work of art is an object end owed with precise properties and [it possesses], as it were, the rigidity of a crystal.'

Chapter 5

Derrida and the Deconstruction of Communication

Jacques Derrida (1930–2002) and the practice that has become synonymous with his name – deconstruction – became widely known in the late 1960s for a new approach to the analysis of texts irrespective of the discipline to which they traditionally belonged. While such an approach has been judged by its adherents as a radical liberation from the outdated categories of thought that permeate Western culture, its detractors accuse Derrida of wilful obscurantism. Derrida's rise to intellectual fame initiated with his publication of three books in 1967: *Of Grammatology*, *Speech and Phenomena* and *Writing and Difference*.

Derrida's notoriety and rejection is closely related to what he conceives of as the practice of deconstruction. This practice entails closely reading other philosophers with special focus on or attentiveness to their written language. Such practice reveals a concern with the literariness of philosophy, with the fact that much of philosophy is communicated through texts in which the language used – ambiguity, metaphor and imagery – ends up disrupting the content that is being expressed. This is not the traditional view of philosophical practice, where philosophers assume that a 'proper' piece of philosophical writing communicates an argument or thesis clearly and logically. Derrida argues that certain words will always escape the control that the author attempts to exert on the text, that the intentions expressed and the language used to express those intentions are not necessarily synchronized.

In this chapter, I am going to elaborate on (1) what are considered to be traditional theories of language, and use this elaboration to introduce some of the terminology associated with the practice of deconstruction. This will be followed by (2) an examination of Derrida's account of the spoken–written hierarchy, which will serve to highlight (3) the role of *différance* in Derrida's philosophy. I will then discuss (4) Derrida's relation to speech act theory and his engagement with John Searle and conclude (5) with suggestions on the way deconstruction can contribute to film theory.

Language

While reading Derrida might initially seem a rather daunting task, once one is comfortable with a number of terms used in his writings, then these become (relatively) more accessible. A good place to start is with the concept of 'presence' as it features throughout Derrida's texts. When an object (a tree) or a thought (a holiday) is present to us, it would not be mistaken to say that the 'tree' is next to us, or that we are thinking about our holiday at the moment. Both the tree and the holiday are present 'here and now' to us, externally (in the world) or internally (as a thought or idea in our mind). This model assumes that there is a truth beyond – and independent of – our language, about which we can only communicate by using our words and language.

Derrida[1] challenges this view by arguing that there is no truth outside language, for language is the 'filter' that prevents any direct access to the world or to our minds. Derrida is critical of traditional theories of language that explain the way meaning is produced in terms of either (1) the relation of language to the world, such that the meaning of a sentence is located in its ability to represent the external world, or (2) the relation of language to the self, where meaning is produced by the mind or consciousness. The underlying assumption operating in these theories is that of 'presence'; in the case of the former the presence of the world acts as a guarantor of meaning, while in the case of the latter, it is the mind or consciousness that acts as a guarantor of meaning. Both the world and the mind are the foundations that offer stability to language.

The notion that there is a truth outside language that is present to the person is one that has 'haunted' Western thinking about reality, and Derrida has labelled this the 'metaphysics of presence'. He argues that Western metaphysics can be read as

> determinates of being as *presence* in all the senses of the word [...] all the names related to fundamentals, to principles, or to the centre have designated an invariable presence – *eidos, arche, telos, energeia, ousia*, (essence, existence, substance, subject), *aletheia*, transcendentality, consciousness, or conscience, God, man, and so forth. (1978: 279–80)

The metaphysics of presence is closely connected to what Derrida calls 'logocentrism' and 'phonocentrism'. Logocentrism refers to the classical use of the Greek word *logos*, meaning 'word', 'speech', 'law' and, over time, having been associated with 'reason'. Through logocentrism, Derrida identifies a close connection in Western thought between the self as a conscious, rational mind and language. According to this view, the self is both prior to and the source of meaning which then expresses itself through the medium of language. This is not an uncommon view of the self, for it is widely believed that each of us is a unique self that communicates its uniqueness through language. The problem with this account according to Derrida is that when we look into our self and listen to the voice 'within us', this voice 'within us' is already an effect of language. The critique of logocentrism is that there is no self that exists prior to and apart from language.

Furthermore logocentric thinking, with its emphasis on reason, promotes a specific way of thinking by subscribing to the values of logic as the tool for the communication of thought. Logical thinking excludes all meaning that cannot be controlled by the principles of identity and non-contradiction. As a result a concept has a single, identical meaning and this meaning is opposed to another, such that to assert it and its opposite at the same time would be a contradiction (e.g. to say a bachelor is a married man). There are three consequences of this way of thinking that Gutting (2001: 293–94) labels as

1. the principle of opposition, where the world is structured into binary opposites (the true versus the false, the soul versus the body, good versus evil and so on);
2. the principle of exclusion, where the meaning of a concept excludes, by definition, that which does not fall within it. Given, for example, the way good is defined, then certain acts would by definition be considered evil;
3. the principle of priority, where thinking is structured not only in terms of oppositions and exclusions, but where the terms in the opposition are value loaded. There is according to Derrida an inherent bias that favours one of the terms in the opposition, so that truth, for example, is privileged over error, the good over the bad, the soul over the body and the masculine over the feminine.

Phonocentrism is intimately tied to logocentrism in the sense that it is a symptom of the logocentric bias of Western thought. Since by communicating our thoughts with language there is the danger that the language used might influence our thoughts, a superior form of communication would be one without language, a kind of 'telepathy' between minds in direct communication with each other. But since this ideal form of communication is unattainable, the spoken word is the next best option. Phonocentrism favours the spoken word, since the voice is closest to the mind and is therefore best suited to communicate our thoughts. In his reading of the history of Western thought, Derrida notices that different writers from different disciplines have always privileged speech while considering writing as a secondary and inferior medium. The problem with writing is that it involves the use of stylistic devices that can prevent the ideal of clarity in communication from being attained.

For Derrida, logocentrism and phonocentrism are the attempt to explain away differences of meaning by reducing them to a single meaning; logocentric thinking is oppressive in that it attempts to control the multiple potential meanings with language. Derrida's goal is to liberate language so that its inherent potential and its many possibilities of meaning are released.

It might be useful at this stage to answer the question: 'what is deconstruction?' The answer, however, is not so simple, for it is the characteristic feature of deconstruction to resist any attempt to be simply defined in terms of an 'is', because the 'is' presumes an ontology which deconstruction works against, working from within it in order to oppose it. In 'Letter to a Japanese Friend' (1983), Derrida suggests to a Japanese translator ways in which the term *deconstruction* can be translated into Japanese, and in the process outlines a number of ways in which deconstruction should not be conceived. For a start, (1) deconstruction is not some nihilistic destruction of everything; and (2) neither is it a type of analysis, for analysis is a process of reducing elements to their basic units, but it is these basic units that deconstruction is engaged with; (3) it does not involve critique of any sort, for the concepts involved in critique – choice, judgement, the Kantian transcendental – are those things that deconstruction operates upon; (4) it is not a method which is in competition against other methods, or which can be taught as a kind of procedure in educational institutions; (5) it is not something that a person or an institution does to a text from the outside. Derrida closes the letter by writing, 'What deconstruction is not? Everything of course! What is deconstruction? But nothing of course!' (1983: 5).

Speech and writing

Most people would be taken aback if they were told that to understand the nature of language, to understand what is essential and unique about it, they should look to writing rather than speech to achieve this goal. It is generally assumed that oral communication is the primary function of language, with writing considered to be an additional and secondary feature. And it is not hard to imagine the basis for this assumption, for when we speak we feel as though we are both producing and in control of the meaning as we speak.

Derrida controversially argues for the priority of writing, but this should be immediately qualified: in arguing for the priority of writing, he is not discussing the chronological evolution of language, that is, whether historically writing came before speaking, but rather the logical preconditions that make a language possible. The deconstruction of the speech–writing opposition is an important feature of Derrida's overall project of undermining the metaphysics of presence, since the spoken word is widely associated with the presence of the speaker. In this section I am engaging with two of Derrida's texts that demonstrate his deconstruction of the spoken–written opposition: these are his reading of Plato in *Dissemination* (1981) and his reading of Saussure in *Of Grammatology* (1976).

In the essay 'Plato's Pharmacy' in *Dissemination*, Derrida offers a sophisticated reading of Plato's *Phaedrus* where towards the end of this text, we find Socrates engaged in defending the priority and superiority of speaking as opposed to the inferiority and secondary aspect of writing. Derrida's deconstructive strategy renders this opposition untenable by questioning those values that the privileged term in this contrast – *speech* – assumes.

A cursory reading of the *Phaedrus* immediately challenges our understanding of Plato's philosophy. Plato was a firm believer in the power of the dialectical process that uses reason and logical deduction to arrive at the truth. But Plato's attempt to justify the superiority of speech over writing is framed within a mythical context. This is highly unusual because Plato had always insisted on the superiority of rational explanations over mythological ones. Derrida will demonstrate that although this is unusual, Plato is obliged – perhaps without knowing – to start in this way, given that mythology and writing share the common feature of repeating without being able to provide reasons for the repetition. In 'Plato's Pharmacy', Derrida's strategy is not merely that of reversing oppositions, but of going further by displacing the entire spoken/rational and written/mythical opposition.

The myth in question concerns the presentation of a number of gifts invented by the god Tholth to the Egyptian king Thamus. These gifts are intended to benefit humanity and include numbers, geometry, mathematics, astronomy and writing. The benefit of writing is that it will make 'the Egyptians wiser and [it] will improve their memories: both memory and instruction have found their remedy' (1981: 96–97). However, King Thamus is not convinced. He approves of all the inventions except for writing, offering a number of interrelated reasons for rejecting it (1981: 102).

The negative assessment of writing can be summarized as follows:

1. Writing replaces the living voice and presence of the speaker with inanimate signs. Instead of the presence of the teacher who can guide and instruct the student, and activate the knowledge within the student, writing offers a system of signs that does not challenge the student in the search for truth, but merely repeats the same thing. When someone reads and re-reads a text, he/she will find exactly the same words. If the person has difficulty in understanding the text, they will remain with their difficulty because there is no author to explain the meaning of the text (1981: 135–36).
2. Writing makes people lazy. The memory of those who rely on writing will decline because they will no longer find the need to exercise their memory, since they can consult the written text whenever they feel like. But the acquisition of knowledge and wisdom is not merely the result of blind repetition, but the active exercise of memory framed within the student–teacher model.
3. The teacher–student relationship will no longer have any importance since the student can dispense with the teacher and just read the text. But true knowledge and wisdom are accumulated over time as a result of the maturity of the teacher, who can transmit this knowledge and wisdom orally to the student. The authority of the teacher is in effect challenged and the natural social order is disrupted.
4. The written text acquires a life of its own. Since a written text can communicate a meaning without requiring the speaker to explain that meaning, the written text in effect makes the speaker redundant: texts can be read and understood even when the author is dead. The problem and danger with writing is its autonomy since the written word is meaningful independently of the author, and as a result it is possible to offer interpretations that differ from what the author originally intended (1981: 143).

There is an evident paradox in the relation between Plato, Socrates and the *Phaedrus* itself. Socrates argues for the priority of the spoken word as the medium for the practice of philosophy while denouncing writing in the process; consistent with this belief, Socrates does not write his own philosophy. But unless the philosophy of Socrates is written down, it would soon be forgotten after his death. And even if he does not explicitly say so, Socrates wants his philosophy to be remembered. Writing down his philosophy is therefore a necessary evil, and this 'duty' is performed by his diligent student Plato, who thereby ensures that what was taught by Socrates is communicated to posterity.

Despite this inconsistency between what Socrates says and what Plato does, Derrida's deconstructive reading goes further: he focusses on certain features of the text that other readings tend to skim over or ignore as unimportant details. With extreme meticulousness he unravels the different senses of certain terms used by Plato to articulate his point of view.

What these different senses show is that there is no single, clear-cut rationality that can communicate the truth of the *Phaedrus*: the values of reason, logic and speech – values that are central to Plato's philosophy – are disrupted by a number of metaphors that are found in the text. Plato, for example, uses the Greek word *pharmakon* to discuss the nature of writing as both a 'poison' and a 'cure'. What Derrida points out is that although these two senses of *pharmakon* are opposed to each other, they are found together when Plato describes writing. Writing is a 'poison' since it threatens the purity of living speech. With the spoken word the speaker knows what he/she means, but with writing the connection between the speaker and the meaning is dislocated, since a written text has no need of the speaker to explain its meaning. On the other hand, writing is a 'cure' for old age, a 'cure' that counters the failure of memory with the passage of time. And as a 'cure' it enables a person to remember what was spoken about in the past, since through writing the original intention of the speaker is preserved forever.

The *pharmakon* reveals the inability of the text to transmit a single meaning. The difficulty is that of deciding which of the two senses Plato intends. Derrida answers that it is not possible to decide and the term *pharmakon* is one that Derrida describes as an 'undecidable'. Writing as *pharmakon* is the sign of irreconcilable opposites, a disruption of the logic of identity:

> If the *pharmakon* is "ambivalent," it is because it constitutes the medium in which opposites are opposed, the movement and the play that links them among themselves, reverses them or makes one side cross over into the other (soul/body, good/evil, inside/outside, memory/forgetfulness, speech/writing). It is on the basis of this play or movement that the opposites or differences are stopped by Plato. The *pharmakon* is the movement, this locus, and the play: (the production of) difference. (1981: 127)

Memory plays an important role in Plato's account of truth, and it is from within this memory-truth axis that writing is considered to be a disruptive influence on the grounds that writing impoverishes memory. However, while Plato sees writing as a threat to memory, he then goes on to distinguish between a 'good' type of memory and a 'bad' one. The 'good' type of memory (anamnesis) occurs when those truths that the soul has forgotten are recalled through proper teaching. The 'good' use of memory involves the living presence of the speaker/teacher who, in dialogue with the student, activates his/her memory so as to repeat what was already known but forgotten. The 'bad' type of memory is the one that replaces the genuine live interaction of the intellect with 'shorthand' signs; it is not genuine knowledge since it is not the product of reflection. The 'bad' type of memory repeats blindly without any understanding of the material under consideration. Derrida's argument is that this contrast is untenable since both the 'good' and the 'bad' type of memory rely equally on the possibility of repetition, on the ability to repeat what happened in the past (1981: 111).

It is on the question of repeatability that Derrida's argument hinges. On the one hand, for truth to present itself as truth it must be repeated in the presence of the teacher, through the use of the spoken word and the exercise of memory; on the other hand, repetition is also the characteristic of non-truth, writing and bad memory: 'The true and the untrue are both species of repetition' (1981: 168).

However, while writing is pejoratively described, it would seem that – at some level – Plato is unable to relinquish writing completely. One of the clearest examples of the conflict between what Plato intends to say and what he actually writes can be seen in his attempt to define speech by using metaphors of writing. When Phaedrus asks Socrates to specify which form of discourse is superior to writing, he replies, 'the sort that goes together with learning and is written in the soul of the learner' (in Derrida 1981: 148). As Derrida points out, it is remarkable that after Socrates puts so much effort into condemning writing, he then goes on to define speech as 'writing' on the soul. Writing must in some sense be necessary after all, and this is why a distinction is made between good and bad writing (1981: 149).

Derrida also argues that the 'instability' of writing, its effect on and disruption of speech were also played out in ancient Greek society, which defined itself in opposition to those persons who did not fit in. But while Greek society excluded its others, it also maintained within its walls a number of individuals who could be used as scapegoats in times of crisis, 'the representative of the outside is nonetheless *constituted*, regularly granted its place by the community, chosen, kept, fed, etc., in the very heart of the inside' (1981: 133). Interestingly, the Greek word for these scapegoats is *pharmakos* (defined as wizard, magician, prisoner and scapegoat), a word not found in the *Phaedrus*, but whose etymology reveals an overlap with *pharmakon*. Derrida argues that there is continuum of sense between the words found within Plato's text and those found outside it. And just as the purity of Greek society was contaminated by maintaining within itself those it wanted to exclude, the purity of speech is likewise 'contaminated' by writing.

Among the other values that constitute the framework of the discussion on the spoken and written are also questions concerning the role of authority and the legitimation of tradition as a way of ensuring the continued existence of the community. This existence is ensured by the tradition which acknowledges the father as the natural authority transmitting orally to his legitimate son the values and knowledge of that community. Within this father–legitimate son framework, writing is an 'orphan' permitted only because it is non-threatening (1981: 77).

Underlying Plato's text is another logic that operates by exclusion with the goal of protecting truth from the corrupting influence of writing. The model of speech as the medium that leads to truth through dialogical interaction can only and necessarily condemn writing as a secondary and impoverished derivative. The *Phaedrus* is situated at a relatively early stage in Western philosophy and is indicative of a certain way of thinking about language, truth and reality. It might lead one to argue that Plato is the 'founder' of this way of thinking. However, despite this prominent historical position, Derrida carefully rejects talk of both 'origins' and 'ends', as these belong to the 'luggage' of logocentric metaphysics, whose assumptions he seeks to undermine. To claim that Plato is the originator of this way of thinking about speech is to return to the framework of binary oppositions that belong to the discourse of the metaphysics of presence. In his close reading of 'Plato's Pharmacy', Derrida has shown the play of differences at work within the text. The term *pharmakon* has the structure of the double that is undecidable since it is used simultaneously as both a poison and a cure.

In *Of Grammatology* (1976), Derrida uses a similar strategy to question Saussure's claim of the superiority of the spoken word over the written word. While Derrida remains indebted to Saussure for the radical innovations he brought to linguistics, Derrida's reading develops these innovations to their logical conclusions. The importance of Saussure's linguistics lies in the fact that it offers a tentative critique of logocentrism. By arguing that a sign is composed of a signifier and a signified, Saussure was, in effect, dismissing the view that a sign is used to communicate ideas that lie outside the sign system. And yet, despite this promising start, Saussure did not realize the implications of his own linguistic model and remained 'trapped' within the metaphysics of presence that has characterized Western culture (1976: 53). And while Saussure considered his linguistics to be a scientific study of language, Derrida argues that his 'scientific' model is tainted with logocentric and phonocentric assumptions.

The starting point for Saussure's linguistics immediately reveals his prejudice in favour of speech: in the study of language, it is the sound or phonology that should be the focus of attention: '[f]or each language uses a fixed number of distinct speech sounds and this is the only sound system which has any reality as far as the linguist is concerned' (1983: 34). This is prejudiced because if one is studying language as a whole then this should include both the spoken and the written word. By stressing sounds or phonology it is evident that Saussurean linguistics – allegedly scientific and objective – values the spoken word from the outset. As a result, writing is positioned as the external other to speech and 'outside' language in general.

The phonocentric bias is even more evident in Saussure's account of the relation between speech and writing. There is a tension in Saussure's thinking on the relation and value of the spoken and the written word, for while the spoken word is exclusively privileged as the object of study for linguists, it seems that the written word should not be dismissed out of hand (1983: 24–25). On the contrary, Saussure warns us to be vigilant since many people continually and mistakenly think of writing as an intrinsic part of language. But Saussure is not only issuing a warning: in his analysis of writing, his rhetoric describes writing as having many 'dangers', as something with the power to 'usurp' the spoken word, exercising a 'tyranny' over language as a whole. It is odd to see writing being condemned with such an outburst of indignation. Derrida asks why Saussure felt the need to resort to such forceful rhetoric: what is it about writing that is so threatening?

One of the threats lies in the ability of writing to disrupt the natural condition of language. According to Saussure there is a 'natural and [...] authentic connection which links word and sound', or meaning and sound (1983: 26). By nature humans have the faculty of expressing themselves through sounds, and this explains why Saussure considered phonology (the study of sound) as the model for the science of linguistics. Implicit in Saussure's view is the assumption that the natural order of the world is one where humans in their natural state use language in the first instance to speak.

But this claim on the way things are by nature is challenged by Derrida who asks: how can Saussure claim that there is a natural connection between the sounds humans produce and the meanings in their minds, when he considers one of the achievements of his linguistics to be the non-natural connection between sounds and meanings? The thesis of the arbitrary nature of the sign gives an account of the relation between the signifier (the sound) and the signified (meaning) as a non-natural relation. These two claims – the natural and the arbitrary – are precisely the opposite of each other, so it is strange to find them next to each other in Saussure's explanation of language. The thesis of the arbitrary nature of the sign has an important consequence for the alleged superiority of the spoken to the written: (1) if the spoken is superior to writing because it is natural; and (2) if writing is inferior because it is unnatural; and (3) if all signs (spoken and written) are arbitrary, then (4) this disrupts the contrast between the natural and the unnatural, a contrast that Saussure wanted to retain.

In addition, Saussure had also introduced the principle of difference to explain the identity of signs. What gives sounds an identity is not something inherent within the sound itself but its relationship to other signs within the linguistic system, a system constructed according to certain conventions of use. The basis of this claim is Saussure's view that the sign is fundamentally a psychic phenomenon as opposed to a material one. Sounds are not defined by their physical manifestation but by the way they relate to other sounds (1983: 116–17).

The evidence for the differential nature of sound could be seen in the way different people could pronounce sounds differently and yet still be understood. This showed that understanding could take place because it was not a question of the sound being related to the meaning, but a question of understanding sounds as different from others within the sound system. As Derrida once again points out, the differential nature of sounds contradicts Saussure's claim that there is a natural connection between sounds and meaning.

Given that Saussure considered the existence of a natural connection between sound and meaning, what is the danger posed by writing? The danger represented by writing is that it threatens the natural order of things. Writing has the potential to disrupt the way words are pronounced since different people can read the same words but pronounce them differently. These variations of pronunciation would eventually lead to modifications within the language itself, and as a result the natural connection between sound and meaning would be weakened. Derrida writes:

> This natural bond of the signified (concept or sense) to the phonic signifier would condition the natural relationship subordinating writing (visible image) to speech. It is this natural relationship that would have been inverted by the original sin of writing [...] (1976: 35)

As Derrida points out, Saussure's way of thinking conceptualizes writing as a phenomenon lying outside (of) language; since by nature language is a spoken medium, then writing is the non-natural, external other of language, posing a permanent threat to the natural order of things.

There is a further interesting twist to Derrida's reading of Saussure. The internal contradiction in Saussure's writing is apparent when, after having condemned writing so vigorously, he uses writing as a model to understand the functioning of language as a whole, claiming that '[a]n identical state of affairs is to be found in that other system of signs, writing. Writing offers a useful comparison, which throws light upon the whole question' (1983: 117). One would think that having expressed so many reservations about writing, Saussure would have adopted some other model. Perhaps, as Derrida points out, he could not do otherwise.

The problem with Saussure's account is that it had privileged speech at the expense of writing by prioritizing sound, but the difference that enables a person to identify a sound is not itself a sound. Difference or the 'space' between sounds is what makes the identification of different sounds possible, and it is also this 'space' that makes meaning possible. As a result the spoken word loses its privileged status, since both the spoken and the written are generated by the same process of difference.

> By definition, difference is never in itself a sensible plenitude. Therefore, its necessity contradicts the allegation of a naturally phonic essence of language. It contests by the same token the professed natural dependence of the graphic signifier. (1976: 53)

Saussure had placed writing in a secondary and derivative position on the grounds that it was a 'signifier of a signifier', but the principle of difference shows that all signs were signs of other signs. As it turns out, the feature that was identified so closely with writing is the same feature that can best explain the functioning of the linguistic system as a whole. Perhaps this is why Saussure increasingly turned to models and examples of writing to support his linguistic theory.

The implication of Saussure's use of writing as a model to explain all of language reveals that writing is not the external other of language, situated in a secondary and derivative position, but rather always already within language. As it turns out, language is a form of writing. Derrida writes:

> [T]he alleged derivativeness of writing, however real and massive, was possible only on one condition: that the "original", "natural", etc. language had never existed, never been intact and untouched by writing, that it had itself always been a writing. (1976: 56)

Derrida calls this generalized concept of writing 'arche-writing' or 'originary writing', and his argument is that the characteristic that was attributed to writing – difference and absence – is the characteristic of language as a whole. Writing, he claims, 'is not a sign of a sign, except if one says it of all signs, which would be more profoundly true' (1976: 43). And by broadening the concept of writing to arche-writing, other systems of meaning production (ideograms, hieroglyphics and cybernetic systems) rather than just the written marks on a page can be explained.

The re-definition of writing as a generalized writing – as arche-writing that includes both the spoken and the written word as signs of signs – leads to a reversal of the speech–writing hierarchy and a reconstruction of the concept of writing. Although arche-writing is the condition for the possibility of both speech and writing, it should be noted that Derrida's notion of arche-writing does not function as a 'master' concept positioned outside of a discourse. Although it is not a transcendental signified that provides a stable foundation for discourse, it can be described, according to Gasche (1988), as 'quasi-transcendental' in that it functions like a transcendental signified but operates within specific texts and discourses.

Derrida's close textual reading undermines the strategies employed within the discourse of metaphysics to erase difference as it seeks to establish the presence of self-identity. Grammatology is the name Derrida uses for the new writing that reveals and revels in its resistance to metaphysics. It would seem that the easiest way of resisting the metaphysics of presence would be to reverse the speech–writing opposition by placing writing in the superior position. This would be a mistake, for to do so would be to succumb once again to the logocentrism of Western metaphysics. Resistance to the metaphysics of presence is not merely a simple reversal of opposites, but rather a reconfiguration of the terms to include both terms in the opposition. The terms Derrida introduces throughout his texts – *différance*, arche-writing, *pharmakon*, supplement and hymen among others – perform this function, and in this sense they can be considered undecidables insofar as they resist the attempt to be straitjacketed into a single, determinate meaning. The two or more meanings of these terms undermine the binary oppositions that inform the discourse of metaphysics.

Différance, traces

As I have already mentioned, Derrida agrees with the Saussurean model of language but develops it to its logical and radical conclusions. One consequence of his reading of Saussure is that of the interrelated notions of 'trace' and '*différance*'. Derrida argues that the relation between signs is not merely one of proximity, where each sign is different from or opposed to the sign that is immediately next to it. Rather, each sign is related to every other sign within the linguistic system. The presence and identity of a sign is also connected to other absent signs within the linguistic system, and this means that the use of a sign entails other signs following in its 'wake'. Each sign leaves a trace of itself on other signs. In *Of Grammatology*, Derrida writes:

> *The (pure) trace is différance*. It does not depend on any sensible plenitude, audible or visible, phonic or graphic. It is, on the contrary, the condition of such a plenitude. Although it *does not exist*, although it is never a *being-present* outside of all plenitude,

its possibility is by rights anterior to all that one calls sign (signified/signifier, content/ expression, etc.), concept or operation, motor or sensory. (1976: 62)

An indication of what Derrida means by trace and *différance* can be found in *Positions* (1972), where he discusses the key Saussurean conceptual opposition between *langue* (system) and *parole* (event). Derrida highlights the paradoxical nature of this opposition, for on the one hand the presence of a sign is established by its difference from other signs within the system. But the system itself can only come about as a result of signs themselves having a meaning in the first place. The speech act (or event) depends upon the system (or *langue*), but the system itself is the product of speech acts (1972: 28).[2] Knowing the meaning of the sign *house* depends on its contrast with other forms of accommodation, but to be able to articulate the different types of accommodation you must have the sign (such as *house*) that enables the system to come into being. Derrida describes this process as circular, in that the speech event and the system depend on or refer back to each other. What is needed is a way of explaining both, and the term *différance* is used to explain the conditions that must be in place so as to account for the generation of meaning.

The term *différance* is a neologism coined by Derrida to capture two characteristics of signs: difference and deferral. It is a combination of 'to differ' (as when we say 'a' is different from 'b') and 'to defer' (as in to postpone, put off). The connotations associated with difference and deferral are spatial and temporal respectively. Signs are spatial because they are connected to other signs within the linguistic network, and they are temporal because they are connected to other signs that come before or after them within the linguistic system.

It is because of différance that the movement of signification is possible only if each so-called "present" element, each element appearing on the scene of presence, is related to something other than itself thereby keeping within itself the mark of the past element, and already letting itself be vitiated by the mark of its relation to the future element, this trace being related no less to what is called the future than to what is called the past, and constituting what is called the present by means of this very relation to what it is not: what it absolutely is not, not even a past or a future as a modified present. (1982: 13)

When Derrida coined the term '*différance*' he pointed out that the English *different* and the French *differant* sound the same, and that this might easily lead to some confusion. This confusion is dispelled when they are written, since their difference is apparent in the spelling. What this highlights is the important Derridean point that certain meanings can only be communicated through the written word.

It should be emphasized that Derrida's *différance* is not merely the combination of two sets of meanings, but 'immediately and irreducibly polysemic' (1982: 8). The use of a sign has within it the potential to generate infinite meanings, as a sign differs from another sign that in turn differs from another in a chain of signification so that, given a different context, a different signification might (though not necessarily) be generated. Meaning is not fixed once and for all but is an ongoing process, 'the indefinite referral of signifier to signifier [...] which gives the signified meaning no respite [...] so that it always signifies again and differs' (1978: 25). One way of showing Derrida's point is that if we look up the meaning of a signifier in a dictionary, we do not find any signifieds but more signifiers. Storey gives an example of this process of endless postponement or deferral of meaning:

> [I]f we look at the signifier 'letter' in the Collins Pocket Dictionary of the English Language, we discover it has five possible signifieds: a written or printed message, a character of the alphabet, the strict meaning of an agreement, precisely (as in 'to the letter') and to write or mark letters on a sign. If we then look up one of the senses, the signified '[written or printed] message', we find that it too is a signifier producing four more signifieds: a communication from one person or group to another, an implicit meaning, as in a work of art, a religious or political belief that someone attempts to communicate to others, and to understand (as in 'to get the message'). (1993: 86)

In *Margins of Philosophy*, Derrida describes *différance* as 'the movement according to which language or any code, any system of reference in general is constituted "historically" as a weave of differences' (1982: 12). But by saying that *différance* is at the core of meaning and history (as their origin), it would seem that Derrida has returned to the language of metaphysics with its emphasis on foundations or first principles. This would re-enact a gesture typical of the tradition of Western philosophy that locates a transcendental first principle to explain differences away. But for Derrida, the 'originary trace' shows that there can never be a pure, first moment, an origin towards which meaning can return. Unlike Saussure, who remained trapped within logocentrism by privileging the signified as that towards which signifiers (phonic or graphic) refer to, Derrida considers the signified as just another signifier.

Thus, although *différance* functions like a metaphysical principle, it has no privileged foundational status: it is transcendental in the sense of the underlying presuppositions or conditions that make something possible. In this sense, *différance* is the condition for the possibility of language and meaning without being situated in an anterior position to language and meaning. For Derrida, *différance* is inherent within or part of language and meaning, and it also makes language and meaning possible. *Différance* is described as 'the non-full, non-simple, structured and differentiating origin of differences. Thus the name "origin" no longer suits it' (1982: 11). There can never be a pure origin or meaning that is independent of all signifiers, since signifiers circulate within the linguistic system.

Opposed to the idea of meaning as grounded in an origin or a goal, Derrida argues that signification is a process of dissemination where each sign substitutes the other in an infinite play of meaning. Consequently, there is no centre that can function as a presence to stabilize signs: on the contrary, the presence that logocentrism took as an unquestioned value is seen as an effect of signification, an effect of the linguistic system. *Différance* undermines the metaphysics of presence. This Derridean position opens up the space for a radical theory of interpretation that no longer claims to have access to things or meanings but produces new interpretations that are in turn interpreted, giving rise to new interpretations ad infinitum.

In his elaboration of meaning as *différance*, Derrida replaces Saussure's static account of language with a dynamic and temporal one that takes into consideration the context(s) within which language is used. Whereas Saussure's account considered signs as expressing a meaning that was already present within the linguistic system, Derrida's account considers meaning as always incomplete, since understanding the meaning of a sign requires taking into account other signs within the linguistic system.

Communication and speech act theory

Traditional theories of communication assume a sender-message-receiver model of communication. The sender intends a meaning that is encoded (phonically or graphically) into a message and transmitted to a receiver who decodes the message to understand what the speaker intends to mean. This model operates on the assumption that (1) communication is the communication of intentions,[3] with the presence of the speaker in oral communication and the absence of the speaker (as a deferred presence) in the case of written communication; (2) there is a strict dichotomy between the signified and the signifier, with the signifier as the optional (but necessary) supplement that enables the signified to be communicated. Interestingly the signified is favoured over the signifier (the meaning over the medium) and is furthermore assumed to remain the same in each instance of communication.

In 'Signature Event Context' (1988), Derrida's critique of the traditional model of communication aims to demonstrate that the signified–signifier opposition is untenable. This opposition fails to take into account the logically necessary features of all signs – the possibility of their repetition or iteration. His critique opens (1) by identifying this necessary feature in writing, as it is in writing that it is most evident, and continues (2) by showing that this feature belongs not only to written signs but to all signs. This is followed by (3) an application of this insight to the speech act theory of J. L. Austin.

Derrida's starting point is a problematization of the concept of communication. Communication is typically defined as the transfer of meaning, such that the other senses of communication – such as the imparting of a non-linguistic force or the delivery of a paper at a conference – are considered secondary. In offering to define *to communicate*, most dictionaries would start by offering the literal sense and then add the figurative ones. But the difficulty is that it already assumes what we are in fact trying to define. What dictionaries show is that understanding or defining the meaning of a concept entails using other words, so to start any discussion one must tentatively agree to use words in a certain way within a context. This is precisely the case with the concept of communication (1988: 1).

Derrida starts his analysis of communication by focussing on written communication, and his analysis focusses on Etienne Condillac's *An Essay on the Origin of Human Knowledge, Being a Supplement to Mr Locke's Essay on the Human Understanding* (1756), an essay explicitly written with the purpose of 'filling' in certain features of language that Locke had neglected in his work. Condillac's essay attempts to account for the origins of writing as an addition or supplement to speech. It serves the important function of enabling the communication of messages to take place over greater distances that are out of the range of the spoken word, but that can be bridged by writing. On Derrida's reading, Condillac justifies writing on the grounds that (1) human beings have to communicate; (2) they have to communicate the ideas or thoughts in their minds; and (3) given that they are already able to communicate to themselves and to others, they invent a new means of communication – writing (1988: 4).

For Condillac the invention of writing is a progressive 'evolution' of linguistic communication since, given that societies are no longer organized as communities using face-to-face communication, then the distancing of members from each other could be reduced through writing:

> [m]en in a state of communicating their thoughts by means of sounds felt the necessity of imagining new signs capable of perpetuating those thoughts and of making them *known* to persons who are *absent*. (in Derrida 1988: 4)

This, however, is not an accurate way of representing absence, and Derrida points out that the absence of the receiver in Condillac's model is not really an absence but a 'modification of presence'. On Condillac's account, to write is to communicate with someone who is present but is beyond the range of the spoken word – who, so to speak, is distantly present. Clearly, this view of writing is still dominated by the framework that thinks of the spoken word as present and immediate, with the written word as a projection across space of the spoken word. On this account writing does not have any characteristics of its own, and it owes its relatively favourable status to its ability to transport the presence of the spoken word.

Derrida adds that a more complete understanding of writing as absence is one whereby the receiver is not merely distantly absent, but absolutely absent, or dead. The meaning of a piece of writing can still be understood if the receiver is dead, for to understand a written text there is no need to assume that there is a reader who will activate the text. It is possible to write a letter to someone who, unknown to you, died before the letter arrived: it will still be possible to understand the letter despite the absence of the receiver. This view on the absence of the receiver applies equally to the sender or producer of the text. The author is not a necessary condition for understanding a text, since we can understand a text even if the author is dead. Furthermore, it is also possible to understand a written text without needing to know what the author intended to mean. Given the removal of the sender and the receiver as the source or origin of the meaning, where does this meaning 'reside'? The short answer for Derrida is that meaning is found within the structure of language itself.

If it is possible to understand a written text without the sender or receiver, then how is it possible for a written sign to function? For the latter to be possible, the written sign must have the possibility of being repeated. Repetition or 'iterability', as Derrida calls it, is a structural feature of writing which enables the recognition of a unit of writing as the same, despite being different. In other words, the power of iteration makes it possible to both identify a string of words as the same and to generate a different meaning, since it is being generated within a different context (1988: 53).

At this stage, it is useful to distinguish between Derrida's notion of a 'generalised writing' and what I am calling 'specific writing' (the written sign: writing in a narrow sense). Derrida points out that the traditional account of writing has certain features that pre-figure his 'generalised writing': these features are (1) that the written sign does not need to be associated with the present moment; (2) that it can be taken out of a context and inserted into another, in a process of 'grafting' and (3) that it is situated at a distance from that which it refers to, so that it can be used again to refer to another thing (1988: 9–10). The absence that is central to 'specific writing' overlaps with the absence that 'generalised writing' is concerned with, and this is why Derrida applies this insight to all signs – spoken, written, human and non-human. The use of any sign does not entail as a necessary precondition the presence of the sender or the receiver. The nature of the sign is that it can be used and reused, that is, repeated. This notion of 'generalised writing' as repetition is the condition that makes all communication possible. Absence is an inherent feature of communication and the relatively permanent marks of 'specific writing' become possible only as a result of this repetition.

> This structural possibility of being weaned from the referent or from the signified (hence from communication and from its context) seems to me to make every mark, including those which are oral, a grapheme in general; which is to say, as we have seen, the nonpresent *remainder [restance]* of a differential mark cut off from its putative "production" or origin. And I shall even extend this law to all "experience" in general if it is conceded that there is no experience consisting of *pure* presence but only of chains of differential marks. (1988: 10)

The second part of Derrida's essay, 'Parasites. Iter, of Writing: That It Perhaps Does Not Exist', is an engagement with the speech act theory of J.L. Austin. In *How to do Things with Words* (1975), Austin had argued that the use of language to describe or represent the world is only one way of understanding language, one that could be subsumed within a broader category of speech acts. A speech act is an utterance that performs an action: it is what we do when we talk, so that when a couple say 'I do' they are not describing a wedding, but are actually getting married. Since all utterances perform an action, we can use language to promise, pray, declare, warn, threaten, joke, describe and so on.

In order to explain these speech acts, Austin does not rely on the presence of the speaker who intends the utterance, since one can think of many instances where the intention is not enough to guarantee the meaning of the speech act. A promise remains a promise even if the speaker does not intend to keep his/her promise. Promises can be explained in terms of the conventions governing their use, the 'formula' used in uttering them, rather than the speaker's intentions. And this is why Austin proposes to explain speech acts by focussing on the conventional context of their production: if certain conditions are fulfilled or satisfied, then the speech act is judged as successful (if not, it is then unsuccessful). These 'felicity conditions' require that (1) the appropriate words must be uttered (one can only say 'I do' when getting married); (2) they must be uttered in the right context (one can only say them in a church for them to be effective as a Christian wedding) and (3) the speaker is sincere in his/her uttering them (saying them as a joke renders them null and void). These are the necessary conditions that guarantee the success of a speech act.

A number of features attract Derrida to Austin's theory, namely (1) his explanation of communication in terms of speech acts; (2) his defining communication in terms of 'force'; (3) his elaboration of the notion of force as transformative, as producing an effect and (4) his rejection of the true and the false as the values that are central to language.

> For these four reasons, at least, it might seem that Austin has shattered the concept of communication as a purely semiotic, linguistic, or symbolic concept. The performative is a "communication" which is not limited strictly to the transference of a semantic content that is already constituted and dominated by an orientation toward truth (be it the *unveiling* of what is in its being or the *adequation-congruence* between a judicative utterance and the thing itself). (1988: 13–14)

But while the feature that attracts Derrida to Austin is the latter's attempt to account for meaning in terms of the context and the associated conventions of production, Austin himself retreats from this explanation when he re-introduces the speaker's intention. In order to account for the transformative power of a speech act, that is, how an utterance does something to transform a situation, Austin realizes that the grammatical structure is not enough to generate the illocutionary force; something else is needed and it is here that the speaker's intentions are re-introduced. Austin therefore distinguishes between the locutionary and the illocutionary aspect of an utterance: the locutionary aspect is explained in terms of the grammatical rules of a linguistic system, while the illocutionary aspect is explained with reference to the way the speaker uses the utterance, to the intentions. The utterance *the bus is arriving* can be explained according to the grammatical rules of the English language, which constitute its locutionary aspect. But it may also be explained according to the way the utterance is used by the speaker – as a fact, as a warning to get back onto the pavement, as a remark on its punctuality.

Speech act theory is Austin's attempt to explain the illocutionary force of utterances by identifying the presence of the speaker intending the speech act as a necessary feature of the illocutionary act. It is only (for example) because the speaker intends to keep the promise he/she is making that it counts as 'genuine' speech act of promising. The speaker must be committed to the promises he/she is making, and Austin calls the making of a promise that one has no intention of keeping an 'insincerity' or an 'abuse'. It is evident that speech act theory relies upon the presence of the speaker as a guarantor for the authenticity of his/her utterances.

The critical point Derrida makes at this stage is that the intentionality and presence that Austin associates with speech acts are not necessary for the speech act to mean something.

It is perfectly possible for an utterance to be repeated in a different context from that within which it was originally uttered by the speaker. For a speech act to function, it must derive its meaning independently of the speaker. In other words, it must belong to a system of conventions that is already in place prior to the speaker's utterance and that makes it possible for the speech act to be repeated in a different context.

This leads Derrida to make a further claim about Austin's theory of speech acts, which has been strongly resisted by commentators sympathetic to speech act theory. If, according to speech act theory, utterances require the presence of the speaker to guarantee their authenticity, what happens then when someone makes a joke of something serious, when a promise or threat is uttered on stage, or when the words of someone else are quoted? These speech acts pose a threat to the claims made by speech act theory since the speaker's intention to mean is being used in a way that undermines the value of intentionality. Austin considers it in the interest of speech act theory to separate performatives into those that are genuine and those that are 'parasitic' or etiolations (1975: 22).

These utterances 'thrive' upon everyday uses of language and represent exceptions or aberrations from the norm. As a result, when Austin describes the 'felicity' conditions that ensure the success of a speech act, he excludes those speech acts that are 'non-serious' since these cannot even claim to function as genuine speech acts.

It is this opposition between the 'serious' and the 'non-serious' that Derrida challenges, for by removing the 'non-serious' from the equation Austin commits an unjustified limitation upon the object of inquiry. If Austin wants to give an account of the way performatives function, he must also be able to explain those that cannot function and not just remove them as irrelevant to the study of speech acts. To account for the possibility of both serious and non-serious speech acts, Derrida introduces the notion of iteration:

> [I]sn't it true that what Austin excludes as anomaly, exception, "non-serious", citation (on a stage, in a poem, or a soliloquy) is the determined modification of a general citationality – or rather, a general iterability – without which there would not even be a "successful" performative? (1988: 17)

The condition that makes it possible for a speech act to be taken seriously is the same condition that makes it possible for it to not be taken seriously. Miscommunication is inherent within the system of communication. Derrida's concept of iteration describes the fact that speech acts can be taken out of one context and used in another without the need to explain the meaning by referring to the speaker's presence in the act of intending-to-mean. The metaphysics of presence that Derrida has detected in such diverse writers as Plato and Saussure has also slipped into Austin's speech act theory, since intentionality is not a necessary 'felicity' condition for the production of meaning. On the contrary, a better explanation for the production of meaning is Derrida's notion of arche-writing as *différance*, since it is the condition that makes the 'iterability' of language possible without the need to posit the speaker and his/her intentions.

Derrida is insistent that a speech act is performed and has a meaning in a context. Its importance is such that it is usually taken for granted that to understand the meaning of a sign or signs one should look at the context of their production. And in this sense it is frequently accepted that the context is a kind of fixed or enclosed entity within which any ambiguity of meaning can be removed. However, various questions arise: does a text lead to the context or is it the context that allows us to understand the text? What are the boundaries of a context? Who decides what is included and excluded from a context? Derrida is explicit: 'I shall try to demonstrate why a context is never absolutely determinable, or rather, why its determination can never be entirely certain or saturated' (1988: 3). While meaning is always context-dependent, the context itself is not a fixed and self-enclosed entity. Derrida claims that a context is 'boundless' and this is for two reasons.

1. The attempt to limit what can be included within a context serves to create another context: to say what should or shouldn't be included within a context has the paradoxical effect of creating another context:

   [A]ny attempt to codify context can always be grafted onto the context it sought to describe, yielding a new context which escapes the previous formulation. Attempts to describe limits always make possible a displacement of whose limits, so that Wittgenstein's suggestion that one cannot say 'bububu' and mean 'if it does not rain I shall go out for a walk,' has paradoxically, made it possible to do just that. (Culler 1982: 124)

2. The addition of new information to the object under investigation in effect creates a new context for the object under investigation.[4] Utilizing Derrida in a book on the philosophy of communication has created a new context for studies in deconstruction.

   [A]ny given context is open to further description. There is no limit in principle to what might be included in a given context, to what might be shown to be relevant to the performance of a particular speech act. This structural openness of context is essential to all disciplines: the scientist discovers that factors previously disregarded are relevant to the behaviour of certain objects; the historian brings new or reinterpreted data to bear on a particular event; the critic relates a passage or a text to a context that makes it appear in a new light [...] [M]eaning is determined by context and for that very reason is open to alteration when further possibilities are mobilized. (Culler 1982: 124)

Despite Derrida's questioning of the limits and possibilities of the context, it still retains an important role insofar as it imposes a limit on interpretation. Contrary to what many think, deconstruction does not advocate an 'anything goes' approach with regard to interpretation, and the often quoted 'there is nothing outside the text' is nothing more than a confirmation of the context as a limitation upon the text. The extent of these limits upon the text can be seen by Derrida's endorsement of what he calls 'interpretive police', where a community establishes the criteria for establishing good or bad, or true or false interpretations:

> [W]ithin interpretive contexts [...] it should be possible to invoke rules of competence, criteria of discussion and of consensus, good faith, lucidity, rigor, criticism, and pedagogy. (1988: 146)

What Derrida shows is that the rules that govern an interpretation are not somehow natural, but rather the product of a community that achieves a minimum of consensus as to what counts as a good or bad interpretation. It is the community that has the possibility of halting the re-contextualization of speech acts, and that functions as an 'interpretive police'. When asked about whether the notion of 'interpretive police' implies a certain amount of repression, Derrida responds by pointing out that while there are restrictions on what counts as an interpretation, restriction should not be equated with repression, just as a red traffic light is restrictive but not repressive (1988: 132).

It should be recalled that Derrida is not denying that meaning is determined by context, as it is this very context that enables communication to take place. His argument that a context is open-ended or underdetermined does not imply that there is no meaning, or that meaning is indeterminate. On the contrary, Derrida insists that 'one cannot do anything, least of all speak, without determining (in a manner that is not only theoretical, but practical and performative) a context' (1988: 136).

What Derrida has argued for in 'Signature Event Context' is that an adequate account of any speech act theory must be able to explain both its successes and its failures. A case in point is that of 'signatures'. The function of a signature is that of acting as a guarantee of the identity of the person linked to whatever is being signed: it represents the speaker in his/ her absence. And signatures function because they have the possibility of being repeated – as when I sign different cheques – and therefore, as with other signs, a signature can be 'misused' or fail (as when someone counterfeits my signature on a cheque). The possibility of 'misuse' or failure is the result of signatures belonging to the same system of iteration that makes 'serious' or 'successful' signatures possible. The example of the signature is an instance of the same structure that applies to all speech acts: (1) meaning is dependent upon both convention and context, but (2) these do not limit the range of use for speech acts. Speech act theory in the hands of Austin attempted to control meaning by first tying meaning down to contextual conventions, and when this seemed inadequate, by tying meaning to the speaker's intentions.

It should be pointed out that Derrida rejects the view that authorial intention should be eliminated and replaced by iterability in the search for meaning. Rather the concept of iterability and the possibility of decontexualization – both of which are inherent within the structure of language – are the conditions that make possible the author's intentions as one of several possible meanings for any speech act. So too the author's intention to mean is not there 'in our face', simply waiting to be read off the text. Rather what counts as the author's intended meaning is also the result of what the community of interpreters operating within a context determine such meaning to be.

One can surmise the benefits of deconstruction as twofold. (1) It demonstrates how meaning is not dependent upon the sender or the receiver of the message, so that any question of intentionality is not exhausted by reducing meaning to subjects. (2) It claims that neither is meaning so tied to the context that it only becomes intelligible in relation to a context. Rather, contexts are multiple and the nature of the sign is such that it can function in other contexts different from the one it 'originated' from. This is why it is always possible to mean something different from that which we intended to mean.

In 'Reiterating the Differences: A Reply to Derrida' (1977), Searle takes issue with Derrida, accusing him of maliciously misreading Austin's work and of undermining the most obvious and common sense view of language as an instrument for communication. Not to be outdone, Derrida responds to Searle's arguments in 'Limited Inc. a b c [...]' (1977) by pitting the 'playfulness' commonly associated with the Yale School of deconstruction against the 'seriousness' associated with Searle and analytic philosophy. Perhaps the most blatant example of this 'playfulness' is his quoting parts of Searle's text (and these quoted parts eventually make up all of Searle's text) within his own and using them out of context to undermine the idea that writing communicates what the author intended to mean despite his/her absence. 'Limited Inc.' (1988) reproduces both Searle's criticism and Derrida's response:

1. Searle argues that Derrida is mistaken in claiming that writing can *only* function in the absence of the receiver (1988: 47). Derrida responds by claiming that he never said that the absence of the receiver is necessary for written communication to take place. As Dooley and Kavanagh (2007) point out, this would mean that when Derrida wrote a text, for the text to acquire a meaning he would have had to leave the room. And while the absence of the receiver is not a necessary condition for the text to have a meaning, it is still possible for it to have a meaning if the receiver is not there. A text will always function irrespective of whether the intended receiver is there or not. Iteration or the possibility of repetition is the condition of possibility for there being a text at all (1988: 49).

2. Searle thinks that Derrida has missed the whole point of Austin's argument by focussing on secondary aspects of language use such as the theatre (1988: 204–05). Derrida comments on the strangeness of Austin's claim, since in his other writings he considered his theory as a

> project of classifying and clarifying all possible ways and varieties of *not exactly doing things* [...][It] has to be carried through if we are to understand properly what doing things is[.] (1979: 271)

In addition, the whole point of *How to Do Things with Words* was to challenge the (then) dominant traditional view of language as the study of constative utterances (true or false statements). So while traditional philosophy of language offered an inadequate theory of language by excluding performatives, Austin himself initiated a series of exclusions from his own theory, a theory that was supposed to explain all languages uses, all speech acts. This is why Derrida challenges Searle's claim that Austin is merely suggesting a method for proceeding with the analysis of language, since this claim is too restrictive in that it fails to explain the conditions that generate all utterances.

On the question of the non-serious utterances Searle reads Derrida differently. The latter's concern with the value of 'non-serious' utterances is a sign that Derrida is not interested in doing 'serious' philosophy, and it therefore explains why Derrida questions both the communicative function of language and the value of the context in understanding the meaning of an utterance. In fact, it would seem that Derrida in Searle's eyes is determined to challenge the everyday commonplace assumptions of language use. In effect, Searle argues that the possibility of non-serious utterances, of pretending to make a promise or to get married, depends upon or is secondary to the possibility of making a promise or getting married in real life (1988: 205).

Derrida's reply is to challenge the notion of the dependence of the non-serious upon the serious by arguing that both of these classes require the repetition of conventionally agreed-upon 'formulas'. According to Austin, the condition that makes promising possible is the following of a conventional procedure, a 'code' or 'formula' that is uttered. Derrida highlights the iteration of speech acts when he writes:

> Could a performative utterance succeed if its formulation did not repeat a "coded" or iterable utterance, or in other words if the formula I pronounce in order to open a meeting, to launch a ship or a marriage were not identifiable as *conforming* with an iterable model, if it were not thus identifiable in some way as 'citation'? (1988: 18)

And since the iterability of 'formulas' is especially evident in non-serious contexts such as the stage, then Derrida argues that the serious uses are a branch of the more general non-serious uses. Culler is exemplary in bringing out this point:

> This is a principle of considerable breadth. Something can be a signifying sequence only if it is iterable, only if it can be repeated in various serious and non-serious contexts, cited and parodied. Imitation is not an accident that befalls an original but its condition of possibility. There is such a thing as an original Hemingway style only if it can be cited, imitated and parodied. For there to be such a style there must be recognisable features that characterise it and produce its distinctive effects; for features to be recognisable one must be able to isolate them as elements that could be repeated, and thus the iterability manifested in the inauthentic, the derivative, the imitative, the parodic, is what makes possible the original and the authentic. Or to take a more pertinent example, deconstruction exists only by virtue of iteration. One is tempted to speak of an original practice of deconstruction in Derrida's writings and to set aside as derivative the imitations of his admirers, but in fact

these repetitions, parodies, 'etiolations' or distortions are what brings a method into being and articulate, within Derrida's work itself, a practice of deconstruction. (Culler 1982: 120)

In addition there is also the question of the 'parasitical' status of fictional discourse, since Derrida denies that fiction is 'parasitic' upon non-fiction. For Searle the relation of non-fiction to fiction is one of logical dependence, with the latter being dependent upon the former in a relationship which he describes – following Austin – as 'parasitic'.

Derrida responds by turning the tables on Searle: if Searle's analysis is supposed to be objective by showing the logical dependence of one to the other, why is his analysis value-loaded, relying as it does on pejorative value judgements (1988: 92)? According to Derrida, Searle's thinking or logic is governed by certain 'pre-logical possibilities' that reveal a hierarchical axiology at work, so that certain concepts are privileged over others. This axiology operates in an exclusive 'all or nothing' way, so that speech and the serious are opposed to writing and the non-serious. But Derrida argues that the opposition of a concept to another does not entail that one excludes the other from the analysis, for to outline or demarcate a concept is in effect to mark what it is from what it is not (1988: 123). To add insult to injury, Searle concludes that Derrida does not believe in 'rigorous and precise' distinctions for concepts. Derrida finds this criticism impossible to believe:

> What philosopher ever since there were philosophers, what logician ever since there were logicians, what theoretician ever renounced this axiom: in the order of concepts (for we are speaking here of concepts and not of the colors of clouds of the taste of certain chewing gums), when a distinction cannot be rigorous or precise, it is not a distinction at all. (1988: 123)

3. Searle argues that Derrida's distinction between the spoken and the written word is grounded in a confusion between the permanence of a text and its iterability. The relative permanence of a text distinguishes it from speech, but in both the spoken and the written word it is the intention that grounds the meaning within a context. The fact that a written text is a permanent object is not the result of the possibility of its iterability or repetition since permanence and repetition are very different concepts (1988: 50–51).

Derrida agrees that the survival of the text cannot be equated with repetition and this is because it is repetition or iterability that makes the survival of the text possible. When Searle talks of permanence, what he has in mind is the book as being the same book, as being a reproduction of the same. This is precisely what Derrida does *not* mean by iterability: iterability is repetition with the possibility of difference. It can be called a structural principle in the sense that it is the condition that makes both difference and sameness (or permanence) possible.

4. Searle criticizes Derrida for denying that a written text can communicate an intention. The important point for Searle is that by understanding the intentions of the writer, using

the intentions as a kind of benchmark, one can resist the temptation to misinterpret the writer (1988: 26).

But this is not what Derrida claims: there is no question of denying the intentions of the speaker or the author, but of whether these intentions can be completely accounted for in every context, since it is always possible for an intention to be interpreted otherwise.

> What the text questions is not intention or intentionality but their *telos*, which orients and organizes the movement and the possibility of a fulfillment, realization and *actualization* in a plenitude that would be *present* to and identical with itself. (1988: 56)

Iterability is not opposed to intentionality, but is rather the condition or the system that makes the communication of intentionality possible. For Derrida, the fact that language can function in different and unpredictable situations shows that an utterance can be understood without reference to the intentions of the person. There is a big difference, Derrida argues, between the assumption that readers need to posit some kind of hypothesis of intentionality to understand a text and a speech act theory that claims that understanding necessitates the interpretation of an intended meaning. It is the latter that Derrida objects to.

From Searle's point of view, if one subscribes to the notion that communication is possible because humans have an innate competence to understand language, then a written text can also draw upon the communicative competence of the reader to understand the intentions of the author as expressed in the text (1988: 27). For Searle, it is these conventional rules of language that make it possible to retain the meaning intended despite the change of context. In other words, the repetitive power of language is what enables the illocutionary force (the intentions) to be 'saved', even if the context of that utterance is different. This is why a text can be read for its intended conclusion even if the author is no longer alive.

For Searle, ordinary language is the ideal medium for communicating the intentions of speakers or writers, with any possible obstacles to this communication as incidental. For Derrida, it is not a question of eliminating intentionality in the communication of meaning, but rather a realization that language itself as a medium has the potential to disrupt the speaker or writer's intentions. It becomes increasingly apparent from this exchange of ideas that the distance between the starting points of Searle as representative of the analytic practice of philosophy and Derrida as representative of the practice of deconstruction is greater than imagined.

Derrida and film theory

While a lot of attention has been given to the relationship between deconstruction and a number of disciplines such architecture, literature, philosophy and cultural studies it has been remarked that less attention has been paid towards the relationship between deconstruction and film theory. Among key texts that examine this relation are Marie-Claire Ropars-Wuilleumier's 'Le Texte divisé' (1981) and Brunette and Wills's *Screen/Play: Derrida and Film Theory* (1989). For the purposes of this section I am focussing on a paper by Peter Brunette titled 'Toward a Deconstructive Theory of Film' (1986), in which he lists a number of possible ways whereby deconstruction can be fruitfully applied to film theory.

1. Deconstruction can be political. While politically minded film theorists with deconstructive sympathies have accepted the notion of texts as sites that disseminate meaning, they have been reluctant to accept the idea that this applies also to political texts, instead seeking to privilege their politics 'outside' and 'beyond' the play of difference. Brunette suggests that the kind of politics that deconstruction can engage in is that of challenging and undermining of accepted hierarchical structures. He notes how Derrida paid increasing attention to institutional structures such as the university and other foundational concepts of Western culture such as reason (1986: 59).

2. Deconstruction should retain its theoretical concern. One 'problem' that many have with deconstruction is that while it has persuasively shown the contradictions and aporias of language, it seems to say nothing about individual texts, so perhaps the time has come to shift emphasis more towards the latter. Brunette disagrees arguing that just as language seems to naturally communicate our thoughts or while the natural functioning of speech in the case of film studies connect with the world, the same – if not more so – occurs in the case of film where we take the image as reality. Deconstruction should retain its theoretical concern because film is itself a kind of writing constituted by the play of light in its presence and absence; and so too, just as language creates an illusion of reality, in the case of film it is even more apparent that film does not represent anything, with the result that it 'will have an all the more violent effect upon the spectator' (1986: 61–62).

3. Deconstruction can help study the question of intentionality. In literary studies the answer to the question of what a text meant had been reduced to the intentions that the author had in producing the text. While this would provide a stable meaning for the text by locating the origin of meaning in the consciousness of the author, the nature of film shows that this account of meaning is too simple. As a medium, film is both the result of the collaboration of a number of persons and inherently disseminative. Brunette claims that the question of intentionality as posed in literary studies can benefit from a deconstructive approach to film (1986: 62).

4. Deconstruction can challenge traditional accounts of film history. Brunette points out that film history is also a form of narrative and therefore subject to the same techniques found in other narrative texts. This has two consequences: the first is that the figurative nature of film should be highlighted as when (for example) a shot or sequence represents the film text as a whole; the second is that film history is often categorized in terms of periods which results in an exclusion of whatever does not fit into that period. Deconstruction can reveal the differences within a period that have been reconfigured as 'other' to that period (1986: 62).

5. Deconstruction can help theorize the relation between film and reality. One of the questions that interested Derrida was that of the 'frame' that surrounds a painting since it is the frame that marks the boundary of what counts as the painting and in so doing showing that what is considered 'outside' the painting, that is, the frame, is important in that it determines what is the painting. Brunette elaborates upon this idea arguing that in the case of film the question of the frame is even more relevant, since the frame constitutes both the inside and the outside. The relation between the inside and the outside raises the questions of how to examine the relation between film and reality as well as the relation between the viewer and the film (1986: 63).

6. Deconstruction can help understand classical and modern film theory. For classical and modern film theory to be articulated, theorists have necessarily put in place a series of exclusions coupled with certain hierarchical oppositions in their construct of reality. Since deconstruction can help in our understanding of the relation between reality and copies of reality, this understanding might be fruitful (for example) in studies on documentaries that claim to reproduce reality (1986: 63).

7. Deconstruction can examine the question of figuration in film. The status of reality as the bedrock towards which language, whether literal or figurative, is ultimately grounded can open a new dimension on film theory that explores the relation between figuration and film. Brunette notes that figuration is receiving more attention in film studies; citing the work of Dudley Andrew, Brunette points out that Andrew both forgets that figures complicate meaning and privileges figures as events by placing them outside and the cause of the system (1986: 64).

8. Deconstruction would enable a more open interpretation of film. On this account, Brunette argues that each audio and visual part of the film is a signifier that contributes to the construction and dissemination of meaning that in turn resists the critics' will to master it. He points out (for example) that in Bergman's *The Seventh Seal* one signifier stands out (the death head hanging on the coach in the background) but just as easily other signifiers can be considered significant (the white canvas of the coach as a sign of hope). With a deconstructive approach to film, the film as a text opens itself up to different possible interpretations that resist the tendency of the critic to dominate the text by 'carving' it into an organic unity (1986: 66).

The strategies of deconstruction have been applied to several fields of study and its range of application is being extended to film theory. In this respect, Brunette has contributed to the way this relation can be formulated by listing a number of suggestions that can be used as points of departure for an examination of the relation between deconstruction and film theory. In *Cultural Theory and Popular Culture* (2000), Storey offers a deconstructive account of the film *Dances with Wolves* (1990). His starting point is that of highlighting the structures inherent within the film: East/West, civilization/savagery and white/native Americans. The privileged term among all of these oppositions is the first, and the film questions our assumptions of what it means to be civilized, for although the central figure in the film is a lieutenant sent from the 'civilised' East to the 'savage' West, it turns out, through the course of the film, that the representatives of the civilized East (the US cavalry) are more barbaric than the presumed 'savage' Native Americans. However, what deconstruction does is not merely reverse the priorities and suggest we start living in a natural Native American way; rather, it challenges or undermines the assumptions that we take on board when we describe our culture as 'civilised'. Deconstruction is a strategy of intervention, for in the process of interpretation it does not leave the text and the concepts underpinning the text as they were. The process of reading a text in effect produces another one.

Critical remarks

Derrida's challenge to Western philosophy has not gone unnoticed. On the one hand, there are those such as Rorty and Butler who consider his undermining of the assumptions of Western philosophy as a breath of fresh air. On the other hand, there are those like Searle, Quine and Chomsky who consider him as nothing more than a charlatan. However, since the early reactions to Derrida there have been a number of re-evaluations of his work, and although not all philosophers are persuaded by its value, an increasing number are more sympathetic. A case in point is the publication by S.C. Wheeler called *Deconstruction as Analytic Philosophy* (2000) and B. Stoker's *Derrida on Deconstruction* (2006).

Since I have already described in detail Derrida's engagement with Searle on the questions of intentionality and communication, I will now present the views of Habermas and Gadamer. Habermas objects to Derrida's views insofar as they tend to dissolve the distinction between reason and rhetoric. Since according to Derrida there is no foundation (in the world or in the mind) to meaning, then what makes a view or interpretation acceptable is its rhetorical force. Habermas counters this view by arguing that Derrida does not realize that there are different ways of using language: what Habermas has called 'the rationalisation of the lifeworld' (1987) entails the ability to recognize and use the different dimensions of language. Rather, Derrida confuses the descriptive or factual use with the poetic or disclosive use of language, in effect confusing philosophy with literature. In addition, Habermas (1988) also describes Derrida (among others) as a 'young conservative', since by abandoning reason in favour of rhetoric, young conservatives renounce the possibility of improving things through rational argument and indirectly open themselves up to manipulation.

Gadamer's engagement with Derrida is not so much a confrontation as a rapprochement of hermeneutics with deconstruction. Gadamer's philosophical hermeneutics, with its emphasis on dialogue and openness to the other, requires a certain amount of good will, that is, a willingness to reach out in order to understand others. Derrida is suspicious of the notion of good will, arguing that what is considered as good will is a disguised form of a good will to power, a will to appropriate others that is symptomatic of the Western tradition. In line with his way of thinking about dialogue as the search for mutual ground, Gadamer modifies his claim, arguing that the understanding that philosophical hermeneutics seek is in fact an understanding of that which is different and where the other can be right (Michelfelder and Palmer 1989).

In this chapter, I have started (1) by examining Derrida's theory of language and (2) proceeded to his discussion of the relation between the spoken and the written word as it is played out in a number of key texts. The following section (3) developed Derrida's views of language with the concept of *différance* while the next section (4) outlined Derrida's engagement with speech act theory and his discussion with John Searle. The final section (5) examined a number of suggestions for the relevance of deconstruction to film theory.

Notes

1. Dooley and Kavanagh rightly point out that 'Derrida is primarily a philosopher of language. He devoted his entire career to demonstrating how all of our experience is mediated by language, writing and textuality' (2007: 21).
2. In *Positions*, Derrida describes the relation between the structure and the event of language: '[t]here is a circle here, for if one rigorously distinguishes language and speech, code and message, schema and usage, etc., and if one wishes to do justice to the two postulates thus enunciated, one does not know where to begin, nor how something can begin in general, be it language or speech. Therefore, one has to admit, before any dissociation of language and speech, code and message, etc. (and everything that goes along with such a dissociation), a systematic *production* of differences, the production of a system of differences – a *différance* – within whose effects one eventually, by abstraction and according to determined motivations, will be able to demarcate a linguistics of language and a linguistics of speech' (2002: 28).
3. Hahn writes, 'Am I not also equally present at the moment of writing? Is it not possible for me in the act of speaking to change my intentions? Is it not possible I am less clear about my intentions – my intention, for instance, to promise and to make good on my promise – than I am in the reflective moment of writing?' (2002: 72).
4. Deutscher offers an excellent example of the multiple intersecting contexts: 'Think of the ambiguity of the status of gay marriage in the United States [...] [T]here is the context of a couple's family and friends; the gay community and contemporary America. There is the perspective of this decade, and the retrospective perspective of this century to come. There is current state and federal law, which may not agree and so provide different contexts. According to the different ways in which we would think of the context, the gay marriage is many different actions (failed or successful) and can be read in many different ways' (Deutscher: 60–61).

Chapter 6

Gadamer on Communication as Hermeneutics

After a lengthy academic career Hans-Georg Gadamer (1900–2002) published *Truth and Method* (1989). It was the culmination of a lifetime's investigation into questions concerning interpretation. Theories of interpretation have been considered a peripheral area of study usually restricted to theology, law or literature departments. Since it is not always clear what certain texts or passages within these disciplines mean, then the question of how to interpret them becomes a crucial one. Gadamer examines questions of textual interpretation in depth, but this concern is ultimately connected to the view that these questions help one understand better the nature of human existence. His concern is ontological rather than epistemological.

Questions concerning interpretation usually belong to the area known as hermeneutics.[1] The word *hermeneutics* has an old history and its etymology is derived from the Greek word *hermeneium*, meaning 'to interpret'. In classical mythology Hermes was the messenger of the gods, and his function was that of bridging the world of the gods and the world of humanity, since the language of the divine and the language of humanity differed radically. Irrespective of whether the gods told the truth or lied, Hermes would interpret and communicate their messages to humanity. His role was indispensable since it was the only way communication between the two separate worlds could be maintained.

Gadamer's literary output is prolific, ranging from theoretical questions of interpretation to specific studies on philosophers such as Plato and Hegel, and poets such as Celan. In this chapter, I am focussing on the text that crowns Gadamer's academic career, *Truth and Method* (1989). Gadamer has pointed out that the title is misleading, for it suggests that the acquisition of truth is to be equated with the use of a particular method. It would have been better, he later suggests, to have called it 'truth against method', so as to show that there are other kinds of truth, truths that go beyond the narrow conception of truth as proposed by the methods of science.[2] This explains why the first two sections of *Truth and Method* address questions of art and history respectively, as central to his project in hermeneutics is the idea that truth also belongs to the domains of art and history.

I open the chapter by providing (1) a lengthy overview of Gadamer's interpretation of the history of hermeneutics. This is followed by (2) his critique of science and (3) his retrieval of the concepts of prejudice and authority. The later sections examine (4) the centrality of understanding in hermeneutics and (5) the role of history in the constitution of the understanding together with the fusion of horizons. The next sections focus on Gadamer's concept of (6) dialogue and (7) language while the final section (8) focusses on the potential contribution of Gadamerian hermeneutics to intercultural communication.

The history of hermeneutics

Gadamer's contribution to hermeneutics is not that of offering another theory of interpretation that is in competition with other rival theories of interpretation.[3] Gadamer's hermeneutics is not just a technique for interpreting texts but involves a much broader and therefore more philosophical account of human understanding. Hermeneutics is concerned with all human activities, from the sciences to the arts; these disciplines are concerned with the human attempt to understand both the world and humanity itself. And since all human understanding can only take place in language, the universality of language transforms hermeneutics into a philosophical discipline (1989: 475–76).

Given the importance of understanding to hermeneutics, Gadamer's point of departure is an interpretation of the history of hermeneutics so as to see the way understanding has been conceptualized.

Before the nineteenth century, hermeneutics as a practice for the interpretation of texts was associated with Protestant theologians and their approach to the Sacred Scriptures. They were concerned with two problems. (1) For most of the time it was possible to understand the Scriptures without the need for hermeneutics, but there were times when hermeneutic procedures were necessary to prevent misunderstanding from taking place. Laying down guidelines for the correct interpretation of the Scriptures was considered important since it was believed that certain allegorical or vague passages in the Bible prevented the word of God from being correctly understood. (2) The true meaning of the Scriptures had been corrupted by the dogmas and the traditions of the Catholic Church. Protestant theologians argued that the meaning of the Sacred Scriptures could be understood on its own terms. This raised a further question: if the Scriptures could be read on their own, should they be read as a unified text, or as a number of texts written at different times with different goals in mind?

Despite the differences in the methods of interpretation, Protestant and Catholic theologians shared common ground in that the whole point of interpretation was to focus attention on the truth claims made by the text. Protestant and Catholic interpreters were interested in the subject matter or content of the texts, and not what they might tell us about their authors or about the historical context of their construction. Gadamer concurs with this view as he is interested in what texts have to say to us in order to teach us. According to him, the act of interpretation entails a conversation with the text itself rather than with the author.

The first major shift in the history of hermeneutics occurs with Schleiermacher (1756–1834), who broadened the concept of understanding from the interpretation of specific texts to interpretation in general. It was not a question of devising a specific hermeneutics for each of the disciplines, for biblical, legal or literary texts, but of creating a general hermeneutics, that is, a theory of interpretation. 'Hermeneutics *as* the art of understanding *does not yet exist* in a general manner, *there are only several forms* of specific hermeneutics' (in Lawn 2006: 58). Hermeneutics as a discipline with its own identity and concerns was born.

The starting point for Schleiermacher's general hermeneutics is that of centralizing misunderstanding in interpretation. Misunderstanding is so frequent that it can even occur in those passages that do not seem to require interpretation. In this respect Schleiermacher distinguished between two kinds of hermeneutical practice: the lax and the strict. The lax practice of hermeneutics is one where the basic assumption is that understanding is the norm, so that hermeneutics is only necessary when misunderstanding takes place. The strict practice of hermeneutics assumes that misunderstanding is the norm: misunderstanding occurs because our prejudices or perspectives influence our interpretation. In this sense, we misread the author by adding or excluding something that the author might have not intended. Schleiermacher even defines hermeneutics as 'the art of avoiding misunderstandings' (1989: 185).

Despite being a theologian and translator of Plato, Schleiermacher was inspired by the Romanticist view that humanity needed to return to the emotional and religious sources of life. From a theological perspective, he wanted to return to the 'special' feelings experienced by the early Christians as they received the gospel orally within their particular Hebraic context. To achieve this goal, he meticulously studied the Greek texts of the New Testament in order to remove the layers of interpretations that had encrusted the original intentions of the author of the New Testament. What he discovered was that many rituals that were celebrated in the Roman cults of Christianity were not related to Jesus or to the Hebraic context, but to the Roman Empire.

In order to reconstruct the original meaning of the text, Schleiermacher distinguished between the grammatical and psychological levels of the text. This distinction is necessary because there is a difference between the grammatical meaning (language) and the meaning the author intended (psychology) in the production of the text. Since the author uses a language to communicate his/her thoughts, for the interpreter to understand him/her it is obvious that both must share the same language. In addition, since words in a language are interconnected, and since one understands words and sentences in relation to other words and sentences, that is, to the totality of language, the interpreter must not only understand the words used by the author, but also understand the way language as a whole was used at the time. Language pre-exists the thinker and conditions his/her thoughts to a degree. The grammatical meaning can be understood through the rules of language, rules that are shared by a linguistic community. Understanding the grammatical meaning entails studying the language used at the time to uncover the historical sedimentation that has accumulated on the text.

On the other hand, a different approach is required to understand the psychology of the author. Through his/her texts the author wants to communicate something different, a new thought that can be understood when placed in relation to the rest of his/her life. This level entails being able to understand the motivations and intentions of the author. This can be achieved through a process of empathy, where one enters the mind of the author to be able to share the original experience that led him/her to produce his/her text. Understanding the psychology of the author means that one must also look at the life and times of the author – in other words at the historical context.

Psychological interpretation involves a further distinction between discovering the thoughts of the author and examining the way these thoughts are expressed. The former is psychological while the latter is technical. To understand the subject matter that the author is communicating it is necessary to see what it is about the subject that induces the author to think and write about it. It is also necessary to see why the author selects a particular genre to communicate his/her thoughts, together with the logical rules that connect the different thoughts of the author. Although the genres and logical rules are conventional, they also contribute in helping to understand the thoughts of the author. The point in Schleiermacher's hermeneutics is that of entering the mind of the author; by reconstructing the original context to discover the background elements of the author's life, Schleiermacher believed it was possible to understand the unique individuality of the author.

The act of interpretation, therefore, involves the twin features of the grammatical and the psychological. Which of the two is given priority actually depends upon the interpreter. If the interpreter is interested in the way the language at the time influences the thoughts of the interpreter, then the emphasis will be placed on the grammatical; if the interpreter is interested in the way the author uses language to communicate his/her thoughts, then the emphasis will be on the psychological. However, despite having more of an interest in one than in the other, the grammatical and the psychological cannot exclude each other completely.

The hermeneutic circle or the part-whole relation of understanding is evident in Schleiermacher's account of the grammatical and the psychological (1989: 291). Understanding an utterance depends upon understanding the utterance in relation to the language as a whole as well as to the author and his/her life as a whole (the social and historical context). But to know the whole, it is necessary to know the parts (the utterances) that make up this whole: there is a to-and-fro movement between the parts and the whole. To know, for example, the meaning of a text it is necessary to know the culture within which the author lived; but to know the culture within which the author lived it is necessary to study the texts (including the author's) pertinent to that culture.

Given the circular nature of understanding, the problem seems to be one of finding a way to enter this circle. Schleiermacher suggests that it is possible to enter the hermeneutic circle by first reading the text so as to get a rough idea of what it is about. With this rough idea, subsequent readings serve to confirm and consolidate the main ideas. In short, the strategy is that of first going through the text to acquire familiarity with the ideas and then proceeding to the grammatical and psychological interpretations. The influence of Schleiermacher's hermeneutics was widespread, but subsequent interpreters tended to emphasize the value of recreating the original creative moment of the author through the process of divination. The quest to enter the author's mind as the goal of interpretation led to the negation of the interpreter in the process of interpretation.

Although Gadamer acknowledges the important role Schleiermacher played in the history of hermeneutics, he takes issue with him on a number of points: (1) the emphasis on the author had the negative effect of ignoring the contribution of the interpreter, to the extent that this contribution was considered problematic. In effect, the subjectivity of the interpreter was eliminated so that the subjectivity of the author could be highlighted; (2) Schleiermacher neglects the contribution of the text itself in the production of meaning: the language used in the text presents a vision of life and the world. The interpretation of a text is the result of the worldview presented by the text in its interaction with the reader; (3) Schleiermacher's attempt to eliminate the gap between the past and the present is solved by negating the present so as to return to the past; it is the distance between the past and the present that constitutes the problem for interpretation. Gadamer argues that this conception of hermeneutics is fundamentally flawed since it is this temporal distance that generates the interpretation. It is a mistake to think of a past 'in itself', a past as it actually happened, a past that can be understood without the filter of the present. The idea that there is a past that can be faithfully reproduced and that can be returned to through the hermeneutic process is a relic of Romanticism that longed for a return to a golden past. (4) Gadamer is also critical of Schleiermacher's negative assessment of misunderstanding. He had argued that the task of hermeneutics was that of avoiding misunderstanding in order to let the original meaning and intention appear. Gadamer does not consider misunderstanding in entirely negative terms, arguing instead that misunderstanding can also be productive in the sense that the misunderstanding of texts has also generated other interpretations. Gadamer sums up the problem with Schliermacher's hermeneutics as one that replaces the communication of truth with the communication of subjectivity (1989: 196).

After Schleiermacher, the next major development in the history of hermeneutics came with the historical school, characterized by Ranke and Mommsen. These applied the insights of Schleiermacher's hermeneutics to the study of history, but this study was broadened to include not only texts but also artefacts and monuments. The historical school was a reaction to the Hegelian interpretation of history as the unfolding of the Absolute Spirit; such metaphysical speculations were rejected outright and replaced by the view that historical texts should be read on their own terms. Objectivity was the desired goal, and according to Ranke this entailed ignoring the present moment – with the beliefs, values and ideas of the time – to capture the spirit of the past.

Following the historical school, Gadamer turns to another leading figure in the history of hermeneutics, Dilthey (1833–1911). Dilthey was explicitly concerned with establishing the scientific and objective credentials of hermeneutics. He read the history of hermeneutics as the history of the progressive development of hermeneutics towards scientific objectivity. And with his hermeneutics, he hoped to provide a method equivalent to the methods used in the natural sciences. The question he set himself mirrored the question asked by Kant in the *Critique of Pure Reason*. Just as Kant asked about the conditions that made objective scientific knowledge possible, Dilthey wanted to know what conditions make objective knowledge of the human sciences possible.

Dilthey distinguished between the knowledge derived from the natural sciences (chemistry, physics, biology etc.) and the knowledge derived from the human sciences, encompassing the human spirit (philosophy, theology, sociology, politics, psychology, history and economics). The difference between these two sciences is grounded in terms of their goals: the natural sciences seek to explain, while the human sciences seek to understand. The basis for the explanations of the natural sciences is that of causality. To say one knows something in the natural sciences means that one can establish a causal relation between the phenomena one is studying. This means that the study of science involves bringing these phenomena under laws. On the other hand, to know something in the human sciences requires understanding, and this entails eliminating the interpreter from the process of the interpretation. Objectivity in the human sciences requires that the historical situation of the interpreter be removed and that the object under observation is studied according to the spirit of its own age. Human life cannot be explained according to the categories used in the natural sciences, since understanding human life requires an interpretation of the intentions, motivations and behaviour of humans; it is in this respect that Dilthey argues that hermeneutics was the method of the human sciences. However, despite the different methods used, Dilthey believes that the ultimate goal for both the natural and the social sciences was the same: objectivity.

Gadamer considers Dilthey's hermeneutics as an advance on Schleiermacher's hermeneutics, since Dilthey replaced the psychology of the author with the category of life or lived experience. To understand life or lived experience in the present moment, Dilthey argued that it was necessary to understand the past as there was a continuity between both moments. The idea of life as a dynamic and ongoing force that lies at the basis of human culture was popular in the nineteenth century. Dilthey was explicit that his account of life should not be construed in strict biological terms, but rather one that demonstrated the interconnection between the part and the whole, so that just as the part is an expression of the whole of life, in a reciprocal manner, the whole determines the significance of the part (1989: 223–24).

The present is the result of what happened before, and the connection between the present and the past is mediated by the texts we have inherited. We can go back in time through the various interpretations of texts, since interpretations of the present are the result of the interpretations that have preceded them. It should be pointed out that hermeneutics was not only concerned with literary texts but with all expressions of life – monuments, works of art, customs – as they are manifested.

Gadamer objects to Dilthey's hermeneutics on the grounds that (1) if hermeneutics is the 'special' method that enables understanding in the human sciences, then this creates a gap between the understanding used in hermeneutics and that used in everyday life, as though understanding was not also a component of day-to-day living. (2) Although – according to Dilthey – the natural and the human sciences are both concerned with attaining objectivity, the goals of the two disciplines are not the same since the human sciences are concerned with the motivation behind particular events whereas the natural sciences are concerned with universal or general laws. As a result, when Dilthey contrasted cultural understanding with scientific explanation, since the latter was privileged as the model for knowledge, cultural understanding was relegated to a secondary and inferior position. What Dilthey failed to realize was that understanding is central to human existence and therefore takes place within a historical context. As a result, understanding at a particular moment entails the assumptions of the tradition to which a person belongs.

Despite his criticism, Gadamer considers the principle of lived historical experience that underlies Dilthey's thought as a vital component of hermeneutics. From this principle he derived two notions, namely that human understanding is limited and finite, and that understanding can never be absolute in the same way as that of the natural sciences.

The writings of Martin Heidegger (1889–1976) and especially *Being and Time* (1962) play a central role in the development of Gadamer's philosophical hermeneutics. Heidegger transformed hermeneutics by shifting its emphasis from that of theorizing about interpretation to interpretation itself as the central feature of human life. Understanding and interpretation are not incidental features of human life but constitute the very nature of human existence. Heidegger is concerned with the way humans strive to understand the world through their interpretative activities. Instead of human existence, Heidegger introduces the term *Dasein* – translated as 'being-there' – which captures the sense of human life as inextricably situated within the world: '[t]he phenomenology of Dasein is a *hermeneutic* in the primordial signification of this word, here it designates the business of interpreting' (1962: 62).

Since the existence of Dasein unfolds within the world it is therefore temporal, and by this Heidegger includes both the past and the future. Human existence is a 'thrown projection' because Dasein is born into a world that is already there with its structures of significance and because it looks to the future with certain expectations. The understanding that Dasein can achieve is grounded in what Heidegger calls the 'fore-structures' of understanding, that is, a context of value and expectations. The fore-structures of understanding are what we inherit from the past and are born into, and given the world that Dasein is born into, certain possibilities for its future are available. Ultimately the understanding that Dasein seeks to find in life is also an understanding of itself because it concerns its own future possibilities.

In *Being and Time* Heidegger develops the notion of the hermeneutic circle (1962: 194–95), and the circularity of understanding involved in everyday life. Since understanding is defined in terms of the projections of possibilities, what Heidegger is offering is an existential account of understanding rather than a cognitive one. Heidegger brings out three characteristics of the fore-structures of understanding: (1) as fore-having, which means that we are born into a world where objects already have significance. A hammer, to use Heidegger's example, shows that it has a significance within the world of the workshop prior to our existence; (2) as fore-sight, where we understand something from a certain point of view, such as the need to fix the chair and (3) as fore-conceptions, where the hammer is interpreted as a tool that is used for the sake of something. In being used, the hammer stands out from its context of equipment even though it has significance within that context: when I see an object 'as' a hammer, '[t]he 'as' makes up the structure of the explicitness of something that is understood. It constitutes the interpretation' (1962: 189). The concept of fore-structures is crucial as it demonstrates first that there is no such thing as 'pure' perception, since perception is always already an interpretation, and second that there is a close connection between understanding and interpretation.

The relationship between understanding and interpretation can be more clearly explicated in terms of Dasein's possibilities and actualizations. The mode of existence of Dasein is that of understanding its environment or world as a number of significant possibilities: in its everyday life Dasein encounters a number of possibilities so that a student, for example, has the possibility of going to class, to the library, to the bar or just sitting idly in the campus. This is why Heidegger writes that Dasein understands itself in terms of its projected possibilities. By *project* he does not mean having a plan in one's head but the world as a number of possibilities that are projected into the future. The concept of interpretation presupposes the concept of the understanding, for while understanding relates to the environment as a whole, interpretation is specific. Thus, I interpret that building as a library because I already understand what the world of the university as an institution entails: lecture halls, the canteen, exams, friends, lecturers, computer labs and the library and so on.

> In interpreting, we do not, so to speak throw a 'signification' over some naked thing which is present-at-hand, we do not stick a value on it; but when something within-the-world is encountered as such, the thing in question already has an involvement which is disclosed in our understanding of the world, and this involvement is one which gets laid out by the interpretation. (1962: 190–91)

In Section 33 of *Being and Time*, Heidegger goes on to examine the movement from interpretation to assertion. Insofar as Dasein is involved in its everyday life, its relation to objects is practical so that the student uses the library in order to research material for his/her assignments. In a situation where a student answers that he/she goes to the library to borrow books, the student is now sharing his/her view of the library as a place with certain characteristics: it is an assertion. A transformation has taken place, for instead of the library actually being used, it has now become an object of thought and is present to the person as having certain characteristics. Heidegger comments that the mode of being captured by the assertion has superseded the practical mode of being that participates in the world.

Dasein is involved with and participates in the world that it interprets; it is no passive observer of the world. It is only because Dasein is a temporal being that has a past – is 'thrown' – and has a future – thereby projecting possibilities – that Dasein can have the kind of existence it does. The point is that there is no such thing as presupposition-less data of perception: I don't see a building as stones and concrete but as the library. The idea that perception is neutral is a chimera of modern science that hoped to acquire knowledge that was free of prejudgements. This is an important point because it is here that Heidegger shows the mistake in thinking that knowledge and understanding are free of all contexts or objective. But although there is no such thing as purely objective knowledge in the modern scientific sense of being non-prejudiced, this does not mean that Heidegger excludes all forms of objectivity. Rather, interpretation is a process that follows the hermeneutic circle where one's presuppositions are challenged in the light of new information so that understanding is more thorough. It is 'objective' in this sense.

Gadamer acknowledges the Heideggerian centrality of interpretation and expectation for human existence. The philosophical project of hermeneutics involves 'working out appropriate projections anticipatory in nature, to be confirmed "by the things themselves"'(1989: 267). The search for meaning that Gadamer understood to be central to the hermeneutic project was always necessarily incomplete for two reasons: (1) the fact of human finitude or the limitations of human existence; and (2) the linguistic aspect of human existence.

So too Gadamer agrees with Heidegger's opposition to Dilthey's notion of hermeneutics as the search for a method appropriate to the human sciences. Underlying this view is the assumption that the appropriate method will lead to objective interpretations. Heidegger and Gadamer both consider Dilthey's project to be a vestige of the Cartesian view of knowledge as objective. However, despite the rejection of objectivity, both argue that the interpretation of history, art or texts led to a form of understanding that was no less valid than that of the sciences.

Science and method

Gadamer's critique of science is directed at the idea that the truths of science do not represent the whole truth of the world, and neither are they the only truths that one should look for. His analysis of the historical conditions that gave rise to the scientific method shows that there was another tradition that did not emphasize the methodology of science but instead focussed on the tradition of history and culture. The domination of the scientific method resulted in the human sciences denying their own historical nature.

Following Heidegger and Husserl, Gadamer rejects the modern Cartesian view that knowledge can only be obtained by eliminating all traces of subjective and cultural influences in order to find a 'pure' starting point for knowledge. The Cartesian strategy is transcendental in the sense that it seeks to establish an ahistorical standpoint from which to operate. In a twist that shows the inherent contradiction of historicism, Gadamer argues that the desire to find an absolute standpoint for knowledge is itself the product of a particular historical situation. While the historicists of the nineteenth century recognized the historical foundations of all human life and knowledge, they still attempted to ground the human sciences in an epistemological method that would yield absolute knowledge. Gadamer points out that this is an impossible quest: we can only understand and acquire knowledge from where we are positioned at the moment.

The general thrust of Gadamer's thinking is to encourage a return to humanistic concepts in education. The concepts of rhetoric, justice, common sense and taste are no longer considered part of a person's education because these are deemed to be subjective and therefore unable to provide any valid contribution to knowledge. There does not seem to be any place for these subjects in the contemporary world, and these are excluded from a person's education. In his attempt to reverse this way of thinking about education, Gadamer rethinks the goal of education as bringing about cultural understanding.

Prejudice and tradition

The starting point for Gadamer's hermeneutics is the revival of the concept of prejudice which he defends against attempts during the Enlightenment to discredit it. For the Enlightenment, the only acceptable form of knowledge, belief or practice was that which passed the standard of reason. Enlightenment thinking valorized rationality and opposed reason to the authority of the tradition and of the person.

Gadamer's concept of prejudice is used in the sense of Heidegger's 'fore-structures' or prejudgements that are already 'in place' before a judgement can be passed. Whenever understanding takes place there are prejudices in the background as part of the tradition within which we belong. It might seem that his use of the word *prejudice* to replace Heidegger's 'fore-structure of understanding' is not such a good one; the word in English has several negative connotations, so that a racist or sexist is a prejudiced person in that he/she judges others on the basis of their race or gender.

But Gadamer is not using the concept of prejudice in this sense, and to argue his case for the rehabilitation of the term he reveals how the negative connotations have been historically derived. These negative connotations started with the Enlightenment, when reason was opposed to (traditional) authority on the grounds that the latter passed judgements and maintained certain claims to knowledge and truth that could not be justified on rational grounds. In addition, Enlightenment thinkers favoured the superiority of the present in the search for knowledge over the inherited wisdom of the past that they considered unreliable. The authority of tradition had no rational justification, and consequently it was prejudiced to accept the wisdom of traditional authority. Paradoxically, this negative evaluation was continued by the Romantics who – in reaction to the Enlightenment – were prejudiced in favour of the past over the present. But by simply reversing the polarities, they still remained within the same framework of thinking that attributed negative connotations to prejudice.

Gadamer's rehabilitation of prejudice and tradition consists of re-establishing their role in the understanding. In defence of the authority of tradition against the Enlightenment, Gadamer argues that the contents of a tradition, having survived over time, prove themselves to be of value, and therefore provide a source of legitimate prejudices. This does not mean that what is of value in a tradition will remain so forever, since it is always possible that the truths embodied in the tradition change. But these changes will in turn further the growth of the tradition. What this shows is that tradition preserves what is best and this explains why Gadamer thinks that the past still has something to teach us. It also shows that understanding is not something subjective occurring only in the mind of a person, but something that is shared:

[U]nderstanding is to be thought of less as a subjective act than as participating in an event of tradition, a process of transmission in which past and present are constantly mediated. (1989: 290)

In response to the Enlightenment's mistrust of authority, Gadamer argues that this is also mistaken, for it assumes that authority is always oppressive. The Enlightenment conception of authority was one of blind obedience to a command, and in this sense it was opposed to reason and freedom. But this is a corrupt version of authority. According to Gadamer, authority is not the expression of irrationality, but rather the recognition of a person's capabilities. When, for example, we are unwell we go to the authority in medicine – the doctor – to ask for help. In this situation we recognize the doctor as the person who is superior to us in judgement and therefore overrides our own judgement. There is, therefore, no contrast between reason and authority because seeking the authority is, in fact, the rational thing to do.

Since we all belong to a particular context, we all inevitably carry with us a certain amount of cultural 'baggage' or prejudices (our values, systems of belief and language) that make it possible for us to understand anything at all. These prejudices can be both conscious and unconscious, the latter operating without us being aware of their influence. We can, however, become aware of their influence and transfer our unconscious prejudices to the domain of reflective consciousness. Since these prejudices are the product of our social and cultural education as part of our belonging to a society, it is evident that they are an inherent part of us, constituting our being. Gadamer writes, '*[t]hat is why the prejudices of the individual, far more than his judgements, constitute the historical reality of his being*' (1989: 276–77). The prejudices that are the result of our historical situation are not an obstacle to understanding, but prepare the way for it.

In everyday life, Gadamer accepts Husserl's claim that perception is never neutral but always involves the projection of a meaning – one that is, strictly speaking, not found in the perception: '[p]ure seeing and pure hearing are dogmatic abstractions that artificially reduce phenomena. Perception always includes meaning' (1989: 92). The same occurs in textual interpretation: being able to understand a text involves projecting its meaning onto the basis of the evidence that one has, so that, for example, the title and the author indicate (as a starting point) what the text is about. The expectations of meaning a reader has of the text are the necessary preconditions or prejudices that enable him/her to read the text; obviously the reader's understanding of the text can change as the reader proceeds through the text. The encounter with the text, therefore, entails the projection or expectation of meaning, which (upon detailed examination) either confirms or highlights the need to revise one's prejudices.

Gadamer's concept of prejudice can be seen in the process of interpreting texts where the hermeneutic circle operates, since when we read we project a meaning onto the parts that are in turn related to the whole. The assumption behind this way of thinking is that the text forms an internal unity that Gadamer calls the 'fore-conception of completeness'. This functions as a regulative ideal that guides our reading by setting a standard by which we can accept or reject an interpretation. The standard implicit in the interpretation of a text is the standard of truth and coherence. It is only because we assume that a text is true that the prejudices we carry with us can be challenged (1989: 299).

Dropping this standard exposes the interpreter to the impossible situation of not knowing whether it is the text itself that is inconsistent or whether it is the interpreter who is unable to understand the text. Gadamer's position is that since the text has something to teach us it should be given precedence over the interpreter: the text is the 'authority' of a subject, offering something different to say to its readers. If the text did not have this priority, then interpretation would merely consist of confirming the reader's view, a view that could possibly be mistaken.

There can be no question of eliminating one's prejudices, but rather a recognition of their presence. This recognition necessitates the realization that the starting point of interpretation is self-interpretation. By recognizing that we are prejudiced, it becomes possible to understand the subject matter in relation to oneself. This is an important step in that it serves as a limit to the always present possibility that our prejudices are mistaken. The consequences of realizing the prejudicial nature of our understanding is that: (1) our prejudices are subjected to a critical analysis that will allow the text to disclose its truth; and (2) there can never be a total elimination of prejudices that would enable the 'pure' meaning to shine through. Just as the understanding of a word takes place because it is located within the larger sentence, the understanding of a text takes place because the text can be located within the context of a tradition. Since the tradition includes all the interpretations that have been generated and transmitted over time, then a crucial feature of the interpretation of a text also includes all the previous interpretations of the text. In the relation between the interpreter and the text, Gadamer argues that the tradition offers a standard of truth. In the interaction between the interpreter and the tradition, some feature of the tradition might be changed or revalued, and what was considered important loses its stature. The tradition – while providing a standard – is dynamic and ongoing.

It is often the case that we take our prejudices for granted, considering them to be the right ones. This is a mistaken assumption that Gadamer seeks to highlight: the goal of his philosophical hermeneutics is to find a way of distinguishing between legitimate and illegitimate prejudices. The one possible help in assessing the prejudices of our predecessors is what Gadamer calls 'temporal distance'. With the passage of time we can look back at the past and identify those prejudices that were legitimate from those that were illegitimate:

> Often temporal distance that can solve the question of critique in hermeneutics namely, how to distinguish the true prejudices, by which we *understand*, from the *false* ones, by which we *misunderstand*. (1989: 298–99)

In the distance between the text and the present other interpreters have been at work, and through their work they understand why a work has value. By way of example, Schmidt writes that 'changes in our understanding of the world may allow Aristotle's *Nicomachean Ethics* to be read with greater insight today than in the Middle Ages' (2006: 104).

Understanding

One could say that the starting point of Gadamer's concept of understanding is a retrieval of the Pre-Romantic views of hermeneutic theorists such as Spinoza and Chaldenius, who considered the content of certain texts – the Sacred Scriptures – to be communicating the truth. To understand these texts is to understand the truth of their content, just as, for example, understanding Euclidean geometry involves understanding the truths of geometry.[4] This view is very different from that of the Romantic theorists, who argued that understanding a text was a question of understanding the creative genius of the author, which led to a search for the authors' intentions: 'understanding means, primarily, to understand the content of what is said, and only secondarily to isolate and understand another's meaning as such' (1989: 294). Understanding and truth are interconnected, in that to understand a text is to agree on the content; this agreement is what Gadamer considers the truth.

By focussing on the truth claims of the text, Gadamer is able to displace the emphasis of hermeneutics away from understanding meaning in terms of what the author intended. This latter view is the source of much controversy since understanding the meaning of a text entails that one must 'exit' the text to discover the author's intentions or the reasons as to why he/she wrote what he/she did. This procedure usually involves examining the biographical, psychological or historical conditions that constitute the background of the author. This view assumes that because the reader cannot see the point of what the author is saying, then the only way to understand this text is by referring to the circumstances surrounding the author's life. Gadamer rejects what he calls the 'genetic' explanation of meaning, arguing that this explanation only comes about when the attempt to understand the content fails: '[i]t is only when the attempt to accept what is said as true fails that we try to "understand" the text, psychologically or historically, as another's opinion' (1989: 294).

Understanding the meaning of a text is not the possession of either the writer or the reader but a mutual process in which both participate, since they both share the same language of the text. To highlight this point Gadamer compares the process of understanding with that of playing games. When a person plays a game, he/she enters the world of the game: his/her private goals and purposes are set aside so as to follow the rules that enable the game to be played. The game takes over the person's life so that it, so to speak, allows itself to be played: 'The real subject of the game (this is shown in precisely those experiences in which there is only a single player) is not the player but the game itself' (1989: 106). The importance of this point is that the game imposes its rules on the players and this means that it imposes its authority on them. And just as a game follows rules, language is governed by rules that are socially formulated, so there can be no communication and understanding that do not abide by these rules. The process of understanding texts is similar in that the texts belong to a tradition that imposes its authority upon the interpreter by making certain claims. In arguing for the predominance of the tradition over the person, Gadamer is reiterating his critique of subjectivism in interpretation, since understanding and interpretation are not something solitary that takes place in the subject; they actually constitute the participation within the tradition.

A crucial aspect of Gadamer's account of the concept of understanding is that all understanding is situated. This means that the position of the interpreter must be taken into consideration. Understanding something depends upon the interests and focus of the interpreter, an interest that might not have been the concern either of the author or of his/her contemporary reading public. Warnke points out that:

> [m]y understanding of Shakespeare's *Hamlet* may be connected to my understanding of psychological issues and existential themes. These may not be issues or themes that motivated Shakespeare himself; neither are they ones of which his public was necessarily aware or of ones that will necessarily always orient the understanding of the play. Nevertheless these issues and themes help determine both the meaning the play can have for me and, indeed, the way in which I understand Shakespeare's intentions. (1987: 74)

There is a further broadening of Gadamer's account of understanding. When the nineteenth century emphasized the value of method, it created a distinction between understanding and application. The goal of nineteenth-century hermeneutics was that of understanding a meaning 'in itself'; this understanding was subsequently applied to particular situations. In the field of jurisprudence an attempt was made to first understand the law, and then to apply it to the case at hand. In the field of theology, an attempt was first made to understand the meaning of a passage from the Scriptures, and this was later applied to the situation at hand.

Gadamer argues that the distinction between understanding and application is untenable: understanding always involves application since the attempt to understand something entails applying a meaning to our context. When we try to understand something we are part of the equation, carrying ourselves along in the flow of meaning. The concept of application is important since it is what enables the interpreter to project the meaning of the text. It is because one applies the text to one's situation that one is able to project a meaning onto the text in the first place. Application is an inherent part of the process of understanding, not an optional and additional extra:

> Application does not mean first understanding a given universal in itself and then afterward applying it to a concrete case. It is the very understanding of the universal – the text – itself. (1989: 341)

Understanding involves the application of a universal to a particular situation – to the horizon of the interpreter. But it is not a question of having a pre-given universal and then applying it to a text: it is in the application itself that the universal is actualized so that the meaning of the text is actualized in the fusion between the interpreter and the text.

The model that Gadamer uses (1989: 317–24) to describe the process of application is the one proposed by Aristotle in the *Nicomachean Ethics*, which shows how universal ethical norms require deliberation so that they can be applied to concrete and particular situations. The Aristotelian model shows that it is not enough to have abstract guiding principles in ethics without a consideration of how these principles connect with practical life. When it comes to the concepts of courage or of right, it is not enough to understand what these concepts mean, but a question of seeing how they can be relevant or are applicable to the particular situation. This highlights the fundamental difference between Plato and Aristotle: Plato sought a theoretical understanding of the idea of the good, whereas Aristotle asked what the good was for humans within a context. Understanding norms without knowing how to use them is useless. It is not enough to know that in principle one should be good to others; it is more important to know when to be good to specific people in specific situations[5] (1989: 324).

There are three points that Gadamer's textual practice derives from Aristotle. (1) The application of the text to the particular situation is part of, and brings out, the potential meaning of the text; in interpreting a text from the past the new circumstances could not have been imagined by the author, and yet the interpreter projects the meaning of the legal text to the new circumstances. (2) The application of the text to the contemporary situation is not one that can be predicted in the manner of a law-like deduction; the interpreter must apply what the original author said to the present situation even though the original author did not know the future possible applications of the text. (3) The application of the text to the new circumstances should be guided by a principle of charity, whereby the best of what the text has to say is brought out.

Gadamer demonstrates his arguments on the importance of application by offering as an example (1989: 324–41) the process involved in the interpretation of legal or theological texts. From legal hermeneutics, he describes the position of the judge and the legal historian: in the case of the judge, when he passes a judgement, he must apply the 'old' law to the present situation even if the lawgiver has not considered the current situation in formulating the law. In the case of the legal historian in the process of understanding the 'old' law, it is not enough to understand the original situation when the law was created because an essential part of understanding the law involves understanding how the law has been applied and how it has developed over time. These developments are part of the potential meaning of the law. It is the same with the interpretation of the Scriptures: the priest who reads the Sacred Scriptures to prepare his homily must take into account his contemporary audience. The homily must be relevant to the lives of the listening audience so that the interpretation of the Sacred Scriptures includes its application to the current situation.

The importance of Gadamer's identification of understanding with application is apparent in that it explains the relationship between truth and the interpreter. The truth that the tradition communicates is not a timeless truth that one blindly accepts, but is rather a truth applied to the situation of the interpreter. The tradition is the framework or a standard with which to approach the text, a framework or standard that enables the interpreter to distinguish interpretations from misinterpretations. Warnke describes this process:

> [...] whether we are familiar with the literature on Shakespeare's work or not we approach his work in a way influenced by a tradition of Shakespeare interpretation so that we assume its excellence, importance and so on. But, just as we cannot apply ethical norms categorically we cannot adhere to a tradition of interpretation dogmatically. Rather, in approaching Shakespeare from the perspective of changed historical circumstances, we necessarily modify and extend the traditional way in which the excellence and importance of his work has been understood. (1987: 96)

Effective history and the fusion of horizons

In order to explain the importance of tradition upon the interpreter, Gadamer introduces the concept of effective history. Effective history has a dual structure: on the one hand it involves the effects of history upon the interpreter, these being the prejudices that influence him/her consciously or unconsciously; while on the other hand, it also includes the awareness of the interpreter that there are historical forces influencing him/her: '[u]nderstanding proves to be a kind of effect and knows itself as such' (1989: 341).

The concept of effective history also shows why there can never be an understanding of the past 'in itself'. Any understanding of the past – whether as an event or a text – entails understanding the effects upon the interpreter. For Gadamer these effects are not something external to the phenomena being studied but an essential aspect of it, so much so that it is these effects that reveal or disclose its true significance. Whereas events in the natural world are causally connected, understanding an event or a text requires interpretation. But this understanding involves an understanding of the history of their interpretations. This highlights the embedded situation of the interpreter since he/she is not neutral or detached from the context but a part of it. The tradition of a text is the history of its interpretations; our interpretation of a text is, therefore, conditioned by the prejudices that we have inherited from the tradition.

The 'power' of effective history is such that although we are aware of its influence on our understanding, we can never grasp or master it completely. When the historicist school in the nineteenth century attempted to eliminate all traces of the interpreter's historical context so as to produce objectivity in history, they failed to realize that this same attempt was a product of their own historical situation.

> Even in those masterworks of historical scholarship that seem to be the very consummation of the extinguishing of the individual demanded by Ranke, it is still an unquestioned principle of our scientific experience that we can classify these works with unfailing

accuracy in terms of the political tendencies of the time in which they were written. When we read Mommsen's *History of Rome*, we know who alone could have written it, that is, we can identify the political situation in which this historian organized the voices of the past in a meaningful way. (Gadamer 1977: 6)

The effect of history upon the reality of human existence is always greater than our consciousness. Even if we recognize the power of effective history, this power is in no way diminished, and this explains why it is always possible to subject an interpretation to revision.

The centrality of the concept of effective history in Gadamer's writings is such that it would be mistaken to think of it as relevant only to the philosophy of history or to the study of the past; this would only suggest that we are conscious of our historical situation as we read the past. Gadamer's account is deeper in that all understanding is affected by history, because history takes place within the broader context of the tradition within which we are situated.[6] This is why he emphatically writes that '[u]nderstanding is, essentially, a historically effected event' (1989: 300).

Central to Gadamer's concept of understanding is the concept of horizon, derived from the Husserlian account of perception but transformed into an account of understanding that is relocated to the broader context of horizons of significance. The horizon (or lifeworld) is the world within which we live and encompasses the values, systems of belief, customs, social practices and rituals of a culture. A horizon offers a perspective of the world viewed from a particular point. The concept of horizon is a fruitful way of describing the complete set of prejudices that constitute the world of the individual. A language is such a horizon and different cultures with their different languages offer different horizons. And just as a physical perspective excludes certain features of the terrain from its range, a language or a horizon allows certain things to be revealed while other things remain hidden. Revelation and limitation are the characteristics of both a language and a horizon.

Interpretation involves the twin horizons of the interpreter and the text. The mistake of the nineteenth-century historicists was that of ignoring the horizon of the interpreter, which was judged as having no contribution to make towards the production of meaning. The idea was that to understand the past it was necessary to leave behind one's horizon (with the issues and prejudices that constitute it) and enter the horizon of the past. But eliminating the interpreter would only result in adopting what the author has said rather than agreeing with the truth content of the text. And even if we wished to eliminate the interpreter from the process of understanding, this would be an impossible task because the horizon of the interpreter is not something that just happens to be there, something incidental that can be removed. Horizons are an essential part of the interpreter's identity because it is the prejudices of the interpreter that make any understanding possible. Finally, the horizon of the interpreter is important because the text communicates or has something to say to the interpreter now, in the present world.

In the interpretative process, an encounter occurs between the horizon of a text and the horizon of the interpreter. 'Understanding is always inevitable *for* a subject as much as it is *of* some object' (West 1996: 108). Gadamer's expression *fusion of horizons* is intended to capture this ongoing process in the production of meaning. He calls the interaction between the horizon of the text and the horizon of the interpreter an event of understanding that enables communication to take place. Although the interpreter anticipates the meaning of the text on the basis of his/her prejudices, the encounter with the prejudices of the text generates a new interpretation: *'understanding is always the fusion of these horizons supposedly existing by themselves'* (1989: 306).

The fusion of horizons is also one way of reacting to the claim made by relativists that each horizon is a self-enclosed world, with no possibility of contact and communication. Gadamer argues that just because understanding takes place within a horizon, this does not exclude – as Rorty does – the possibility of understanding between horizons taking place. The 'borderline' between horizons is not rigid but allows for movement between them. While we realize that there are differences between horizons, mutual understanding involves merging these differences rather than abandoning them.

Given that the fusion of horizons involves the horizon of the interpreter and the horizon of the text, Gadamer argues that there is no standard that enables one to judge an interpretation as better or worse. Rather, understanding can only be considered as different: understanding a text involves understanding what the text has to say, and what it has to say to me in my particular situation. However, the emphasis on the application to the particular situation should not be interpreted as implying a subjectivist or private concept of the understanding, since Gadamer considers understanding to be something public, an event that belongs to the happening of the tradition. The truths that texts communicate are not truths in themselves, truths that eternally represent an unchanging object, but they are true to a community of interpreters, true from the point of view of the community of interpreters rather than the individual.

The concepts of effective history and the fusion of horizons go hand in hand. In the encounter between the horizon of the interpreter and the horizon of the text, the consciousness of the effects of history by the interpreter helps in the formation of critical judgements and in maintaining or eliminating prejudices. Clearly, the interpreter is not a passive recipient locked in his/her horizon of prejudices. The text – with its horizon – has the potential to disrupt the prejudices of the interpreter. What is taken for granted can be challenged and subsequently modified or rejected. But whether prejudices are modified or not, the new interpretation is the product of the fusion of horizons and with it the tradition continues to reproduce itself.

Dialogue

The model for the understanding that takes place in the fusion of horizons is that of a dialogue or conversation, where the goal is to understand the truth of the subject matter or the content that the text is communicating. It is not a conversation that is intended to find out something about the psychology of the other person or the context of the other, but to agree on the subject matter. This agreement on the subject matter is an agreement that is concerned with truth (1989: 385).

In the understanding or dialogue that takes place between the interpreter and the text, it is not the case of an interpreter projecting a meaning onto a (now) meaningless past, but on the contrary, of the past speaking to the present through the text. The fusion of horizons describes the process whereby the horizon of the text speaks to the horizon of the interpreter. While the horizon of the past imposes itself and communicates its truth to the interpreter, since the horizon of the interpreter changes with different historical periods, there can never be a final objective meaning. The emphasis is on 'different': for Gadamer, the successive interpretations cannot be called 'better' because different historical situations can only produce varied interpretations. There is no point outside history from which to judge whether one interpretation is better than another. Those interpretations that are false have not withstood the test of time. Tradition as the preservation and transmission of what is true eliminates those prejudices that are false or illegitimate. Although there is no in-itself of meaning to a text, the opposite conclusion – that each meaning is subjective or that each interpretation is a misinterpretation – is likewise mistaken. For Gadamer, each interpretation belongs to the potential interpretations of a text, where 'the verbal explicitness that understanding achieves through interpretation does not create a second sense apart from that which is understood and interpreted' (1989: 398).

The otherness of the text puts into sharp relief our assumptions and prejudices by challenging them. It is the difference in time between the production of a text and the world of the interpreter that enables a new interpretation to be generated. The point of the interpretation is not that of travelling to the past world when the text was produced, but to learn from the text, to discover the truths that the tradition has to communicate. And as the tradition unfolds, new insights are discovered; the text reveals or discloses new meanings that would not have been previously noticed. The distance in time between the production of the text and its reception by the interpreter is one of the means that enables one to judge between legitimate and illegitimate prejudices. Warnke writes:

> our understanding of Mark Twain's Huckleberry Finn may differ from Twain's understanding of it or the understanding of it by his immediate public. Because of our heightened awareness of racial stereotyping we may find the portrait of Jim more problematic than people did at the time that the book appeared and this may affect our understanding of the content of the book as a whole [...] Understanding is primarily an understanding of the claim a work of art imposes on us and this means that we understand a work in its relevance to our own situation. That situation does not affect simply the significance of a work but rather enters into the interpretation of meaning itself, into what is shocking, what is unclear and into what the work "really" says. (1987: 68)

Gadamer describes the process of understanding and application by using the model of dialogue defined in terms of question and answer. The meaning we are trying to understand is the answer to our question, and the process of interpretation and understanding is formulated in terms of a dialogical situation – 'for the dialectic of question and answer that we demonstrated makes understanding appear to be a reciprocal relationship of the same kind as conversation' (1989: 377). Some might argue that in dialogue we exert 'power' over the other, seeking to dominate or criticize them. This is not Gadamer's view, for rather than confrontation, Gadamer seeks mutual understanding. This is why he distinguishes between authentic and inauthentic dialogue. Authentic dialogue is concerned with listening to what the other has to say while inauthentic dialogue is concerned with being right, with 'winning'.

In everyday life, a conversation has a life of its own with no pre-established objective that the conversation must arrive at. The interesting feature of the nature of dialogue is that a dialogue always has a temporary ending: it can be picked up and continued another day. Dialogues are not structured conversations in the sense that topics should follow a rigidly scripted sequence. Gadamer's description of a dialogue as something that happens to us is brought home when we recall conversations over the phone with our friends. Many times we are amazed at the range of topics that we have spontaneously spoken about, shifting from a serious point to a silly one with ease.

But the central issue for Gadamer is the conversation itself rather than the subjectivity of the participants. In our conversations with the other, the subject matter comes more fully to the forefront, and as a result a better understanding of it takes place:

> What emerges in its truth is the logos, which is neither mine nor yours and hence so far transcends the interlocutors' subjective opinions that even the person leading the conversation knows that he does not know. (1989: 368)

In a conversation both participants belong to the bigger issue of the subject that is being spoken about, something that escapes their possession and which opens them up to each other.

There are parallels between the conversations we have in everyday life and the interpretations of texts. In the case of both, we are mistaken if we think that the participants are either in control of the conversation with each other or in control of the meaning of the text. The difference between them is that with texts it is through the interpreter that the voice of the text is brought out.

To explain the dynamics involved in the interpretation of texts, Gadamer approves of the method suggested by R.G. Collingwood, who is credited with introducing the expression *the logic of question and answer*. He used this expression to argue that understanding a text is not the result of assessing its internal logic, but is rather an answer to a question. Collingwood argued that the 'context' surrounding the text should be acknowledged: the motivations, concerns and historical issues within which the author is situated contribute to the meaning of the text. While it is not possible to enter the author's mind, it is necessary to understand the background context within which he/she has worked.

By understanding the issues that were at stake in the text, it is possible to achieve a more complete understanding of it. Interpretation involves retrieving the questions that made the text possible, with the latter having been formulated as an answer to such questions/ as an answer to such questions.

However, while Gadamer considered Collingwood's position as an advance upon previous attempts that judged texts merely according to the binary logic of true and false values, Collingwood failed to realize that the other pole of interpretation is that of the interpreter, who is also a product of a historical situation. What this means is that the interpreter must also be taken into consideration since the questions asked of the text are relevant to the present-day situation of the interpreter. As a result of the dynamic interaction between the interpreter and the text, both the questions and answers change. The text is not a passive, 'dead' object with a meaning waiting to be discovered by the interpreter, and neither is it merely the projected meaning of the interpreter. Rather, the process of question and answer is mutual: the text also confronts or questions the interpreter while the interpreter directs questions towards the text in the search for answers.

There are two questions[7] that one might ask initially, but these merge into each other. In the first case, it is the interpreter who is asked a question: '[t]he voice that speaks to us from the past – whether text, work, trace – itself poses a question and places our meaning in openness' (1989: 374). Something from the past speaks to the interpreter who turns to the text to see what it has to say about the subject. But to answer the question that the text poses to the interpreter, the interpreter needs to look for the question that the text itself is an answer to. In the process of reconstructing this question, the other interpretations of the text that belong to the tradition cannot be ignored; the interpreter is aware of these as he/ she formulates the question from the context he/she is situated in. As we have already seen, understanding a text involves its application to the interpreter:

> [R]econstructing the question to which the meaning of a text is understood as an answer merges with our own questioning. For the text must be understood as an answer to a real question. (1989: 374)

The two questions merge into one, and the fusion of questions is a restatement of the fusions of horizons. Understanding is 'the interplay of the movement of tradition and the movement of the interpreter' (1989: 103). Schmidt describes this movement as follows:

> One example of the movement of tradition is the different ways that Plato's *Republic* has been found to have something illuminating to say in the course of its preservation within tradition. The movement of the interpreter includes not only the reading of the original text but also an examination of that reading in light of other interpretations of Plato and the goal of establishing a unity of meaning for the text. The tradition, as inherited language, provides for the anticipation of meaning, while the interpreter, through her critical judgement, continues to form tradition. (2006: 103)

This explains why different periods and different individuals find different answers to their questions. Again the idea that there are 'different' interpretations might easily lead some to think that an interpretation is purely subjective. This is not Gadamer's position: even when we think that an interpretation is completely our own, in that we decide what the text means because we are in control of its meaning, there is a historical process always already affecting us. Before we start to interpret, the tradition pre-exists us: others have already been engaged in a dialogue with it and our interpretations are continuations of that dialogue which we modify, elaborate or reject. In turn our interpretations become an ongoing part and continuation of the tradition itself. The dialogical process that takes place within the tradition to which we belong enables us to become aware of our prejudices – our assumptions and value judgements. Although these operate, so to speak, 'behind our backs', they can be made known to us and are therefore a valuable and positive contribution to understanding and self-understanding.

For Gadamer, it is the spoken word that must be revitalized. In the dialogue with the text the written word must speak again. However, although Gadamer favours the spoken word, he is not (pace Derrida) trying to reinstate the 'metaphysics of presence' that Derrida claims is the founding error of Western philosophy. The nature of writing is that it is 'alienated': writing is alienated from speech and the task of hermeneutics is to transform it back to a living dialogue. The way to do this is not to think of the text as having a 'fixed' and stable meaning, but rather as the product of a dialogue between reader and text. Meaning is always tentative, and successive generations will produce different interpretations of the same text. Better still, the text will speak differently to different generations. This is why although understanding can be complete, it can never be final since there will always be the changing horizon of the interpreter in dialogue with the text. The difference between the spoken word and the written word is that the latter has broken free of the limitations of the space and time of its production and acquired a relative permanence within the tradition. The subject matter – or what the text is about – is the common element between the text and the interpreter, so that the task of the interpreter is to make the text speak again.

The difference between an actual dialogue and a textual dialogue is that, in the case of the latter, the interpreter must bring the text to communicate (what it has to say and) its truth claims. When the interpreter interacts dialogically with the text, he/she listens to what the text has to say, using the principle of charity to adopt and develop the claims made by the text to see if they challenge his/her prejudices. Understanding what the text has to say involves the interpreter applying his/her own understanding – through the medium of language – to the language of the text. Just as language is the medium through which humans understand each other, understanding a text replicates the dialogical model of mutual understanding. It is with and through language that the text can speak to the interpreter so that an understanding about the subject matter can be agreed upon. An illuminating way of understanding Gadamer's hermeneutic enterprise is that of translation, where a speaker must translate what the other has said into his/her own language: to understand what the other has said it is necessary to apply the latter to the speaker's own language. Translation involves understanding as application, with the speaker having understood what the other has said once they have agreed on the content that they have been communicating.

The relationship between the interpreter and the text can be characterized in three possible ways (1989: 358–60). (1) As an object that can be subsumed under general laws and that therefore can be predicted: this is the method associated with the natural sciences where the interpreter can objectively describe what the text says. (2) As a person, but with the qualification that the interpreter can understand the author better than the author could understand himself/herself. (3) As an other that speaks to me: the text as part of a tradition has something to say to the interpreter who is open to what the text has to say. Being open does not mean passively agreeing with everything, but realizing that there are some things we must accept even if we do not agree with them. This position describes the hermeneutic experience, for, in the act of interpretation, the interpreter experiences the truth of something new in the interaction with the tradition.

The importance of the dialogical model is that it reveals the attempt to understand both oneself and the world as the shared experience of humanity, rather than the experience of an isolated consciousness. Dialogue is described as a consensus because it goes beyond the original views of the participants and takes into consideration the possible objections and counter examples of the other. In a nutshell, consensus can be reached by agreeing to disagree, but what is crucial is that both have a greater understanding of the issues, having 'raised' the dialogue to a higher and more informed level:

> At the conclusion of a conversation, the initial positions of all participants can be seen to be inadequate positions on their own and are integrated within a richer, more comprehensive view. For hermeneutic understanding it follows that we are not limited to the premises of our tradition but rather continually revise them in the encounters with and discussion we have of them. In confronting other cultures, other prejudices and, indeed, the implications that others draw from our own traditions we learn to reflect on both our assumptions and our ideas of reason and to amend them in the direction of a *better* account. (Warnke 1987: 170)

Language and truth

Following Heidegger, Gadamer subscribes to the view that a human being's relation to the world is that of making sense of it, of attempting to understand a world that exists before them and that comes to them always already interpreted. The world humans are born into is constituted by tradition and the vehicle for the transmission and preservation of tradition is language. Language precedes humans and makes possible human experience and thought. It makes human experience possible both in terms of understanding others and in terms of understanding oneself.

Gadamer's valorization of language is encapsulated in the following key sentences: *'the fusion of horizons that takes place in understanding is actually the achievement of language'* (1989: 378) and *'Being that can be understood is language'* (1989: 474). It is only through language that humans have a world at all. Clearly language is not an optional or incidental feature of human existence but an essential one, for the world discloses itself though language, and language comes into being by disclosing the world. The relationship between language and the world is one of complementarity rather than opposition, with language on one side and the world on the other (1989: 443).

The place of language in Gadamer's hermeneutics cannot be underestimated, and it is one of those domains (together with history and art) that make the experience of truth possible. However, while Gadamer considers language as the source of truth, he distances himself from correspondence or representational theories of truth. According to these theories, language represents facts about the world and communicates their truth-value. Gadamer's criticism of this view lies in its assumption that one can treat language as an object of analysis, studying the way it corresponds to the world. This view of language suggests that one can step outside language to examine the relationship between propositions and the world. But it is evident that there is no position outside language with which to evaluate the relation between propositions and the world; the study of this relationship can only take place from within language itself. The criticism of propositional logic is part of Gadamer's ongoing criticism of the use of method in the human sciences. When we talk about method in the natural sciences we are talking about the control of objects that are isolated, manipulated and repeated. In the case of the human sciences, understanding is not merely the ability to isolate a meaning but that of belonging to and participating in a tradition. It is this notion of understanding as participation that Gadamer contrasts with understanding as making things or meanings at our disposal.

Gadamer's analysis takes as its starting point one of the first texts in western culture that examines language. In the *Cratylus* the question that Plato attempts to answer concerns the relationship between language and the world: is this relation a conventional one, with the community agreeing upon the words used to name objects, or is the relationship one where words naturally represent objects? The answer in the *Cratylus* favours the conventional argument, with language described as a system of signs. However, Gadamer points out that both theories mistakenly assume that objects exist and can be known without any intervention of language. Gadamer rejects this when he argues that language is disclosive, by which he means that it is language that brings the world into being, and that it is only after this disclosure that language can function to represent the world.

The work of Humboldt plays an important role in the development of Gadamer's thinking on language. Humboldt had argued that each language expresses a vision of reality or a way of life. The differences between languages could be accounted for in relation to the different linguistic structures of a particular language. However, Gadamer does not merely appropriate Humboldt's claim, but argues that the vision of life that each language presents is not a question of its formal or structural features but a question of the content that language expresses. What is important is 'what is said or handed down in language' (1989: 441). The language of a community communicates the 'form of life' of the community: without their language, the world of a particular community – with their shared values, beliefs and norms – would not exist.

Gadamer's account retrieves the original sense of communication by identifying communication with the expressivist theory of language. Originally the meaning of the concept of communication was closely tied to that of community, but in the twentieth century the meaning was narrowed down to the transmission of information. In Gadamer's hermeneutic analysis of language, the concept of communication is redefined as the expression of the values, beliefs, customs and social practices of the community – in other words, the world of the community and the community's experience of the world.

The centrality of language in Gadamer's philosophy is highlighted in the distinction between 'world' and 'environment'. All living things have an environment, but it is only humans that have a world, or an orientation towards the world. The difference is that while living things depend upon their environment, human beings develop attitudes and behave in certain ways to relate to the world. To have a world means that humans can stand back from the world whereas other living things are 'absorbed' into the environment. It is in this sense that they are free from their environment (1989: 444–45).

While all humans interact in a particular environment, they are not passive in relation to it but can think about it and attempt to understand it through their language. As a result they transform their world. Different cultures have coped with their environment in different ways and have therefore developed different concepts. The linguistic heritage of the community – its linguistic tradition – encapsulates the experiences of the community.

This raises the question of whether – given that each community has its own language and therefore its own linguistically constructed world – it is possible that there is a world in itself, an extralinguistic world that can be contrasted to the linguistic world. Gadamer argues that although each language is a perspectival vision of the world, this does not mean that there is a position outside language from which one can compare language to the world in itself. Just as Husserl's account of perception had demonstrated that each perception is a partial perspective of the world, and that the world in itself is nothing more that the totality of perspectives, Gadamer argues that each language is a perspective of the world and that the world in itself is nothing more than the totality of linguistic perspectives. The important difference between Husserl's account of perception and Gadamer's account of language is that a language (unlike a perception) can assimilate the views of another language. And while a language can assimilate the experiences of another language, no one language can ever attain the status of describing the world as it really is because 'we never succeed in seeing anything but an evermore extended aspect, a "view" of the world' (1989: 447). And just because we enter another linguistic world, this does not mean that we abandon ours. When we learn another language we do not forget the world we come from.

Gadamer's view on language makes a strong claim since language is said to construct the world. The concept of linguistic construction here does not just refer to the organizing or structuring of nature, of giving form to an unformed environment. Rather, the disclosure of the world by language is a disclosure of something, of some subject matter. This is why Gadamer considers the primary mode of being of language to be dialogue which he defines as the coming to an understanding or agreement about a subject. But this view of language should not be interpreted in terms of purposes, with the sole purpose of language being that of achieving understanding. This would reduce language to the status of a medium or tool at the disposal and control of the participants rather than enabling the world to appear as a world.

But while language discloses the world it is unable to dominate it. The world overflows the categories of language. This insight explains why unexpected experiences can overwhelm us to the extent that we fail to find the words to describe them. As a result of his analysis, Gadamer argues that language both discloses and hides the world. This double-edged quality of language can be seen in the distinction between the said and the unsaid. While a proposition is 'the said' by virtue of communicating a content, the 'unsaid' is the background of the proposition. The 'unsaid' is the 'more' that frames the proposition or the text; it is the question to which the proposition is the answer, with '[t]he hermeneutic task [being] to uncover and lay bare the unsaid by drawing it into an explicit dialogue with the said' (Lawn 2006: 84).

The hermeneutic structure of language parallels the hermeneutic structure of human experience. Just as an experience is the result of the interaction between the background of the unfamiliar and the familiar, a sentence can be understood against a background of social and cultural conventions. The hermeneutic parallelism between the structure of experience and the structure of language is no coincidence, since understanding an experience requires language for this understanding to be communicated. It is only through language that our understanding of a personal experience, a work of art or social institution can be communicated. And language itself is a tradition since it transmits the experiences and knowledge that have been acquired over time.

Gadamer distinguishes between two senses of experience. Empiricist accounts of experience tend to consider an experience as something that can be repeated, as something that can be verified through a process of experimentation. Rather than pointing to something new, the sense of experience is that which conforms or repeats what has already happened. On the other hand, Gadamer argues for a broader sense of experience that includes both its unexpectedness and novelty. Experience for Gadamer means that one is open to the future. But although one is always open to future experiences, what experience teaches us is that there are limits to what humans can achieve with their life. Even with the impressive advances in science and technology, life can never be completely controlled or mastered. This is why experience is self-experience: ultimately what we learn is always about ourselves in our capacity as human beings. 'The experienced man knows that all foresight is limited and all plans uncertain. In him is realised the truth value of experience' (1989: 357). The emphasis here lies with the concept of experience as something primary, as something that happens to us or that we have undergone.

The hermeneutic element in Gadamer's account of experience is the interplay between the part and the whole, or the new and the old. It is the background of the 'old' that makes what is 'new' an experience of truth: the true is produced in the dynamic that takes place between the part and the whole. And while the experience of something as 'new' lies in its 'conflict' with the 'old' background, it is the background that gives meaning to the experience. The experience of truth in Gadamer is an 'eye-opener'. Lawn describes this from the perspective of literature:

> [N]o matter how many times a poem or novel are read they always manage to open up new lines of enquiry, new possibilities. The written text does not change but the interpretive possibilities, that is, for Gadamer, the truth possibilities, do, as they are endless. (Lawn 2006: 62)

Gadamer's model of dialogue helps us understand his concept of truth. In a dialogue something is revealed or disclosed about the participants: we are surprised by the truth that has been expressed. What we take for granted is disrupted and we see ourselves and the world differently. Likewise, in our dialogical exchanges the assumptions or prejudices we carry with us can be challenged, such that we learn something about ourselves. Although language is never value-free, since it always embodies the prejudices of a culture, this does not mean that we are forever trapped within the tradition from which we speak.

In textual interpretation, the relation between the interpreter and the tradition is bridged by the language that both share. It is through language that the content of the tradition is communicated: the question posed to the interpreter enables the potential meanings of the tradition to be actualized. The interpreter translates the question posed to him/her by the tradition into a new interpretation, since something new is disclosed by language. This in turn perpetuates the tradition. Because we belong to a tradition that precedes us, and since tradition is communicated linguistically, Gadamer argues that the tradition takes precedence over us (1989: 463).

This is why the idea of interpretation as subjective, with the subject enacting complete control over the text, is mistaken. In fact the subject is acted upon by language and tradition. When Gadamer writes that 'the content of tradition itself is the sole criterion and it expresses itself in language' (1989: 472–73), he is arguing that it is tradition that provides the standard for interpretation. This is not to say that tradition is always right or provides the correct interpretation, but that it is tradition that 'decides' if an interpretation continues to belong to that tradition or is dismissed and forgotten.

In his discussion of the realizations of the different interpretations that are inherent within the text, Gadamer introduces the notion of 'speculation'. Each interpretation is a speculative event in the sense that each interpretation is different and yet is part of the same subject. For example, the different interpretations of a play all belong to the same subject. It is not the case of one subject manifesting itself in different presentations; rather, the presentations are the different ways in which the subject presents itself. Being is one but it manifests itself as many (1989: 473).

Gadamer and intercultural communication

Reading *Truth and Method* might leave one with the impression that Gadamer's hermeneutics is oriented solely with the interpretation of texts from the past. However, this orientation does not exclude the application of Gadamer's philosophical hermeneutics for understanding the processes involved in intercultural communication since the 'fusion of horizons' that constitutes the act of interpretation can take place both vertically (from the present to the past) and horizontally (across cultures). In 'Hans-Georg Gadamer, Language, and Intercultural Communication' (2001: 6–20), Roy and Starosta point out that the use of Gadamer's philosophical hermeneutics remains virtually untapped in intercultural research conducted by American scholars (2001: 6). In their article, Roy and Starosta identify a number of areas in which Gadamer's philosophical hermeneutics can profitably inform intercultural communication. These involve:

1. The temporal dimension of understanding. One of the main theses proposed by Gadamer in *Truth and Method* concerns the nature of understanding and knowledge. While knowledge of natural phenomena entails understanding the causal connections that generate the phenomena so as to establish law-lie regularities, such an approach cannot be used to understand texts or human beings. Instead, for Gadamer understanding is contextual so that the significance of texts, events and people entails an understanding of their historical context. In terms of intercultural communication, Roy and Starosta suggest that an awareness of the temporal dimensions of what it is one is trying to understand. What the historical context shows us is that over time cultures change so that it is necessary 'to critically examine the subtleties of context that influence such communication patterns' (2001: 12). In addition since the interpreter or intercultural researcher is also situated within a historical context then he/she is also conditioned by prejudices. As Gadamer pointed out, understanding is always prejudiced but not all of them are necessarily negative. In fact, he thinks that they are the productive ground for all understanding. In terms of intercultural communication this means the interpreter should not let his/her own prejudices hinder one's understanding of other cultures by being open or receptive to other cultures (2001: 12–13).

2. The moral dimension of understanding. The second future of Gadamer's hermeneutics that is of interest to intercultural communication scholars is the notion of praxis. Given his contention that humans relate to each other as moral actors then the search for human knowledge should be grounded in moral considerations of the other. When this is transposed to sphere of intercultural communication Roy and Starosta argue that intercultural communication researchers should be aware of the potential for emancipation within other cultures and not merely restrict themselves to describing communication patterns in those cultures. This is where the moral dimension comes in: a responsible intercultural communication researcher is aware of the other culture as being a possible

site of tension and conflict; the task of the researcher is to 'demonstrate linkages between communication, identity, power and knowledge across cultures' (2001: 13).

3. The problem of generalization. The philosophical hermeneutics of Gadamer stresses that the relationship between the interpreter and the text should be dialogic in order for understanding to be achieved. The text should be treated as another person, as someone with a contribution to make to the relationship; in other words, it should not be treated like an object. This notion resonates well with intercultural communication research. Other cultures should not be objectified, as Roy and Starosta point out, into fixed types such as collectivist/individualist, masculine/feminine, high/low and so on (2001: 14). This way of thinking only perpetuates stereotypical generalizations, neglecting the differences that can be found in the other culture. In addition, the dialogical relationship is based on equality between the communication researcher and the culture he/she is researching. This means that the creation of knowledge is a mutual undertaking with the contribution of the cultural other as equally significant. By adopting a Gadamerian perspective, the cultural other is transformed into a significant other as opposed to a subservient or dominated one (2001: 15).

Roy and Starosta suggest that Gadamer's concept of Bildung provides the basis for the training of the intercultural communication researcher. Bildung is roughly translated as 'cultured' but the cultured person on Gadamer's account is not only one who knows the facts but who can discriminate or judge between good and bad, beautiful or ugly and so on, and incorporates them into his/her own life. Although the starting point for the cultured person is his/her own culture he/she goes beyond it to see the 'big picture'. It is, therefore, a practical concept that describes the process that contributes to a person's self-understanding.

The intercultural communication scholar should be one who has assimilated his/her own culture but who has not stagnated within its confines; on the contrary, he/she is aware of the limits of his/her own culture and is able to go beyond it in the desire to discover new things. The intercultural communication researcher leaves the familiarity of his/her own culture to explore the unfamiliarity of the other culture. This person 'is not bound by his/her community or group but adopts a cosmopolitan view of the world and cultures' (2001: 16). While recognizing the differences that exist between (and within) cultures the 'competent' intercultural researcher understands that there is something that unites all of humanity.

The value of Gadamer's philosophical hermeneutics has been underestimated in intercultural communication theory, and Roy and Starosta have pointed this out suggesting that intercultural communication should be reconfigured in such a way so as to take into account Gadamer's notion of praxis as a moral relationship between researchers and participants.

Critical remarks

When Gadamer died, he was considered one of the key contributors to hermeneutical theory, and while he is perhaps better known on the Continent, his work is steadily attracting the increasing attention of Anglo-American philosophers. However, the hermeneutic vision that Gadamer offers has not been without its detractors. Gorner (2000) points to a number of problems in Gadamer's account. (1) The dialogue or conversation that takes place between individuals, and which culminates in an understanding of the thing itself, seems to take place 'behind' the back of individuals, given that the individuals belong to or participate in a tradition that both pre-exists them and 'uses' them to communicate its truths. (2) The dialogical structure of the question and answer that is central to Gadamer's concept of understanding is used mostly as a model for the interpretation of texts, but it is hard to see how a model taken from human life can be applied to the relation between a text and a person. It seems that one can apply the dialogical structure of the understanding to the general field of hermeneutics only in a secondary sense. (3) One consequence of the concept of effective history is that we would not understand something that happened in the past if it had no effect, no subsequent interpretation. This would entail the false view that we would not be able to understand Aztec culture since we have no effective historical connection with it.

In 'A Review of Gadamer's *Truth and Method*' (1986), Habermas has critically engaged the work of Gadamer on a number of counts, but perhaps his most pertinent criticism is that Gadamerian hermeneutics miscalculates the force of ideology at work within society. It is not enough to equate the prejudices that hermeneutics uncovers with ideology, for ideology is also at work in those situations that are 'normal' and that in fact are constituted by ideology, with the consequence that it would be difficult to recognize them at work. It is in this respect that Habermas considers hermeneutics as lacking a 'reference system' that is, a theory of society that would enable it to go beyond the surface to the deeper level within which ideology operates.

Finally, given the centrality of language in hermeneutics, several commentators thought that Gadamer had collapsed everything into language, and was advocating a sort of linguistic idealism. But to understand Gadamer's thesis, it must be remembered that his philosophy is a phenomenological analysis of the act of understanding, an act that does not reduce understanding either to a subjectivist or an epistemological function. His view is that something can only be understood through language; language is the necessary condition for understanding to take place. Language transforms understanding into an event. Against his critics, it is possible to formulate two lines of defence: (1) they fail to understand the target of Gadamer's assertion of the centrality of language. This assertion is directed against the entrenched view of propositional logic that dominates Western philosophy. Dialogue replaces propositional logic in that the propositions of logic are themselves embedded within a context of dialogue; propositional logic does not exist on its own but falls within the ambit of speakers and their motivations. (2) Within a genuine conversation, things crop up in the minds of participants; it is not a question of the speaker's intention to reveal things, but a question of common understanding that is achieved by speakers.[8] Clearly Gadamer's hermeneutics is not subjectivist since understanding is not the exclusive 'private' domain of the subject, but it incorporates the other with whom the conversation is taking place. *Dialogue* is a key term in Gadamer's vocabulary because it is the model within which understanding between persons and texts within a tradition takes place.

In this chapter I have started by outlining (1) Gadamer's reading of the history of hermeneutics, so as to prepare the way for (2) his critique of the claims of science, (3) a critique that retrieves the concepts of prejudice and tradition. This was followed by (4) an analysis of the kind of understanding that belongs to the social or human sciences, (5) an analysis that brings to life the notion of effective history as the foundation of understanding, together with an elaboration on the way understanding involves an interaction between a fusion of horizons that is (6) modelled upon a dialogue of question and answer. The following section provides (7) an overview of Gadamer's account of language while the last section ends (8) with examining the possible contribution of Gadamer's hermeneutics to intercultural communication.

Notes

1. Hamilton (1996: 51) offers the following definition of hermeneutics: 'Hermeneutics is the science of interpretation. It stresses the individuality of each human expression and, against scientific generalizations, claims that we choose between the several meanings any utterance might have in the light of the special circumstances under which it is made.'
2. West quotes Bubner on Gadamer as 'a matter of explicating the *reciprocal relations between methodical science* and an original truth which transcends the methodical' (in West: 106).
3. Gadamer writes: 'the purpose of my investigation is not to offer a general theory of interpretation and a differential account of its methods (which Emilio Betti has done so well) but to discover what is common to all modes of understanding and to show that understanding is never a subjective relation to a given "object" but to the history of its effect; in other words, understanding belongs to be being of that which is convinced' (1989: xxxi).
4. However, it has been pointed out that Gadamer at times overemphasises this outright rejection of the genetic origins of meaning (Warnke 1987: 9), since knowing the historical conditions of Greek geometry can help us understand why these principles of geometry appeared when they actually did.
5. Warnke elaborates on what is entailed in understanding the concept of courage: 'Courage may involve a willingness to die but also a refusal to die, standing up for one's rights as well as yielding to others[…] [What] the virtue of courage involves [is] not so given but rather depend[s] to a far greater extent on individual circumstances' (1987: 93).
6. West brings this out very clearly: '[W]e are products of a particular history and tradition just as much as we are interpreters of other historical traditions. History is not simply an object to be known; history is also what has made us into the particular "subjects" who attempt to understand it' (1996: 109).

7. There are both right and wrong questions to ask of a text, and for Gadamer, to ask about the author's intentions rather than about the meaning of the text is to ask the wrong question. Asking the right kind of question is a skill that has no ready-made rule, '[t]here is no such thing as a method of leaning to ask questions, of learning to see what is questionable' (1989: 365).
8. Gadamer writes: 'a genuine conversation is never the one we wanted to conduct' (1989: 383).

Chapter 7

Wittgenstein on Language as a Form of Life

The writings of Ludwig Wittgenstein (1889–1951) have had an enormous impact on the development of philosophy in the twentieth century. This impact can be gauged both from the variety of topics he discusses and from his own peculiar way of conducting philosophical analysis. As a result, his writings have attracted both professional philosophers and those more generally interested in philosophy.

The texts that have received most attention are the *Tractatus Logico-Philosophicus* (1921) and the posthumously published *Philosophical Investigations* (1953). For some time, it was customary among scholars to divide Wittgenstein's work in two main periods, each focussing around these two texts. The problem was that this schema neglected his other writings and there is now a growing consensus on a middle period in which a number of other posthumously published texts (such as *The Blue and Brown Books* and *Philosophical Grammar*) should be placed.

In this chapter, I am only taking into consideration the *Tractatus* (hereafter T) and the *Philosophical Investigations* (hereafter PI). I will first outline (1) the views of two key figures in the analytic tradition of philosophy, followed by (2) the early Wittgenstein's picture theory of language (3) with the subsequent distinction between saying and showing; this is followed by (4) the later Wittgenstein's introduction of the meaning-as-use thesis (5) and the concept of language games. The final section (6) shows the way some of Wittgenstein's ideas can be applied to film theory.

Philosophical background: Frege and Russell

The writings of Gottlieb Frege (1848–1925) and Bertrand Russell (1872–1970) can be said to constitute the starting point of analytic philosophy in the twentieth century. They also form the background to Wittgenstein's thinking on the nature and scope of philosophy, and a general overview of this background influence is both necessary and useful.

In the *Grundlagen* (1884), Frege made a number of important contributions to the study of language. The first of these is his critique of psychologism, which is the view that the meaning of a word is the image or idea that we have of it in our mind (e.g. the meaning of the word *table* is the image or idea of a table in a person's head). For Frege, the meaning of a word has nothing to do with the mental image we might have of it and this popular view is the result of trying to understand the meaning of words individually. The rejection of psychologism leads to the principle of contextuality, which states that one should never ask for the meaning of a word in isolation but always see it within the context or the role it plays in a sentence. A sentence is a combination of words such that each contributes to the sense of the sentence as a whole. The third contribution concerns the structure of the sentence as a whole: a sentence has a subject and a predicate position and these are connected to each other. For Frege, the subject position is filled by a proper name and refers to an object while the predicate position is filled in by a general term and refers to a concept. In the sentence *Socrates was a philosopher*, the sense of the proper name *Socrates* is descriptive and refers to a person while the sense of *philosopher* is that it completes the sentences and refers to a concept. Problems arise with those sentences that have concept words in both subject and predicate positions, a situation that Frege considered could only be generated in natural language.

Frege is also known for introducing a distinction between the colouring, the sense (*sinne*) and the reference of a word (*bedeutung*). The colouring is the subjective associations a word might arouse in a speaker or hearer, and from a philosophical point of view, he considered these to be unimportant. On the other hand, the sense of a word is objective and this permits us to decide if a sentence is true or false. The reference of the word is what it is about so that the reference of a proper name (a singular term) is the object and the reference of the predicate is the concept. Frege furthered his analysis so that it applied not only to individual words or phrases, but also to complete sentences such that the sentence as a whole can have a sense and a reference. On this account, therefore, the sense a declarative sentence expresses is a thought and the reference is what the declarative sentence names, either the True or the False.

Furthermore, the distinction between sense and reference enabled Frege to show how two phrases might have a different sense but refer to the same object: on this account the phrase 'the morning star' communicates the sense of a celestial body that appears in the morning while also referring to the planet Venus, and 'the evening star' communicates the sense of a celestial body that appears at night while also referring to the planet Venus.

The question that Frege and Russell attempted to answer concerned the way language and the world are connected: given that language and the world are qualitatively different how is it possible that a series of sounds or written marks can communicate something to us about the world? The typical answer is that the connection between the two is one of correspondence with words in the sentence describing objects in the world. This conception of language neatly combines the popular view that words refer to objects and that the words that compose the sentence create a meaning. With the sentence *Socrates lived in Athens*, the name *Socrates* refers to a person and the name *Athens* refers to a place so that the sentence as a whole has a meaning precisely because the words mean their objects.

The difficulty this theory of language and meaning generates arises when one talks about things that do not exist. If the words we use have a meaning because they refer to objects that exist then what is going on when we talk about things that do not exist? In sentences such as *Santa Claus lives in Greenland* the sentence is meaningful, even though it refers to someone who does not exist. Clearly, the view of language and meaning as corresponding to reality needs to be modified.

Frege's distinction between the sense and the reference shows the way in which an expression might have a sense and communicate a thought even if it had no reference. We can understand the phrase 'the greatest natural number' even though it does not refer to anything that exists; in this case, the expression has a sense but no reference. With the proper name *Santa Claus*, Frege would argue that the sense of the name functions as a descriptive phrase so that *Santa Claus* can be redescribed as *the man who delivers presents to children in Christmas*. This sentence has a sense because we can understand it even though it cannot be either true or false since the name *Santa Claus* does not refer to someone that exists.

This led Frege to consider everyday natural language as 'defective' since it is possible to use names or sentences that do not refer to anything in the world. For this reason, he argued that any philosophical analysis should be conducted in an ideal language such as mathematical logic where there is both a sense and a reference even though the reference might be an ideal entity.

Russell agreed with Frege on the 'defective' nature of everyday natural language but argued against the notion that proper names have a sense, claiming instead that proper names mean the objects they refer to; on this account, the proper name *Venus* means the object it refers to. However, this reintroduces the problem of those names that do not refer to anyone who exists (Santa Claus) and Russell provides a very interesting solution with his theory of descriptions. His central argument is that these proper names are nothing other than descriptive phrases and must be therefore analysed differently from real proper names, even though they might refer to the same person. The definite description, 'The Head of the Roman Catholic Church' currently applies to Pope Benedict but in the future it will apply to someone else (just as it used to apply to Pope John Paul II in the past). By adopting the symbolic language proposed in the *Principia Mathematica* rather than everyday natural language Russell's analysis shows the way the difference between descriptive phrases and proper names can be explained.

The descriptive phrase 'The present King of France is tall' seems, from a grammatical point of view, to be a singular sentence (the article 'the' captures singularity). Upon closer inspection, the sentence turns out to be a complex general sentence and the complexity is shown in the way the sentence is 'unpacked' to reveal its logical form as (1) at the moment there is at least one person who is male and the king of France; (2) at the moment, there is only one person who is male and king of France; (3) whoever is, at the moment, male and the King of France is tall. The singularity of the King of France is captured in (1) and (2) such that if these are true then the property of being tall is true for the sentence as a whole. But because the King of France does not exist then (1) and (2) are false, and in logic, if part of a conjunction is false then the sentence as a whole is false.

The importance of this analysis is that Russell shows the way that a sentence can be meaningful even if it is false. Since each of the component sentences that make up the complex one is meaningful then the sentence as a whole is meaningful too. Sentences that do not refer to things or persons that exist can therefore be also meaningful.

Frege and Russell's distrust towards everyday natural language as a means towards the resolution of philosophical problems is inherited by the early Wittgenstein. Such problems are more adequately dealt with through the use of mathematical logic, which is purposely constructed to avoid the defects inherent to everyday natural languages. In the *Tractatus Logico-Philosophicus* (1922), Wittgenstein outlines his proposals for the 'ideal language' that would solve such problems.

The Picture theory of language

In the preface to the *Tractatus*, Wittgenstein clearly states that by understanding the way language works it will then be realized that philosophical problems are actually pseudo-problems in that they have arisen as a result of misunderstanding the workings of language. This notion of understanding the way language works involves establishing the limits of what can be said meaningfully, but the limits of what can be meaningfully said is likewise the limit of what can be meaningfully thought. For Wittgenstein, a proposition is an expression of thought (T 3.1) and to go beyond what can be said or thought would be to venture into the realm of nonsense. One important aim of the *Tractatus* is to demarcate the limits of what 'can be said' and thought but also to create the space for what cannot be said but shown.

The *Tractatus* presents the reader with more than the usual difficulties associated with reading a difficult philosophical text. It is 79 pages long and consists of 525 aphorisms usually of a sentence or two in length; there are seven main points followed by a number of comments and subcomments on six of them. The decimal system used to number these points, comments and subcomments is such that each sentence relates to the previous one in terms of relative importance. The fact that each sentence is so short with only a comment, rather than an explanation, requires considerable interpretative skill in understanding them. In addition, the fact that Wittgenstein uses the logical symbols of Russell's *Principia Mathematica* together with some other symbols that he invented only compounds the difficulty in understanding him.

A large portion of the *Tractatus* focusses on the nature of propositions, meaning, the world and the connection between them. Since it is the world that conditions our representation of it, Wittgenstein starts by talking about it and the opening line in the *Tractatus* is 'The world is all that is the case' (T 1). Here he is immediately alluding to the fact that since a proposition represents whatever is the case in the world (whether it is true or false), then the totality of propositions represents the totality of possibilities in the world. This is followed by 'The world is totality of facts, not of things' (T 1.1.), and what Wittgenstein has in mind is the idea that the world is composed of a number of objects or entities in combination with each other. In other words, contrary to the popular view, the world is not a series of objects that exist independently of each other (tables, rocks, trees) but exist in relation to each other, composing what Wittgenstein calls 'states of affairs'. And these in turn combine to make up facts.

There is a parallel between Wittgenstein's ontology and language: corresponding to the objects, states of affairs and facts hierarchy we find names, elementary propositions and propositions. Just as objects are the building blocks of reality, likewise, names are the building blocks of language: names mean their objects by referring to them. The combination of names constitutes an elementary proposition and there is a direct, one-to-one correspondence between the elementary proposition and the state of affairs. Elementary propositions are combined through the use of logical connectives such as 'and', 'or' and 'if, then'. Elementary propositions can be true or false of the world and the truth and falsity of a proposition depends upon the truth and falsity of its elementary components. 'A proposition is a truth-function of elementary propositions' (T 5). What makes a proposition true or false is its relationship to the world and it must be kept it mind that these are the only two values possible; there is no middle ground.

In order to explain the way propositions and facts, or language and the world, are related Wittgenstein introduces the idea of language as picturing: 'a proposition can be true or false only in virtue of being a pictures of reality' (T 4.061). Wittgenstein had been inspired to the concept of language as picturing after he had read a newspaper account of how toy cars and dolls were used in a court to describe a car accident. The models were placed in such a way that they corresponded to the way the accident happened. The model was a representation of something that had happened in the world (T 2.12). The possibility of models being pictures of reality is the result of the picture and the reality having something in common: this common feature is the structure. In other words, the elements that constitute the picture are organized in the same way as the objects that constitute reality (T 2.1514).

However, while this might be true for pictures how does a proposition function as a picture? For Wittgenstein the necessary conditions for something to be a picture is that first, it has a structure in common with the reality it is representing and that, second, a picture correctly or incorrectly represents that reality such that a picture can be true or false of reality (T 2.21). When it comes to discussing the way propositions picture reality, Wittgenstein offers the analogy of the way the music played by a musician is a picture of the musical score in front of him/her: the musician is able to translate the notation into the sounds because he/she understands the shared structure between the notation and the instrument he/she is playing. There is, according to Wittgenstein an essential connection between them and this essential connection is also found in the relation between propositions and reality. 'A proposition communicates a situation to us, and so it must be *essentially* connected with the situation' (T4.03). It is the sense that the proposition is picturing (T 4.022) and this sense is derived by comparing the proposition with the world, a comparison that allows us to judge the proposition as true or false (T 2.223).

What Wittgenstein's account brings out is the correlation between propositions and the world; it is only meaningful propositions that have the possibility of telling us something about the world because they acquire their meaning, their sense by being pictures of the world. It is the world of facts that guarantees a sense or meaning to propositions so that any talk beyond the world of facts is meaningless, is without any sense.

Saying and showing

Given that the only meaningful propositions are those that say something about the world, then the only meaningful propositions are those of the natural sciences. With this argument the propositions of logic are excluded on the grounds that they are tautologies: 'For example, I know nothing about the weather, when I know that it is either raining or it is not' (T 4.461). They are true but empty. Tautologies, like the propositions of philosophy, are senseless because they tell us nothing; they do not picture anything in the world. And this is what leads us to realize that we do not need the *Tractatus* itself. There is, however, one positive purpose to the propositions of philosophy: they clarify our thoughts (T 4.112).

But apart from the category of what 'can be said', Wittgenstein introduces another category for that which 'can be shown'. This category is broad and includes moral, religious, aesthetic values and 'the problems of life'. The basis of the distinction between what 'can be said' and what 'can be shown' is that there are features of human life that do not pertain to the domain of science because they cannot be analysed with the methods of science. This is not to say that they are unimportant, but on the contrary, that they are too important to be handled by science. The domain of science is the contingent, that is, it deals with those things that happen but do not have to happen. Questions concerning values, on the other hand, are too serious to be considered as chance events in human life. They are beyond or transcend the world since science only deals with what is in the world. If only the propositions of the natural sciences belong to the said, then the propositions concerning moral, aesthetic or religious values can only be shown. 'There are indeed things that cannot be put into words. They *make themselves manifest*. They are what is mystical' (T 6.522).

Interestingly, the class of things that can be shown also includes the 'logical form'. This is because the logical structures of language, the world and the connection between them is something that cannot be pictured by propositions because propositions can only picture what is in the world and there is no picture of the 'logical form' in the world. It just shows itself: '[p]ropositions cannot represent logical form: it is mirrored in them. What finds its reflection in language, language cannot represent' (T 4.121).

With the aim of resolving philosophical problems by understanding the workings of language over and above its everyday, natural use, Wittgenstein held that this kind of understanding language required discovering its nature or essence. In the *Tractatus*, he argued that there was a single essence to it, a single 'logic of language' that could be discovered through an analysis of the relationship between language and the world. In this relationship, the nature of language is to picture the world and the foundation of this picturing relationship is one where names refer to objects.

Description and explanation

Over time, Wittgenstein came to reject most of the claims that he had proposed in the *Tractatus*. In the *Philosophical Investigations* he approaches the study of language from the perspective of its communicative role. What is emphasized now are the many different practices of language, each of which follows its own logic: meaning is no longer considered to be the relation between a name and an object but the way an expression is used within a community.

The stylistic differences of both texts are immediately apparent: instead of the minimalist remarks that characterize the *Tractatus* we find an assortment of short paragraphs, aphorisms, maxims and fragments, a style that Stroll (2002: 93–100) calls the 'broken text'. There is no account at the end of which one reaches a conclusion but remain open-ended as though they are part of a conversation. This conversational approach is further supported by the way topics are repeated so as to be able to see the problem from different angles.

In the *Investigations*, Wittgenstein's aim is to dislodge certain puzzles that are the result of misusing language or of misunderstanding its nature. These puzzles occur when one thinks there is only one way of understanding language or when one uses an expression outside of its everyday context. Philosophers usually think that a puzzle can be solved if one can discover the underlying or hidden causes of the puzzle; they have been captivated by a certain model of thinking that assumes that if one digs 'deeply' enough one will be able to explain the puzzle away. This is the mistake that Wittgenstein is now warning us about: rather than attempting to find underlying causes of explanation, we should observe the way language works. This approach is emphasized by the expression 'Don't think, but look!' (PI 66) and it reconceptualizes the task of philosophy as that of describing the way language is used in everyday life, rather than seeking underlying explanations. The philosopher describes the way expressions are used in everyday life without attempting to change anything; philosophy will 'leave everything as it is' because, rather than discover new information, it is simply rearranging properly what we already know.

The central premise in Wittgenstein's argument is that philosophers have taken a step back from everyday natural language in their attempt to define concepts. Instead of trying to define the concepts of time, knowledge, belief and so on, they should 'bring words back from their metaphysical to their everyday use' (PI 116). Paradoxically, while they seem to be perplexed over how to define such concepts, they seem to know how to use them perfectly well in their everyday lives.

In the *Investigations*, there is an intimate connection between the descriptive method that Wittgenstein employs and the philosophical content of that text. The emphasis on describing the way language is used can be seen in the numerous examples, metaphors and analogies that serve to challenge the traditional (including his own earlier) view that an explanation or a single theory can explain away the misunderstandings generated by language. There is no need to devise theoretical explanations for philosophical problems because the problems can now be 'dissolved' if we remove the original misunderstandings. Philosophy is now viewed as a therapeutic activity (PI 255) and this is one of the many examples or 'cases' that Wittgenstein offers:

> Compare *knowing* and *saying*:
> How may feet high Mont Blanc is---
> How the word 'game' is used ---
> How a clarinet sounds

> If you are surprised that one can know something and not be able to say it, you are perhaps thinking of a case like the first. Certainly not of one like the third. (PI 78)

Here, Wittgenstein describes the differences in the way we use the concepts of knowing and saying in everyday life. If someone told us they know how high Mont Blanc is but then tell us that they cannot say how high it is, we would find this extremely odd. But we would not find it odd if someone told us they know what a clarinet sounds like but they cannot tell us for the simple reason that no such words for the sound of the clarinet exist. The important lesson that Wittgenstein wants to teach us here – both here and in the *Philosophical Investigations* in general – is that we are confusing different ways of thinking when we think that to know something is to be able to say it.

The purpose of these examples, metaphors and analogies is precisely that of reminding people what they know but seem to have forgotten. In this particular case, they are being dominated by a certain way of thinking that assumes one can always say what one knows. While at times it is perfectly possible to do this, as when I know how tall I am and can tell you, there are other instances when this is not possible. And this highlights the virtue of using numerous descriptions of the way language is used, for it is by describing the world that the differences between concepts can be brought out. It is the ability to discriminate between those situations that seem to resemble each other but which have subtle differences that mark the new approach.

Language games

One of the key concepts introduced in the *Philosophical Investigations* is that of language games. It is a concept used to describe the many different ways language is used within a community or a 'way of life'. As opposed to the abstract view of language in his early work, Wittgenstein is now interested in the activity of language and the way it is intermeshed with other social practices. By introducing the concept of language games, Wittgenstein wants to show that the way of thinking about language that had dominated him in the *Tractatus* is misleading.

In the *Tractatus*, he had argued that the only function of language was that of picturing the world with names referring to objects and meaning those objects. This idea of language is fairly common and he cites St. Augustine's view of language (PI 1) as a case in point of the extent to which it has dominated philosophical thinking about language. Wittgenstein shows that the flaw with the idea of language as naming is that it relies on ostension or pointing. If one argues that the meaning of a name is its object, then one would know the meaning of the word *cat* by pointing to a cat. The problem with this answer is that it assumes what it wants to prove: to know that the word means the cat, one would already have to have knowledge of English. Otherwise, how would one know if one was pointing to the colour of the cat, or its legs or its agility of movement? Pointing makes it impossible to learn a new language. In sum, the criticism of naming reveals two main difficulties: it fails to account for the way we acquire meaning and it fails to take into consideration the many different roles that language fulfils.

The idea of language having many functions is one of the key ideas of the *Investigations*. Wittgenstein calls the different functions or uses to which language is put *language games* and in Section 23, he lists many different kinds of language games, such as asking questions, giving orders, describing something, singing, translating, telling a joke and so on. What emerges from this list is the notion of language as constituting a series of communicative activities; Wittgenstein uses an analogy to bring home the point: 'Think of the tools in a tool-box; there is a hammer, pliers, a saw, a screwdriver, a rule, a glue-pot, nails and screws. The functions of words are as diverse as the functions of these objects' (PI 11).

The concept of language games is clearly opposed to the traditional essentialist account of meaning as a kind of object that can be defined. On this account, a word has a common meaning 'behind' all its different manifestations. For example, Wittgenstein asks, why is it that because we use the word *game* in so many ways (board-games, card-games, ball-games) then there must be something that all the different games have in common; otherwise we would not use the same word. But the sheer variety of games – some are played alone, some with others, some are competitive while others are not – puts paid to the idea that there is a single defining feature for all games. Since, in everyday life, we know how to use the word *game* despite the similarities and differences between the various games, Wittgenstein explains this ability we have by introducing the concept of family resemblances (PI 67): he describes individual family members as different even though they resemble each other in some respects. One might have the same hair colour as the other; another might have the same physique. Just as there is no one single characteristic that belongs to all the family, by analogy, there is no single feature that is common to all games.

It should be pointed out that Wittgenstein's emphasis on understanding the meaning of a word or expression by seeing the way it is used is not a return to theory building. The *Investigations* does not define meaning in terms of use but, more importantly, highlights the ability a person must have to be able to use expressions within their appropriate language game. In fact, Wittgenstein also talks about words and sentences in terms of their functions (PI 11), aims and purposes (PI 5), among others. On his account, there is a close connection between meaning and understanding, a connection that articulates understanding in terms of know-how, where one understands the meaning of an expression if one knows how to use it, if one knows the rules that are entailed in its usage.

Wittgenstein is here targeting those accounts that suggest that understanding the meaning of an expression is an inner mental process, something that goes on in one's head. This account is reminiscent of the *Tractatus* theory of meaning, where the meaning of an expression is like a picture or image in one's mind. This account is clearly empiricist in that it mistakenly equates the experience of something with its image as the meaning. While it is not unusual to associate certain experiences or memories of experiences with words, these associations do not constitute their meaning. Wittgenstein offers a number of reasons for rejecting the inner-mental view of understanding. I will mention two: the first is that if the meaning of a word is the mental association with that word, then different people will have different associations for that word, making communication impossible. The second reason is that even if we have an image in our mind, we would still not know what the meaning of that image is because we can associate any number of expressions with it. So, using Wittgenstein's example, the image of a cube still does not tell us what its meaning is, because we can associate any number of expressions with it (a cube of sugar, a box, an ice cube) and are therefore left in the predicament of not knowing how to understand the meaning of the word *cube* (PI 139–141).

Understanding the meaning of a sentence is therefore not a mental process such as imaging, but an activity or ability to do something (PI 199). On this account, understanding is a question of know-how and in the case of language it is a question of knowing how to use language. To understand the meaning of a sentence is, in effect, to understand how to use that sentence appropriately. Understanding the meaning of a word or a sentence entails being able to utilize it in various contexts with specific aims in mind. The notions of appropriateness and ability tie the concept of language games to that of the 'form of life': 'the term "language-*game*" is meant to bring into prominence the fact that the speaking of language is part of an activity, or a form of life' (PI 23).

By 'form of life', Wittgenstein means the total set of linguistic and non-linguistic (customs, traditions, beliefs) practices that are shared by a community. Language is not detached from the life of the community but intimately connected to it. Through language the continued existence of the community as a specific 'form of life' is ensured, for when the language is learnt it is also the way of life that is being transmitted and learnt. When it comes to questions of justification, there is nothing beyond the 'form of life' for the 'form of life' is the point at which justification is impossible. Understanding certain concepts cannot be explained further other than by pointing out that this is the way they are used within a form of life (PI 217).

Rules and the private language argument

Wittgenstein's emphasis on understanding the meaning of a sentence in terms of being able to use that sentence is clearly connected to the idea that there are specific rules for each language game that one must follow or observe (PI 143–242). The crucial point concerning the notion of rules that he wants to establish is that something counts as a rule only if a community has agreed upon it. 'The word "agreement" and the word "rule" are related to one another, they are cousins. If I teach anyone the use of one word, he learns the use of the other with it' (PI 224).

Rules are, therefore, not imposed externally on the person and neither are they independent of the actual practices of members of a community. Rather, rules are created by the community and manifested in their public usage. Just as the rules of a game are a product of convention and are activated through their being used, the same argument applies both to rules in general, and to linguistic rules. Wittgenstein's example of a signpost brings the point home: a signpost's function of guiding us to our destination is not a matter of imposition, but a matter of a practice that has been conventionally established coupled with our understanding of that convention (P 85). Rules, like the signpost, guide members of a community.

This emphasis on the communal aspect of rule formation and adherence serves to counter the view that it is possible for a single person to create his/her own rules which only he/she is obliged to follow. The problem with this view is that there would be no way of knowing if that person was following the rule or not, since it would be a private affair. And, as Wittgenstein points out, there is a big difference between thinking one is following a rule and actually following it (PI 202). For the latter to take place it must be possible to check whether the rule was being obeyed or not, and hence the need for public criteria. Rules are external to the individual but internal to the community.

Wittgenstein's discussion of rules and language as a 'form of life' brings out the social dimension of language. This social dimension plays an important role in Wittgenstein's critique of what has become known as the private language argument (PI 243–363). The private language argument takes its cue from the Cartesian view of the world as composed of two substances, mental and physical. Mental substances are immaterial and as a result have no spatial location, while material substances exist in a particular space and have certain properties, such as mass and weight. The mental and the material are completely opposed to each other, and this creates a number of problems: (1) the problem of explaining their interaction. If a person is composed of a mind and a body then how is it possible for the immaterial mind to cause the material body to do something as when I decide to go for a coffee? An unbridgeable gap between the mental and the physical has been created because the mental is equated with the inner or private and the physical with the outer or public. (2) This problem follows from the first: since there is this unbridgeable gap between the mental and the material, then the only knowledge of which we can be certain of is that concerning what we are immediately acquainted with, such as our own mental states. Any knowledge of the external world or other mental states can only be inferred. For Descartes, while I might not be sure about what has happened in the world, I can be certain about what is happening in my mind; his thinking has established a distinction between an inner (mental) world and an external (material) world.

Wittgenstein's criticism of the private language argument is, in effect, a criticism of this inner–outer distinction. There are parallels between the Cartesian model and the private language argument: with the Cartesian model, a person is certain only about his/her own mental states, while with the private language argument, a solitary person names objects or experiences, and alone knows what the words he/she has invented refer to, making it intelligible only to him/her. Many people might be comfortable with the private language argument because they think of their own mental states as private, as something to which only they have access. But to be able to construct his/her own private language there must be set of rules that enable the speaker to connect words to things or experiences.

Wittgenstein employs a number of reasons to demonstrate the inherent mistake of the private language argument. The first of these involve the concept of rules: a language is a rule-governed system and for something to count as a rule it must have some criterion for establishing when the rule was being followed or broken; if it were not possible to break a rule, then the whole notion of rules would itself not make sense. The second reason connects the concept of rules to that of the form of life: it is the community that creates the rules that are transmitted and learnt by successive generations of that community; this is what makes the rules public. When we use language to talk about our private mental states, we are using a medium that has shared public criteria for establishing ways of talking about mental states. Since the rules for using expressions are public, there can be no private language to talk about private experiences. It is the fact that rules are embedded and shared within a 'form of life' that makes communication between members of a community possible. By highlighting the publicness of rules and language, Wittgenstein undermines the subjectivity of 'private' mental states, for any talk about such mental states is only possible with a language that is itself always already social. This is why, Wittgenstein argues, when we use expressions to talk about pain, what we learn as children, is to associate expressions of pain with behaviour: 'A child has hurt himself and he cries; and then adults talk to him and teach him exclamations and, later, sentences' (PI 244). What is thought of as private mental states (happiness, pain) is, in effect, a natural expression of human behaviour (smiling, grimacing); and this natural behaviour has been replaced with a language that can be used to talk about that behaviour.

Wittgenstein and film theory

Various theorists from a spectrum of disciplines have elaborated upon Wittgenstein's ideas in the context of their own studies. Thus (for example), in 'Nishida and Wittgenstein: from 'pure experience' to *Lebensform* or new perspectives for a philosophy of intercultural communication' (2003) Thorsten Botz-Bornstein has compared Wittgenstein with Nishida to identify a common ground for intercultural communication; and in 'Wittgenstein's Tractatus Project as Philosophy of Information' (2004), R. A. Young finds in the early Wittgenstein a contribution to information theory. Another area in which Wittgensteinian ideas have been used is that of film theory, in (for example) Rupert J. Read and Jerry Goodenough's *Film as Philosophy: Essays on Cinema after Wittgenstein and Cavell* (2005) and Edward Branigan's *Projecting a Camera: Language-Games in Film Theory* (2006). For the purposes of this section

I am focussing on a short paper presented to the Society for Cinema and Media Studies by Edward Branigan, namely 'Wittgenstein, Language-Games, Film Theory (2005).

Branigan's concern in this paper is to utilize Wittgenstein's concept of language games so as to better understand the '*iconography* of grammatical objects' ('image', 'frame', 'shot', 'camera', 'point of view', 'editing', 'style', 'realism', 'auteur', 'performance', 'spectatorship' and 'medium specificity') that constitute the staples of film theory. Branigan selects one of the aforementioned grammatical objects – the camera – to describe how the many various uses of the camera are connected to the form of life of the cinema (2005: 2).

While at first sight, it would seem that the camera is a fairly easy object to theorize this simplicity is beguiling in that it would be mistaken to conceptualize the camera as having some sort of identity that constitutes the basis or a common ground throughout its various usages. If we say that it is the camera that creates the feeling of movement in a film, would it therefore make sense to say that a specific weight with a specific serial number is the cause of the feeling of movement? The problem is that since a specific camera is used for certain shots and other cameras for other shots would it make sense to say that the spectator is referring or knows which camera is being used in a particular sequence of shots (2005: 2)? And Branigan adds that even a more generalized account of the camera, as the total weights and numbers of the cameras used in a particular film, is inadequate in that one would still have to account for all the other films together with their cameras. The apparent solution would be to construct a highly abstract camera defined by a number of very general features such as a box with a lens, diaphragm, shutter and film, and so on, and if the list of defining features proves to be too long, then the opposite tack might be taken and just say a 'box' (2005: 2–3). Despite all these possibilities Branigan argues that they fail to take into account one key feature of film: the experience of viewing a fiction. Being able to use a camera and knowing that cameras have been used to create films is very different both from knowing how to use a camera to construct a fictional narrative and from the actual experience of a fictional and narrative movement (2005: 3).

Perhaps, some might suggest, a camera is an object that functions as a guide, guiding the viewer in the film. Once again, Branigan points out, this assumes that there is an essential core meaning to the concept of guiding as though it has some invariant meaning throughout its different usages. The notion that the camera guides the viewer assumes that the film is a linear and ongoing movement in a certain direction that creates the effect of guidance for the viewer. But, the question this raises is, how does one know which parts of the film one is to focus on to create the effect of being guided? From the many different parts of a film, how would one put the parts together to produce the action of guiding and the effect of being guided? Instead of such an approach, Branigan argues for a more 'cautious' approach, reminding us that there are many different ways of being guided but these must include the feeling of being guided and that we feel that we are being guided in a film on account the influence that the film has upon us. It is our performance or the generation of expectations, memories, surprises, fantasies and so on as well as our responses to being guided that contribute to the feeling of being guided (2005: 3).

Branigan suggests that a better approach to understand the concept of a camera is to examine the way the word functions to describe the experience of watching a film. This Wittgensteinian approach to the language-game of film specifies that there are as many cameras in film theory, each of which depends upon a specific context of use, on what is expected or wanted of a particular film theory. He writes, '[t]here are many film theory language-games and all must be evaluated on the basis of changing, pragmatic criteria as well as evaluated on the basis of their interface with the *practices* that count for us' (2005: 6).

On Branigan's account an iconography of film theory that derives its inspiration from Wittgenstein would be:

1. Grammatical: film theory would only consist of a specific grammar ('frame', 'shot', 'camera', 'editing', 'sound', 'style', 'realism', 'auteur', 'performance', 'spectatorship' and 'medium specificity').
2. Intersubjective: film theory would not be considered as dealing with objective or universal propositions but tied closely to the social practices and values of the context of film.
3. Fragmentary: given an acceptance of the lack of objectivity or uniformity of film theory then it should be realized that film theory is partial, temporary and historical.
4. Figurative: film theory is no longer the domain of abstraction but rather of metaphoric projections that find their origin in bodily experiences, concepts and so on.
5. Connected: film theory should explain film not analytically, that is, by breaking a film down into simpler units and forming a hierarchy, but as a network of interconnections that form a *heter*archy.
6. Impure: film theory is impure in the sense that there is nothing exclusive to film theory as though it were isolated and pure; on the contrary, film is impure because it is situated within a culture and a history.

In this section, I have shown one of the many ways in which ideas from the philosophy of Wittgenstein have been explored within the discourse of film theory. There are, as I have mentioned in the introduction to this section, many other areas of exploration and it is evident that richness and complexity of his thought will also penetrate other areas of communication studies.

Critical remarks

Wittgenstein has exerted considerable influence on philosophy in the twentieth century. This influence can be seen in both traditions of contemporary analytic and continental philosophy with the result that there is a virtual publishing industry offering different interpretations of various aspects of his philosophy. The variety can be seen in the way studies on Wittgenstein were, for some time, divided into two stages, characterized by the *Tractatus* and the *Investigations*, an approach that is being increasingly challenged; and there is an increasing consensus among scholars that there is a third Wittgenstein, characterized by the text *On Certainty* (1969).

Moreover, even in the early-later approach to Wittgensteinian studies there is considerable debate over the relationship between the two texts. Wittgenstein himself thought that both texts should be placed next to each other if only for the latter to expose the defects of the former. However, while some argue that these two texts complement each other, others argue that they are opposed to each other. K.T. Fann (1969: xii) suggests a more nuanced approach in that the texts complement each other on questions concerning the nature and tasks of philosophy but are opposed to each other with regards to the method Wittgenstein uses in his philosophical analysis.

Others point to problems internal to the respective texts. Grayling, for example, argues that (1) while it might seem obvious to say that a proposition pictures a fact, what it is that constitutes a fact is not so obvious. The proposition *The cat is on the mat* can be construed as having two names (cat, mat) and a relation connecting them (on) but what the proposition represents, that is, the fact, is different for there is only a *cat* and a *mat* but no *on*, for this is an abstract relation. In addition, Wittgenstein had argued that when words function as names for objects that are simple, that is, they cannot be further broken down. But clearly it is mistaken to say that *cat* names the object cat since cats are not simple objects as they can be broken down further into colour, size, changing properties and so on. Wittgenstein's own account makes it difficult to see what is an object or a name (1988: 52–53). (2) There also are difficulties with the notion that some things cannot be spoken about but shown: since values do not belong to the world of facts, Wittgenstein places them beyond the world, in effect, dislocating them from everyday life. But it seems that values and ethics are part and parcel of everyday life since many times our moral choices need to take into consideration the facts of the situation. In addition, Grayling points out that if values merely showed themselves, then there should be no disagreements between people about them and nobody would defend or attack the ethics of one another (1988: 55).

The early Wittgenstein exerted considerable influence on the Logical Positivists, who, perhaps mistakenly, appropriated him as the father figure of this movement. Wittgenstein, however, did not accept their conclusions, and the distance between their respective ways of thinking can be measured with the ideas that were then published in the *Philosophical Investigations*. Habermas (1987a, 2001), among others, recognizes the value of the later Wittgenstein as central to the linguistic turn of philosophy away from questions of epistemology that had dominated modern philosophy. The emphasis of modern philosophy had been directed at consciousness, which prioritized the solitary individual such that considerations of both language and knowledge had been reduced to an examination of the thought processes and perceptions of the isolated individual. With the linguistic turn that characterized twentieth-century philosophy, the centrality of language to the formation of self-identity, perception and knowledge displaced the individual with the social.

Another philosopher who has made extensive use of the later Wittgenstein is J. F. Lyotard who, in *The Postmodern Condition: A Report on Knowledge* (1979), has adopted the concept of language games in his analysis of contemporary society. Lyotard argues that the proliferation of discourses that characterize contemporary society can be likened to the language games of a community within which norms and values are internally justified. There is, therefore, no external standard with which to assess a discourse just as there is no external standard with which to assess a 'form of life'. While Lyotard uses Wittgenstein's concept of language games to account for the different discourses within the postmodern world, not everybody would concur with his account as it seems to justify relativism.

In this chapter, I have outlined (1) the philosophical context that provide the starting point for Wittgenstein's philosophy (2) an overview of the picture theory of language and (3) the fundamental distinction between saying and showing. The rest of the chapter is taken up with (4) the new distinction between describing and explaining (5) the concept of language games and Wittgenstein's critique of the private language argument. The chapter ends (6) with an account that demonstrates the use of Wittgenstein in film theory.

Chapter 8

J. L. Austin and Speech Act Theory

J. L. Austin (1911–60) inaugurated a branch in the philosophy of language that subsequently came to be known as ordinary language philosophy. Unlike those philosophers who focussed on the construction of formal or idealized languages, he studied the workings of everyday natural language as used in different situations of communication. As a result, the emphasis of his study shifted towards the role of the speaker, listener and context within which communication takes place. The emphasis upon the context reveals that the study of communicative processes entails not only an examination of the actual utterances, but also a crucial evaluation of the conventions that underlie such utterances.

Although Austin did not publish much during his lifetime, his writings have been published posthumously and include the *Philosophical Papers* (1961), *Sense and Sensibilia* (1975) and *How to Do Things with Words* (1975). In these writings, Austin examines various philosophical problems, and his innovative approach to the way they should be analysed has guaranteed his legacy.

In this chapter I will first outline (1) Austin's suggestions on the methodology of ordinary language philosophy and will follow this with (2) an examination of the distinction between constative and performative utterances. The next section will focus on (3) Austin's analysis of performatives that leads to (4) the development of speech act theory. The last section will show how (5) Austin's insights have been put to use by Butler in her analysis of hate speech.

The method of linguistic analysis

In 'A Plea for Excuses' (1979: 175–204), Austin outlines his particular method of linguistic analysis as a way of proceeding from ordinary everyday language 'by examining *what we should say when*, and so why and what we should man by it' (1979: 181). He justifies this method on the following grounds:

1. to avoid being misled:

> [W]ords are our tools, and, as a minimum, we should use clean tools: we should know what we mean and what we do not, and we must forearm ourselves against the traps that language sets us. (1979: 181–182)

2. to learn more about the world:

> [W]ords are not (except in their own little corner) facts or things: we need therefore to prise them off the world, to hold them apart from and against it, so that we can realize their inadequacies and arbitrariness, and can re-look at the world without blinkers. (1979: 182)

3. to avoid specialization or technical jargon:

> [O]ur common stock of words embodies all the distinctions men have found worth drawing, and the connections they have found worth marking, in the lifetimes of many generations: these surely are likely to be more numerous, more sound, since they have stood up to the long test of the survival of the fittest, and more subtle, at least in all ordinary and reasonably practical matters, than any that you or I are likely to think up in our arm-chairs of an afternoon – the most favoured alternative method. (1979: 182)

After having elaborated the reasons for his choice of method, Austin offers some more suggestions on the method with which he conducts his philosophical analysis of the concept of excuses in 'A Plea for Excuses' (1979: 175–04):

1. the use of the dictionary. Using the dictionary to find the relevant definitions must be *'thorough'*, and there are two ways in which the dictionary can be used – (a) by listing all the relevant words and looking them up; and (b) by selecting a large number of relevant words, looking up the definition and carefully noting other relevant words that are in turn also looked up. Eventually repetitions will occur. 'This method has the advantage of grouping the terms into convenient clusters – but, of course, a good deal will depend upon the comprehensiveness of our initial selection' (1979: 187).
2. the use of textbooks. Austin considers the resources of the law and those of psychology as invaluable:

> With these sources, and with the aid of the imagination, it will go hard if we cannot arrive at the meanings of large numbers of expressions and at the understanding and classification of large numbers of 'actions'. (1979: 189)

3. imagined or actual cases. Elsewhere, in 'Three Ways of Spilling Ink' (1979: 272–87), Austin suggests starting his philosophical analysis by considering 'imagined or actual cases'. By this he means that one either selects an actual conversation for analysis to see what is appropriate to use in a particular situation or imaginatively reconstructs a possible conversation to see what should be said in a particular situation. Having collected the 'data', one must then proceed to explain it, and Austin suggests that the use of 'such

methods as "Agreement" and "Difference" [show] what is in fact present in the cases where we do use, say, "deliberately", and what is absent when we don't' (1979: 274). It is by using this method of comparison and contrast that what is specific to each expression can be highlighted.

4. 'the "grammar", "etymology" and so forth of the words' (1979: 274). The point of examining both the grammar and the etymology is that over time, the grammar and morphology that has 'survived' will teach us a lot about the meaning of the expression (1979: 282).

An essential part of Austin's philosophical practice required a conscientious involvement with minute details concerning idioms and expressions. There are a number of instances in the *Philosophical Papers* (1979) that demonstrate this concern: he looks for the difference between knowing that a bird is a gold finch from its red head and knowing that it is a gold finch because it has a red head (1979: 84); or the difference between acting deliberately, acting intentionally and acting on purpose (1979: 275). In *How to Do Things with Words* (1975), Austin distinguishes between what I do in saying something and what I do by saying something (1975: 121–31).

This scrupulous attention to detail raises an important question: are these details philosophically important or are they merely the historical variations of a language that offer interesting insights but seem philosophically trivial? Austin's position is that if there is a difference then there is a rational explanation for this difference, and this implies that it is not just an unimportant coincidence but something that should be looked into. The difference might not be evident, but the point of linguistic analysis is to find the difference that makes the difference.

Austin justifies his belief in the value of ordinary language on the grounds that it has evolved into its current usage and that it therefore represents the best there is. Given that the language available – ordinary language – embodies all the necessary features for our understanding, why should this be replaced by a jargon that creates more confusion than clarity? The general thrust of Austin's philosophical method is to leave everything as it is, to describe what the 'plain man' says, without trying to improve upon it.

Constatives and performatives

One of the movements that dominated the Western philosophical tradition for a relatively brief period was that of logical positivism. The logical positivists devised what came to be known as the verification principle, which stated that for a statement to be meaningful it must be verified either as true or false; if there is no way of verifying it, then the statement is 'condemned' to meaninglessness. This theory faced two fundamental difficulties: the first one was that the verification principle itself was impossible to verify and should therefore also be considered meaningless; the second difficulty was that a large number of things we talk about – beauty, morality, religion – cannot be verified, so that these utterances would be considered meaningless. However, although meaningless, the logical positivists did not advocate eliminating such utterances from our everyday discourse. They explained these utterances as expressions of subjectivity, so that, for example, the utterance *the cake is good* is another way of saying 'I like the cake'.

It is against this background that Austin can be read. Throughout his writings, Austin resists the fairly common idea that the primary function of language is that of describing reality. To this end, he coined the phrase *descriptive fallacy*. In his posthumously published work *How to Do Things with Words*, Austin declares that his goal is to demonstrate that the truth-conditional theory of meaning is not central to the study of language. Austin introduces the terminology of 'constatives' to discuss the use of statements whose function it is to 'constate' something of the world, something that is true or false (1975: 3). According to this view, we have language on one side and the world on the other; when a statement represents the world we consider it to be true, and when it does not we consider it false. However, it is evident that there are many other uses of language that have been largely neglected by formal semantic theorists. Particular attention should be paid to the use of language from the point of view of the speakers, and Austin coins the term *performative* to describe the way speakers use language to perform actions. He offers the following examples:

(E.a.) 'I do (sc. take this woman to be my lawful wedded wife)' – as uttered in the course of the marriage ceremony.

(E.b.) 'I name this ship the *Queen Elizabeth*' – as uttered when smashing the bottle against the stem.

(E.c.) 'I give and bequeath my watch to my brother' – as occurring in a will.

(E.d.) 'I bet you sixpence it will rain tomorrow.' (1975: 5)

These utterances cannot be assessed in terms of the true and the false; rather by uttering them one is, in fact, performing an action. Utterances such as *I bet you sixpence it will rain tomorrow* or *I hereby christen this ship the Queen Elizabeth* are not the sort of utterances that one claims as true or false. It just would not make sense to answer 'false' to *I hereby christen this ship*. The point of these utterances is not to describe facts or states of affairs, but crucially to do things. When the prime minister utters 'I declare war on Zanzibar', he/she is going to war, with the various issues that such an utterance involves – listening to the military, persuading the nation and so on. After war has been declared, the world is not the same place for something has happened: the words uttered have transformed the world. Likewise, when a person says 'I do' (within the context of a wedding ceremony), the person is not describing his/her wedding ceremony but getting married. The couple's life is different from the life they enjoyed before they got married.

But Austin is at pains to show that getting married is not a question of 'just' uttering a few words (1975: 8), since these words acquire their performativity through the established conventions of a particular society. He offers an analysis of the conventions that need to be fulfilled for the utterance to perform its function:

(A.1) There must exist an accepted conventional procedure having a certain conventional effect, that procedure to include the uttering of certain words by certain persons in certain circumstances, and further,

(A.2) the particular persons and circumstances in a given case must be appropriate for the invocation of the particular procedure invoked.

(B.1) The procedure must be executed by all participants both correctly and

(B.2) completely.

(Γ.1) Where, as often, the procedure is designed for use by persons having certain thoughts or feelings, or for the inauguration of certain consequential conduct on the part of any participant, then a person participating in and so invoking the procedure must in fact have those thoughts or feelings, and the participants must intend so to conduct themselves, and further

(Γ.2) must actually so conduct themselves subsequently. (1975: 14–15)

In the case of (A. 1), by saying 'I do' one is in effect getting married, as long as (A.2) there are witnesses, a priest or magistrate, and neither of the couple is already or still married. In the case of (B.1), the whole procedure of getting married must be enacted correctly, so the right words must be uttered. In response to the question of whether the bride wants to take the bridegroom, the performative would fail if she answered 'maybe'. And (B.2) what is meant by completion is that the utterance is acknowledged, so that if, for example, one makes a bet, the other person must acknowledge that he/she is taking part in a bet by shaking hands and saying 'you're on'. Austin calls this acknowledgement 'uptake'. In the case of (Γ.1), we are in the domain of the sincerity with which the speaker expresses his/her intentions; to accuse someone of something that the speaker knows is not the case is a violation of (Γ.1) just as it is a violation of (Γ.2) if one promises to do something that he/she has no intention of keeping.

The early Austin distinguished between performatives and constatives, identifying the different characteristics of each. While constatives are descriptive utterances that can be either true or false, the values associated with performatives are those of success or failure. Austin introduces the terminology of 'happy' and 'unhappy' to describe the success or failure of performatives through the fulfilment of certain conditions that he calls the 'felicity conditions'. While performatives might not be true or false, they might succeed or fail and it is always possible for them to go wrong. Austin calls failed performatives 'infelicitous'.

In the doctrine of infelicities, Austin outlines the ways in which performatives can fail (1975: 14–44):

1. they 'misfire' when there is no conventional procedure in a particular context. If I say 'I order you to chop wood' in a context where there is no conventional system for ordering or accepting orders, then the order has misfired; likewise, when someone does not follow the procedure completely, as when I write a will saying 'I leave everything to my son' and inadvertently forget to sign it.
2. they can be 'abusive': these are the more serious of the unhappy performatives for they are associated with the insincerity of the speaker. If I say 'I promise to return the money tomorrow' when I have no intention of returning the money, this is not merely a case of the conventional procedures failing, but of an abuse of the conventional procedures. Another abuse occurs when I apologize but do not mean it: in this case, my apology is an insincere one.

Although both misfires and abuses are instances of performative failure, Austin differentiates between them on the grounds that abuses involve an act of deception and are therefore more serious than misfires.

The emphasis here is on the relation between the speaker and the world. In the case of the constative, it is a question of whether the statement matches or fails to match the world. In the case of performatives, the world is changed by virtue of the performative being uttered: to say 'I do' successfully is to change the world, since it is now a different place, one in which I am married.

The analysis of performatives

Since Austin places so much emphasis on the performative–constative distinction, his next step is to identify the specific characteristics of the performatives so as to find out why they constitute a class of their own. Their characteristics are the first person, present indicative active (1975: 57). Despite being couched as a question, it seems that these are the characteristics of a performative utterance, and they are justified on the grounds that since the speaker is doing the action through the act of uttering it, it would necessarily involve the first person.

Before conducting his analysis, Austin pre-empts two possible objections to his use of the grammatical form to identity performatives:

1. the first objection is that they constitute an incidental feature of language and cannot really be the identifying sign of a performative. But Austin points out that if a

performative is the doing of something, it must be something that is done by an agent, and this agent is the speaker. The use of the grammatical form of the first person shows precisely this.

2. the second objection is that the grammatical form can also be used with constatives (e.g. 'I want to have a drink'). Austin responds by pointing out that performatives are asymmetrical while constatives are symmetrical so that, for example, a performative is effective only if it is uttered by the speaker: to say *he promises* does not constitute a promise (1975: 63).

Despite this defence of the grammatical form, Austin still finds a number of faults with them:

1. the use of the first person in the active voice is not necessary since a performative can be uttered in the passive voice, so that 'You are hereby authorised to pay [...] and Passengers are warned to cross the track by the bridge only' (1975: 57) are both performatives (1975: 57).

2. there are even more serious challenges to the criterion. (a) The present tense: instead of using the present tense 'I find you guilty', I might say 'you did it'; (b) the indicative mood: instead of the indicative mood 'I order you to turn right', I might say 'Turn right'(1975: 58).[1]

3. there is also the problem that the first person can be also used to describe routine actions rather than the doing of things, such as, for example, 'I bet him (every morning) sixpence that it will rain' (1975: 64).

4. while the first person in the present tense differs from that of the continuous tense, the latter can be used at times in a performative manner, so that 'I can say 'I am protesting' when performing the act, by, in this case, means other than saying 'I protest', for example by chaining myself to park railings' (1975: 64).[2]

The attempt to establish characteristics that identify performatives faces increasing difficulties. There are some utterances that have the requisite grammatical form, but which we would not want to allow into the class of performatives as it would broaden the class of performatives excessively: ' "I state that" seems to conform to our grammatical or quasi-grammatical requirements: but do we want *it* in?' (1975: 68). So too, Austin points out, the use of the grammatical form as a criterion for performativity can be too narrow: by telling someone 'I insult you', I am not doing anything, I am not insulting the person. The grammatical form does not indicate the presence of a performative and is misleading (1975: 68).

Another problem with the performative–constative distinction is the class of utterances that do not seem to fit within either of the two, where it is unclear whether the utterance is a performative or a constative. It is evident that when we say, 'I feel repentant' we are describing our state and are therefore issuing a constative. Likewise, when we say 'I apologise' we are doing something – apologizing – and are, therefore, issuing a performative. But some utterances are dubious: 'I am sorry' and 'I am grateful' can be considered both as performatives and constatives (1975: 79).

In his analysis of performatives, Austin introduces a further distinction between primary performatives and explicit performatives. An example of a primary performative is *I shall be there* while an example of an explicit performative is *I promise that I shall be there* (1975: 69). The distinction shows that without the explicit formula the first utterance can be understood in different ways, for example, as the expression of an intention or as a hopeful desire. The function of the 'explicit' is parallel to certain non-linguistic actions: Austin describes the convention of bowing and saying 'Salaam' at the same time. If I say 'Salaam' as I bow before you, I am performing the action of greeting you and not examining your shoes. By bowing and saying 'Salaam' I am making explicit my greetings to you. In a similar fashion, explicit performatives 'make plain how the action is to be taken or understood, what action it is' (1975: 70).

Austin also realizes that although performatives are explicit, since they are unambiguous or specific ways of saying what one is doing, there are other indirect ways of saying that achieve the same results. These are (1) the mood, so that instead of saying 'I order you to shut it', I say 'Shut it'; (2) the intonation, where one uses a different tone of voice to express 'it's going to charge', either as a warning or a question; (3) the use of adverbs, where instead of saying 'I promise I'll be there', one says 'I'll be there without fail'; (4) connecting particles, where instead of saying 'I conclude that X', one says 'therefore X'; (5) non-verbal accompaniments, such as frowns, pointing and so on; (6) the context, where, for example, the health of the speaker influences the way the utterance *I shall die some day* is understood (1975: 73–77). What this list shows is that primary performatives can perform the same function, or do the same things as explicit ones; in other words, to perform an action it is not necessary to have the grammatical form of the explicit performatives.

Austin's inability to identify performatives shifts his analysis towards a questioning of the strict dichotomy that separated performatives from constatives. He points out that:

1. they are not mutually exclusive. The utterance *I warn you the bull will charge* is performing an act of warning, but it can also be judged as true or false. In a similar vein, there is no reason why a constative could not be described as true or false, and in addition also perform an action (1975: 55).
2. there are features common to both performatives and constatives that Austin calls 'presupposition', so that both constatives and performatives can fail if certain presuppositions are not in place. For instance, if a person says 'when I die you will inherit my Caravaggio', without having any Caravaggio painting then the utterance is a failure because it is stating things that should not be assumed in the first place. Similarly with performatives, if I advise you to join the French Foreign Legion without knowing anything about the military, I fail to give you good advice (1975: 50–51).
3. furthermore, the distinction between the performative and the constative is undermined by observing the sincerity of the speaker. Sincerity is not only related to performatives

but also to constatives, so that a promise must be uttered sincerely for it to succeed just as a description requires the sincerity of the speaker to establish its truth claim (the Earth revolves around the Sun but I don't believe it) (1975: 50).

It might be claimed that the difference between constatives and performatives could lie in the area of their respective values: while performatives admit of degrees of success and failure, in the domain of constatives there are no degrees of truth and falsity. A performative can be more or less successful, while a constative is either true or false. Austin questions this claim, arguing that there are many constative utterances that are not formulated with a strict demarcation of their truth. The utterance *France is hexagonal* is not the description of the precise shape of France, but a rough estimate which is not meant to be answered as either true or false (1975: 143).

Speech act theory

By the second half of *How to Do Things with Words*, Austin gives up on his goal of identifying the specific features of performatives and broadens his inquiry into an analysis of how saying something is also doing something. It is the study of language as a whole that is now being considered. However, despite abandoning his early performative–constative distinction, Austin realizes that although the insight that some utterances perform actions was correct, the way this insight was generalized was mistaken. As a result, Austin proposes a new theory that subsumes within it the insights that were learnt from the performative–constative distinction. This new theory is called the Theory of Speech Acts and its central thesis was that all utterances – whether performative or constative – involved the doing of an action. In 'Performative Utterances', Austin writes:

> besides the question that has been very much studied in the past as to what a certain utterance *means*, there is a further question distinct from this as to what was the *force*, as we call it, of the utterance. We may be quite clear what 'Shut the door' means, but not yet at all clear on the further point as to whether as uttered at a certain time, it was an order, an entreaty or whatnot. (1979: 251)

Before elaborating on the details of Austin's theory of speech acts, it might be fruitful to examine the sense in which speech can be said to constitute an action. There is the act of producing a sound, of producing sounds in a sequence to form a sentence and of producing sentences that have a meaning. These three features are called the phonetic, the phatic and the rhetic, respectively. The phonetic is the basic level of sound production through the use of the vocal chords; the phatic involves the use of sounds that have been transformed into words and that are stringed together according to the rules of grammar to generate sentences

---

and the rhetic aspect is that involving the meaning of sentences, dressing sentences with a sense and reference (1975: 95).

Taken together these constitute what Austin calls the locutionary aspect and distinguishes it from the illocutionary and perlocutionary act. These are the differences between them.

1. the locutionary act: this is the basic and fundamental level of a speech act because it literally involves doing something. When we speak, we produce sounds that are words which are combined into sentences to generate a meaning.
2. the illocutionary act: although it is evident that someone has said something it is not necessarily evident what the force of that utterance is. Austin uses the example of 'it's going to charge': should this be understood as a warning or a statement (1975: 98)? The illocutionary force can take different forms such as making promises, praying, joking, ordering and – crucially within speech act theory – making a statement. So too the illocutionary force involves taking into consideration the speaker and the intentions with which he/she communicates. The illocutionary act is a form of saying that qualifies as doing something such as promising, asking, announcing and so on (1975: 98–99).
3. the perlocutionary act: the saying of something can also affect another person. In this sense, our saying is also a doing: we did something to the other person, such as convince them, make them laugh (1975: 101).

However, Austin is chiefly interested in the illocutionary aspect of the speech act, and his working method consists in comparing it with the locutionary and perlocutionary acts. In relation to this he examined

1. the difference between an illocutionary and a perlocutionary act. According to Austin, while perlocutionary utterances are the subject of empirical investigation, since they can be verified, illocutionary utterances are the subject of an a priori philosophical analysis. Austin maintained that any utterance can produce a perlocutionary act, so what is required is an empirical analysis of which utterances produce a certain effect. In the case of illocutionary utterances, it is not an empirical examination that will tell us whether the utterance is illocutionary or not.

However, there is a further and perhaps more significant way of bringing out the difference between illocutionary and perlocutionary acts revolving around the question of 'effect': 'the performance of an illocutionary act involves securing of *uptake*' (1975: 117). In the case of illocutionary acts, all that is required is that the listeners understand the utterance, while with perlocutionary acts the listener not only understands but changes his/her views or behaviour.

For an action to count as an illocution it is enough that the listener understand the speaker's intention, for it to count as a perlocution the listener's attitudes, his beliefs –

what, for want of a better expression, we may call roughly his 'mental state' – must be affected in some way. (Friggieri 1991: 206)[3]

Given this identification of illocutionary acts as not having consequences, then Austin's claim that they are the a priori material for philosophical investigation might be justified.

Austin also took great interest in the conflicts and misunderstandings that arise between the illocutionary force of the utterance and its perlocutionary effects. The locutionary act 'shoot her' has the illocutionary force of urging or advising or commanding, with the perlocutionary effect being that of persuading me to shoot her. In this case, the intention as expressed by the speaker is understood by the hearer. But the relationship between the speaker's intention and the hearer's response are not necessarily synchronized: the hearer could be frightened by the speaker's utterance, and object to the speaker's utterance –regarded as dangerous or unwarranted – in the first place. The perlocutionary effect is unpredictable and context-dependent (Levinson 1983: 236–37).[4]

2. the difference between the locutionary and the illocutionary acts. This is an important question because if we take the locutionary act to be the production of a meaningful utterance, then what is the scope of the illocutionary act? Austin insisted that this was an aspect of the philosophy of language that was of crucial importance (1975: 100), but his difficulty lay in how to formulate the nature of illocutionary acts. On the one hand, he had to prevent illocutionary acts from being 'reduced' to locutionary acts (meaning), while at the same time he had to show that they were different from perlocutionary acts, being subject to empirical verification. Austin's difficulty lay in carving out the specific domain of illocutionary acts.

Austin starts by claiming 'a locutionary act is in general, we may say, also and *eo ipso* to perform an illocutionary act' (1975: 98). Here he is bringing home the point that by virtue of uttering something, I am producing a sentence with a meaning (locutionary act) and simultaneously doing something else such as asking, commanding and/or promising (illocutionary act). They are not two separate actions, but one.

However, Austin clearly distinguishes between the meaning of the locutionary utterance and the force of the illocutionary utterance. The meaning of the locutionary utterance should be understood in the sense of Frege's distinction between the sense and reference of an utterance, while the force of the illocutionary should be understood in the sense of what we do, or how we use the locutionary (1975: 100). One can understand what is meant by 'The bull is about to charge', but might not understand if it was meant as a warning or a statement (Friggieri 1991: 189).

3. the question of whether it is possible to identify an illocutionary act through its grammatical form. Austin offers these examples: 'He said "get out"', 'He told me to get out', [and] 'He said "Is it in Oxford or Cambridge?"'; 'He asked whether it was in Oxford

or Cambridge' (1975: 95). From these examples Austin concludes that *tell* and *ask* are the illocutionary acts of ordering and asking, respectively. Given that there is no indication of the context of their production, it would seem that there is a grammatical form that enables us to identify illocutionary utterances: in these examples, they are the grammatical forms of the imperative and the interrogative. Perhaps this is why Austin insisted that illocutionary acts are conventional, since they followed conventional grammatical forms (1975: 103; also, 105, 118).

The problem with this view is that while there are certain grammatical forms for asking and telling, there are no grammatical forms for warning, toasting or making an appeal. Clearly the grammatical form is not applicable to all illocutionary utterances, and Austin goes on to suggest another possibility for identifying illocutionary utterances. When talking about illocutionary utterances it should also be possible to say 'he meant it as […]' (1975: 100), highlighting the point that it is what the speaker intends to mean by his/her utterance that is important. And if the illocutionary force is not communicated, then this is a failing of the speaker.

However, the emphasis on speaker intentionality is not entirely successful. For a start it is difficult to maintain the view of illocutionary acts as conventional and intentional at the same time. Austin himself acknowledged this when he wrote that the illocutionary 'act is constituted not by intention or by fact, essentially but by *convention*' (1975: 128). It would seem that Austin favours the conventional at the expense of the intentional, so if an utterance is understood as an order or a warning it is because of the conditions of ordering and warning, and not because of the way the speaker used the utterance (as an order or a warning). And it is also possible to perform an illocutionary act without intending to: to overlook and to neglect are cases of illocutionary acts that are performative without the relevant intention.

A third possibility suggested by Graham (1977) (the other two being the conventional grammatical form and the speaker intention) is that of highlighting the context of communication. This is something Austin advises us to always keep in mind:

> [T]he occasion of an utterance matters seriously, and that the words used are to some extent to be 'explained' by the 'context' in which they are designed to be or have actually been spoken in linguistic interchange. (1975: 100)

Austin's point is that the contextual situation of the speaker and the listener, coupled with the grammatical conventions appropriate to that context, can explain illocutionary acts.

But the emphasis on the context also has certain difficulties, for while some explicit contexts explain illocutionary acts it is possible to use an illocutionary act without a specific social context. Consider the difference between these two situations: within a military context the lieutenant might warn his troops to dispel any notion of surrendering, but when I warn you that the bull is about to charge the situation is different for there is no specific context for the utterance to count as a warning.

Austin and discourse analysis

With Austin a whole new dimension to the study of language was introduced. The value of his studies on language has been picked up by others who have used his conceptual tools in their respective studies. One can mention J. Hillis Miller's *Speech Acts in Literature* (2001) and Judith Butler's *Excitable Speech* (1997) as cases in point. In the following section, I will focus on Judith Butler and the way she uses Austin in her analysis of hate speech.

Butler opens *Excitable Speech* (1997) with a number of questions:

When we claim to have been injured by language, what kind of claim do we make? We ascribe an agency to language, a power to injure, and position ourselves as the objects of its injurious trajectory. We claim that language acts, and acts against us, and the claim we make is a further instance of language, on which seeks to arrest the force of the prior instance. Thus, we exercise the force of language even as we seek to counter its force, caught up in a bind that no act of censorship can undo. (1997: 1)

In this citation, the issues that concern Butler – language, censorship, politics and agency – are thematized, and while focussing principally upon the writings of J. L. Austin and L. Althusser, her theoretical background is informed by both M. Foucault's account of power and J. Derrida's account of context and iteration. Interestingly the word *excitable* in the title of her book refers to the legal term 'excitable speech', a term that refers to speech considered beyond the control of the speaker because it is uttered under duress. Butler will argue that in a sense all speech is excitable (1997: 15).

Within democratic societies, the value of freedom of speech is unquestioned; the free exchange of ideas is considered an essential ingredient that characterizes Western democratic cultures. But freedom of speech also raises the problem of whether it should include all speech. Should offensive speech – racist or sexist discourse – be also permitted? Do these situations justify censorship?

Several theorists have in fact argued in favour of state intervention by censoring racist or sexist discourses. In the 1980s feminist antipornographers and critical race theorists argued (1) that pornography and racial speech should no longer be protected by the First Amendment of the American Constitution (the First Amendment protects freedom of speech); and furthermore, (2) the active intervention by the state to censor such discourses was justified in terms of the Fourteenth Amendment (the Fourteenth Amendment guarantees equality and respect for all citizens).

Butler positions herself against those legal theorists and scholars who support the introduction of censorship. This is not to say that she condones offensive speech or that she is unaware of the possible injury that such speech can cause. But she views the question of censorship by situating it within the framework of democratic politics, with the possibility of the subject contesting such speech without recourse to state censorship.

The First Amendment of the US Constitution concerns the protection of free speech: all ideas have the right to be expressed and the freedom to express them should be protected. There are exceptions to the First Amendment, and include speech that is defamatory, libelous, plagiaristic, threatening (to an officer of the law), and false advertising. But what is known as hate speech – sexist or racist discourse – is also protected by the First Amendment since it belongs to the marketplace of ideas; and while we might find these ideas reprehensible and disagree strongly with them, this does not justify their exclusion. Hate speech is not harmful but merely represents the point of view of a person or groups of persons who are expressing their opinion; such opinions can be countered with other ideas.

This is where the issue of censorship has its origins. Those seeking to regulate hate speech argue that such speech is in fact harmful: it is not a question of 'just words', but rather of words that actually hurt the people they are addressed to. Matsuda writes about the 'deadly violence that accompanies the persistent verbal degradation of those subordinated' and later remarks that 'Racist hate messages, threats, slurs, epithets, and disparagement all hit the gut of those in the target group' (in Butler 1997: 166).

Butler disagrees with the notion that the state should intervene to prevent such speech. It is not that Butler denies that hate speech can injure and hurt those towards whom it is directed, but rather regards it as a question of strategy. Her view is that leaving hate speech within the public domain provides a better way of dealing with it, for the conditions that make hate speech possible are also those that make 'defiant' speech possible. It is defiant speech that can challenge and defuse the harm of hate speech.

Proponents of state censorship claim that hate speech is harmful and that the person towards whom it is directed undergoes an injury. This raises a number of questions: how does language have this force to injure others? Where did this force come from? To answer this question Butler turns to Austin's theory of speech acts, where she sums up the difference between illocutionary and perlocutionary acts as follows:

> [T]he former are speech acts that, in saying do what they say, and do it in the moment of that saying; the latter are speech acts that produce certain effects as their consequence; by saying something, a certain effect follows. (1997: 3)

Butler's argument centres upon the temporal difference between them: while illocutionary acts are immediate and their happening instantaneous, perlocutionary acts occur later, their effect taking place at a different temporal moment.

But while the illocutionary act takes place at the moment of its utterance, its force is derived from elsewhere. Following Austin's analysis, the power that gives illocutionary utterances their force is derived from the institutional framework that specifies the words or formula that is to be uttered, the persons who can utter them and the circumstances within which they can be uttered. If a speech act derives its force from previously established conventions, then it is much harder to identify what Austin calls the 'total speech situation' that he claimed was necessary for understanding the speech acts.

Butler argues that if the difference between the illocutionary and the perlocutionary act is one of time – the former occurring immediately and the latter happening later – then (given that illocutionary acts are the result of conventions or what she calls 'historicity') it is not the case that there is a direct and immediate effect between speech and conduct. The force that gives illocutionary acts their power is accumulated over time. The performative act 'echoes prior actions, and *accumulates the force of authority through the repetition or citation of prior and authoritative set of practices*' (1997: 51).

Whereas Austin thought that to understand a speech act one needs to examine the 'total speech situation', it turns out that there is more to the total speech situation than he had in mind. Butler's introduction of the 'historicity' that gives the illocutionary act its force transforms the present moment of the speech act to include both the past and the future. The historical derivation of the force shows that there is a space between the (illocutionary) act and conduct. As a result, the distinction between the illocutionary and the perlocutionary cannot be maintained since both can be construed as 'effects', the former of its (vertical) historical development and the latter of its (horizontal) temporal recognition. And this constellation of past, present and future gives signs their potential for unexpected meanings; an utterance has the potential to transcend 'the moment it occasions' (1997: 14).

In the case of hate speech, it is the use and repetition of injurious names that constitute their historicity. Injurious names carry their history with them, a history that

> has become internal to a name, has come to constitute the contemporary meaning of a name: the sedimentation of its usages as they have become part of the very name, a sedimentation, a repetition that congeals, that gives the name its force. (1997: 36)

And it is because such hate speech has been used before in an offensive manner that we now know that it is offensive. It is by being used and re-used that it succeeds in acquiring its effects.

The next step in Butler's strategy is to show that the censoring of hate speech is mistaken because it is grounded in the belief that the illocutionary act always and necessarily succeeds in hurting the other. Hate speech theorists assume that the illocutionary act is always successful, that it efficiently achieves its effect of hurting the other: 'a speech act is said to act – as efficacious, unilateral, transitive, generative' (1997: 74). It is towards this assumption that Butler applies Austin's doctrine of infelicities to show that an illocution does not necessarily achieve its goal. As Austin pointed out, one feature of performatives is that they are vulnerable to 'misfires' and 'abuses'. If this is the case, if hate speech always has the possibility of failing to achieve its goal, of failing to hurt, then perhaps censorship is not the best way to counter hate speech.

Paradoxically, hate speech theorists who attempt to censor certain terms fail to realize that in the process of taking these words out of their context they are creating new contexts through the process of repeating these words. And by repeating these words in different contexts, they are taking the 'sting' out of them: they are using these words not to hurt, but to exemplify, to educate or to seek legal redress. In other words, they are deflating hate speech and it is this, rather than censorship, that Butler thinks is a more productive approach to hate speech. The way a sign can be defused through a process of resignification can be seen, for example, in the way the word *nigger* was appropriated by the black community and used as an expression of identity rather than humiliation.

Butler's critique of hate speech theorists is further developed in her critique of the subject. It would seem that hate speech posits a subject as the origin of hate speech, who in turn uses it to hurt the other. It should be recalled that while Butler is critical of the notion of the sovereign subject, this does not absolve users of hate speech from their responsibility. Care should be taken not to equate responsibility with sovereignty: the speaker is responsible for the language he/she uses even if it is language that transforms the speaker into a subject.

Butler's argument against the sovereignty of the subject relies on the work of Althusser and his concept of interpellation. According to Butler, the use of speech by a figure of authority inaugurates the subject, so it is language that constitutes the subject. Although this view contrasts with that of Austin, who assumes that the subject is prior to the speech act that he/she uses, Butler argues that for hate speech to have its injurious effects, it must be necessary to take on Althusser's account of interpellation of the subject, for if there is no subject then how can words hurt anyone? As a result, Althusser's account of the interpellation of the subject, 'appears to constitute the prior condition of those subject-centered speech acts that dominate Austin's domain of analysis' (1997: 24).

According to Althusser, a person becomes an ideological subject as a result of his/her response to the voice of authority hailing him/her. His example is that of a police officer who calls out to a person with 'Hey you there', and the person, recognizing that he/she is being addressed, is transformed or constituted into a subject. This enables Althusser and Butler to argue that the subject is linguistically constituted and is an effect of – rather than being positioned outside of or prior to – language. But Butler's further point is that while it might seem that the police officer is a sovereign power, he/she is actually citing or repeating formulas that are already in existence. For the citational address to be effective the police officer must rely upon the context and convention of address: 'the police *cite* the convention of hailing' (1997: 33), using a language that pre-exists them and which they are not in control of.

Butler adds to the Althusserian analysis by arguing that (1) the subject can be interpellated without consciously knowing it; (2) the person is subjectivized even when he/she resists, refuses or counters the terms that are being addressed to him/her; (3) interpellation does not require an actual person, such as the police officer in Althusser's example, but can be the system itself that interpellates with its bureaucratic forms, adoption papers and so on. Here we can see the parallels between interpellation and illocutionary speech acts, in that they both rely upon established conventions. For interpellative and illocutionary acts to work, they must belong to a conventional system that pre-exists the subject.

The Althusserian model of interpellation makes it possible to explain hate speech. Through the act of calling the other with a hurtful name, the other is transformed into a social being. Butler generalizes this argument to include non-harmful interpellations: these are also injurious because the act of constituting persons as social subjects creates certain possibilities and denies others. When the doctor utters 'it's a girl', the child is being interpellated or constituted as a female subject with all the possibilities (or lack of) that this entails.

Contrary to the popular view of the subject as the originator or author of his/her discourse, Butler argues that the subject is produced as an effect of discourse. As the subject uses offensive language, he/she is produced as a racist or sexist subject at the same time as he/she transforms others into 'sexualised' or 'raced' beings. The racist or sexist subject is produced because of the 'long string of injurious interpellations' that pre-exist him/her and that are already used in a sexist or racist manner. The subject is not at the origin of the discourse but rather an effect of it: the *subject who "cites" the performative is temporarily produced as the belated and fictive origin of the performative itself* (1997: 49).

Although Butler does admit that there are times when hate speech should be prosecuted, she does not offer a detailed account of when this should occur. The reason for this lack is that her focus is directed mainly towards the institutionalization of hate speech as opposed to the individual one-on-one interaction that underlies the claims of responsibility made by hate speech theorists. Thus, while racists and sexists are responsible for their utterances, Butler's point is that the language they are using is not their responsibility but rather an inherited language, although this does not justify their using it.

Butler promotes counter-speech as a form of resistance to hate speech:

[T]he gap that separates the speech act from its future effects has its auspicious implications: it begins a theory of linguistic agency that provides an alternative to the relentless search for legal remedy. The interval between instances of utterance not only makes the repetition and resignification of the utterance possible, but shows how words might, through time, become disjointed by their power to injure and recontextualized in more affirmative modes. (1997: 15)

While Butler's critical analysis is directed at the concept of the subject as a sovereign in control and able to calculate the effects of his/her utterances, this does not entail an elimination of agency. Rather, it is the elimination of the subject as traditionally conceptualized that makes possible her radical views of agency and resistance. Using the Derridean critique of the context and the related notion of iteration, Butler argues that agency is possible because hate speech can be appropriated and made to resignify. The agent can transform hate speech into a tool of political subversion and be used to challenge those that attempt to injure. Butler writes:

Such reappropriations illustrate the vulnerability of these sullied terms to an unexpected innocence; such terms are not property; they assume a life and a purpose for which they were never intended. (1997: 161)

In her critique of the censoring of hate speech by the state, Butler elaborates on what it is about the state and its exercise of power (through the courts) that she considers a hindrance to a more democratic politics. She claims that

1. the state is arbitrary in the operation of power: Butler reaches this conclusion after examining the decisions taken by the American Supreme Court with particular reference to *R.A.V vs St Paul*. She contends that in its decision on racist hate speech, the Supreme Court made it harder to prosecute those who burnt a cross in front of an African American home (racist hate speech), while making it easier to prosecute obscene hate speech as was the declaration of being homosexual in the military, which was tantamount to being obscene and therefore liable to prosecution. Clearly the courts were not neutral in their judgements.
2. the state increases its power by being allowed to adjudicate hate speech. Allowing the state to decide (through the courts) which type of speech is permitted and which type is forbidden is another way of entrusting it with more power. It is, after all, the courts that decide what is to count as 'hate speech' in the first place, and while there is a difference between the courts' judgements on racist and sexist discourse and the state's decision on what constitutes the content of hate speech, Butler argues that attempts to challenge the state have tended to result in discrimination against the very groups it was supposed to protect (1997: 97–98).
3. state regulation decreases the possibility for resignification within the public domain. Butler argues that state censorship has the effect of diminishing the potential for resignification by dictating what can and cannot be said. Her vision of an alternative democratic practice is one where there is no state involvement, with the result that the threat of hate speech can be challenged, undermined or used to empower in the process of resignification within the public domain (1997: 108).

Butler's disagreement with the notion that the state should intervene to prevent such speech is based on her radical vision of democratic politics. It should be pointed out that question of resignification has been challenged by Salih, who argues that just because a person ignores or resignifies an abusive term, it still depends upon the abuser to recognize that he/she has been ignored or that the term is not being used in the same way. If the abuser fails to recognize this then nothing much seems to have happened, in the same way as the meaning of a word does not depend upon what one person decides to make it mean. It seems that some kind of 'semantic consensus' is needed for resignification to be effective (2002: 115).

Critical remarks

Austin has been subjected to a number of critical comments, both with regard to his philosophical method and in relation to his theory of speech acts. Hanfling (2000: 26–37) points out that Austin did not help reject the charge that his contributions were 'merely verbal', which would imply that his method did not contribute to the resolution of philosophical problems. Austin also claims that his analysis is not the 'last word', but rather the 'first word' for the analysis of philosophical problems. However, Hanfling points out that the words that Austin examines are the ones that are currently in use, so as it turns out, the 'end' and the 'beginning' of philosophical analysis revolve around the same words. A more serious criticism of Austin's method of focussing upon words is the view that words and the world are two separate entities, with words representing the world, so that an examination of words should reveal a better understanding of the world.[5] Hanfling asks: if this is the case then why not look at the world directly so that the 'inadequacies and arbitrariness' of words can be avoided? Take Austin's examination of the difference between 'succumb to temptation' and 'losing control of oneself'; here he was clarifying the different uses of these words to describe different forms of behaviour. But to bring out the differences between them it is not necessary to contrast them against a non-verbal world.

In relation to the details of Austin's analysis of language, Friggieri (1991: 155–58, 161–62) raises an important point. The distinction between primary or implicit performatives and explicit performatives misled Austin. The similarity of the grammatical form (the first person singular in the present perfect tense) led him to think that they both belonged to the same category, whereas they actually belong to different categories: (a) the reference of the primary performative is an object or name (the reference *I name this ship* is the ship), while the reference of the explicit performative is the content of the sentence (in the utterance *I warn you that the bull is about to charge* the reference of 'I warn you' is 'the bull is about to charge', which makes explicit the force of the primary utterance); (b) Austin's primary performatives had been conceptualized within the framework of non-linguistic or institutional conventions, whereas the explicit performatives were not bound by these non-linguistic or institutional conventions, so the 'mishaps' that were characteristic of the former were not surprisingly inapplicable to the latter.

Graham (1977: 108–09) points out that the interesting question that Austin's work raises for other disciplines concerns the degree to which one can achieve an accurate translation of their texts. In taking as examples intercultural communication, history or the social sciences, while it might seem that the requisite to understand the past, another culture or another people is that one can get to the core meaning of their texts or – in Austin's terminology – the locutionary content, what Austin demonstrates is that the illocutionary force of utterances in other cultures is not necessarily the same as ours. Problems with interpretation are common enough with utterances in one's own culture, so one can imagine how these problems increase with distances in space and time.

In this chapter, I have first (1) outlined the method that Austin used in the analysis of philosophical problems. The second section (2) introduced the key distinction between constative and performative utterances, while following it was a (3) description of Austin's criticism of the performative class, a criticism that leads (4) to his reconfiguring this distinction into the new speech act theory. The last section (5) broadened the study of speech acts to the domain of social analysis.

Notes

1. Graham points out that Austin's examples differ from those he had offered earlier. The early examples had closely tied the felicity conditions of their production to their content, so that to say 'I promise' is in effect to promise, but to say 'you did it' does not tell us what it is that you did, that is, which action was performed (1977: 61).

2. Levinson elaborates upon this point, showing that only the first of the following is a performative: '1. I bet you five pounds it'll rain tomorrow. This utterance describes an action, the act of betting; 2. I am betting you five pounds it'll rain tomorrow. This utterance is used by the speaker to remind the hearer of their bet.
3. I betted you five pounds it'll rain tomorrow. This utterance, since it is in the past, is used to report something that the speaker and listener did.
4. He bets you five pounds it'll rain tomorrow. The utterance in the third person also functions as a reminder to the hearer by a third party' (1983: 232).

3. An example of the different misfires characterizing illocutions and perlocutions: 'If you want to convince me that she is an adulteress, you may show me her handkerchief saying "I found this in his bedroom". But I may not understand your words, or I may not understand what you are getting at. You do not succeed in securing uptake. Your action misfires at the illocutionary level. On another occasion, however, I may understand the words and also see what you are getting at, but still you do not convince me that she is an adulteress: your speech action comes off at the locutionary as well as at the illocutionary levels, but misfires as a perlocution' (Friggieri 1991: 205–06).

4. Levinson offers a clear account of the distinction between illocutionary and perlocutionary utterances: 'in sum then, the illocutionary act is what is directly achieved by the conventional force associated with the issuance of a certain kind of utterance in accord with a conventional procedure, and is consequently determinate (in principle at least). In contrast, a perlocutionary act is specific to the circumstances of issuance, and is therefore not conventionally achieved just by uttering that particular utterance, and includes all those effects, intended or unintended, often indeterminate, that some particular utterance in a particular situation may cause' (1983: 237).

5. On the relation between words and the world, Austin writes: 'Words are not (except in their own little corner) facts or things: we need therefore to prise them off the world, to hold them apart from and against it, so that we can realize their inadequacies and arbitrariness, and can re-look at the world without blinkers' (in Hanfling: 28).

Chapter 9

P. Grice and the Theory of Conversation

The primary contribution of P. Grice (1913–88) to the philosophy of communication can be found in his theory of conversation which focusses on the analysis of language in everyday contexts of interaction and the implications that arise in its usage. He was the first who directed attention towards the value of inference in communication, a view that was adopted by later pragmatists. The kinds of inferences Grice was interested in were those that cannot be deduced from the actual content of an utterance but belong to the complete process that enables comprehension between participants to take place.

Grice can be situated within the debate in the philosophy of language on whether meaning should be understood in terms of formal linguistic rules or formal semantics (Frege, Russell, the early Wittgenstein, Chomsky) or in terms of context of use and participants (the later Wittgenstein, Austin). The debate between the two approaches to linguistic meaning can be understood in the difference between what people say and what they mean, since it frequently happens that these two do not coincide. This disjunction between what is said and what is intended poses the problem of how to study language. The first group of philosophers think that since everyday language can lead to such difficulties, it would be best to study it at a formal level: it is therefore the logical meaning and not the everyday meaning that should be emphasized. Using deductive inferences, logic studies the transition from premises to conclusions that are automatically generated. This view of what constitutes the study of language is associated with Russell, who dismisses ordinary, everyday language as such a 'messy' affair that it cannot be considered a proper field of study. On the other hand, philosophers such as the later Wittgenstein did not consider everyday language as flawed in any way, but rather argued that the question of meaning should be grounded in the way language is used in the contexts of everyday life. To focus on the logical meaning of language is to abstract it from such contexts.

Grice's position in the debate is singular in that while he rejected the idea of language as dependent upon truth conditions, that is, the formal semantic view, he was not wholly persuaded by the idea that the use of language in everyday life was the best way to understand meanings. Although a member of the ordinary language philosophy movement, Grice still thought that logic could help with explaining conversational meaning.

Throughout his career, Grice wrote a number of essays that have been collected into a volume titled *Studies in the Way of Words* (1989), and it is this volume that I shall be referring to when I examine his writings. In the first section I focus on the (1) relationship between intention and meaning, and follow this (2) with an analysis of conversational interactions concerning perceptual statements that reveal the way these could be true, but misleading.

The next section examines (3) Grice's theory of conversation followed by (4) the relationship between the tools of logic and implicatures that can be raised within conversational settings. The final section describes (4) a number of areas within which Grice's work has been fruitfully applied, focussing in particular on humour studies.

Meaning and intention

Although Grice was clearly influenced by the work of J. L. Austin, there are a number of differences between them: (1) Grice agreed with Austin on the value of ordinary language, but he considered Austin's approach, with its reliance on particular linguistic examples, as failing to differentiate between what is philosophically important and what is philosophically trivial. Grice himself attempted Austin's method of going through the dictionary to analyse the language of emotions, but gave up at the end of the letter B when he realized that the verb 'to feel' could also be used with 'Byzantine'; (2) while Austin favoured remaining at the level of describing linguistic uses, Grice wanted to put together these descriptions to formulate a general theoretical account; (3) Grice also retained the distinction between the meaning of words and the way words are used, while Austin emphasized use at the expense of sentence meaning.

In 'Meaning' (1989: 213–24), Grice's central thesis is that an account of meaning must be offered within the explanatory framework of the speaker's intention to mean something when he/she is communicating: 'the meaning (in general) of a sign needs to be explained in terms of what users of the sign do (or should) mean by it on particular occasions' (1989: 217). The analysis of meaning is seconded to the use of language for communicating intentions.

Grice applies the method of ordinary language philosophy to analyse the concept of meaning in order to see the different ways in which it is used. He concludes by grouping the different uses into two sets. The first set is that of natural meaning where we find sentences such as 'those spots mean measles' and 'the recent budget means that we shall have a hard year'. Natural meaning explains events that are symptomatic so that it is natural that the spots on a patient mean that he/she has measles and that the slashes in the budget mean that we will not have much money to spend next year. The second set is that of non-natural meaning (or meaning$_{NN}$), where we find sentences such as "[t]hose three rings on the bell (of the bus) mean that 'the bus is full' and [t]hat remark, 'Smith couldn't get on without his trouble and strife' meant that Smith found his wife indispensable" (1989: 214). In this case non-natural meaning is linguistic meaning where something is meant by being uttered; the speaker means something with the utterance, so that when he/she utters 'the patient has measles' there is no natural relation between the patient and the measles.

> When the expressions "means," "means something," "means that" are used in the kind of way in which they are used in the first set of sentences, I shall speak of the sense, or senses, in which they are used, as the *natural* sense, or senses, of the expression in

question. When the expressions are used in the kind of way in which they are used in the second set of sentences, I shall speak of the sense, or senses, in which they are used, as the *nonnatural* sense, or senses, of the expressions in question. I shall use the abbreviation "means$_{nn}$" to distinguish the *nonnatural* sense or senses. (1989: 214)

The differences between these two sets are specified as follows:

1. in the first set, the sentence entails the truth of what is said. This, however, is not the case with the second set, for while it does not make sense to say '[t]hose spots mean measles but he hasn't got measles' (the first set), it is perfectly possible to say '[t]hose three rings on the bell (of the bus) mean that the bus is full'. 'But the bus isn't in fact full – the conductor has made a mistake' (1989: 213–14).
2. it would seem strange to say that the speaker who uttered 'those spots mean measles' intended to communicate something more by the spots. There is no question of trying to further understand the intentions of the speaker. On the other hand, with the second class of examples it would not be strange to say that the speakers intended to mean something more by their utterance: the 'rings on the bell' mean or communicate that there is no more place on the bus; likewise, the speaker – remarking about Smith – intended to communicate Smith's dependence on his wife.
3. finally, it is only with the second set of examples that we can add 'mean' followed by quotation marks: 'those three rings on the bell "mean" the bus is full', but we cannot say 'those spots "mean" measles'.

It should be pointed out that although the difference between these two classes is characterized by Grice as a difference between natural and non-natural meaning – or meaning$_{NN}$, the latter is not restricted to linguistic meaning. Grice uses 'utterance' in a broad sense such that it includes non-linguistic meaning: human behaviour which is used to communicate something to someone on a particular occasion is also an utterance.[1] In the later 'Utterer's Meaning, Sentence-Meaning and Word-Meaning' (1989: 117–37), this view is specified: 'I use the term "utter" (together with "utterance") in an artificially wide sense, to cover any case of doing x or producing x by the performance of which U meant that so-and-so' (1989: 118).

In his analysis of meaning$_{NN}$, Grice considers causal explanations of meaning as similar to behaviourist accounts of meaning, an account that he firmly rejects. The causal explanation of meaning was suggested by C. L. Stevenson, and although Stevenson did not favour a strict behaviourist account of meaning on the ground that it was too simplistic, he did assume a causal model when explaining linguistic meaning. Stevenson had argued in *Ethics and Language* (1944) that a sentence such as *John is a remarkable athlete* causes in the listener the effect of associating *athlete* with *tallness*. This is obviously not a linguistic rule but an association that the sentence suggests that 'we should not ordinarily say that it "meant" anything about tallness, even though it "suggested it"' (in Chapman 2005: 65). Grice's reply is that it is possible to talk about 'non-tall athletes' without contradicting oneself. The trouble with Strawson's account – as Grice shows – is that, given the notion of suggestion, all forms of behaviour might be considered as communication, including those forms of behaviour that we would not normally consider as communication. For example, putting on a tailcoat might lead to the belief that one is about to go dancing because we conventionally associate tailcoats with dancing. But just because we conventionally associate wearing tailcoats with dancing, this is not what is necessarily being communicated.

> [T]he causal theory ignores the fact that the meaning (in general) of a sign needs to be explained in terms of what users of the sign do (or should) mean by it on particular occasions; and so the latter notion, which is unexplained by the causal theory, is in fact the fundamental one. (1989: 217)

This explains why the concept of intention is crucial to the Gricean account of meaning. Intentionality provides the framework for understanding communication by shifting the emphasis away from conventional behaviour. It is the intention to mean, rather than the convention, that explains what is meant through the act of communication.

It seems that another major influence upon Grice's essay is that of Peirce (Chapman 2005: 71–72). The starting point of Grice's analysis concerns Peirce's use of the term *sign* that he equates with *means*: by using *means* Grice is able to bring out the similarities as well as differences in relation to Peirce's concepts of 'index' and 'symbol'. Using the following sentence, *the position of the weathercock meant that the wind was North East*, to analyse the category of index, Grice brings out two important points: (1) that it truly was a north-east wind and (2) that there was a causal connection between the wind and the weathercock.

However, if instead of 'means' one says 'the position of the weathercock was an indication that the wind was North East, but it was actually South East', it is clear that 'was an indication' cannot be used interchangeably with 'means': 'indication' does not entail the truth of what is said. Likewise, the word *mean* does not necessarily imply a causal relation: if one says 'the position of the weathercock meant that the wind was North East' then, in this case, there is a causal relation between the weathercock and the north-east wind. But if during a conversation at a bus stop one says 'those three rings of the bell meant that the bus was full', there is no causal connection since one might ask 'was it full?' By applying the method of ordinary language philosophy, Grice concludes that the way Peirce uses the term *sign* is not consistent with everyday usage.

Grice introduces a distinction between the 'timeless meaning of an utterance' and what speakers mean to communicate with these utterances – the 'utterer's occasion meaning'. Although Grice seems undecided on whether meaning is something stable (or 'timeless') or whether it depends upon the speaker, he eventually places greater emphasis on different levels of intentionality and communication.

This account of intentionality is further developed since it is realized that it is not only the speaker's intention that is important, but equally important is the hearer's recognition of that intention. When a speaker wants to produce a certain effect or a belief in a hearer, the intention is to communicate meaning$_{NN}$ as well as to ensure that his/her intention be recognized by the hearer as the communication of certain information. It is the recognition of this intention that causes the hearer to accept or change his/her beliefs. Grice's analysis here concerns descriptive sentences:

'*A* meant$_{NN}$ something by x' is (roughly) equivalent to '*A* intended the utterance of x to produce some effect in an audience by means of the recognition of that intention'; and we may add that to ask what *A* meant is to ask for a specification of the intended effect.... (1989: 220)

Grice's main contribution to understanding what is entailed by the concept of communication is the recognition of the speaker's intentions by the hearer. He introduces a number of examples that highlight the pivotal role of intentionality and its recognition in communication. The difference between 'I show Mr X a photograph of Mr Y displaying undue familiarity to Mrs X' and 'I draw a picture of Mr Y behaving in this manner and show it to Mr X' is that in the former, the effect upon Mr Y (surprise, anger) would still take place irrespective of the intention to communicate the meaning$_{NN}$. Seeing the photo is enough. In the case of the latter, it is the intention to communicate that characterizes the example: the art of drawing is my way of communicating my intentions to reveal or expose Mr Y's behaviour, and it is this that would normally be considered as communication.

Likewise, intentionality plays an important role in the types of communication that influence the actions of others. Take Grice's example of the police officer who stops the car by standing in front of it: the action of stopping the car will take place whether the motorist recognizes the police officer's intention or not. On the other hand, when the police officer waves the car to stop, an act of communication has taken place because this depends upon the motorist's recognition of the wave as an act intended to communicate the message of stopping. Grice identifies two levels of meaning$_{NN}$: first, and primarily, in the relation between the speaker, the listener and the context where intentions are communicated and recognized; second, and derived from the first, is the meaning$_{NN}$ of words and phrases.

However, despite conventional meaning being secondary to intentional meaning, Grice adds that the way some intentions are recognized cannot be included as part of the meaning$_{NN}$:

[I]f (say) I intend to get a man to do something by giving him some information, it cannot be regarded as relevant to the meaning$_{NN}$ of my utterance to describe what I intend him to do. (1989: 221)

As Grice points out, the actual explicit formulation of the intention is 'comparatively rare', but should there be any doubt about the intention, the context serves as a useful way of understanding it:

Again, in case where there is doubt, say, about which of two or more things an utterer intends to convey, we tend to refer to the context (linguistic or otherwise) of the utterance and ask which of the alternative would be relevant to other things he is saying or doing, or which intention in a particular situation would fit in with some purpose he obviously has (e.g. a man who calls for a "pump" at a fire would not want a bicycle pump). (1989: 222)

Conversational statements: 'true but misleading'

A clue to the development of Grice's theory of language can be seen in his essay 'The Causal Theory of Perception' (1989: 224–47), where he offers a defence of the causal nature of perception. Traditional empirical theory maintains that if our knowledge is derived from our senses, then it is this sense data that we are immediately aware of. While it has been presumed that the material world is the cause of the sense data, there is no way of proving with certainty the existence of the material world, since all we have access to is the sense data and not the material world. Grice defends this scepticism of the material world, arguing that it is a challenge that should not be dismissed but is to be listened to.

However, the value of the discussion on sense data is that of offering insights on language use: when one utters the sentence *'so and so' looks Q [red] to me*, one is assuming that the notion of sense data is relevant; otherwise, there is no way of explaining the subjectivity of the experience. Grice calls such statements '*L*-statements', and his general argument is that if I perceive a red object, then this object causes me to 'seem to see something red'. He claims that *L*-statements are 'true whenever a perceptual statement is true' (1989: 227) since the perceptual statement entails the *L*-statement.

When someone makes such a remark as "It looks red to me," a certain implication is carried, an implication which is disjunctive in form. It is implied either that the object referred to is known *or* believed by the speaker not to *be* red, *or* that it has been denied by someone else to be red, *or* that the speaker is doubtful whether it is red, *or* that someone else has expressed doubt whether it is red, *or* that the situation is such that though no doubt has actually been expressed and no denial has actually been made, some person *or* other might feel inclined toward denial or doubt if he were to address himself to the question whether the object is actually red. (1989: 227)

L-statements make sense only if one is doubting or denying the sense data: when a speaker says 'it looks red to me' this utterance can only be construed as an answer to a query on the colour, and Grice points out the strangeness of the speaker 'saying "that looks red to me" (not as a joke) when I am confronted by a British pillar box in normal daylight at a range of a few feet' (1989: 227). The speaker would only say 'it looks red to me' if someone else was doubting or denying the colour.

But the conditions of doubt and denial are not part of the meaning of *L*-statements and this is why the implication of *L*-statements is 'cancellable'. This point is illustrated by another of Grice's examples from a non-perceptual angle: [2] when a tutor is asked to write a report on the standard of philosophy of his/her student and his/her response only mentions the student's excellent use of English and regular attendance at tutorials, it is evident that he/she is implying that the standard of the student's philosophical ability is not worthy of note. However, if the tutor goes on to say 'I do not of course mean to imply that he is no good at philosophy', then clearly the implication is cancelled with the qualification. With the case of *L*-statements and the aforementioned example, Grice shows the way a statement might be true, even if it is misleading.

To explain this use of language, Grice offers both a weaker and a stronger account. In the weaker case, if there is no doubting or denial involved, then the sentence demonstrates a plain misuse of language. In the stronger case, if there is no doubt or denial and Q has the relevant property (red), this use is misleading even if true. Grice resolves the question in favour of the second case as it seems more applicable to language in general. He formulates a general principle of language use as the 'preference to the making of a stronger rather than a weaker statement in the absence of a reason for not doing so' (1989: 236). The difference between perceptual statements and *L*-statements is that perceptual statements are stronger since they entail *L*-statements, while *L*-statements do not entail perceptual statements. To utter an *L*-statement when one could utter the stronger perceptual statement is misleading even though, as such, the *L*-statement is not untrue. According to the causal theory of perception, *L*-statements are always true, even though using them in everyday contexts of communication is misleading. In his later writings on the maxims of conversation, Grice replaces the principle of the stronger and the weaker with the maxim of relevancy.

Chapman (2005: 96) describes the benefit of the principle of the 'stronger' as twofold: (1) it is prescriptive in that it recommends the way language should be used; and (2) it allows for reasonable exceptions, since in terms of Grice's overall project the principle would provide an explanatory account of language rather than merely provide a list of linguistic rules. Grice's conclusion regarding the use of the language of sense data is that it is legitimate to use such statements because they are true irrespective of whether one is in a condition of doubt or denial, and although true, people tend to avoid using them because they are misleading.

The theory of conversation

In the 1960s Grice's research focussed on the difference between speaker and sentence meaning, paying special attention to the context of speaker meaning:

Philosophers often say that context is very important. Let us take this remark seriously. Surely, if we do, we shall want to consider this remark not merely in its relation to this or that problem, i.e., in context, but also in itself, i.e., out of context. If we are to take <u>this</u> seriously, we must be systematic, that is thorough and orderly. If we are to be orderly we must start with what is relatively simple. <u>Here</u>, though not of course everywhere, to be simple is to be as abstract as possible; by this I mean merely that we want, to begin with, to have as few cards on the table as we can. Orderliness will then consist in seeing first what we can do with the cards we have; and when we think that we have exhausted this investigation, we put another card on the table, and see what that enables us to do. (in Chapman 2005: 96)

In the aforementioned passage, Grice emphasizes the values of systematicity and order as a counterweight to the tendency of some ordinary language philosophers – Austin being a case in point – to produce open-ended lists without some form of generalization.

Grice's operating strategy for the analysis of context consisted in narrowing it to linguistic contexts, these being conversational situations with two persons in the changing roles of speakers and hearers. The model of conversation adopted by Grice is one whereby meaning is communicated by one speaker to one listener with the aim of producing some effect on that listener. It seems that according to Grice's account, the goal of communication can be defined in terms of the values of success and effectiveness (Cosenza 2001: 20). However, while Grice acknowledges the position of the hearer in the process of conversation, his account is structured in terms of the contributions of the speaker's intention to communicate a meaning to a hearer. In this respect, the hearer's contribution to the conversation is limited to the recognition of the speaker's intentions: [3]

A general pattern for the working out of a conversational implicature might be given as follows: "He has said that p; there is no reason to suppose that he is not observing the maxims, or at least the Cooperative Principle; he could not be doing this unless he thought that q; he knows (and knows that I know that he knows) that I can see that the supposition that he thinks that q is required; he has done nothing to stop me thinking that q; he intends me to think, or is at least willing to allow me to think, that q; and so he has implicated that q." (1989: 31)

Although Grice restricts the concept of context to conversational exchanges, he does use some ideas from non-linguistic situations. In the situation of two persons passing through a gate, it is expected of the first person to hold or leave it open for the second. Should the first person shut the door without any good reason then this would be considered rude. Just as helpfulness is a normal expectation in human behaviour, so too helpfulness is part of our conversational behaviour, especially since conversations are joint, collaborative ventures between partners. Both partners share a mutual goal and therefore help each other in achieving it.

Grice later changes the terminology of 'helpful' to that of 'co-operative': in trying to understand the nature of this cooperative activity, Grice uses the terms *object* and *desiderata* to describe the principles that regulate the behaviour within a conversation. There are two desiderata: (1) of candour where speakers should, as a rule, make the strongest possible statements with the qualification that they do not attempt to mislead; and (2) of clarity, where speakers should contribute to the conversation by speaking clearly and by providing relevant information to the conversation. Other principles that form part of the conversational setting are (3) the principle of conversational benevolence, where contributions to a conversation are geared towards the agreed principle of conversation; and (4) the principle of self-love, where the participants will not go to unnecessary trouble towards their contribution. These principles will later be renamed Quantity, Quality, Relation and Manner, where the components of this loose assemblage of principles are united into a generalized schema.

Grice's theory of conversation mapped out a new area of study in the philosophy of language. As such he preferred using the term *conversation* over *communication*, and it was only subsequent critics who labelled his work as an attempt at elaborating a theory of communication (Cosenza 2001: 20). Although studies in the philosophy of language were divided between a concern with the formal analysis of language and that towards speaker meaning and intention, Grice argued that both could be subsumed under a broad principle that explained all human behaviour (linguistic and non-linguistic behaviour) as directed towards a goal. In 'Logic and Conversation' he developed this theme and introduced the Cooperative Principle: 'Make your conversational contribution such as is required at the stage at which it occurs, by the accepted purpose or direction of the talk exchange in which you are engaged' (1989: 26). When people communicate they expect to achieve certain purposes, and in order to achieve them they follow a number of principles or maxims. For Grice, conversation implies cooperation between participants and he lists four maxims that they should follow in the pursuit of understanding. These are as follows.

1. The maxim of quantity were the participants should offer the right amount of information.
2. The maxim of quality where the participants should strive to be truthful.
3. The maxim of relation where the contribution of the participants should be relevant to the conversation.
4. The maxim of manner where the participants should strive to be clear.

Grice offers some examples of the aforementioned maxims:

1. *Quantity*. If you are assisting me to mend a car, I expect your contribution to be neither more nor less than is required. If, for example, at a particular state I need four screws, I expect you to hand me four, rather than two or six.
2. *Quality*. I expect your contributions to be genuine and not spurious. If I need sugar as an ingredient in the cake you are assisting me to make, I do not expect you to hand me salt; if I need a spoon, I do not expect a trick spoon made of rubber.

3. *Relation.* I expect a partner's contribution to be appropriate to the immediate needs at each stage of the transaction. If I am mixing ingredients for a cake, I do not expect to be handed a good book or even an oven cloth (though this might be an appropriate contribution at a later stage).
4. *Manner.* I expect a partner to make it clear what contribution he is making and to execute his performance with reasonable dispatch. (1989: 28)

The difference between what is said (the literal meaning) and what is meant (or as Grice says 'implicated') can both be explained and resolved by an appeal to the principle of cooperation: listeners can and do reinterpret literal sentences to achieve the goal of successful communication. It is by integrating these principles of language use that Grice hoped to create a broad philosophical theory of language.

While Grice favours the analysis of language in a particular context, he is critical of the notion that sentence or conventional meaning has one 'meaning'. The concept of sentence meaning is analysed as

1. the 'what is said', where the speaker is committed to the truth of what is said.
2. the conventional implicature, where it is not the speaker's intention but the words that generate the implicature. If we compare the following sets of examples: (a) Set A: 'she was poor but honest' and 'he is an Englishman; he is, therefore, brave'; with (b) Set B: 'she is poor and honest,' and 'he is an Englishman and brave,' the meaning of Set A is not the same as the meaning of Set B, since it is only in Set A that the idea of contrast and consequence is introduced. As a result, we would not say the sentences in Set A are false, although we would consider them to be misleading. With conventional implicatures, Grice shows how it is the conventional meanings of words that can implicate (Chapman 2005: 101).
3. conversational implicatures are those implicatures that result from the fact that something is being said. With conversational implicatures, participants in a conversation 'add' to the actual utterance so as to achieve understanding. One can say the participants go beyond the 'surface' of the utterance to fill in what has been implicated. For example, A says *'Smith doesn't seem to have a girlfriend these days'* and B replies *'He has been paying a lot of visits to New York lately'.* (1989: 32)B's reply does not seem relevant to A's remark, but the relevant connection can be made because B is conversationally implying that A has a girlfriend in New York.

The opposition between 'conventional implicature' and 'conversational implicature' is fundamental. In the case of conventional implicature, it is the meaning of the words that determines the implicature, but in the case of conversational implicature, the meaning is inferred from the context and the observation of the principle of cooperation. With conversational implicatures it is not what is said that is the goal of the conversation but what is meant, and conversational implicatures are generated when a maxim is not fulfilled.

There is, therefore, a close connection between the principle of cooperation, maxims and conversational implicature.

Grice lists the different ways in which a maxim can fail to be fulfilled:

1. a maxim can be 'violated' deliberately: this is the situation of people who do not say what they mean but pretend to be open and transparent. The list includes liars, con-artists, grifters and tricksters. Although they violate the maxims uncooperatively they still have reasons for their behaviour.
2. a participant can 'opt out' by not following the relevant maxim: 'He may say, for example, *I cannot say more; my lips are sealed*' (1989: 30). Again the participant has reasons for not saying what he/she means and therefore opts out of cooperating in the conversation.
3. a participant might be faced with a 'clash' of maxims, so that fulfilling one maxim entails a clash with another one. Therefore, the maxim of quantity (be informative) is in conflict with the maxim of quality (have adequate evidence for what you say).
4. a participant may 'flout' a maxim where he/she blatantly fails to fulfil it without, however, trying to deceive, opt out or resolve a clash of maxims. In this case, the participant does not say what he/she means but hints at it in such a way that the hearer understands what the speaker means. It is these 'floutings' of the maxim that are typical of conversational implicatures, and it is these that Grice focusses on by offering a number of examples that demonstrate that

> though some maxim is violated at the level of what is said, the hearer is entitled to assume that that maxim, or at least the overall Cooperative Principle, is observed at the level of what is implicated. (1989: 33)

In these conversations, the speaker is uncooperative at the level of what is said. Once again we are given the example of the professor's reference for the student who has applied for a job in philosophy: 'Dear Sir, Mr X's command of English is excellent, and his attendance at tutorials has been regular. Yours, etc.' (1989: 33). This example shows that cooperation is not taking place at the level of what is said, but at the level of what is implicated: the maxim of quantity is flouted by not giving enough information and therefore producing the implicature in which the professor is indirectly saying or implying that the student is not good at philosophy.

For the hearer to figure out the conversational implicature, a number of features must be taken into account. These include the conventional meanings of the words; the principle of cooperation and its maxims; the linguistic and non-linguistic context; any background information and that the participants are aware of the aforementioned features (1–4).

Logic and conversational implicatures

In 'Indicative Conditionals' (1989: 58–85), Grice discusses the relationship between logic and natural language, arguing that no 'such divergence exists' while focussing primarily on conditionals (although he does discuss other logical constants to a lesser degree). Chapman (2005: 106–07) suggests that the target of Grice's essay is P. Strawson, who in *Introduction to Logical Theory* (1952) states that the logical implication 'p>q' is very different from the way it is used in ordinary everyday language. The use of 'if, then' in ordinary language suggests a causal connection between the antecedent and the consequent: when we say 'if it rains, then the party will be a failure' the suggestion seems to be that one is causally connected to the other. There is the further possibility, according to Strawson, that when the 'if, then' formula is used in everyday life the speaker is expressing some doubt about the 'if […] ' or knows that it is false. As a result, Strawson concludes that while the ordinary language use of 'if, then' entails its logical counterpart, the contrary is not the case: there is more to ordinary language usage than can be accounted for by the logical form.

Grice disagrees with Strawson and he introduces the 'Indirectness Condition' to describe the causal connection between p and q. For Grice (Chapman 2005: 107), the literal meaning of 'if p then q', of the 'what is said' on any particular occasion of utterance, is simply equivalent to the logical meaning of 'p>q'. He argues that the causal connection is a conversational implicature and can therefore be cancelled out by the context or by denial.

> To say "If Smith is in the library, he is working" would normally carry the implication of the Indirectness Condition; but I might say (opting out) "I know just where Smith is and what he is doing, but all I will tell you is that if he is in the library he is working." No one would be surprised if it turned out that my basis for saying this was that I had just looked in the library and found him working. The implication is also contextually concealable, that is, I can find contexts which, if known to participants in a talk-exchange, would make an explicit cancellation unnecessary. (1989: 59)

The question Grice tackles concerns how implicatures produce the indirect condition. His first answer refers to the maxim of Quantity which enjoins us to use the stronger or more informative statement in our conversations. In this case, the more informative statement would be 'p and q' rather than 'if p then q'. In the weaker case, there is no definite information about the truth values of p and q; and the use of 'if p then q' leads (unless cancelled by the context) to conversational implicature. The same argument applies to other logical forms: for example 'p or q' has common features with the logical form 'p v q', but the ordinary language use leads to conversational implicatures. The conversational implicature arises because it seems strange to use 'p or q' if both p and q are known to be true. While the truth conditional meaning of the logical form 'p v q' states that at least one of the propositions should be true, in the conversational use of 'p or q' it is implied that not both are true. If both were true it would, within a conversational setting, be better to offer 'p and q' since this would be providing more information.

Grice's second answer to the question of how conversational implicatures are produced regards the way they contribute to everyday human interaction. The use of conditionals enables people to understand the choices available to them, although these uses depend upon the context. It does not make sense to say on a hot sunny day 'if it is hot and sunny, I shall go to the beach'. Likewise, the use of disjunctions helps people in everyday life to think about alternatives: this or the other possibility. It would not, for example, make sense to say at 4.30 p.m. 'which show shall we go to? The 3 p.m. or the 6 p.m. show?'

In 'Presupposition and Conversational Implicature' (1989: 269–82), Grice returns to the question of expressions that refer to non-existing things and picks up the debate between Russell and Strawson. Once again Grice here applies his theory of conversation to traditional philosophical problems, retaining the overlap between logic and language use rather than their opposition. Chapman (2005) points out that when this essay is read within the larger context of Grice's writings, it can be seen as part of a study of the way language refers to the world with the question of reference as pivotal to the philosophy of language.

In the theory of descriptions Russell had argued that in

1. 'the king of France is bald,' the sentence entails that there is one unique person (the king of France) and this unique person is bald.
2. 'the king of France is not bald,' it is possible to deny that there is one unique person (i.e. there is no king of France) and that this unique person (who does not exist) is not bald. According to Russell, this sentence is ambiguous.

Strawson challenges the supposed 'ambiguity' that Russell claims on the grounds that in everyday language use, 'the king of France is not bald' means that there is a king of France who is not bald. Speakers are thus committing themselves to the existence of the king of France while denying his baldness. The ambiguity of the kind Russell describes rarely crops up in everyday conversation:

[W]hen one is asked such a question as whether the king of France is, or is not, bald, one does not feel inclined to give an answer; one does not feel very much inclined to say either that it is true that he is bald or that it is false that he is bald, but rather to say things like *The question does not arise* or *He neither is nor is not bald*, etc'. (1989: 269)

Grice's response and defence of Russell focusses on the different types of commitment by speakers to 'the existence of the king of France' and to his 'baldness'. These, Grice argues, do not necessarily involve the same kind of commitment. Grice's defence involves pointing out the distinction between (1) the use of negation when applied to the whole sentence (it is not the case that the king of France is bald): in this sentence there is no commitment to the king of France or to the baldness; and (2) the use of negation when applied to the latter part of the sentence ('the king of France is not bald'): in this sentence, there is no commitment to the baldness. Russell's theory of descriptions allows for two sentences that entail a commitment to the existence of the king of France: (1) the positive assertion (the king of France is bald) and (2) the sentence that denies only his baldness (the king of France is not bald).

But, Grice points out, 'without waiting for disambiguation, people understand an utterance of *The king of France is not bald* as implying (in some fashion) the unique existence of the king of France' (1989: 272). The denial of the commitment to the existence of the king of France only occurs in the denial of the whole sentence. Such a denial, Grice argues, is not the result of logical entailment, but rather the result of conversational interaction. The implicature arises on account of the form or way that the speaker formulates his/ her utterance: it belongs therefore to the category of manner. However, Grice adds a new element when he says. '"Frame whatever you say in the form most suitable for any reply that would be regarded as appropriate"; or, "Facilitate in your form of expression the appropriate reply"' (1989: 273). The point here is that participation in conversation should take into account the range of possible responses. This further reinforces Grice's defence of Russell against Strawson, since it can be argued that the speaker did not frame the utterance in such a way that allows for a possible reply. Strawson had argued that upon hearing 'the king of France is bald', the hearer would not deem it false but be nonplussed as to what you were talking about. But when the speaker utters 'the king of France is bald', one of the possible replies does not include denying the existence of the king of France because information or knowledge that is commonly shared is not usually denied.

This leads Grice to distinguish between common knowledge and controversial information:

> For instance, it is quite natural to say to somebody, when we are discussing some concert, *My aunt's cousin went to that concert*, when we know perfectly well that the person we are talking to is very likely not even to know that we have an aunt, let alone know that our aunt has a cousin. So the supposition must be not that it is common knowledge but rather that it is noncontroversial, in the sense that it is something that we would expect the hearer to take from us (if he does not already know). That is to say, I do not expect, when I tell someone that my aunt's cousin went to a concert, to be questioned whether I have an aunt and, if so, whether my aunt has a cousin. This is the sort of thing that I would expect him to take from me, that is, to take my word for. (1989: 274)

In both the positive and negative sentences, it is not the existence of the king of France that is being challenged or considered controversial, but the baldness.

Grice and humour

One area to which Grice's analysis seems especially amenable is that of popular culture and what makes plays, TV shows and films interesting to watch occurs as a result of the violating, infringing and opting out of the maxims of conversation. While the ideal of clarity in the everyday use of language is important for mutual understanding, within popular culture the use of language with the ideal of clarity would lead to boredom. It is not difficult to recall situations in films where the protagonist needs to convince the addressee to reveal what he/she knows so as to save, for example, someone else or the environment. The participant fails because the addressee refuses to cooperate by saying nothing, that is, by opting out; or the addressee misleads the protagonist by shifting attention to something else (rather than communicating the information he/she knows): this is a violation of the maxim of quantity.

The interest in applying Grice's maxims and their violation has been taken up a number of theorists involved in the study of humour. In 'Pragmatic Interpretation of Humour Production and Comprehension' (2007), Yan Lin-qiong outlines the way that the violation of Grice's maxims generate humour. This occurs when (1) the maxim of quantity is violated through the exchange of more or less information than is required for the purpose of the conversation; (2) the maxim of quality is violated when false information, or information without sufficient evidence is purposely offered; (3) the maxim of relation is violated when irrelevant information is offered deliberately and (4) the maxim of manner is violated when participants are not clear in their conversation. Lin-qiong argues that there are two pragmatic features of humorous utterances, namely being non-bona fide and incongruous (though emphasizing the former) and that these are evidenced in the conversational implicature that is the result of violating the aforementioned maxims.

In *Logic, laughter and laughter-provocation* (2006) Cassar examines, among other issues, the way laughter is generated. She suggests that although one way of explaining laughter provocation could be that of examining what Grice calls 'utterer-meaning', this might not be a fruitful approach, as the question of meaning itself is broader than the way Grice conceptualized it. As a result,

> [i]t follows that the first imperative task that has to be carried out in order to determine the meaning of laughter-provocation is to establish what laughter is, since only then can the investigation of the mechanisms, logical or otherwise, which connect provocation and response be undertaken, taking into account the diversities of both ends of the operation. (2006: 13)

In other words, it is not enough to examine Grice's codes or maxims and argue that laughter provocation is the result of inverting these codes, because these codes are framed as ways of achieving effective communication. Merely inverting them would only result in restricting our understanding of the way laughter can be provoked without any guarantee that this would be successful. For example, by breaking Grice's maxim 'Be relevant' one does not necessarily produce laughter. Cassar concludes by pointing out that an account of laughter provocation is limited if it focusses on Gricean codes, as such an account fails to take into consideration the temporal process underlying the generation of laughter.

Critical remarks

Although Grice is remembered mostly for his theory of conversation, it should be added that his contributions to philosophy are wide ranging, offering solutions to problems in the fields of epistemology, perception and ethics. However, while he applied his theory of conversation to these fields, he never used actual conversations in his analysis of language use. Over time Grice realized that rationality played an important part in his theory of conversation: by following the Cooperative Principle a person was behaving rationally by pursuing the goals of a conversation. It was this rational activity that constituted the very essence of human life that Grice tried to explain. And this is why the criticism of Grice's theory of conversation – for its failure to take into account the conflictual nature of actual conversations – might be misplaced. As a rationalist, he was attempting to outline the conditions that allow for the production of meaning and effective communication, rather than formulate an empirical description of actual conversations.

Hanfling (2000: 186–88) argues that although Grice champions the cause of ordinary language in the analysis of philosophical problems, as it turns out the analysis undermines ordinary language. In his account of perception and *L*-statements, he supports his arguments with a number of ingenious examples, but the result is that he employs a very non-ordinary use of everyday language. In this case, the meanings that are attributed to certain words such as *seem* or *see* deviate from their everyday ordinary use. The principle that the stronger statement should be adopted over the weaker one is therefore challenged. According to the theory, one should not say that 'Grice is in England' if I know that 'Grice is in Oxford'; but if both contribute equally to the conversational exchange, then – unless one had a point for doing so – there is no inherent reason for choosing the stronger statement and not the weaker one.

Grice also argues in favour of the thesis that to understand the meaning of an utterance one must understand what the speaker intended by that utterance, and in so doing eliminate the class of locutionary acts. In other words, the speaker would reduce the sense of the utterance to the force or the way that it is used. Again Friggieri (1991: 199–204) points out that understanding the way the speaker intends to use the sentence presupposes an understanding of what the sentence means, so that to understand the utterance *You're standing on my foot* as a request to get off my foot, you must first understand the meaning of the sentence.

Chapman (2005: 191) points to a number of criticisms regarding Grice's account of language: (1) his failure to define conversation, taking it to mean language used in a context, or a number of sentences following each other without any empirical data; (2) the theory of conversation was supposed to explain a number of traditional philosophical problems, but the casual conversations used seem to develop a life of their own with the point of their original introduction forgotten; (3) on the one hand, Grice generalizes from particular conversations, coming to a generalization that is the result of describing what participants bring to the conversation; but on the other hand, he considers his maxims as rules that prescribe the way language should be used; (4) Grice's conversations are between persons of equal social status and mutually interested in the exchange of information. However, not all conversations are of this kind, and within different contexts – for example a university – participants resort to different maxims.

The influence of Grice's writings has been chiefly achieved through the essays 'Meaning' and 'Logic and Conversation', and this success has been recognized by philosophers of language and linguistics. It is not uncommon to come across the term *Gricean pragmatics*, even though he never used the term himself. It could be said that Grice's contribution to the debate between formal semanticists and pragmatists on the issue of literal meaning and speaker meaning was that of bridging the two through the Cooperative Principle and conversational maxims. In addition the concept of conversational implicatures – a concept that includes the possibility of alluding, implying or insinuating something – highlights the difference between what speakers literally say and what they mean or implicate. One way of evaluating Grice's place within the philosophy of language is by contrasting his views on language with those of Chomsky. Chomsky had argued that to understand linguistic meaning there was no need to take into consideration the use of language to communicate, arguing that it was not even necessary to consider communication as the primary function of language. For Grice the opposite is the case: the only way to explain language is from the point of view of communication.

In this chapter, I have outlined (1) the concepts of intention and meaning in Grice's philosophy of communication; followed by (2) his analysis of statements that are true but misleading within conversational settings. The following sections discussed (3) his theory of conversation and (4) the relation between the procedures of logic and conversational implicatures, ending with (5) a brief look at the way his ideas have been applied to the study of humour.

Notes

1. Grice writes 'surely to show that the criteria for judging linguistic intentions are very like the criteria for judging non-linguistic intentions is to show that linguistic intentions are very like nonlingusitic intentions' (1989: 223).
2. This example is taken from his essay 'Logic and conversation' (1989: 22–40).
3. Grice's recognition of the hearer is also mentioned in the earlier essay on 'Meaning': 'for x to have meaning$_{NN}$, the intended effect must be something which in some sense is within the control of the audience, or that in some sense of "reason" the recognition of the intention behind x is for the audience a reason and not merely a cause' (1989: 221).

Chapter 10

Searle and the Intentionality of Speech Acts

Throughout his career John Searle (1932) has focussed on a number of philosophical problems, but he is chiefly known for his innovative contributions to three areas of philosophy: philosophy of language, philosophy of mind and philosophy of society. In this chapter, I am mostly focussing on Searle's early studies of speech acts, although I also touch upon his philosophy of mind and of society when they overlap with language. Searle's theory of speech acts is an attempt to develop further the insights made by Austin with his groundbreaking work on speech act theory. This development involves a description of the structure and processes that allow communication to take place.

The tradition Searle draws inspiration from is that of analytic philosophy, where emphasis on detail is part and parcel of the practice of these philosophers. Searle, however, differs from the typical analytic philosopher, in that while analytic philosophers tend to avoid putting together their detailed arguments into larger wholes, Searle has no qualms about synthesizing his arguments into a 'big picture'. In the process of creating a synthetic philosophy Searle also incorporates the views of others, and this has resulted in criticisms from many different quarters.

In this chapter I start by looking at (1) the foundations of Searle's analysis of speech acts (intentionality and rules), followed by (2) an analysis of the structure of the speech act (reference and predication). The next section outlines (3) the conditions for the generation of speech acts and (4) his elaborate taxonomy that highlights the differences between speech acts, and which culminates in (5) a revamping of Austin's classification of speech acts. (6) Other speech acts such as double and indirect speech acts are also examined. The chapter ends with (7) an examination of the important concept of context and (8) an overview of the relation between language and society. The final section examines (9) Searle's account of computer communication.

Speech acts: Intentions and rules

The starting point for Searle's analysis of linguistic communication is the speech act rather than the word or the sentence. For a speech act to count as an act of linguistic communication 'it must be produced with certain kinds of intentions' (1969: 16). Intentionality in communication marks the difference between linguistic communication and an emotional or non-verbal reaction. Saying 'ouch' after bumping one's head is not an act of communication since one did not intend to say it. The importance of intention within linguistic communication can be restated as follows: even if a squiggle and a sound were identical to a spoken or written word, unless there is an intention motivating the squiggle or word, then they cannot be considered acts of linguistic communication. In addition the intentionality that characterizes speech acts is of a particular sort. There is a difference between understanding a speech act and understanding the arrangement of furniture in a room: both entail understanding intentional behaviour, but such behaviour relates to different sorts of intentions.

The analysis of the intentions that are expressed through speech acts is rather complex because intentions are, so to speak, multilayered. If, for example, I tell Peter 'the movie starts at 9.00 pm', there are a number of intentions taking place, for not only do I intend to inform Peter about the time the movie starts, but I also intend for Peter to recognize my intention. The recognition of my second intention is important because if I only intend to inform Peter about the actual time the movie starts, then I cannot be blamed if he thinks I am hurrying him up (it is not my intention to hurry him up). The third intention is connected to the rules of language. Meaning is communicated by the rules of language, and for communication to take place Peter must understand the intentions expressed through the rules of the English language. This is why understanding a foreign language also entails understanding the intentions expressed through the rules of that language. If the rules were not recognized as an intention to communicate, then the fact that a message was communicated and understood would only be a fluke.

Searle is aware of the distinction between what we say and what we mean. This is frequently labelled as the difference between speaker and sentence meaning. There are many situations where we know what the sentence means, but we still ask ourselves: what did the speaker intend by it? When Peter tells David 'it's beautiful today', does he intend to describe the weather? Or suggest that they spend the day outdoors? Or both? Or none? To resolve this issue Searle introduces the principle of expressibility, whereby 'whatever can be meant can be said' (1969: 19).[1] The value of this principle is that the speaker, if need be, can help the hearer understand his intention by expressing it in a more direct way: the sentence can be restated so that speaker meaning and sentence meaning become one.

> We might express this principle by saying that for any meaning X and any speaker S, whenever S means (intends to convey wishes to communicate in an utterance, etc.) X then it is possible that there is some expression E such that E is an exact expression of or formulation of X. (1969: 20)

In addition the principle of expressibility shows that even in those cases where I cannot say exactly what I mean, it is always possible for me to do so either by – if no term exists – introducing it, or by learning more about the language. The importance of the principle for Searle is that it aligns the rules for performing speech acts with the rules for using certain linguistic units. He points out, for example, that studying the speech act of promising involves studying those sentences that are the literal and correct performance of a promise (1969: 21).

In his analysis of intentionality Searle takes issue with Grice, who considered the speaker's meaning as the intention the speaker has in producing an effect upon the hearer by getting the hearer to recognize that intention:

> [W]hen I say 'hello', I intend to produce in a hearer the knowledge that he is being greeted. If he recognizes it as my intention to produce in him that knowledge, then he thereby acquires that knowledge. (1969: 43)

Searle disagrees with this analysis and offers two counter-arguments, with the first stating that an account of speech acts must also take into account the rules and conventions of language. While Grice's account of intentionality and speaker meaning is useful as a starting point, it does not offer a complete picture of what is entailed as an act of communication. To illustrate his criticism, Searle offers the story of an American soldier captured by Italian troops in World War II. In order to persuade his Italian captors that he is in fact German, the American soldier repeats the only sentence he knows in German: '*Kennst du das Land wo die Zitronen bluhen*?' (1969: 44). His intention is to produce in his captors – as an effect of his utterance – the belief that he is German. But Searle asks, does uttering this sentence mean 'I am a German soldier'? (1969: 44). The German sentence does not mean this, even if that is what the speaker intends by it. What the words mean is also dictated by the language, and the sentence uttered by the soldier means 'Knowest thou the land where the lemon trees bloom?' (1969: 45).

The second counter-argument states that the focus upon the effects of the intention confuses perlocutionary acts with illocutionary ones:

– Many utterances have no perlocutionary effects. When one says 'hello' to someone else, no action is being expected from the hearer except that he/she understands that what is said to him/her counts as a greeting.
– Grice's account is limited in that it applies to certain utterances such as 'Get out', where there is a perlocutionary effect expected of the hearer, but fails to explain the differences between 'I promise', 'I predict' and 'I intend'.
– I might say something and produce an effect without intending to produce that effect. I might say and mean 'poverty is immoral' without the least interest in producing any effect upon the hearer.
– Telling someone to believe what I say because it is my intention to make him/her believe it does not qualify as a reason for believing it.

Searle concludes that 'the 'effect' on the hearer is not a belief or a response. It consists simply in the hearer's understanding the utterance of the speaker. It is this effect that I have been calling the illocutionary effect' (1969: 47). Strictly speaking, the perlocutionary effect should not be considered part of the speech act because the speech act has been completely executed.

Given that language plays a crucial role in generating the meaning that is part of the communicative act, Searle proceeds with his analysis of language by defining it as a 'rule-governed form of behaviour' (1969: 41). To belong to a linguistic community is to share in the rules that make linguistic meaning and communication possible. By learning the same rules, speakers of a language can communicate a message and have it understood by hearers. In his analysis of the rule-governed nature of language, Searle distinguishes between regulative and constitutive rules.

Regulative rules are those which regulate actions that already exist. The human action of eating exists independently of the rules, and yet there are rules that guide our eating habits. Likewise, our interpersonal relations exist independently but there are rules of etiquette that guide our behaviour.

> Regulative rules characteristically take the form or can be paraphrased as imperatives, e.g., "When cutting food, hold the knife in the right hand", or "Officers must wear ties at dinner". [...] Regulative rules characteristically have the form or can be comfortably paraphrased in the form "Do X" or "If Y do X". (1969: 34)

Constitutive rules differ in that with these rules we are creating the actual forms of behaviour out of nothing. One of the prime examples of constitutive rules is the playing of games: without the rules of football there would be no game, as it is the rules that bring the game into existence. Without the rules there would be 22 men running around a field chasing a ball. The 'formula' that captures constitutive rules is 'X counts as Y in context C' (1969: 35). There are two points that need to be kept in mind when understanding constitutive rules. The first is that the rules are usually a system of rules. It might be the case that one rule does not have the 'counts as' formula, but when this rule is seen as part of the whole system then it is the whole system that constitutes the 'counts as'.

> Thus, though rule 1 of basketball – the game is played with five players to a side – does not lend itself to this form, acting in accordance with all or a sufficiently large subset of the rules does count as playing basketball. (1969: 36)

The second point is that the Y term in the 'counts as' formulation is not a neutral term in the sense that it usually describes consequences:

> '[O]ffside', 'homerun', 'touchdown', 'checkmate' are not mere labels for the state of affairs that is specified by the X term, but they introduce further consequences, by way of, e.g., penalties, points, and winning and losing. (1969: 36)

Having established the importance of constative rules in understanding both games and language, Searle still needs to tackle the question of why and how it is that speech acts generate illocutionary force. How is it possible that the speech act of promising – which is fundamentally an act composed of words following the rules of language – creates an obligation? To answer this question Searle forwards these claims:

1. Languages are conventional: to use a language is to use the conventions of that specific language, whether it is English or Swahili.
2. Illocutionary acts are rule-governed: while there are some illocutionary acts that can be performed 'naturally' by getting the viewer to recognize the intentions through the person's behaviour, this does not eliminate the fact that many perlocutionary acts cannot be performed without language. Not only would it be impossible learn complex issues, (an account of the computer systems of the space shuttle) but, Searle adds, 'I wish to argue, some system of rule governed elements is necessary for there to be certain *types* of speech acts, such as promising or asserting' (1969: 38–39). To highlight the difference between the rule-governed nature of illocutionary acts and 'natural' forms of behaviour, Searle points out that the rules for making a promise or asserting and so on cannot produce a natural effect. To state that 'I have a headache' is very different from actually having a headache, as I can have a headache whether I state it or not.
3. Languages are rule-governed. While particular languages use their own conventions, each language follows the same underlying rules so that 'fact that an utterance of a promising device (under appropriate conditions) counts as the undertaking of an obligation is a matter of rules and not a matter of the conventions of French or English' (1969: 39–40).

Referring and predicating

A speech act has two components: reference and predication. In 'Sam smokes habitually' (1969: 22), the speech act refers to or is about 'Sam' and it predicates 'smoking' of him. Together, referring and predicating constitute a propositional act, which entails what we are talking about. On its own the propositional act fails to show its communicative value so that an account of communications must include an account of what the speaker intends to do with his/her speech act. This is why the propositional act is coupled with an illocutionary force indicating device: the latter tells us what type of speech act the sentence is, such as whether it is a question, an assertion or a request. Together the illocutionary force indicating device and the propositional act form the basis of the process of verbal communication.

In both his analyses of reference and predication, Searle introduces a number of conditions that bring out their respective features. In the case of reference some preliminaries should be noted: referring requires that the normal input and output conditions are in place, so that to refer requires that the speaker can vocalize the words and that the hearer can hear them. Referring also belongs to a larger speech act since the act of referring takes place as we are communicating. The conditions outlined by Searle as enabling reference are:

1. The axiom of existence which states that proper referring entails that the object being referred to exists. So when talking to my friends about my new plasma television set I am referring to a specific object that we are all admiring. If I do not own a plasma television set, then a condition for referring successfully has failed.
2. The principle of identification, which refers to the way an object can be redescribed. Thus to talk or refer to an object we can use the demonstrative *that* and point to it – 'that (pointing to the television set) is mine'. Or we can also describe the object so that it stands out from other objects in the room, saying 'the flat screened, 30-inch thing hanging on the wall is mine'. Both conditions (a) and (b) enable us to pick out objects during the course of our communication.
3. The principle of intentionality. The speakers must (a) intend to use words and sentences that point to an object, and (b) want the hearer to recognize both the intention to refer to the object and the intention that the speaker has in referring to the object. This recognition is achieved through the rules of language that both speaker and hearer share in common. In explaining this point Searle asks us to imagine this situation:

> I may call my hearer's attention to an object by throwing it at him, or hitting him over the head with it. But such cases are not in general cases of referring, because the intended effect is not achieved by recognition on his part of my intentions. (1969: 95)

A question that has drawn considerable attention in contemporary analytic philosophy of language is the problem of proper names. Some, Searle notes (1969: 162–64), have argued that a name functions as a label so that although it is attached to a person, it does not have any sense attached to it. If this is the case, then how does it refer or point to persons who no longer exist or who live far away? Searle responds to the problem posed by proper names by invoking the principle of identification. If we ask 'who is Richard Nixon?', we answer by offering a number of descriptions that are attributed to that person, such as ' […] was a president of the United States', ' […] resigned on account of the Watergate scandal' and so on. The benefit of Searle's account is that it enables a person to be described in many ways, and yet these different descriptions still refer to the same person.

Searle's analysis of predicating ties up with his account of referring. He adds three further conditions to those already mentioned:

1. It is necessary to satisfy the condition for referring before we can predicate. This is obvious enough for we cannot predicate if what one is predicating does not exist. I cannot predicate successfully of the tiger that 'it sure looks hungry' if there is no tiger.
2. The application of predicates. When I predicate a quality of an object, that predicate must be relevant to the object. It makes no sense to say 'the rock has died': to be able to predicate reveals that we know a lot about the world.
3. The application of the values as true and false for all utterances. Searle's point is to show that it is not only assertions that can be judged for their truth or falsity, but also requests,

commands, promises and so on. Whatever forms a predicate might have (requests, promises, commands, etc.), the values of truth and falsity still apply. When the general commands his troops to 'attack the bunker', it is true that they have not yet attacked and it will be true once they do. This is an important point for Searle who shows how truth values apply to all uses of language and not merely one type.

It should be noted that although predicates are important in that they bring content to the speech act, that is, what the speech act is about, they still depend upon the way we talk about that content. In other words, it is the illocutionary force that conditions the way the predicate is used (as an assertion, question or command). This highlights the difference between predicates and reference, for although referring is also about part of a speech act, what is referred to is independent of the speech act. To sum up, understanding predicates involves both understanding the content and the illocutionary force.

Conditions for speech acts

Given that Searle accepts Austin's view that speech acts are used not only to describe facts but to do things, he considers it fundamental for the study of speech acts to outline the conditions that are necessary for the understanding of speech acts. Although Searle offers a number of conditions, these can be reduced to four main ones.

1. The propositional content condition: this focusses upon the content of the speech act, on what it is about. It is the content that must satisfy certain conditions for it to be successful. Promises, for example, must be future oriented, while apologies look to the past since we apologize for the things we have done.
2. The preparatory condition: such a condition varies, ranging across the different social, mental and physical states of the speaker and the hearer, and must be in place before the speech act can be issued correctly. If you congratulate someone, something positive must have happened (although we can be sarcastic in our congratulations); and for the general's command to take effect, it must be directed at his inferiors, not his superiors.
3. The sincerity condition: this describes the speaker's relation to his or her utterance. A promise is sincere if I intend to keep it; a command is sincere if the general wants the soldier to do what he commands. The sincerity condition can be satisfied in different ways and the conditions of satisfaction depend upon the type of speech act: promises and commands differ in their respective conditions of satisfaction. However, we are all familiar with people saying 'I didn't mean it' as though that negates or justifies not keeping their promises. Searle disagrees, arguing that a promise is a promise and the speaker who promises but fails to keep it is insincere.
4. The essential condition: the essential condition of a speech act is that it is intended. A promise is intended as a promise, and it therefore places the speaker under an obligation

to do something; a command places the hearer under an obligation to follow some action. With the essential condition the speech act is intended to fulfil something linguistically. Searle considers this condition as the most important one.

An analysis of speech acts must take into account what Searle describes as normal input and output conditions. Thus, for example, for any speech act to take place both the speaker and the hearer must understand the same language, know what they are saying, do not suffer from any speaking or hearing impediment and so on. These do not actually contribute to the analysis of the various speech acts but are necessary for any speech act to take place.

Differences between speech acts

Searle continues to develop the ideas he introduced in *Speech Acts* in a number of essays that make up the book *Expression and Meaning* (1985). In 'A taxonomy of illocutionary acts' (1985: 1–29) he provides a list of twelve ways in which these differences between speech acts can be generated, although some of these ways overlap with the conditions established in the earlier analysis of speech acts. The taxonomy accounts for the way speech acts can differ from each other.

1. The point or purpose of the speech act

   The point or purpose of an order can be specified by saying that it is an attempt to get the hearer to do something. The point or purpose of a description is that it is a representation (true or false, accurate or inaccurate) of how something is. The point or purpose of a promise is that it is an undertaking of an obligation by the speaker to do something. (1985: 2)

This aspect is similar to the earlier essential conditions, and the idea is that the speech act has an illocutionary point or purpose. Thus, in a promise the speaker commits himself/herself to what he/she has promised. Again Searle distinguishes between the illocutionary point and the *illocutionary force*. The latter is the broader term that includes the illocutionary point together with the other dimensions of speech acts. The illocutionary point concerns the effect of the speech act: both a command and a request want the hearer to do something, but the way this is done – the 'force' used to get the hearer to do what the speaker wants – is different.

2. The 'direction of fit', which describes the relation between the word and the world (1985: 3). When the speech act fits or corresponds to the way the world is, then it has succeeded in describing the world: when I say 'the door is shut' and the door is indeed shut, the direction of fit is word-to-world. There is also, however, a 'direction of fit'

that goes in the opposite direction, the world-to-word. In this case the world must be changed to fit the word: if the door is open when I say 'shut the door', then by shutting the door the world changes to match my utterance. Other possibilities include no direction of fit and a dual direct of fit.

3. The psychological dimension (1985: 4). This dimension repeats Searle's earlier concern with the speaker's sincerity in expressing his/her utterances. The person who utters a belief, a promise or request must be sincere in his belief, promise or request: failing to do so is not only inappropriate but abusive.

4. The strength of the speech act. 'Both "I suggest we go to the movies" and "I insist that we go to the movies" have the same illocutionary point, but it is presented with different strengths' (1985: 5). The strength or force of a speech act may vary – I might speak loudly or softly – but the illocutionary point remains the same. It still remains a promise whether I shout or utter it quietly.

5. The status of speakers and hearers (1985: 5–6). Speech acts differ according to who is uttering them. This point concerns the social standings of the person, so that the utterances of the general differ from those of the private, and so on.

6. The interests of the speaker and hearer (1985: 6). The speech act varies according to the situation of the speaker and hearer, so if a person gets a promotion then congratulations are in order; if a person is in mourning, condolences are appropriate.

7. The utterance within the discourse (1985: 6). Certain speech acts are part of a larger set of speech acts or discourse. If I say 'I conclude' it is fairly obvious that other things have already been said.

8. Differences in propositional content. Speech acts are generated by devices that tell us the content of what is being uttered (1985: 6). Certain devices such as verbs can indicate whether the content refers to the future or the past.

9. Public and non-public issuing of speech acts (1985: 6). Although some speech acts can start or end with 'I classify this' or 'I conclude that', this does not mean that what follows must be publicly stated. We can classify or conclude whatever we like without saying what it is that we are classifying or concluding. On the other hand, it makes no sense to say 'I promise' without publicly saying what it is we are promising, or to issue a command without publicly saying what the command is.

10. Institutional contexts (1985: 7). Some speech acts require non-linguistic institutions to acquire their force. Excommunication requires the institution of the Church; marriage requires either the Church or the state. It is useful to keep in mind that language is also an institution, albeit different from non-linguistic institutions. A promise functions as a speech act on account of the institution of language that regulates what counts as particular kinds of speech acts.

11. Differences in illocutionary verbs having a performative use and not others. Most illocutionary verbs have a performative use (stating, concluding and pleading) but 'one cannot perform acts of, for example, boasting or threatening, by saying "I hereby boast" or "I hereby threaten." Not all illocutionary verbs are performative verbs' (1985: 7).

12. Differences of style in performance. The way the speech act is delivered can vary even though there might be no differences in the illocutionary point (1985: 8). Other stylistic differences are those between speaking and writing, or an academic use of language and ordinary language.

The classification of speech acts

There is, however, more to the study of speech acts. It might seem that the study of speech acts is open-ended in the sense that there are an infinite number of speech acts without any order to them. Austin himself, towards the end of *How to Do Things with Words* (1975), had suspected that despite the vast array of speech acts it was possible to classify them into certain basic types. He proposed a tentative classification but died before this classificatory system could be established. In 'A taxonomy of illocutionary acts' (1985), Searle takes up and refines Austin's task.

Searle is critical of Austin's attempt to classify speech acts by concentrating on verbs in the first person, such as 'I promise' or 'I state', because in so doing the difference between these speech acts is lost. By way of contrast, Searle's proposed list of dimensions of speech acts brings out the differences between 'I announce' and 'I promise': '[a]nnouncing [...] is not the name of a type of illocutionary act, but of the way in which some illocutionary act is performed' (Searle 1985: 9). When we say 'I announce' we are invoking the twelfth dimension because of the way we perform the speech act, its means of presentation.

An examination of Austin's classification shows that it has no order to it but bounces around from one dimension to another (1985: 8–12).

1. Commissives are a basic and fundamental category and Austin defines them as committing the speaker to a certain course of action (1975: 157). It is as though by saying 'I intend to go to the party' we are promising or committing ourselves; Searle rejects this, arguing that 'I intend' is not a commissive but rather a description of what the speaker has in mind; it is a report of what he intends to do.
2. Expositives are described by Austin as 'the conducting of arguments, and the clarifying of usages and of references' (1975: 161). But what Austin calls expositives belong to Searle's seventh dimension where a speech act is part of a larger discourse.
3. Executives involve the giving of decisions (1975: 155). Searle argues that these speech acts can be explained by looking at the social status of the speaker and hearer (fifth dimension), and also by locating them within an extralinguistic institution (tenth dimension).
4. Behabitives are reactions or expressions of attitudes to others (1975: 160). Searle finds the behabitives ill-defined, arguing that they can be better explained with reference to the interests of the speaker or the hearer (sixth dimension), plus the expression of the psychological states of the participants (third dimension).

5. Verdictives are the judicial act of delivering findings (1975: 153). Although Searle does not comment, Fotion has commented that

> it should be clear that verdictives involve appeals to the 7th dimension (*differences in relations to the rest of the discourse*), the 10th dimension (requiring extra-linguistic institutions) and perhaps the 5th dimension (status of speaker and hearer). (2000: 46)

Searle's review of Austin's taxonomy shows its failings and the need for a more systematic account of speech acts. 'What I propose to do is take illocutionary point, and its corollaries, direction of fit and expressed sincerity conditions as the basis for constructing a classification' (1985: 12). He is critical of Austin's attempt at classifying speech acts on the grounds that they are disorganized, since there is no principle of explanation that tells us how to separate the different types of speech acts. Searle is not simply presenting a new taxonomy of speech act types but – and this is of fundamental importance – presenting a method that explains why one type is more fundamental than the other. Out of Austin's original list he only retains the commissives.

1. Searle (1985: 14) agrees with Austin that commissives are the basic type of speech act because they are oriented towards what he has already emphasized as the point or purpose. However, there is more to Searle's account of commissives and he introduces the notion of the 'direction of fit'. A commissive has a world-to-word direction of fit so that the world changes to fit the words. By uttering and fulfilling a promise the world has changed to match the words. This can be schematized as follows: (C) represents the commitment, the arrow pointing upwards stands for the world-to-word direction of fit, (I) shows the sincerity condition (of intent) and (S does A) refers to the propositional content (in the future).

$$C \uparrow I \ (S \ does \ A)$$

Commissives are the basic category because a number of dimensions apply to them, such as the point of the speech act, the direction of fit and the sincerity condition. Other dimensions can also play a secondary role so that within the rubric of commissives variations (vows, swearing) can take place.

2. Assertives commit the speaker to a proposition that can be judged as true or false (1985: 12). This can be schematized in the following way: ⊢ represents the assertion, the downward pointing arrow describes the word-to-world direction of fit, (B) represents the sincerity condition (of belief) and p represents the propositional content:

$$\vdash \downarrow B \ (p)$$

Like the commissives, the assertive category has a number of variations so that a number of other speech acts fit the assertive model. To say 'I state' or 'I affirm' is both to say that something corresponds to the world and that the speaker believes in what he/she is saying. Variations take place if the speaker is unsure of what he/she says (the dimension of strength of point), or if the speaker complains about losing something (the dimension of interest to the speaker) or if the speaker can be saying something that is part of a larger discourse (the dimension of the rest of the discourse).

3. Directives attempt to get the hearer to do something (1985: 13). Directives can be schematized as follows: the exclamation mark (!) represents the illocutionary point of getting the hearer to do something, the direction of fit is world-to-word ($\uparrow$), the sincerity condition W (of wanting action A to get done) and the propositional content showing it is the hearer who should do it (H does A).

$$! \uparrow W \text{ (H does A)}$$

Once again other secondary dimensions can come into play and these make variations possible. One can, for example, ask for something aggressively or politely (the fourth dimension) or one can ask something in virtue of one's institutionally defined status (the fifth dimension).

4. Expressives communicate the psychological state of the speaker (1985: 15). Other examples of expressives are to thank, to congratulate, to apologize, to console, to deplore and to welcome. Searle's analysis of expressives is a subtle one in that it does not involve what we typically consider as responses to our emotions. Weeping with joy at having won the national lottery is not considered by Searle to be an expressive act of communication. Nor do expressives include saying what one did, as when I tell you how angry I was yesterday. This is a description or a report of an action. Expressive speech acts are those where linguistically one implies that one has had a certain emotion: to say 'Good Morning' implies that the speaker has a positive, cheerful emotion, just as saying 'I'm sorry' implies that I have the emotion of sorrow. These are legitimate speech acts that can be schematized as follows: (E) represents the illocutionary point of expressives, (Ø) represents the fact that there is no direction of fit for expressives, (P) represents the various psychological states and the propositional content is represented by (S/H + property).

$$E \text{ (Ø) (P) (S/H + property)}$$

As usual there are variations in relation to the dimensions used. For example, winning the lottery and grieving at the loss of a close relative require different expressives: clearly the propositional content (the eighth dimension) and the interests of the speaker (the sixth dimension) come into play. Other variations can be produced with the fourth dimension describing the strength of the illocutionary point. The strength of an apology can vary: there is a difference between brushing against someone in a corridor and crashing into someone else's car through neglect.

5. Declaratives are a unique type of utterance because once uttered they have the power to change things: when the couple are declared man and wife, they are in effect married (1985: 16–17). Just by being uttered the speech act changes the status or condition of the hearer. Declaratives are also unique in that they include both directions of fit: by uttering them one is bringing about a change in the world and simultaneously the world is changing or 'adapting' to one's utterance. The schema for declaratives is as follows: (D) represents the illocutionary point of declaratives; the double arrow (↕) shows that the direction of fit is two way (from world-to-word and vice versa at the same time); the symbol (P) represents the propositional content and the (Ø) represents the lack of sincerity condition.

$$D \updownarrow (Ø) (P)$$

The variations of the declaratives depend upon specific dimensions but probably the most important dimension concerns non-linguistic institutions as described by the tenth dimension. Declaring war or excommunicating someone requires that the relevant speech acts be embedded within an institutional framework such as the state or the Church. Other variations on declaratives emerge relative to the social position of the speaker (the fifth dimension) so that, for example, only the queen can knight certain personages.

Searle's classification of speech acts accomplishes two goals: on the one hand, it is broad enough to show the multiplicity of speech acts that can be found within natural language, and yet, on the other hand, it also creates an order or a system out of this multiplicity. The different speech acts – promising, requesting, baptising, commanding and so on – can be grouped systematically with reasons offered as to why each speech act should be within its respective category (1985: 29).

Complex speech acts: Double speech acts and indirect speech acts

In his analysis of speech acts, Searle stated that he would follow the strategy of starting by examining straightforward speech acts to establish a basis for his theory while leaving complex speech acts to be dealt with later. In 'Taxonomy' he begins to examine non-standard speech acts such as assertive declaratives: these are single speech acts that function doubly. By way of example, Searle describes the failed attempt by the runner to reach another base when the empire calls 'You're Out' (1985: 19–20). This speech act is both an assertive, since the umpire has passed the judgement that the ball has reached the second base before the runner, and a declaration, since the status of the runner has changed from being in the game to being out of it. Assertive declarations can be schematized as follows:

$$D \downarrow \updownarrow (B)\, p$$

While (D) represents the declaratives, (B) represents the sincerity condition (of belief that characterises assertions), the arrow downwards represents the assertive direction of fit, and the double arrow the declarative direction of fit.

In 'Indirect speech acts' (1985: 30–57) Searle uses his theory of speech acts and his classification of speech acts to elaborate on the much used linguistic phenomenon of indirect speech acts. 'The problem posed by indirect speech acts is the problem of how it is possible for the speaker to say one thing and mean that but also to mean something else' (1985: 31). When a person tells you 'you're standing on my foot', then he/she is not merely providing information that can be judged as true or false, but indirectly telling you to take your foot off theirs. In other words, they are issuing a directive even though at face value the utterance is an assertive.[2]

What needs to be examined is the way indirect speech acts actually operate and how they can be explained within the framework of speech act theory. Searle offers the example of a dinner conversation between Dr Phixum, an orthopaedic surgeon and his patient. When Dr Phixum asks 'can you pass the salt'?, is he asking about his patient's ability to literally lift the salt off the table? If this were the case then the patient would reply with something of the sort, 'Yes today I can, though 3 days ago it would not have been possible'. The patient's reply would consist of a series of assertives. However, if Dr Phixum actually wanted to add salt to his food then maybe uttering an assertive ('here you are') or just passing the salt silently would be sufficient. The conversational sequence in this example is that of a directive followed by an assertive should the patient respond verbally, with another directive involved if the salt is passed (1985: 46–47).

Although Searle's rather elaborate breakdown of the speech act seems long, it must be remembered that this takes place in an instant. Just as behavioural acts can be broken down and redescribed in terms of smaller acts that constitute one large act, the same applies to speech acts.

However, some important considerations are introduced by Searle as he develops his account of indirect speech acts:

1. An indirect speech act is a literal utterance. It is not a question of ambiguity, since if it were ambiguous the hearer would ask for clarification. Rather it is (directly) a question about whether the hearer can pass the salt (his arm might be broken, there might be no salt on the table, the salt container might be empty) and (indirectly) a directive to pass the salt. This explains why the hearer might respond to Phixum's question by saying 'I cannot as my arm is broken'; in this case, he is responding to a question about his ability. Should he be able to physically lift the salt off the table, then (if he wants) he can also

oblige Dr Phixum and pass him the salt. What this shows is that indirect speech acts are indebted to speech act theory. For the indirect speech act to work what is directly uttered and indirectly implemented must be connected to certain preparatory conditions such as the speaker or hearer's abilities, wants or social setting; or to the propositional content so that what is directly uttered can be connected to the indirect aspect of the speech act.

2. In everyday life indirect speech acts do not cause too much trouble since their frequency has given them an idiomatic status. Idioms are like formulas that listeners have no trouble identifying as conventional uses of language.

3. Searle acknowledges the work of P. Grice, who pointed out that the conversational setting required the cooperation of participants. In this case, the hearer cooperates with the speaker by understanding the indirect speech act; this is important because without the assumption of cooperation it would be difficult to explain how speech acts worked.

4. The broad picture Searle gives of indirect speech acts is that they are a polite way of talking, rather than the perhaps abrupt way a directive sounds. When, for example, you want the hearer to leave your apartment, there is a difference between saying 'it's getting late now' and the harsh sounding 'get out'. The problem is that politeness makes it possible for the hearer to not comply since he/she might reply 'yes it's late, but the movie's really good'. Politeness works because it offers a choice, even though the speaker really does not want the hearer to choose.

Searle's analysis of double speech acts shows that his classification can handle more sophisticated uses of language.

Contexts

Unlike indirect speech acts, where speaker and sentence meaning can be distinguished separately, literal speech does the opposite by bringing them together. The sentence says what the speaker means it to say and this applies to any of the speech act types listed in Searle's taxonomy: commissives, directives and so on. In literal sentences it is often claimed that the meaning of the sentence is independent of any contextual concerns, a view that has been called the 'zero or null context view'. In 'Literal Meaning' (1985: 117: 136) Searle explicitly rejects this view:

> I shall argue that for a large class of sentences there is no such thing as the zero or null context for the interpretation of sentences, and that as far as our semantic competence is concerned we understand the meaning of such sentences only against a set of background assumptions about the contexts in which the sentence could be appropriately uttered. (1985: 117)

In his early writings, Searle's notion of preparatory conditions already indicated the importance of contextual considerations for the realization of successful speech acts. Thus, excommunicating someone requires a social and institutional context where the speaker has the authority to excommunicate; to promise something assumes that the speaker can fulfil the promise, that it is future-oriented; to make assertive claims the speaker must provide some evidence.

However, in 'Literal Meaning' Searle is making a further and stronger claim that describes the context independently of the preparatory conditions and beyond the use of reference.

> For a large class of unambiguous sentences such as "The cat is on the mat", the notion of literal meaning of the sentence only has application relative to a set of background assumptions. The truth conditions of the sentence will vary with variations in these background assumptions; and given the absence or presence of some background assumptions the sentence does not have determinate truth conditions. These variations have nothing to do with indexicality, change of meaning, ambiguity, conversational implication, vagueness or presupposition as these notions are standardly discussed in the philosophical and linguistic literature. (1985: 125)

When one says 'the cat is on the mat', this sentence might seem context-free since it can be understood without needing to know anything about the context of its utterance. Searle wants to imply that even if we ignore the referential aspects (this cat and this mat) and if we ignore the preparatory conditions of the speaker, there is still an underlying context playing its part in the sentence. This can be seen by the 'on' in the sentence: by saying 'the cat is on the mat' we are assuming the existence of a gravity-conditioned world, where cats can be on mats precisely because the laws of gravity are in operation. We also assume that the mat remains rigid on the floor even though it is not rigid, and that the cat does not transform itself into another creature from minute to minute. Perhaps, to avoid confusion or for the sake of clarity, it might be useful to add these contextual features – taken for granted – into the sentence itself. This would, however, be an extremely daunting task, as (1) it would transform simple sentences into long and complicated ones; and (2) each new sentence we bring would itself have a context, and this would entail elaborating these other contexts ad infinitum.

Searle reinforces his argument concerning the implicit contextual assumptions operating and conditioning our speech acts with an example of a directive: the request for a hamburger with relish and mustard and so on carries with it a large amount of information related to 'institutions of restaurants and money and exchanging prepared foods for money' (1985: 127). But the presence of the context can be brought out even in contexts that are not explicitly institutional:

> Suppose for example that hamburger is brought to me encased in a cubic yard of solid Lucite plastic so rigid that it takes a jackhammer to bust it open, or suppose the hamburger

is a mile wide and is "delivered" to me by smashing down the wall of the restaurant and sliding the edge of it in. Has my order "Give me a hamburger medium rare, with ketchup and mustard, but easy on the relish" been fulfilled or obeyed in these cases? My inclination is to say no, it has not been fulfilled or obeyed because that is not what I meant in my literal utterance of the sentence. (1985: 127)

The point about Searle's example is that we take it for granted that hamburgers are served in ways that allow them to be eaten. We never think of reminding the waiter that the hamburger should fit into the plate so that we can eat it.

In *Intentionality: An Essay in the Philosophy of Mind* (1983), Searle introduces a further distinction between the context as Network and the context as Background. Speech acts and mental states are not isolated, individual entities, but are part of, or connected to, other speech acts and mental states. Searle uses the example of a person deciding to run for political office: to do so and for us to understand what he/she is doing, it is necessary that he/she does a number of things such as announce his/her candidacy, have awareness of the rules of eligibility, gain the approval of a number of party members and so on. In other words, taking part in politics is part of a set of practices that have been elaborated upon by the political institutions of the land. The network, therefore involves an awareness of social and institutional conditions.

Although the line separating the Network from the Background is not rigid, a useful way of distinguishing between the two is to say that the utterances related to the Network possess Intentionality, while those of the Background are pre-Intentional. The question Searle's analysis raises concerns our knowledge of the background: if it is pre-Intentional, how do we know about it? To answer this question, Searle introduces the distinction between knowing that and knowing how, arguing that it is the latter know-how that points to the background:

The Background is a set of nonrepresentational mental capacities that enable all representing to take place. Intentional states only have the conditions of satisfaction that they do, and thus only are the states that they are, against a Background of abilities that are not themselves Intentional states. In order that I can now have Intentional states that I do I must have certain kinds of know-how: I must know how things are and I must know how to do things, but the kinds of "know-how" in question are not, in these cases, forms of "knowing that". (1983: 143)

We look at a table and know that it is a table, just as we know that a table is a solid object. Accompanying this belief is the knowledge of how we can use tables – to read, eat and place laptops, books or television upon. We know how to deal with or use tables because we know that it is solid: the know-how is the background knowledge that we carry about with us and we become aware of it through a secondary reaction, as when something that we usually take for granted is questioned.

Searle illustrates the way the Network and the Background are the conditions that enable the following speech acts to succeed:

1. The chairman opened the meeting.
2. The artillery opened fire.
3. Bill opened a restaurant.

With sentences (1) to (3) the meaning of *opened* is the same and it is literal in each case: if it were not, then the meaning of *opened* would be multiplied indefinitely. To understand the use of *opened* in each sentence, it is necessary to refer to the Network and Background of each sentence, since different assumptions are brought to bear upon them. By examining the Network and Background we can answer the question of whether they are true or false. On the other hand, the following sentences are grammatically correct but leave us perplexed as how to interpret them:

4. Bill opened the mountain.
5. Sally opened the grass.
6. Sam opened the sun.

Searle explains the difference between the two sets of sentences:

> Each of the sentences in the first group is understood within a Network of Intentional states and against a Background of capacities and social practices. We know how to open doors, books, eyes, wounds and walls; and the differences in the Network and in the Background of practices produce different understandings of the same verb. Furthermore, we simply have no common practices of opening mountains, grass or suns. It would be easy to invent a Background, i.e., to imagine a practice, that would give a clear sense to the idea of opening mountains, grass and suns, but we have no such common Background at present. (1983: 147)

All this talk of Background and Network raises the question of where they are located. Are they metaphysical entities existing out there independently of us or are they mental, entities existing in our heads? Searle favours the latter mental view because the Background and Network 'spring' into being or 'capture' our awareness as a reaction to them. Although the assumptions that constitute the background concern things in the world, it is the way people are disposed towards them that counts. For example we assume that broken glass is sharp, so we are disposed not to walk on it barefoot; or we assume that sofas are heavy and that, therefore, we are not able to lift them on our own. It is because of our reactions towards these assumptions that Searle considers the Background as mental. But this does not entail that the Backgrounds vary for each and every person such that communication becomes impossible with every person inhabiting a world on his/her own. This view – solipsism – is rejected on the grounds that the world we share is a common one and it includes gravity, hard pavements and global warming.

Searle also broadens his study of language from its internal workings to an account of the relationship between language and the mind. In *Intentionality* he shifts his focus to language as being 'directed' towards something, and as it turns out the concept of Intention comes to play a crucial role in explaining both language and the mind: '[i]ntentionality is that property of many mental states and events by which they are directed at or about or of objects and states of affairs in the world' (1983: 1). There are two features that should be further explained:

1. An intentional state has two components: a psychological aspect (the mental states of belief, desire, etc.) and a content (what the beliefs and desires are about). Both the psychological aspect and the content are directed towards something or someone, so that when a speaker says 'I believe that Gandhi was courageous' the belief is not about the content but about Gandhi. As can be deduced from Searle's earlier writings on language, Intentional states have a direction of fit. Obviously the direction of fit depends upon the psychological mode of the speaker: a belief about the world implies a mind-world direction, so, for example, if I believe it is sunny then my mental state matches the world. But if I wish that tomorrow will be sunny, since I am wishing that the world (tomorrow) matches my wish, then the direction of fit is world-to-mind.

2. Intentional states are tied to conditions of satisfaction or success. When a belief is satisfactory it turns out to be true, and when an intention is satisfactory then what is intended is performed. Searle argues that there is a striking similarity between his speech act theory and his theory of the Intentionality of the mind: illocutionary forces are similar to psychological states. Both speech acts and intentional states have a content, are about or directed towards objects and have a direction of fit: both require conditions of satisfaction. However, Searle qualifies this distinction by arguing that the Intentionality of the mind is the foundation upon which the intentionality of language depends. In other words language depends upon the mind but not vice-versa.

> Since sentences – the sounds that come out of one's mouth or the marks that one makes on paper – are, considered in one way, just objects in the world like any other objects, their capacity to represent is not intrinsic but is derived from the Intentionality of the mind. The Intentionality of mental states, on the other hand, is not derived from some more prior forms of Intentionality but is intrinsic to the states themselves. An agent uses a sentence to make a statement or ask a question, but he does not in that way *use* his beliefs and desires, he simply has them. A sentence is a syntactical object on which representational capacities are imposed: beliefs and desires and other Intentional states are not, as such, syntactical objects (though they may be and usually are expressed in sentences), and their representational capacities are not imposed but are intrinsic. (1983: vii–viii)

By saying that Intentional states are foundational, Searle is arguing that the mind's Intentionality is projected onto the world through language. Both mental states and language are directed towards the world, but while language has meaning, mental states do not: it is through language that mental states are expressed. The Intentionality of the mind uses language to express its psychological states with the conditions of success revealing whether that psychological state has been successfully expressed or not.

An overview of Searle's concept of intentionality reveals its importance in two senses:

1. in the narrow sense, every speech act involves some kind of intentionality, since it enables us to describe a particular state of mind. In describing the hot and humid weather I intend to express my belief that it is hot and humid; likewise, when the general issues a command his intention is to order his troops into battle.
2. in the broad sense, language is configured or directed towards the world. Our language is about the world, so in talking about the weather my language is directed towards the world. This notion of Intention (written in capitals to distinguish it from the other sense) captures the way language and the mind hinge onto the world.

Language and social life

The social dimension of language has already been alluded to since many speech acts would not be successful unless they had the appropriate social background. Thus for a command to be successful it must be uttered by the general to the lieutenant within a military system that is organized hierarchically. Searle develops his account of social reality using ideas from his earlier accounts of language and mind but also introducing new ones.

In *The Construction of Social Reality* (1995) Searle uses the concept of constitutive rules to show the extent to which the institutions of society can be said to be constructed. It should be pointed out, however, that when he uses the concept of institutions what he has in mind is a much broader concept than that which we usually understand by an institution (such as the military or educational institutions), which we tend to associate with certain buildings. For Searle, it is only within an institution that his formula (X) counts as (Y) in (C) can be meaningful. Take for example the game of chess: when the king is checked, we are faced with an institutional fact because the constitutive rules of chess make it so. The game of chess is, therefore, also an institution and institutions are composed of a number of interrelated constitutive rules. Clearly, given the way Searle explains institutions in terms of constitutive rules, there are a very large number of institutions that cover most social practices, including perhaps the most fundamental institution with society – language.

Fotion (2000: 192–8) demonstrates the way social reality is created by asking us to imagine what goes on when a person invents a game (such as the game of Chaos). The first and obvious step in this process involves establishing the rules of the game; to do so this person uses Searle's formula: X (the first to cross the line) counts as Y (five points) in

C (when played on a certain field, watched by certain officials). The concept of collective intentionality plays an important part in the acceptance of rules and social reality. By accepting the rules of the game of Chaos, the players and coaches together intend to play according to the rules. Since there is a tendency to associate intentions with a person, the concept of collective intentionality has an aura of mystery about it, because it suggests that over and above our individual intentions there is a kind of 'super' or 'mega' intentionality. Searle wants to dispel this 'aura' associated with collective intentionality but retains the concept to show how frequently it is used within our social lives. Collective intentions are we-intentions: just because we think of intentions as taking place in an individual mind, this does not mean that it is not possible to have group intentions. The importance of this concept in Searle's account of social reality lies in the fact that it allows for the introduction of social facts: collective intentionality makes social facts possible.

In addition, while observing the game is subjective, understanding it is objective or independent of the person, since to understand it means knowing the rules of the game. Both the spectators and the players know the rules of the game, and – by playing against each other – both teams agree to play by the rules. This agreement highlights a crucial feature of Searle's account of social reality: unlike natural reality, social reality is self-referential, which means that humans are aware of – or can be made aware of – what they are socially describing. Talking about social life includes necessarily accepting it for what it is since there is always a human component or attitude towards it.

> Something can be a mountain even if no one believes it is a mountain; something can be a molecule even if no one thinks anything at all about it. But for social facts, the attitude that we take toward the phenomenon is partly constitutive of the phenomenon. If, for example, we give a big cocktail party, and invite everyone in Paris, and if things get out of hand, and it turns out that the casualty rate is greater than the Battle of Austerlitz – all the same, it is not a war; it is just one amazing cocktail party. Part of being a cocktail party is being thought to be a cocktail party; part of being a war is being thought to be a war. This is a remarkable feature of social facts; it has no analogue among physical facts. (1995: 33–34)

An interesting and pertinent question concerns the way constitutive rules create forms of behaviour from nowhere: how do constitutive rules create institutional facts? The answer involves the normative aspect of constitutive rules: if we see the constitutive rules of games it is evident that the goal or point of the game is to win. These rules prescribe the purpose of the game and therefore the norms that the players of both sides set out to follow. Do these normative features of constitutive rules also apply to other domains of social life? How do they translate into a marriage ceremony? Applying the formula of constitutive rules to a wedding, to say 'I do' (X) counts as getting married (Y) within a church with a priest, witnesses and so on (C).

The normative features of getting married entail knowing the rules of marriage, and because getting married is a serious event these rules are repeated during the ceremony. Once the rules are clear then the normative feature is implied: if one gets married one should behave in a certain way – one has, in effect, changed his/her lifestyle. Furthermore, all those taking part in the ceremony – the officials, the couple, the witnesses and the best man – show their approval of marriage as an institution and of the specific marriage taking place. All the individuals attending the wedding ceremony express their intentions (we-intentions) by participating in the ceremony even though they might not know all the rules associated with getting married.

What Searle has shown in effect is the way the institutional fact of getting married has been generated. The two persons have changed their status and this is an objective fact since all the rules for getting married have been followed. The sophisticated nature of social life is highlighted by two further points: (1) an institutional fact is not a solitary fact, but usually interconnected with other institutional facts. Using money to go shopping (one institutional fact) is connected to the wider system of exchange (another institutional fact); (2) institutional facts involved a degree of repetition: the act of getting married involves the multiple repetitions of constitutive rules by the couple, the officials and the witnesses within a specific context. Searle's argument applies not only to games and marriage but constitutes the very fabric of social life.

The issue that seems troubling concerns the appearance (or not) of the constitutive rules. It seems that most of the time the constitutive rules operate despite remaining hidden. When I go shopping the institutional fact of purchasing new items takes place on account of the constitutive rules that make up the institution of money and the institution of exchange. I go about the business of shopping without reminding myself of the relevant constitutive rules. Probably the best example of the unconscious operations of constitutive rules is the institution of language which I use without knowing why I use it the way I do. Most people use language without knowing the grammatical rules that allow them to use it. How can I, Searle wonders, be said to follow the constitutive rules (knowing how) if I do not even know them (know that)? Searle's solution to this puzzle is formulated in the terminology of 'sensitivity':

[One] doesn't need to know the rules of the institution and to follow them in order to conform to the rules; rather, he is just disposed to behave in a certain way, but he has acquired those unconscious dispositions and capacities in a way that is sensitive to the rule structure of the institution. To tie this down to a concrete case, we should not say that the experienced baseball player runs to first base because he wants to follow the rules of baseball, but we should say that because the rules require that he run to first base, he acquires a set of background habits, skills, dispositions that are such that when he hits the ball, he runs to first base. (1995: 144)

In the case of games, therefore, one plays without consciously knowing the rules because he/she has become second nature to the player who performs the role habitually and routinely:

it is an unconscious way of behaviour. This explanation makes sense for games where one first learns the rules, and having learnt how to play the game over a period of time one no longer refers to the rules. But what about language, where the rules are not specifically learnt by most speakers but only by a minority such as philosophers of language and linguists? How does Searle explain the use of language without the knowledge of the rules that are necessary for its use?

> I am saying that if you understand the complexity of the causation involved, you can see that often a person who behaves in a skilful way within an institution behaves as if he were following the rules, but not because he is following the rules unconsciously nor because his behaviour is caused by an undifferentiated mechanism that happens to look as if it were rule structured, but rather because *the mechanism has evolved precisely so that it will be sensitive to the rules*. The mechanism explains the behaviour and the mechanism is explained by the system of rules, but the mechanism need not itself be a system of rules. (1995: 146)

Searle claims that humans have evolved a neural system that permits a system of rules to operate; clearly the neural system is the machinery that makes the rules possible, but it is not identical to the rules. This answer explains how, given that both adults and children have a neural system, when adults speak (therefore implicitly following the rules of language) the neural mechanism of the children is activated into using the same rules.

Searle's analysis of social reality concerns the functional nature of both institutions and language. In the case of institutions, it is their function that explains their actions: the institution of marriage has the function of protecting and raising children (among other things); the judiciary has the function of adjudicating between competing claims of innocence and guilt. Social life is dominated by different institutions with their own specific functions. Those with functions can be divided into two groups. Non-agentive functions are those without intentionality, such as the heart's pumping blood throughout the body. Agentive functions are those involving humans inputting intentionality into an object, process or institution. Language belongs to the function of the agent insofar as humans impose meaning onto sounds: they do this intentionally with the goal of communicating with others, who in turn communicate with them. The importance of language is, however, not only restricted to this 'horizontal' function of mutual communication: rather, language and communication have enabled humans to create other functional objects. Through the transmission of information enough knowledge has been accumulated to transform society into an advanced society with cars, mobile phones and pacemakers.

Searle on computer communication

In his studies on the philosophy of mind Searle tackles the question of whether the fact that computers can communicate is a sign that they have a mind. One of the chapters in

Minds, Brains and Science (1984) is titled 'Can Computers think?' and here Searle starts by pointing out that a common view shared certain philosophers, psychologists and those working in artificial intelligence is that the brain is to the mind as computer hardware is to the computer program.

Searle calls the computer hardware to software relationship 'strong artificial intelligence' and it is provocative in that it suggests that the brain is merely one type of computer hardware out of many possible kinds. Given the right program, that is, a system that processes inputs and outputs, then any hardware can be considered intelligent. And this view is not restricted to digital computers. Searle describes an encounter with John McCarthy, the inventor of the label 'artificial intelligence' and he goes so far as to claim that any machine that is capable of solving problems has a degree of intelligence and has a number of mental states. McCarthy claims that even the common thermostat has three beliefs: 'it's too hot in here', it is too cold in here' and 'it is just right in here' (1984: 30). One can imagine how incredible this all sounds – few people would entertain the idea that their fridges have mental states yet people like McCarthy consider such machines having beliefs.

Searle takes it upon himself to refute this claim offering a thought-experiment to show the inherent problem with claims of this sort. Imagine a computer program that can simulate understanding Chinese so that if it is given a question in Chinese it will match the question with its memory and provide a Chinese answer. The answer is in excellent Chinese but, can one say that the computer understands Chinese in the same way as a Chinese person? Clearly not, because when a Chinese person understands something this entails understanding its meaning; a Chinese person would understand the meaning of both the question and the answer. Searle then develops the thought-experiment and describes the situation in which a person is in a room with several baskets full of Chinese symbols and a rule book in English for manipulating these symbols. The rule book specifies that (for example) if one sees a certain symbol then one adds another symbol next to it; and if one see another symbol one adds something else and so on. Imagine that a series of Chinese symbols are handed in from the outside to the person inside the room. Unknown to the person on the inside the Chinese symbols were questions and the person, by manipulating the symbols in the baskets according to the rules, provides an answer in excellent Chinese. The question is, can the person in the room be said to understand Chinese? Just by manipulating the symbols there is still something missing from the whole exchange in that the person has no idea of what the symbols mean. And to say one understands something then one must be able to say what it is that one understands (1984: 31–32).

This thought-experiment highlights the inherent flaw with the claims made by computer scientists that support this view of the mind. Computers operate by following formal or syntactical processes, that is, following a sequence of symbols without any semantic content. But there is more to the human mind than the following of symbols. In the case of mental states, these have content: if a person says he/she has a belief or a wish then it is a belief or a wish about something. 'If my thoughts are to be *about* anything, then the strings must have a *meaning* which makes the thoughts about those things. In a word, the mind has more than a syntax, it has a semantics' (1984: 31).

The claim that computers have mental states – with thinking being one of them – is rejected precisely on the grounds that while computers have a syntax that enables them to communicate, they do not have a semantics. In other words, computers, unlike humans, do not know what it is that they are communicating. Some computer scientists believe it is only a matter of time that there will be computers that will think in the same way as humans. Searle's argument dispels even the possibility of such an eventuality. As long as computers function using formal and syntactical processes, they will never be able to think because thinking is more than the manipulation of symbols.

Critical remarks

Searle's elaboration of speech act theory has raised considerable interest that has in turn raised a number of questions. Fotion (2000 70), for example, argues that Searle's account of politeness as an explanation of indirect speech acts is too narrow. Indirect speech acts are frequently performed for utilitarian purposes rather than out of politeness: when you say 'there is a large rattler near your left elbow' you are providing information and indirectly telling the hearer to move away and why they should do so. In addition Fotion points out that we use indirect speech acts precisely because we want to be impolite. To the driver who is told 'can't you see you are blocking the road?', the force of this indirect speech act is 'aggressive' and further insults can be added to it, such as 'you – fool, can't you see you are blocking the road?' (2000: 58).[3]

Although Searle is clearly indebted to Austin's account of speech acts, he considers the distinction between the locutionary and the illocutionary act to be redundant and retains only the latter. According to Searle, the meaning of the utterance is established by examining the intentions of the speaker in the act of communicating. His argument is that every literal sentence has within it, as part of its meaning, force indicators so that there is no need to establish the locutionary act as a separate class. This view is challenged by Friggieri (1991: 195–98), who defends the distinction between the two as established by Austin. If there were force indicators within every speech act then it should be possible to identify them, but one can assert something without knowing what the illocutionary force is. Friggieri offers an example: the utterance 'I am waiting for Joseph' can be used in a number of ways – as a warning, a refusal to go to the cinema, a hint, a secret and so on – and there is nothing within the sentence that tells us what the speaker intends to achieve. We can always understand the utterance as an assertion without necessarily understanding the speaker's intentions in uttering it.[4]

In this chapter I have outlined (1) the pivotal role that both intention and rules play in speech act theory; this was followed by (2) an analysis of the reference-predication distinction and (3) the conditions that enable an understanding of speech acts to take place. Having outlined these conditions, I then highlighted (4) Searle's account of the differences between speech acts and (5) his classification of the speech acts into types or classes. The focus is upon (6) more complex speech acts while the following sections deal with Searle's analysis of speech acts in relation to (7) context and (8) society. In the final section, I examine Searle's discussion of computer communication.

Notes

1. Searle elaborates: 'Often we mean more than we actually say. If you ask me "Are you going to the movies?" I may respond by saying "yes" but, as is clear from the context, what I mean is "Yes, I am going to the movies", not "Yes, it is a fine day" or "Yes, we have no bananas"[…]In such cases, even though I do not say exactly what I mean, it is always possible for me to do so – if there is any possibility that the hearer might not understand me, I may do so' (1969: 19).
2. Fotion provides a number of examples of indirect speech: ' "I think he is angry with me." (Directly this is an assertive about what the speaker thinks, indirectly it is also an assertive concerned with someone's anger' i.e., he is angry after all). "I intend to study harder." (The temptation here is to read this example directly as a commissive. But "I intend […]" reports the thoughts of the speaker. It says that the speaker has an intention. So directly, this is an assertive. It is a commissive, then, by indirection.) "I'm sorry I did it." (This one on the face of it looks like an apology, and thus an expressive, but directly it is an assertive about the speaker's sorrow. Indirectly it is indeed an apology)' (2000: 65).
3. Fotion concludes that '[i]t seems that the varied nature of indirect speech acts allows for more varied reasons for invoking them than Searle allows' (2000: 70).
4. Friggieri offers another example using imperatives: 'Consider: 'Give me that weapon'. In issuing that utterance, whose meaning is, once again, totally unambiguous, I may be (1) ordering you to lay down your arms; (2) inviting you to start negotiations; (3) hinting that you are ambushed; (4) making it clear that it is too early to go hunting; (5) suggesting that we should go fishing instead; (6) asking you to lend me your pistol; (7) pleading with you not to shoot the piano-player; (8) daring you to fight unarmed. And so on. There is no *particular* speech-act which can be determined by the meaning of the sentence' (1991: 197).

Chapter 11

Habermas on Communication and Social Theory

Jurgen Habermas (1929) is a leading exponent of the Frankfurt School and has been instrumental in reviving its influence. The Frankfurt School offers a new and updated version of Marxism that is intended to retain the critical and emancipatory dimension of Marxism within the context of the developments that have characterized the twentieth and the twenty-first centuries. Orthodox Marxist theory of the nineteenth century was situated in the Industrial Age and articulated social phenomena in terms of a materialistic outlook. On the other hand, the technological innovations of the twentieth and the twenty-first centuries have radically transformed society into what is described as an 'information society'. Habermas has 'upgraded' Marxist theory to account for these social changes.

Habermas's intellectual background draws upon a wide number of influences from the Continental tradition, but quite unusually he is one of the first to exploit the resources of the analytic or Anglo-American tradition of philosophy. Within the tradition of twentieth-century Western philosophy, analytic philosophers have shifted their focus onto the study of language, and in so doing they replaced the focus upon consciousness that had characterized modern philosophy since Descartes. This shift toward language had the advantage that, unlike consciousness, it was more conducive to analysis and study. However, the interest in language and communication should be situated within his concern with social questions, these being questions concerning social order and cooperation. This qualification is necessary as his critics have pointed out that his writings on linguistic communication might at times seem to be overstretched. But given the question of how social order is indeed possible in a society composed of a large number of individuals, Habermas's writings on language and communication provide an answer to this question.

In this chapter, I will start by developing in detail (1) Habermas's theory of communication, and will continue (2) with an examination of his concept of validity claims in the next section. Following this, I shall place (3) Habermas's theory of communicative action within the broader picture of society and outline (4) his analysis of contemporary society from the perspective of the lifeworld and the system. The chapter continues with an overview of (5) Habermas's contribution to ethics within the framework of this theory of communication and ends (6) with his analysis of the function of the media in political communication.

Communication

The cornerstone of Habermas's project for the revival of critical theory involves an analysis of the way language is used in communication. Habermas has written widely on linguistic communication, with a number of his well-known essays brought together in *On the Pragmatics of Communication* (2002). In addition, his *Theory of Communicative Action* (1987) demonstrates the way his pragmatic account of language ties in with his theory of society: by reconstructing the competences of speakers in their everyday life within society, Habermas's theorizations can be considered as a reconstructive science that explains the way society operates.

A central question to the study of communication is the question of what it is a person understands when something is being communicated. The answer to this question necessarily entails an examination of the concept of meaning, since communication is the communication of meaning (as opposed to noise). In the case of linguistic communication we might ask: what it is that we know or understand when we know or understand the meaning of a sentence? Is the meaning in the sentence itself or in the way the speaker uses that sentence?

According to the account of those theorists interested in what is known as 'formal semantics' (Frege, early Wittgenstein and Dummett), a person knows the meaning of a sentence when he/she knows the conditions that would make it true or false. Their claim is not that to understand the meaning of a sentence is to understand its truth, since it is possible to understand a sentence that is false ('the earth is the centre of the universe'). Rather, they claim that to know the meaning of a sentence one would have to understand what sort of evidence would be required for it to be true or false. Given that there is a clear correlation or correspondence between the meaning of a sentence and the way that sentence is verified, formal semantic theorists consider the primary use of language as that of stating facts about the world, events or people. Cooke summarises Habermas's critique of the formal semanticists approach to language as follows:

> Traditional formal-semantic approaches to meaning have been guilty of three kinds of abstractive fallacies: a semanticist abstraction, a cognitivist abstraction, and an objectivist one. The semanticist abstraction is the view that the analysis of linguistic meaning can confine itself to the analysis of *sentences*, abstracting from the pragmatic contexts of the use of sentences in utterances. The cognitivist abstraction is the view that all meaning can be traced back to the propositional content of utterances, thus indirectly reducing meaning to the meaning of *assertoric* sentences. The objectivist abstraction is the view that meaning is to be defined in terms of objectively ascertainable truth conditions, as opposed to the *knowledge* of the truth conditions that can be imputed to speakers or hearers. (2002: 6)

Habermas considers the pragmatic approach to meaning as offering a more fruitful approach to the study of communication: (1) it focusses on utterances, that is, on usage rather than sentences. (2) It focusses on the many different kinds of utterances that can be communicated though a language (promises, requests, orders etc.) rather than narrowing the domain of language to descriptive sentences; and (3) it focusses on the relation between the utterance and the social conventions within which they are embedded. Utterances are used within a framework of human interaction so that within a specific context certain uses of language will be employed and considered meaningful, while other uses within the same context will be meaningless. If, for example, I am in a restaurant, I can ask the waiter for a glass of water, but if I ask for permission to practise my knife-throwing skills he will either laugh it off or ask me to leave.

Despite Habermas's preference for pragmatic theories of meaning there is, in his view, a defect with the way they have restricted truth to context. For pragmatic theorists who have adopted the meaning as use by the later Wittgenstein, meaning is relative to the local context or the way of life of the community. Habermas hopes to rectify this by explicating a theory of meaning that is context-independent such that the validity of an utterance is something that transcends the local context.

In his early writings, Habermas uses the label of 'Universal Pragmatics' to describe his project, while in his later writings he changes the title to 'formal pragmatics'. There are two major differences between the pragmatics of Habermas and the pragmatics that interests linguists and philosophers of language. While the study of pragmatics has tended to focus on language use within specific contexts, and therefore fragmented into a series of smaller contexts of use, the pragmatics of Habermas is broader in the sense that it is concerned with the use of language by all speakers. Unlike, for example, sociolinguists, who collect empirical data to examine particular situations of language use, universal pragmatics is a generalized study of the presuppositions involved in speech. It is a concern with the conditions that are necessary for any speaker to be able to communicate and this is why Habermas describes his pragmatics as universal. In addition, Habermas is not interested in pragmatics per se, but in relating pragmatics to his larger concern with social and political theory. His project of reviving critical theory entails an investigation into what it is that constitutes the fabric of society, and since language use enables social integration, the study of pragmatics is a necessary first step.

In his pragmatics, Habermas carefully observes the work of Noam Chomsky, who as a linguist is interested in uncovering the rules that every speaker of a language – irrespective of the particular language – must have to be able to generate a sentence. In other words, Chomsky studies the 'deep rules' of language that a speaker must have so as to be competent in his/her language, such as the ability to form grammatically correct and meaningful sentences, and to recognize when others do not form them correctly. The interesting thing is that the speaker uses these rules even if he/she is not able to articulate them; the speaker uses them 'unconsciously' in the sense that being competent in a language is a question of 'know how' as opposed to knowing the rules of the language, which would consist in 'knowing that'. The fundamental difference between Chomsky and Habermas is that while Chomsky is interested in the rules that generate sentences, or assertions, Habermas is interested in the rules that generate utterances, or speech acts. This difference brings out the point that Habermas develops: language is an intersubjective affair connecting people together. The social dimension of language establishes relations between people, since a speech act is uttered by someone (the speaker) to someone else (the listener) in order to do something within a particular context.

The influence of the later Wittgenstein is also evident in Habermas's account of language and society where he develops Wittgenstein's analogy between language and games. According to Wittgenstein, although there are many varied games all of them are characterized by the following of certain rules: it is the rules that define the particular game and a competent player is one who follows the rules of the game. Again, like the rules of language, the player need not consciously know the rules of the game in all their detail to be able to play it. Playing is a question of ability rather than being able to list the rules. And the ability to play entails using the rules even in situations that one has not encountered before – different situations arise during a game of football or chess that the capable player reacts to. There is a parallel with language in that a competent speaker can understand sentences that he/she has never heard before as well as construct sentences that he/she has never uttered before.

Given that language is a rule-governed activity, Wittgenstein concludes that (1) language cannot be explained in terms of the solitary speaker, and in terms of a private language whose meaning the speaker alone can understand. The use of rules necessitates a community of speakers who can confirm whether those rules have been used correctly or not. Without the community to provide a standard of communication, we could never know if the words we use today were the same as those we used yesterday. (2) The nature of the rules inherent within language shift the question of meaning away from the relationship between language and the world, and towards the way speakers follow rules within specific social contexts. Given that there are different contexts, the way a speech act is used will vary according to its context: the rules governing the way a speaker asks a question within the context of religion is different from the rules governing the discourse of science. Different contexts or language games generate different sets of rules to the extent that there might be no compatibility between the language games.

Habermas objects to the relativistic implications of Wittgenstein's reduction of language to contexts and ways of life. On this account, the many different uses of language have nothing in common so that language is merely a series of disconnected games, the study of which would be to clarify the confusion that results when 'language goes on holiday'. The problem with Wittgenstein's approach is that (1) it fails to realize the degree with which competent speakers relate to each other; and (2) it underrates the importance of the cognitive use of language (1971: 56–65).

In opposition to the potential slide toward relativism implied by Wittgenstein's language games, Habermas proposes the project of universal pragmatics as the rational reconstruction of the competences that every speaker must have in order to be able to communicate at all. The analysis of communication presupposes that both speaker and hearer always already have this competence. The early programme of universal pragmatics had the goal of establishing the dynamics of communication as an essential component for the maintenance and reproduction of society.

Speech act theory is the starting point for Habermas's analysis of society because it clearly demonstrates the intimacy between language and social life. The writings of J. L. Austin provide Habermas with the theoretical framework for his analysis of interpersonal linguistic communication. It was from Austin that Habermas derives both the concept of the utterance (as opposed to the sentence) and the notion of the illocutionary force of the utterance, where by uttering something a speaker is doing something. The weakness of Austin's account is that he separates the force of the utterance from its meaning, so that the force is found in the illocutionary act while the meaning belongs to the sentence uttered. Habermas rejects this distinction because (1) the meaning of an utterance is different from the meaning of a sentence used in that utterance; (2) the separation proposed by Austin is connected to his concern with establishing criteria for differentiating between constatives and performatives, with the result being that only constatives can be subjected to validity claims and finally because (3) Austin's concept of illocutionary force lacks a rational foundation (Cooke 2002: 7).[1]

Habermas's analysis of the utterance reveals that it is composed of a 'dual structure' (2002: 64): these are the performative aspect (or illocutionary aspect) and the propositional content. The propositional content of an utterance is what the sentence is about, or what it refers to. The performative aspect concerns the use, or what can be done with the propositional content, and it is this pragmatic use of utterances that interests Habermas. The sentence *the sun is shining* does not float around, independent of people who use it. It is embedded within a context of usage with the meaning of this sentence conditioned by the way it is being used. The question here concerns the illocutionary force with which utterances are used. According to the context one can ask: is it an invitation to go to the beach? Is it a warning to use suntan lotion? Is it a confirmation of the weather report? Habermas is explicit:

> One simply would not know what it is to understand the meaning of a linguistic expression if one did not know how one could make use of it in order to reach understanding with someone about something. (2002: 228)

The dual structure of linguistic communication shows that an utterance is a combination of both the illocutionary force and the propositional content, a combination that involves both the doing of something with words and the saying something about the world. The communicative act takes place when the intention of the speaker is understood in the process of communicating some content. The content can be cognitive or non-cognitive so that with cognitive utterances the emphasis is upon the world, and further disagreement will concern the truth or falsity of the content, with the social dimension taking secondary place. For example, if I say 'the sun is shining' the emphasis of my utterance is on the cognitive side, informing you about the world, with the social aspect (although present) as secondary since I might be casually talking to a friend. If I say 'let's go swimming' the emphasis is on the social angle since what is primary is my suggestion, while the cognitive side is secondary ('the sea is lovely today'). There is, therefore, always a social dimension to language use: communication entails an intersubjective element of understanding of both the content and the intention of the speaker, since the content must be understood as something specific, that is, as a fact, an invitation, promise, command and so on. Whatever type of utterance I use, a social relation is always involved.

Both the illocutionary aspect and the propositional aspect can be reused in several ways. The propositional content in 'the sun is shining' can be added to several different illocutions that bring out the social angle. I can warn you that the sun is shining, I can inform you that the sun is shining and I can pretend to you that the sun is shining. Likewise, the same illocution can be used with different propositional content: I promise that the sun is shining, I promise to take you out to dinner and I promise to start eating more fruit.

Habermas formulates his universal pragmatics by delineating the conditions that must be met for linguistic communication to take place. This use of language entails (1) grammatical competence; (2) a relation to an external reality (the objective world); (3) an inner reality (the speaker's relationship with his/her own utterances, i.e., his/her intentions) and (4) a normative reality (the values, norms and rules of society).

1. Speakers and listeners must share the same rules that allow them to generate sentences. Participants in communication must be competent in the language such that they understand the sense of what is being communicated. The communicative class involves uttering something that is understandable or intelligible:

    The first class of speech acts, which I want to call *communicative*, serves to express different aspects of the very purpose of speech. It explicates the meaning of engagements via engagements. Each instance of speech presupposes an actual preconception of what it means to communicate in a language, to understand and misunderstand the engagements, to bring about a consensus, to dissent: in general, to know how to deal with language.
    [E]xamples: say, express, speak, talk, ask, answer, respond, reply, agree, contradict, object, admit, mention, repeat, quote, etc. (in Horster 1992: 28)

2. Speakers can communicate their representations of the external world. It is the cognitive use of language insofar as it informs us about the external world. The constative class involves the imparting of something about the world that needs to be understood:

    [T]he second class of speech acts, which I want to call *constative*, serves to express the purpose of the cognitive use of sentences. It explicates the meaning of engagements through engagements. In the prototypical word for the assertoric modes, in "assert" two instances are united that appear separately in the two subclasses of these speech acts. On the one hand, "assert" belongs to the following group of examples: describe, report, inform, tell, elucidate, remark, set forth, explain, predict, etc. These examples stand for the assertoric use of engagements. On the other hand, "assert" belongs to the following group of examples: assure, protest, affirm, deny, dispute, doubt. These examples elucidate the pragmatic purpose, especially of the truth claim of engagements. (in Horster 1992: 28–29)

3. Speakers can communicate their intentions and it is important that these intentions are understood. It could happen that when the speaker is communicating he/she is lying or being sarcastic; failing to recognize these intentions can result in the collapse of the communicative interaction. Questions of sincerity arise since the utterance is used to express the speaker's intentions and whether the speaker was sincere when he/she expressed his/her intentions. The representative class involves making oneself understood; it involves the expression of the subjectivity of the speaker:

> The third class of speech acts, which I want to call *representative* (expressive) serves to express the pragmatic purpose of the self-portrayal of a speaker before an audience. It explicates the purpose of the speaker's engagement of intentions, views and experiences. The dependent clause of propositional content and intentional clauses with verbs like know, think, mean, hope, hear, love, hate, like, wish, want, decide, etc. Examples are: expose, reveal, divulge, admit, express, conceal, veil, pretend, obscure, hide, keep secret, deny. (These speech acts appear in negated form: 'I am not hiding from you that [...]') (in Horster 1992: 29)

4. Speakers communicate according to the norms of behaviour within society. It is a question of the appropriateness or the right of the speaker to communicate. Within the context of a lecture, it is usually assumed that a student has the right to ask the lecturer clarification on some point made during the lecture, but not about the lecturer's hobbies. At issue are the respective roles of the speaker and the hearer, roles that are normatively conditioned. Clearly what and where something is said – the context and the conventions – are an important feature of the communicative act:

> The fourth class of speech acts, which I want to call *regulative*, serves to express the normative purpose of the established interpersonal relation. It explicates the meaning of the relation that the speaker/listener has with respect to behavioural norms. Examples are: command, ask, request, demand, warn, forbid, allow, suggest, refuse, oppose, obligate oneself, promise, agree, accept responsibility, confirm, support, vouch for, terminate, excuse, pardon, suggest, reject, recommend, assume, advise, warn, encourage, etc. (cited in Horster 1992: 29)

The four classes are frequently referred to as the domains of (1) meaning or comprehension, (2) truth, (3) truthfulness and (4) rightness. In his later writings Habermas leaves out (1) as the other three depend upon it. The possibility of saying the truth, being truthful and having the right to say something are all predicated on the possibility of language use.

Although Habermas is clearly indebted to the speech act theory of J. L. Austin, he finds that the latter's analysis of speech acts is directed chiefly upon those speech acts that are institutionally framed, that is, in terms of the institutions that set the rules or conditions for their successful performance (of a marriage or baptism). Habermas's theory is less reliant on the institutional context of speech acts, and in this respect his work is much closer to that of John Searle who elaborated on the conditions that must be met for the success of any speech act. For Habermas the non-institutional success of communicative actions is grounded on the ability of the listener to challenge the speech act; it is here that the notion of validity claims comes into force:

> *In the final analysis, the speaker can illocutionarily influence the hearer, and vice-versa, because speech-act-typical obligations are connected with cognitively testable validity claims* – that is, because the reciprocal binding and bonding relationship has a rational basis. (2002: 85)

Discourse and validity claims

Although communication is defined as achieving an understanding between the speaker and the hearer, this definition is not restricted to understanding the meaning of an utterance but also includes reaching an agreement on the utterance: 'reaching understanding aims at consensus formation' (2002: 294). From the way Habermas articulates the concept of understanding it is evident that it is employed to carry a fairly large load, ranging from the everyday use of understanding the linguistic aspects of an utterance to the more specialized use of understanding in the broad sense of including the reasons that enable a consensus to be reached.[2] The possibility of arriving at a consensus is an inbuilt feature of language. According to Habermas, communication always entails a relation between understanding and agreement, and in the early universal pragmatics this is expressed as follows:

> The aim of reaching understanding (*Verständigung*) is to bring about an agreement (*Einverständnis*) that terminates in the intersubjective mutuality of reciprocal comprehension, shared knowledge, mutual trust, and accord with one another. Agreement is based on recognition of the corresponding validity claims of comprehensibility, truth, truthfulness, and rightness. (2002: 23)

This is stressed again in *The Theory of Communicative Action*: 'We understand a speech act, when we know what makes it acceptable' (1987a: 297). The point that Habermas wants to establish is that to understand the meaning of an utterance is to understand and accept the reasons for that utterance. This is why he considers his account to be consensual or pragmatic, since the 'internal connection' between meaning and understanding is based upon speakers and hearers communicating and offering reasons for their utterances.

In everyday life communicative interaction continues undisturbed and in this interaction a number of things are taken for granted. By uttering something the speaker makes a number of claims with regard to (1) the meaningfulness of the utterance (it follows the syntax of the language); (2) its truth (it says something about the world); (3) its appropriateness (the speaker has the right to say what he/she is saying) and (4) its being truthful (the speaker is consistent in what he/she says and does). But all these features of the utterance can be challenged: the hearer might question each of the implicit or explicit claims made, and the onus lies on the speaker to provide reasons for what he/she is claiming.

Habermas calls the providing of reasons that are acceptable 'validity claims', and these claims describe the conditions that enable successful communication to take place. When, for example, the speaker tells the person who has just turned up at his/her office 'I am going for a coffee', the speech act follows the rules of English and assumes that the coffee shop is open, that you understand that I have the right to have my break (it's ten o'clock) and that I am sincere (that I am not inventing excuses to avoid you). These four dimensions of communication are taken for granted in everyday interaction and are therefore never questioned. But should they be questioned or challenged, Habermas – as a rationalist – argues that genuine communication entails the possibility of providing reasons for one's utterances. The speaker should be able to defend himself/herself and it belongs to the very nature of communication that participants can offer reasons for their 'validity claims'.

Given that every act of communication involves all the validity claims, it is not necessary to challenge each validity claim. While one validity claim might be explicitly challenged, the other validity claims are implicitly maintained and could in turn also be challenged. Habermas writes that

> [w]e have seen that communication in language can take place only when the participants, in communicating with one another about something, simultaneously enter two levels of communication – the level of intersubjectivity on which they take up interpersonal relations and the level of propositional contents. However, in speaking, we can make either the interpersonal relation of the propositional content more centrally thematic; in so doing, we make a more interactive or a more cognitive use of our language. In the *interactive use of language*, we thematize the relations into which a speaker and hearer enter – as a warning, promise, request – while we merely mention the propositional content of the utterances. In the *cognitive use of language*, by contrast we, thematize the content of the utterance as a statement about something that is happening the in the world, (or that could be the case). While we express the interpersonal relation only indirectly. (2002: 75–76)

In listening to the meteorologist, the explicit claim he/she is making concerns the truth of the content (that a tornado is approaching our town), while implicitly it is assumed that the meteorologist is the appropriate person to tell us this information (we should take the advice of moving to a safer area), and that he/she is being sincere (and is therefore someone we should trust).

Discourse is that process that occurs when communication is suspended and utterances are challenged; it is the process that asks for the reasons that justify the utterance. Of the four validity claims informing a communicative act, each has a different mode of what Habermas calls 'redemption'. The validity claims can be grouped into two different sets as there is a fundamental difference between them: one set includes the validity claims of comprehension and sincerity, while the other set includes the validity claims of truth and correctness. The difference between the two sets is that it is only the second set that can be redeemed in discourse. In the case of comprehension, when an utterance is challenged with regard to its meaning the speaker can always use other words to convey the meaning. In the case of sincerity, the validity claim is redeemed if the actions of the speaker conform to his/ her intentions (such as keeping a promise). On the other hand, the validity claims of truth and correctness involve discursive argumentation: whether it is a question of establishing the truth of a statement or the correctness of a norm, the speaker must defend his/her claims by offering reasons or justifications.

Habermas has narrowed down his account of validity claims to three, such that speech acts relate to (1) the external world; (2) the subjective world of the speaker and (3) to others within the domain of interpersonal relations (1987a: 308). These speech acts can be challenged respectively on the question of (1) their factual status: they are judged according to whether they are true or false; (2) their value system: they are judged according to whether the speaker is sincere or not and (3) their normative rightness: they are judged according to whether they are right or not right. Habermas offers an example of the professor who asks a student to get him a glass of water. The student can challenge the professor (1) on factual grounds since there is no water nearby; (2) with regard to his sincerity, since the professor might be testing the student to see his/her reaction in front of the other students and (3) on normative grounds, since the student might object that it is not right or appropriate to ask this of a student.

> What we have shown in connection with this example [of the professor] is true for *all* speech acts oriented to reaching understanding. In contexts of communicative action, speech acts can always be rejected under each of the three aspects: the aspect of the rightness that the speaker claims for his action in relation to a normative context (or, indirectly, for these norms themselves); the truthfulness that the speaker claims for the expression of subjective experiences to which he has privileged access; finally, the truth that the speaker, with his utterance, claims for a statement (or for the existential presuppositions of a nominalised proposition). (1987a: 307)

The benefit of showing the internal connection between rational justification and communication is that the domain of reason is now expanded to areas that have for some time been considered outside its legitimate domain. Rational justification can be offered not only for the domain of facts and objectivity, but also for the domains of morality/norms and subjective experiences. In the case of morality, one's actions can be rationally examined in the light of legitimate moral principles, or if those principles are challenged they can be defended or rejected through reasoned argumentation. With the world of subjective experience Habermas includes the expression of evaluations and desires: contrary to what many think, this is not so personal that it lies beyond rational justification. When one passes an aesthetic judgement, calling something 'good' (or beautiful), one is not just expressing one's taste but can offer reasons for his/her judgement; these reasons are subject to agreement or disagreement. Habermas gives an example of friends discussing a film, with the person who claims that the film is good being expected to offer reasons for his/her assessment:

> In this context [of art] reasons have the peculiar function of *bringing us to see* a work or performance in such a way that it can be perceived as an authentic expression of an exemplary experience, in general as the embodiment of a claim to authenticity. (1987a: 20)

With the concept of discourse, Habermas offers an account of the processes that take place when validity claims are challenged. Discourse is a meta-communicative process since it involves a suspension of everyday communication that in turn requires more communication to resume the communication. Communication breakdowns can only be resolved through further communication. This is where the notion of 'illocutionary force' is particularly relevant for Habermas's account, since the communicative act is more than the minimalist notion of involving two persons, but a relationship grounded in reasons and their acceptance. The hearer wants to know the reasons for what the speaker is saying and therefore challenges him/her. However, it is not enough to just offer reasons since the reasons must be acceptable to the hearers: there is a big difference between being asked to close the window because there is a cold draught and being asked to close it because ghosts might enter the room and possess everyone.[3] Once the hearer is satisfied with the speaker's reasons then the process of everyday communication resumes. James Gordon Finlayson offers a narrative that describes this process:

> Suppose you ask me not to smoke in my office when you are present, and I demur at your request because I know that you too are a smoker. I ask you for the reasons behind your request. You may reply that you have recently given up smoking and do not wish to be tempted back into the habit. At this point, I might accept your reason and put my cigarettes away. On Habermas's view, we have entered into discourse (however briefly), and reached a rationally motivated consensus (this phrase is the accepted English translation of *rationales Einverstandnis*), and returned smoothly to the context of action. (2005: 41)

Habermas discusses the logic of discursive argumentation because he is concerned with the logic of speech acts that are used in rational argumentation (rather than deductive logic which is concerned with the relation between sentences), since the purpose of these arguments is the strengthening or weakening of a validity claim. The logic of discursive argumentation applies to the domains of truth and of norms, and these are called 'theoretical-empirical' discourse and 'practical' discourse, respectively. The difference between the two is that while 'theoretical-empirical' discourse demands an explanation, practical discourse demands a justification. The arguments for the respective discourses are listed by Habermas (in Held 1980: 342).

	Theoretical-empirical discourse	Practical discourse
Conclusions	statements	precepts/evaluations
Controversial validity claim	truth	correctness/propriety
Demanded from opponent	explanations	justifications
Data	causes (of events) motives (of behaviour)	grounds
Warrant	empirical uniformities hypothetical laws, etc.	behavioural/evaluative norms or principles
Backing	observations, results of surveys, factual accounts, etc.	interpretation of needs (values), inferences, secondary implications, etc.

It is clear from the above schema that both the statements of the 'theoretical-empirical discourses' and the evaluations of 'practical discourse' belong to an interconnected set of concepts that form a hierarchical arrangement within arguments: [4]

> [T]he conclusion that is to be grounded (particular statements in theoretical discourse, commands or evaluations in practical discourse); the data that is submitted as pertinent (causes, grounds); the warrant which establishes the link between data and conclusions (general laws, moral principles), and the backing which makes this link plausible (observation reports, considerations of secondary implications of following a particular norm). (Held 1980: 342)

The standard by which one judges whether an argument is acceptable or not is called 'the persuasive force of the better argument' in Habermas's later writings (1990: 158–59), and here it is reason that adjudicates whether to accept or reject a validity claim. This is understandable because Habermas equates the use of arguments and the offering of more reasons with an increase in the freedom of reflection.[5]

When a discursive argument ends, the presumably satisfied participants return to everyday communication, and on Habermas's account, their agreement arrives at the truth of the matter. However, a discourse cannot challenge all validity claims simultaneously: a discourse is grounded in an actual way of life so that rational argumentation takes place within a background context of values and beliefs. When a truth or a value is challenged, other truths and norms remain in the background and are taken for granted. It is impossible to challenge the whole background of truths and values at once. Equally, what is accepted at any moment might – given the availability of new evidence – need to be revised. As a result, the truths or values that a discourse establishes are temporary and open-ended: it is always possible that they will in future be subject to investigation.

It should be pointed out that the concept of discourse describes the practice that takes place in the course of everyday life by ordinary people in the attempt to arrive at rational agreements about their disagreements. This should immediately show that it is not the exclusive domain of philosophers or linguists, but it occupies a central position in modern societies as the mechanism that deals with conflict resolution. The importance of Habermas's analysis of discourse lies in the fact that it ties his pragmatic account of meaning with his broader concern with social theory. It is important to his social theory because it shows the way social order can be maintained in spite of conflict. After the validity claim of a speech act is challenged in discourse, its acceptance or rejection leads to the re-establishment of communicative interaction between members of society. The function of validity claims in Habermas's theory of communicative action is fundamental to his restoration of reason. By showing that reason is inherent in the course of everyday language, Habermas is able to offer a form of social analysis that places reason at its centre.

Communicative, strategic and instrumental action

As part of his social analysis, Habermas introduces a distinction between communicative action and strategic action. Both types of action are goal-oriented but the way these goals are achieved differs greatly: communicative action relies on consent while strategic action relies on influence. Communicative action is that way of interacting whereby meaningful relations are established between members of society either through physical actions or through verbal actions (speech acts). One attempts to achieve one's goals by coordinating one's actions with others. At times, physical actions are accompanied by language or can be redescribed with language, and when communication fails or breaks down then more language is used to re-establish communication. On the other hand, it is also possible to obtain one's goals through influencing others: rather than trying to achieve one's goals by agreeing with others, strategies are used to persuade others to do things that are in one's own interest (2002: 203).

The goal of communicative action is to reach agreement and consent between participants on what is being communicated. This is made possible by the 'common knowledge' of shared convictions that can be rationally challenged and redeemed. It is because humans live in a shared world – of facts or norms – that agreement and disagreement are possible. 'I call knowledge *common* if it constitutes *consent* whereas consent relies on the intersubjective recognition of criticizable validity claims' (in Sutton 2003: 53). In this sense, Habermas opposes 'common knowledge' to a shared body of similar opinions or to convictions that result from sacred or secular authorities: in these cases, the question of validity does not arise.

To support his claim that an analysis of modern society necessitates prioritizing the role of communicative action in the everyday world, Habermas utilizes the distinction between the illocutionary and the perlocutionary aspects of a speech act. While the illocutionary aspect involves the speaker communicating his/her intentions so as to bring about a consensus with the listener in a rational and voluntary way, the perlocutionary effect of a speech act involves the attempt to influence others. The point of this distinction is that in the case of illocutionary acts the purpose of my uttering the speech act is clear, so that the listener understands my intention when I utter it. With perlocutionary acts, however, this intention is not manifest since there is a gap between what I intend and what is understood. Listeners 'can understand what I am *saying* but have no idea what I am really *doing* with the utterance, since the perlocutionary aim of my utterances is not open to view' (Finlayson 2005: 50). Habermas considers the illocutionary aspect to be fundamental and primary because it is transparent, and the speaker's intentions are evident and open. The perlocutionary aspect, on the other hand, is secondary or 'parasitic', since the possibility of manipulating others depends upon them first understanding what one is saying. The success of strategic action involves hiding one's intentions:

> I term those effects strategically motivated that come about only if they are not declared or if they are brought about by deceptive speech acts that merely pretend to be valid. Perlocutionary effects of this type indicate that the use of language oriented toward reaching understanding has been put at the service of strategic interactions. (2002: 202)

Communicative actions require understanding the reasons for one's actions while strategic actions require hiding the reasons for one's actions so as to get the other to do what one wants. By 'understanding' Habermas does not merely mean drawing up a list of reasons for accepting a proposition but a process of participation in which agents evaluate the reasons given for the claim. The participant judges whether the reasons offered are acceptable or not, and similarly the participant can defend his/her own reasons for the evaluation if challenged. On the other hand, strategic action operates differently: to achieve his/her goals the agent uses a number of strategies ranging from bribery to threats of violence or blackmail. Words are transformed into tools used to influence others and no attempt is made to hide the fact that they are not being used for understanding and consent. There are also more subtle means of persuasion in the use of emotional language, whereby the speaker plays on the emotional vulnerability of the other person to mask the defects of his/her arguments.

The goal of strategic action is to control and manipulate others without their agreement or consent; it is success-oriented and the only interest of the person is that of achieving their goals irrespective of the other. The other is reduced to the status of an object so that the relationship is a causal one, with language used to bring about the desired effects. Strategic action is evidenced in game playing: players in the game of chess hide their intentions from each other so as to win. The players try to predict the way the other will react to their moves; they try to establish a causal relation between their moves and the effect it will have on the other player. And this is why one can play chess with a computer rather than another person. The relation between the players is therefore not one of communication since they are not trying to understand each other, but rather a question of strategic action since success in chess is predicated upon the ability to hide one's intentions.

The emphasis on causality shows that there is a similarity between strategic action and instrumental action. However, Habermas differentiates between them since strategic action is a form of social action while instrumental action is concerned with the natural world and not with people. The difference between communicative action and instrumental action is that while communicative action entails reaching an agreement on the validity claims in the course of communication, instrumental action entails both (1) the choice of a goal that is independent of the means used to reach it and (2) a causal explanation of the relationship of the means to attain the goal. Unlike instrumental reasoning, communicative reasoning is not independent of its goal: if the goal is to achieve understanding and acceptance of the validity claims, this can only be achieved through the process of communication itself. There is, therefore, no separation of the means to attain the goals from the goals themselves. The reaching of goals in communication is through participation and interaction, and not the result of a causal relationship: understanding people is not the same as understanding the processes of nature.

In terms of Habermas's theory of society, the benefit of this analysis is that it enables Habermas to argue that the understanding of society entails accepting communicative action as the 'gel' that keeps society together. On the other hand, strategic action offers a vision of society as composed of solitary individuals, each working on one's own and treating each other as means to their own ends.

The lifeworld and the system

In his analysis of contemporary society, Habermas remarks on the widespread mistrust of reason for dealing with human problems. Although there are historical reasons for the decline of reason, a more pertinent explanation is the way it has been conceptualized in terms of efficiency: reason establishes the most efficient means for achieving a particular goal. This use of reason is known as 'instrumental reason' and its success is due to the assumption that there are causal relations between the means and the ends. Scientific thinking follows the model of instrumental reason and it has been credited with solving problems in the natural world. Instrumental reason is also dominant in the way its applications have spread throughout contemporary society, as can been seen with the constant innovations of technology. However, Habermas argues that while instrumental reason has its place, it is not the only way reason can be used.

Historically it was Weber (1864–1920) who had offered an analysis of instrumental reason, identifying it as the dominant – though not the only – mode of reasoning in the capitalist world. While the scientific application of instrumental reasoning had succeeded in resolving a number of problems in the natural world, Weber argued that it was being used in an ever-increasing manner in the human world, namely in the functioning of government and bureaucracies. The analysis of instrumental reason in terms of means and goals takes the following pattern: (1) the means for attaining the goals must be rationally chosen. (2) The goals that are chosen must conform to a person's value system (thereby making these choices rational). (3) These values and their rational exercise are transformed into principles so that they apply completely to a person's life situation. For Weber, Calvinism offered a model of rationality in its choice of means and goals, and in the pursuit of actions according to principles. The ordering and prioritizing of a person's goals enables the person to give his/her life a stable direction, since it would be an absurd life if one changed goals every day.

It is the conclusion of Weber's analysis that leads to serious difficulties:

1. Since instrumental reason is only concerned with the means of attaining certain goals efficiently, then the emphasis upon the application of reason ignores the status of the goals or values themselves. The value of tradition as the basis within which to live our lives is discounted in the modern world, a view eloquently captured by Weber's phrase 'the disenchantment of the world'. As a result, traditional meanings and values are replaced by whatever succeeds. There is a further consequence: if the only way of thinking permitted within a modern-capitalist society is that of instrumental reason, then the value system of a person as a whole cannot be rationally justified. The ends are not anchored in something bigger than the individual (the tradition) but are chosen by the individual in a subjective manner. In other words, there are no criteria that justify the lifestyle one chooses: one chooses from the many different values and goals that are offered to him/her. There is no rational standard by which one can judge another person's choice of ends as mistaken.

2. Weber had also argued that the rationalization of modern society had led to the fragmentation of society into different value spheres or domains, with each of these following their own inner logic:

> [O]ne of the features of Western rationalism is the creation in Europe of expert cultures that deal with cultural traditions reflectively and in so doing isolate the cognitive, aesthetic-expressive, and moral-practical components from one another [...] into what Weber calls "spheres of value" (i.e., scientific production, art and art criticism, and law and morality). (Habermas 1990: 107)

Since Weber conceptualized reason instrumentally there was no standard for assessing these competing value schemes. This generated a sense of fragmentation that left people feeling 'lost' or 'confused', with the typical reaction to these 'feelings' being the rejection of reason itself.

Habermas responds to these claims by arguing that:

1. Successfully achieving an action is not a sufficient condition for claiming that the nature of reason is necessarily goal-oriented; one might successfully achieve something purely by chance, such as 'choosing' the right winning lottery ticket. This is why one of Habermas's fundamental concerns throughout his writings is the transformation of reason into the broader category of communicative reason, such that the rational reflection upon goals can be re-inserted as a legitimate domain.

2. The instrumental model of rationality does not explain the rational choice of goals. The instrumental model assumes that the goal is arbitrary and is therefore opposed to a rational choice that can be challenged. To overcome the limitations of Weber's analysis, Habermas argues that the externalization of a person's actions must be taken into account. A person who acts in the world so as to achieve his/her desired goals holds an implicit view of the world, a certain way of understanding of reality. In going about attaining these goals the person might be questioned by someone else about the reasons for his/her actions, and the response might involve an elaboration of the implied worldview. The elaboration and its subsequent justification could then be assessed by both participants in the discussion. It is clear that the strength of Habermas's argument lies in the ability to offer reasons in the defence of one's actions, just as reasons can also be offered to explain actions that fail.

3. The fragmentation of society can be interpreted in another way: unlike Weber, who interpreted the consequence of fragmentation within modern society as the cause of continuous struggles between the different domains, Habermas interprets modern society as the space where a number of 'voices' have the possibility of communicating with each other. This communication takes place both at the level of argumentation and at the level of everyday life. The problems that people encounter in contemporary society – the loss of freedom and meaning – are not problems about the value of reason, but rather about the need to restructure reason to certain domains of society.

   > Communicative reason finds its criteria in the argumentative procedures for directly or indirectly redeeming claims to propositional truth, normative rightness, subjective truthfulness, and aesthetic harmony. (1987c: 314)

It is not reason that is problematic but its misapplication in contemporary society. As a defender of the Enlightenment Habermas reinserts reason in human life and rejects the 'decisionism' or subjectivism that dominates contemporary moral and cultural theory.

Given the centrality of communication in modern society, Habermas is able to claim that

> [t]he theory of communicative action can make good the weaknesses we found in Weber's action theory, to the extent that it does not remain fixated on purposive rationality as the only aspect under which action can be criticised and improved. (2002: 170)

The dialogic or communicative dimension of reason dispenses with the solipsistic idea of the subject, replacing it with an intersubjective account that Habermas calls communicative reason. The intersubjective dimension guarantees that the world is shared by people engaged in conversation while providing reasons so that agreement can be established.

In 'Actions, Speech Acts, Linguistically Mediated Interactions and Lifeworld' (2002: 215–55), Habermas specifies the importance of the relation between communicative action and the lifeworld:

> The concept of communicative action must prove its worth within the sociological theory of action. The latter is supposed to explain how social order is possible. In this respect, the analysis of the presuppositions of communicative action may be helpful. It opens us the dimension of the background of the lifeworld, which enmeshes and stabilizes interactions to form higher-level aggregates. (2002: 227)

As a social theorist Habermas reformulates the question of the possibility of social order in terms of communicative action. The question of social order is central to social theory in that it seeks to establish how it is possible that a society composed of distinct persons – each with their goals, ambitions and so on – are able to live together. In the early *Legitimation Crisis* (1988), he theorized modern society in terms of a distinction between the lifeworld and the system, a distinction that parallels the distinction between communicative action and instrumental or strategic action. Communicative action is the medium of the lifeworld, while instrumental and strategic actions are typical of the system. Similarly, Habermas introduces the distinction between social integration and systems integration so as to explain the different ways in which social order is possible.

The concept of the lifeworld is originally derived from Husserl, who had introduced it to explore 'the forgotten foundations of meaning underlying everyday life-practices and world experience' (2002: 237). Husserl described the world of everyday life, a world shared by members of a community and opposed to the world of the scientist. The latter is in effect a spectator onto the world, objectifying and quantifying it rather than living in it. For Husserl, the world of the scientist was parasitic upon the world of everyday life, since the scientist depends upon the meanings and interpretations found in the everyday world before he/she could even start his/her own work. As a result, the traditional privilege accorded to science as the primary mode of access to the world was overstated.

The difference between Habermas and Husserl is that whereas Husserl focussed on the lifeworld in terms of the way a person structures his/her perceptual experiences of the world, Habermas focusses on the lifeworld as the world of meanings that is linguistically maintained and challenged. The lifeworld consists of the shared stock of knowledge, values, assumptions and beliefs that make understanding and consensus possible:

> Communicative action takes place within a lifeworld that remains at the backs of participants in communication. It is present to them only in the prereflective form of taken-for-granted background assumptions and naively mastered skills. (2002: 172)

Clearly it is a social concept since the world we share includes both the meanings and understandings that permit communication with others. The function of the lifeworld is that of making social integration possible since the use of general communicative competence is entwined with the cultural competence of members of the lifeworld.

Since communication is the lifeline of the lifeworld, it is evident that language plays a pivotal role in the transmission of communication and in repairing any disruption of the communicative process. The possibility of breakdown in communication takes place because the lifeworld operates, so to speak, 'behind our backs'. Most of the time communication takes place without any feature of the lifeworld being questioned, but at times disagreement and dissent occur and this continues until consensus is once again achieved through discourse. It is, therefore, the lifeworld which provides the conditions for both social integration and critical discussion. To illustrate his point, Habermas offers a story: at a construction site a new foreign worker is asked by one of the older workers to fetch some beer for the morning break. This request can be challenged by the younger worker on a number of grounds: the validity claim to intelligibility (perhaps the young worker is foreign and does not understand German well); the validity claim to appropriateness (the young worker does not think it is part of his duties to fetch beer and not right of the older worker to ask him); the validity claim to factual assumptions (there are no shops selling beer near the construction site) and the validity claim to sincerity (the young worker thinks that the older worker is trying to humiliate him in front of the other workers). What Habermas wants to illustrate is not only the possibility of challenging claims (the general communicative competence of participants) but the further point that communication also entails participants bringing their cultural competence and assumptions (their lifeworld) into the situation. In this story, the lifeworld of the foreign worker is different from that of the older worker, and this explains why the young worker might think it odd that beer is drunk during the morning break. He might not recognize that there is an informal hierarchy at the construction site that allows the older worker to 'order' the younger one. When there is a problem it is not the lifeworld as a whole that is subjected to discussion, but rather a specific topic such as the timing of the morning break or whether all must drink beer:

> Single elements, specific taken-for-granteds, are, however, mobilized in the form of consensual and yet problematizable knowledge only when they become relevant to a situation. (1987b: 124)

But following a breakdown in communication a new consensus is achieved, and this new consensus feeds into the lifeworld. Habermas's concept of the lifeworld is therefore a dynamic one in that the lifeworld enables communication between members of society to take place, and in turn communication enhances the dynamics and growth of the lifeworld: 'the reproduction of the lifeworld is nourished through the contributions of communicative action, while the later simultaneously is nourished through the resources of the lifeworld' (2002: 191). This is why communication is not only a force for social integration, but it contributes to the reproduction of society. Through the medium of communication the identity of a society – its symbolic and cultural features – is revised, revitalized and transmitted to the younger members of society; in so doing it perpetuates that society. In his analysis of modern society, Habermas notes that as society has evolved,

> traditionally customary contexts of action oriented to mutual understanding get shoved out into the environments of systems. Using this criterion, we can locate the boundaries between system and lifeworld in a rough and ready way, such that the subsystems of the economy and the bureaucratic state administration are on one side, while on the other side we find private spheres of life (connected with family, neighbourhood, voluntary associations) as well as public spheres (for both private persons and citizens). (1987b: 310)

Habermas describes the system in terms of the abstract structures that regulate life in modern societies. He calls them the 'non-symbolic steering media' and these include the subsystems of money and power. These subsystems enable modern societies to maintain themselves by generating the necessary material goods and services. Money is the force that 'steers' the capitalist economy, while power – as the mechanism that directs the country – is manifested in the administration of the state (the civil service, the judiciary, the military) and through the officially recognized political parties. Habermas points out that although both money and power operate to integrate society, they do so in different ways. Money functions along a horizontal axis since it integrates society by bringing people together, while power is vertical in that it functions by ordering society into different hierarchies.

The lifeworld, which is grounded in communicative action, is opposed to the system which functions either instrumentally or strategically. Just as instrumental and strategic actions are parasitic upon communicative action, the system is parasitic upon the lifeworld. While the lifeworld is self-sustaining, since communication is beneficial for the lifeworld itself, the system on the other hand depends upon the resources of meaning that it finds in the lifeworld. This also applies in social interaction, where while communicative action in the lifeworld requires competent persons to coordinate their actions in accordance with each other – which is also known as mutual understanding – the system requires the coordination of action in terms of the consequences without the need for the persons to know what these actions mean.

Through the use of money and power, the system does not require communication – which entails understanding the reasons for what one does – but the mere fulfilling of one's role. This is precisely the crucial feature of the non-symbolic steering media: for them to function they must rely on automated or predictable responses. When, for example, I pay the bill at a restaurant, the waiter is not interested in where I got my money from or if perhaps I should have saved it to go on holiday instead. Similarly with power, a soldier is part of a hierarchical military system that follows a chain of command: the soldier must follow the commands of his superior whether he agrees with them or not. For the system to function such that a number of people coordinate their actions, what it requires is a few simple rules that are consistent with each other so that there will be no conflicts between the persons following them. As a result, the system itself tends to gravitate towards a status quo; it is conservative in that it does not encourage change.

The advances of modernization and industrialization have made the twin tasks of managing the economy and the administration of power as functions that are too complex to remain at the level of the lifeworld: it has, therefore, fallen upon the system to coordinate these activities. In the past it was the lifeworld that provided the backdrop for meaningful interaction between members of a community: social interaction was maintained through the medium of language and the communicative competences of participants. This situation has changed with the growth of modern societies and the need to maintain social order over large populations. By coordinating the economy and the state the system makes complex tasks possible: 'system integration' is the name of the process that coordinates people within sophisticated networks. In the case of money, it is possible to purchase goods from all over the world (you can buy coffee from Brazil without going there), so your action of buying is tied to the network that eventually arrives at the coffee producer. Likewise, power coordinates a number of people from different spheres to pool their resources to build dams, organize armies and so on. Performing these large-scale tasks cannot be managed with the communication resources available in the lifeworld: system integration requires that each member of the system perform his/her role mechanically without the need for communication. It is the predictability of responses that enables the system to function as a means for organizing society. For example, I can go to the library and borrow a book without needing to know anything about the librarian, just as he or she does not need to know anything about me (except see my library card). Strategic action can be used in a non-manipulative manner, and Habermas develops this theme in relation to his study of social systems and the way people interact within them. In the course of our everyday life, a large amount of interaction does not take place at the level of mutual understanding and agreement through communicative action; most of the time we live our lives in agreement with others without raising validity claims. Social interaction in modern society involves being able to predict how others would react without the need to challenge them.

In an advanced, modern society there is no escape from the system as it is an integral part of the way these societies are organized and essential to their functioning. This is the positive aspect of system integration: by relieving the lifeworld of the twin burdens of managing the economy and the administration of power, the system has made it possible for the lifeworld to focus on the task of social integration. Social integration is grounded in communication, where coordination between members of society is produced through meaningful communication with the possibility of asking questions and offering answers, thus providing the context for social interaction. On the other hand, system integration does not rely upon communication but upon the predictability of actions, so that persons interact with each other as though they were machines that function automatically.

Despite the necessity of the system in modern societies, Habermas describes the tendency inherent in the system to both dislocate itself from the lifeworld and then attempt to take over it. He calls this process the 'colonisation of the lifeworld': 'the imperatives of autonomous subsystems make their way into the lifeworld from the outside – like colonial masters coming into a tribal society – and force a process of assimilation upon it' (1987b: 355). The systemic imperatives of economics and bureaucratic administration intrude upon the lifeworld so that communicative action is increasingly replaced with instrumental action. This can be seen in the way both economic factors and the intervention of the state dominate the way society is maintained. The evolution of society into complex forms of social organization has developed systems that enable actions to be coordinated. But problematically these systems have developed a life of their own such that their functioning imposes restrictions upon the freedom of persons. Since it is the nature of the system to structure the pattern of action that a person is obliged to follow, then it 'limits' the possibilities of freedom. As a result, market forces dictate economics and the structures of power dictate one's behaviour. In the case of money, for example, freedom is restricted because (1) what we purchase is limited to the amount of money we have and (2) the economics of money operates independently of symbolic institutions. A company that produces pharmaceutical products for human immunodeficiency virus (HIV) is not interested in whether they should be making a profit over something that is needed by suffering people. It is beyond the purpose of the pharmaceutical company to ask such questions as they operate within market economies concerned with profits rather than people.

The problem of colonization is exacerbated when the system imposes its own values on the lifeworld. This can be seen when the system enters the domains of the family and culture, or when it takes over the domains of the public sphere such as the mass media. The markets or the specialists take over areas that previously belonged to agents in the lifeworld and who are now no longer in a position to assess or contribute to decisions that are taken for them. If the characteristic of the system is instrumental thinking and efficiency in the attainment of ends, when instrumental thinking is applied to human life humans are transformed into objects, becoming subject to calculation and quantification. When, for example, a hospital is interested in the numbers of patients rather than the quality of the nursing provided, it is difficult for an individual nurse to provide the care required since the whole system is working against him/her. In effect the system seems to develop a world of its own – a world that follows its own laws that are external to and beyond human agency – and imposes it upon the lifeworld. An inversion occurs since, instead of the system serving the lifeworld, the system becomes an end in itself with the lifeworld transformed into a subsystem operating along instrumental values.

The degree with which the system has succeeded in colonizing the lifeworld is such that challenging the system itself through the resources of communication becomes a difficult task: it is hard work – though not impossible – to resist the notion that efficiency and money are not necessarily conducive to a person's happiness. Everyday language provides a sign of this increasingly dominant view, where one hears people talking about 'retail therapy' as the quick fix to happiness. The encroachment of the system upon the lifeworld has produced a number of social pathologies such as 'loss of meaning, anomie, and mental illness (psychopathology)' (1987b: 142).

Discourse ethics

In his later writings on discourse, Habermas broadens the discussion away from the narrow conceptual concern with 'objectivity' and 'facts' to the broader domain of ethical issues. In a sense this was implied in this earlier writings, since one of the validity claims of the theory of communicative action involved the rightness or appropriateness of what the speaker says. It covered, in other words, the ethical relation between participants in communication. When disagreements arise concerning questions of norms, ordinary communication is temporarily suspended and discussion or argumentation takes place, enabling the speaker to defend himself/herself against the challenges directed towards the rightness or appropriateness of his/her normative utterances.

In his account of discourse ethics Habermas develops the programme outlined in his theory of communicative action, but here he is interested in the kind of argumentation that leads to valid answers concerning moral questions that are generated out of the interaction between people in the lifeworld. The purpose of such argumentation is that of achieving consensus in norms: this might be difficult because new situations have arisen and the 'old' norms are no longer valid ways of coping with these new situations. New norms are required that need to be validated so that persons can adjust to the new situation that life has presented.

In today's world there seems to be a widespread tendency to view moral issues as subjective ones: 'emotivism' is the idea that moral questions can only be at best expressions of subjective opinion. Habermas strongly disagrees with this view of morality as a private domain, positioning himself as a cognitivist: his argument is that the criterion for deciding the rightness of some normative issue is also that of rationality. His theory of discourse ethics is formulated along the same lines as his theory of communicative rationality, since both are cognitively grounded. Moral actions and choices can be defended by an appeal to moral principles, and if these principles are challenged then they can be defended. In his work on ethics, Habermas shows the parallelism between moral statements and factual statements since both presuppose the use of reason. When a person asks about the legitimacy of a norm, he/she is actually asking about its 'rightness' or 'correctness', and although many people think that this question can only be answered with reference to the psychological motivation of the speaker, such an answer is inadequate as it fails to take into consideration the rationality of the norm. When we communicate our values we can offer reasons for why we hold them, reasons that others in a similar context would concur with. Habermas's account of communicative rationality shows that subjectivity in ethical issues is not the last word. A subjective evaluation can always be re-evaluated after the reasons for accepting another evaluation proves to be better.

And since normative utterances are evaluated rationally, they can be also considered objective. This claim needs to be qualified as there is a major difference between normative and epistemological utterances: whereas a statement can be true or false of the world (it is not the world that is true or false), the validity of a norm is not dependent upon the way the world is. Rather, a norm is an expression of how a speaker or others should act in the world. It is evident that the objectivity we find in epistemological utterances is not the same as that of normative ones, but this does not mean that norms have no objectivity. On the contrary, Habermas defends the objectivity of norms by pointing to a 'weaker' version of what has been traditionally considered objective:

> Owing to the fact that normative validity claims are built into the universe of norms, the latter reveals a peculiar kind of objectivity vis-à-vis regulative speck acts, an objectivity that the universe of facts does not possess vis-à-vis constative speech acts […] [N]orms are dependent upon the continual reestablishment of legitimately ordered interpersonal relationships […] Normative claims to validity, then, *mediate a mutual dependence* of language and the social world that does not exist for the relation of language to the objective world. (1990: 61)

There is, therefore, an objectivity of the natural world and an objectivity of the social world; epistemological validity claims belong to the former, and normative validity claims to the latter.

But in spite of the objectivity of normative validity claims, what is the 'force' generated by normative utterances such that one feels obliged to accept it? The use of 'ought' in normative discourse is such that it brings together participants who have agreed upon and who cooperate in following such norms. A norm is followed when a consensus is achieved as a result of the cooperation of each participant: normative propositions depend upon the offering of reasons that justify not only one's behaviour but also that of others. On this account there is a big difference between accepting a norm on the grounds that it has been agreed upon and following a norm out of obedience or conformity. Debates or discussions concerning norms stimulate questions on behavioural expectations, so that achieving a consensus on norms is a process that is informed by a willingness to undergo rational critique. What gives a discourse its power is that it expresses a common interest in its search for consensus. A discourse is universal in the sense that the interests it expresses are not particularized but generalizable, involving shared participation.

Before any discussion of normative validity can begin, Habermas outlines certain presuppositions or rules of discourse. These rules are connected to the competence of those participating in the discourse, and all participants must accept these rules for validity of the discussion. The rules are:

1. Every subject with the competence to speak and act is allowed to take part in a discourse.
2. (a) Everyone is allowed to question any assertion whatever.
   (b) Everyone is allowed to introduce any assertion whatever into the discourse.
   (c) Everyone is allowed to express his attitudes, desires and needs.
3. No speaker may be prevented, by internal or external coercion, from exercising their rights as laid down in 1 and 2. (1990: 89)

The legitimacy of a discourse presupposes a situation where participants understand each other, where every participant has the possibility of using any speech act (raising questions, expressing doubts), where no one is excluded from the discussion and where no one is forced to accept any opinion. It must be possible to challenge an opinion and if a participant cannot defend his/her opinion rationally then he/she is obliged to modify or reject it. It is only in this way that a justified consensus can be achieved since it would be the result of the 'force of the better argument' (1990: 158–59). The challenge to a claim can only be defended if the participants have the possibility of freely entering and moving between the different levels of discourse. Finlayson describes the ideal speech situation as follows:

> [T]he rules of discourse are *idealizing* in that they direct participants towards the ideal of rationally motivated consensus. A discourse in which the voices of all concerned are listened to, in which no argument is arbitrarily excluded from consideration and in which only the force of the better argument prevails, will, if successful, result in a consensus on the basis of reasons acceptable to all. (2005: 44)

Habermas elaborates upon the two fundamental principles that are at stake in the programme of discourse ethics:

1. The principle of universalization (U) is formulated in the following way:

> *All* affected can accept the consequences and the side-effects of its *general* observance can be anticipated to have for the satisfaction of *everyone's* interests (and these

consequences are preferred to those of known alternative possibilities for regulation). (1990: 65)

2. The principle of discourse (D) is formulated in the following way: 'Only those norms can claim to be valid that meet (or could meet) with the approval of all affected in their capacity *as participants in a practical discourse*' (1990: 66).

Taken together the two principles constitute a powerful basis for establishing the validity of moral norms. Those who participate in the process of argumentation are implicitly accepting the idea that a valid moral norm has universal applicability, in other words, that it applies not just to oneself but also to others. It would be a strange moral norm if it applied to you ('do not steal') but not to me. We expect moral norms to be binding on everybody and this is what the principle of universalization caters for. But the principle of universalization on its own is not enough, since one could use other non-moral ways of bringing about universal consensus (threats, intimidation or through the prevention of certain topics). Habermas argues that establishing the validity of norms requires a certain type of reasoning: moral principles need to form a bridge between the logical techniques of argumentation and the data that arise from the social world. This is why both deduction and induction are tools in the formation of norms. The principle of discourse ensures that the solution to moral problems entails reasoning with others, and that any agreement or consensus reached must have been subjected to a process of open and free rational debate. The two principles are in effect a combination of Kantian universality and public participation: a norm is valid only if it is recognized by all those affected by it and if it is validated by participants engaged in a rational debate.

> [T]he categorical imperative needs to be reformulated as follows: "Rather than ascribing as valid to all others any maxim that I can will to be a universal law, I must submit my maxim to all others for the purposes of discursively testing its claim to universality. The emphasis shifts from what each can will without contradiction to be a general law, to what all can will in agreement to be a universal norm." (1990: 67)

The necessary involvement of others in moral discourse shows the extent of Habermas's differences with the views of John Rawls. In his attempt to formulate the grounds for a principle of justice, Rawls hypothesizes a fictional 'original position', where each person imagines himself/herself without the trappings of social class, wealth or capabilities. Since nobody knows how his/her life would turn out, it is in the person's own interest to make sure that all material resources are equally and fairly distributed, since the person himself/herself might be the one who needs it most. While for Rawls this imaginary return to an 'original position' ensures that justice is operating in society, for Habermas this position neglects the very important point that morality takes in particular contexts in the real world. The solutions to moral problems are not discovered in the solitary world of the theorist speculating in his/her office, but in cooperation with others: people argue to reach an agreement or consensus on the issues at hand.

Habermas's discourse ethics emphasizes the role of intersubjectivity in moral discourse. This role had been neglected in earlier moral theories (Kantianism or utilitarianism), as it was assumed that without some objective grounding or foundation there would be no basis for their moral principles. So as to achieve an objective moral position, the views or perspectives of the speaker and of the participants were removed from the discourse. But Habermas points out that removing one's point of view or that of others does not lead to objectivity; rather, it is by taking into account all points of view that a valid moral position can be reached. As Habermas puts it, moral questions are questions in the first person plural involving the use of 'we' or 'us' rather than 'I' or 'you'.

The possibility of formulating universal moral statements is one that pits Habermas against many contemporary philosophers who have questioned the traditional role of philosophy as the discipline concerned with the search for universal truths. And if this contemporary view is accepted, when applied to morality it would lead to a renunciation of universalism in morality. For many philosophers influenced by postmodernism, the attempt to universalize morality is a projection of Western values onto the rest of the world, an attempt that is outdated and Eurocentric. Habermas needs to demonstrate that this charge is unfounded, for otherwise his whole project for the renewal of critical theory collapses. His strategy for countering the anti-universal bias of contemporary Western thought relies upon the work of Karl Otto Apel, who argues that the person who denies the possibility of moral discourse is in actual fact engaging in it. There is no position outside morality just as there is no position outside language: we can only talk about morality by expressing a moral point of view, just as we can only talk about language by using language. Denying any of these entails a performative self-contradiction, and the fact that one cannot engage in moral discourse from a position outside morality is called the 'transcendental presupposition of argumentation'. In other words we have to accept that it is possible to argue about moral issues that concern everybody for the conversation on morality to continue. Habermas uses this insight to claim that all moral argumentation presupposes a universal basis; since it is not possible to talk about morality from a position outside morality, then this is the universal precondition for the production of all discourse on morality.

Given that moral judgements are the result of rational argumentation between participants in every society, Habermas rejects the claim that morality is context-bound or specific, as in fact moral relativists claim. It is the 'force of the better argument', rather than the values and beliefs that social agents bring to the discussion, that validate a moral norm. One would think that if moral norms are universal then they always were universal. This is, however, not the case, and Habermas argues that the process of testing moral norms for their rationality is a historical achievement: it is only found in what he calls 'post-conventional' societies. This paradoxically implies that the whole notion of a universal ethics is conditioned by a historical context. Habermas is aware of the paradox but considers the acceptance of a universal ethics as a sign of the progressive evolution of that society (1990: 109).

The practice of discourse ethics involves a negotiation between members of a community. A person belongs to a community – a lifeworld – within which he/she shares values and beliefs: these shared values and beliefs enable the person to understand others and himself/herself. It is through this community that a person acquires a social and personal identity. But given that changes take place as communities evolve, the values and norms of the community are no longer acceptable. While the community can be a source of solidarity, providing support and a sense of belonging to its members, it can also be oppressive; Western societies have – at various moment in their history – oppressed persons on the basis of their race, gender or social status. This is where the utility of discourse ethics as a critical tool comes in: it enables persons to challenge those norms or values that they find unacceptable. Rather than blind acceptance and conformity, discourse ethics is the medium where the values and norms of a community are either revitalized or discarded. When this critical challenge occurs, it does not take place wholesale; in other words it is not the entire value system that is challenged, since this would lead to the collapse of the community. Instead it is specific norms and values that are challenged.

Given that universal ethics has evolved historically as part of a post-conventional society, there is also the possibility that it will evolve in other ways in the future, ways that might be repressive. Habermas attempts to solve this paradox by describing discourse ethics as a minimalist one (following from Adorno's *Minima Moralia*), in the sense that it does not offer the solutions to moral problems. It does not pretend to stand 'above' everybody, telling them what to do, but points out that it is up to the people themselves to find solutions to moral problems since they are the ones who are going to live with whatever they agree upon. What Habermas does provide is a procedure that shows how a solution can be achieved. In other words, discourse ethics is formal and not substantial in that it highlights the necessary conditions that enable a fair moral decision to be reached. It does not tell us what moral norms and values should be debated, but that they can be debated: '[t]o that extent discourse ethics can properly be characterized as formal, for it provides no substantive guidelines but only a procedure: practical discourse' (1990: 103). Habermas is consistent with the claim that moral discourse belongs to the intersubjective domain so that norms can only be validated in discussion with others. The only role left for the moral philosopher is that of offering his/her contributions to the public domain.

The advantage of Habermas's programme of discourse ethics is that by offering a formal procedure, rather than the actual content of values and norms, it minimizes its relation to the cultural values and norms of a particular historical moment. With this procedure, it is always possible to challenge the values and norms so that they are retained if they remain relevant and replaced if they are outdated. The critical dimension of discourse ethics is that by proposing a minimalist and formal approach it becomes possible to challenge what is taken for granted. As Edgar puts it, the role of discourse ethics is 'to expose false consensus, rather than to affirm or anticipate any true consensus. It is suspicious of any existing consensus' (2005: 164).

The need for Habermas's programme of discourse ethics arises in connection with his analysis of Western culture; as society has developed, it has moved away from a centred view of the world to a decentred one. As a result, there is a distinction between the way the world is and our experience of the world, an experience which might vary for different individuals. Ethical issues arise when the experience of the world differs between participants, and it is through communication that these differences in norms, facts or life experiences are expressed. And yet, despite these differences, it is still possible to communicate and understand each other. Morality, in Habermas's view, provides the double function of protecting both the individual and the social, a function that in turn is a sign of the degree of rationality and progress within a society.

The shift from the early writings on communicative rationality to the writings on discourse ethics is a shift of emphasis. While the moral dimension was considered as one of the four validity claims, the early writings subsumed the moral dimension under the broader category of the political, where the rightness of a political system is justified as in *Legitimation Crisis* (1988). In the writings on discourse ethics this political concern remains, but it is no longer a neo-Marxist analysis of ideology as it is situated within the debates on the nature of justice within a liberal context.

Habermas and political communication

Habermas is one of those philosophers who actively grounds his philosophical ideas in contexts of action and this can be readily seen in his engagement with the political discourses that characterise contemporary society. In 'Political Communication in Media Society: Does Democracy Still Enjoy an Epistemic Dimension? The Impact of Normative Theory on Empirical Research' (2006) Habermas argues in favour of a deliberative model of political communication (as opposed to a liberal or republican one) that emphasizes cooperation between citizens who together look for solutions to political problems (2006: 413).

Habermas argues that the success of the deliberative model of political communication is connected to the interaction by the public sphere in the media. This success depends upon two conditions: (1) the existence of a 'self-regulating media system' that is independent from its social environment and (2) the presence of 'anonymous audiences [that] grant feedback between an informed elite discourse and a responsive civil society' (2006: 411–12). These two conditions are important for the deliberative model of political communication because this model requires the active participation of citizens and/or the creation of public opinions.

The deliberative model coexists with a democratic political system that assumes choices taken are rationally motivated. Habermas's theory of communicative action, with its insistence on the giving of reasons, provides the theoretical framework for ongoing rational deliberations that are essential to the democratic process. Without it political communication would be reduced merely to routine reactions rather than a space of discussion and evaluation. However, as Habermas points out within contemporary Western societies there are two main differences between media format of political communication and the practice of deliberative politics; these are (1) the lack of face-to-face interaction and (2) the imbalance between speakers and addressees (2006: 414–15). Despite these differences Habermas does not consider mediated communication as destructive for deliberative political communication. Rather, he envisions society as a multileveled network in which political communication circulates throughout with the public sphere positioned at the periphery of the political system and channelling political communication to the different parts of the network (2006: 415). In its functioning the public sphere includes 'news, reports, commentaries, talks, scenes and images and shows and movies with an informative, polemical, educational, or entertaining content' (2006: 415).

While the political public sphere requires media professionals (especially journalists) and politicians, the media circulation of political communication requires a number of players such as advocates, experts, moral entrepreneurs and intellectuals. The function of deliberation in the political public sphere is to ensure that there are a number of various opinions on the relevant issues. (2006: 416). Habermas points out that public opinion is central to a dynamic democratic process and it exerts a kind of 'political influence' that differs from that of 'political power' insofar as it is a form of pressure on the minds of others without any institutional settings. The movement of public opinion is twofold: it is directed towards the government that monitors it, but it also returns to the public from where it was generated for possible reappraisal and revision. When public opinion has been filtered according to the relevance of the issues, in relation to the information required and in the light of the appropriateness of the contributions then this is described by Habermas as 'considered public opinion' (2006: 418).

The contemporary world of mass communications is double-edged insofar as it can contribute to the generation of considered public opinions; it can also distort public opinion if the aforementioned conditions are not fulfilled. The world of mass communications is a form of 'media power' because those involved in this media select the politically relevant material as well as the formatting and style of programs. Newspapers in particular function as opinion leaders since their circulation allows for the dissemination of political views with these views taken over by other forms of the mass media. While politicians and political parties have a particular relationship with the mass media, the way the media interpret political messages is not under the control of the government (2006: 419).

The mass media have an inherent power structure that can limit intervention by actors. Despite this limitation, Habermas points out that any intervention must still play by the 'rules of the game' namely that of producing considered public opinions. Two conditions must be kept in mind: (1) the media, as a self-regulating system, must remain independent from the environment and yet bridge the world of civil society with that of politics; (2) citizens must be empowered in civil society to participate in public debates and respond accordingly (2006: 419–29). In turn, these two considerations – when not adhered to – can point to the 'pathologies of political communication'.

In the case of condition (1) Habermas distinguishes between temporary and total interference of the media from the environment. As an example of total interference, Habermas refers to the total domination by the state over public broadcasting in Italy in the decades after World War II. As an example of temporary interference, he mentions the lack of alternative views in the press to the so-called 'war on terror'. Other cases where the media does not remain independent from its environment are those involving special interest groups who use the media to influence politics or when the owners of the media (television and print) blatantly use their media to influence the public and to exert political pressure. In the case of condition (2) which concerns the lack of participation by citizens, Habermas identifies two main causes: these are the lack of access to the media due to 'social deprivation' and 'cultural exclusion' and the domination of the public sphere by market forces. In the case of the first cause, there is an obvious correlation between social status and cultural background and the level of participation in the media. While there seems to be an increased involvement of people in mass communications and politics, Habermas cites empirical evidence that suggests that these people have a lower level of trust in politics. In this case, it might seem that the nature of the media itself contributes to the alienation of citizens from politics. In the case of the second cause, what Habermas has in mind is the way that political discourse is commercialized as a form of entertainment so that 'the dramatization of events, the simplification of complex mates, and the vivid polarization of conflicts promote civic privatism and a mood of antipolitics' (2006: 422).

Given the media-saturated world we live in, Habermas has elaborated on the way the media can contribute to a politics centred upon deliberation. Interestingly, in a footnote to this essay he also comments on the role the Internet – as an egalitarian space – has played in political communication arguing that while it has proved invaluable towards undermining totalitarian regimes, within democratic contexts it has produced a more fragmented public in that users focussed on isolated issues at the expense of national ones (2006: 423).

Critical remarks

The writings of Habermas have generated considerable controversy from both those sympathetic to his project and from those critical of it. With regard to the narrow claims made of speech acts, it has been pointed out that Habermas's attempt to replace a truth conditional account of language with a pragmatic one fails to explain the complexity of speech acts. Finlayson (2005) argues that in everyday life speech acts could easily include all three domains of meaning as one;[6] and while Habermas does recognize that a speech act can simultaneously communicate different aspects (truth or norms or subjectivity) with the possibility of challenging each aspect, he stresses that it is only one that is usually thematized.

Sutton (2003: 52) raises the question of whether communication can ever be interest-free. Strategic interests are part of discourse and therefore the neutrality described in the process of discussion and agreement seems to be highly optimistic. In response Habermas has formulated the notion of 'idealisations' – a term that replaces his earlier 'ideal speech situation', which described the assumptions inherent in language use to achieve understanding. 'Idealisations' are those elements presupposed or assumed within language use so that communication and understanding can take place. They are not over and above language even though they are objective. When talking about facts we assume that an objective world exists. When initiating a discussion with others, one 'minimum' assumption underlying the discussion is that participants believe that the other is sincerely motivated in the search for truth or morality. It might be the case that one finds out that the other is insincere, and in effect seeking to influence others through strategic actions. Whatever the case, one starts by assuming the sincerity of the other person; otherwise no discussion will ever take place.

It is clear that Habermas's theory of communicative action is a theory of argumentation. Participants in a dialogue rationally defend their views and criticize others. By argumentation Habermas accepts the tools used within the discourse of philosophy, for example, the soundness of an argument, the logical or reasoning processes of deduction and induction. A number of critical points are raised by Calvin O. Schrag (in Ramsey and Miller 2003: 15–16), who argues that by reducing the concept of communication to that of argumentation Habermas is neglecting other forms of communication. Argumentation is placed at the service of philosophy, with arguments deployed to justify the validity of claims in the respective the cognitive, ethical and aesthetic domains. As a result, the validity claims serve an instrumental end. Ironically, as Schrag points out, the instrumental reason that communicative reason was supposed to counteract returns under the disguise of the validity claims. Communication, as it turns out, is instrumental.

The value of Habermas's theory of communicative action is that it locates the lifeworld as the context within which everyday communication takes place: it enables the reproduction of a society and provides it with the resources for change. The theory of communicative action also highlights another crucial feature in that the communicative competence of speakers and hearers create the very contexts of communication. In their ability to respond to various speech acts participants are establishing relations among themselves. This is why successful communication involves both understanding and accepting reasons for what is claimed. Moreover, Habermas's analysis also reveals that the bigger threat to modern society comes from the impersonal forces of the system that operates without meaningful communication. The main goal of his critical theory is that of restoring rationality to its proper and central place in human life. Since it is language that defines us as humans, and since understanding and rationality are inherent to language, it follows that humans are rational beings. By combining rationality with communication – communicative rationality – he is able to show the dynamics of social life both in terms of social order and its disruption. Social integration is achieved through the mechanics of communicative action while social conflict has its roots in strategic action.

In this chapter I have first outlined (1) the foundation of Habermas's theory of communication and developed it with (2) the concepts of discourse and validity. These were then situated (3) within the analysis of action as communicative, strategic and instrumental. The subsequent section continued exploring (4) the relationship between the lifeworld and communicative processes set in opposition to systemic ones. The next section narrows (5) its focus towards discourse ethics and the final section examines (6) political communication within a media-dominated world.

Notes

1. Cooke writes: 'Habermas's objection to this is threefold: first, Austin's distinction between force and meaning overlooks the fact that utterances have meaning distinct from the meaning of the sentences they employ; second, it is connected with a problematic classification of speech acts into constatives and performatives, whereby initially, for Austin, only constatives are connected with validity claims; third, it neglects the rational foundation of illocutionary force' (2002: 7).
2. The broad sense of the concept of understanding is further elaborated: 'The term "reaching understanding" (*Verständigung*) means, at the minimum, that at least two subjects capable of speech and action understand a linguistic expression in an identical way. The meaning of an elementary expression consists in the contribution that it makes to the meaning of an acceptable speech act. And to understand what a speaker wants to say with such an act, the hearer has to know the conditions under which it can be accepted. To this extent, understanding an elementary expression already points beyond the minimal meaning of the term *Verständigung*' (2002: 142).
3. Cooke writes: 'although the set of reasons constituting a given *kind* of reasons is always in principle open-ended, in everyday contexts of communication contextual considerations act as a constraint on the kinds of reasons that are relevant to justification' (2002: 12).
4. As an example of argumentation Habermas adopts an argument from Stephen Toulmin: 'The assertion, "Harry is a British subject" (conclusion), can be explained by the identification of a cause: "Harry was born in Bermuda" (data). This explanation is reached through the deductive application of a generalization: "A man born in Bermuda will generally be a British subject" (warrant). The plausibility of this generalization is justified [...]"on account of the following statutes and other legal provisions" (backing)' (in Held 1980: 342).
5. Habermas calls the increase in the freedom of reflection 'radicalisation of argument' (in Held 1980: 343).
6. Finlayson argues that 'natural language seamlessly combines normative, epistemic, and expressive features: "the student has plagiarized my book!" may be at once reporting a fact, expressing an attitude of disapproval because a norm has been transgressed and disclosing subjective feelings' (2005: 40).

Chapter 12

Halliday on Language and Social Semiotics

M. A. K Halliday (1925) is recognized as being one of the leading linguists in the contemporary world for having introduced a new and original approach to the study of language known as systemic functional linguistics. While this is already an achievement in itself he went on to incorporate his linguistics into a larger framework that theorized language from a social perspective.

Halliday's work originates in its reaction to the then dominant view of linguistics as exemplified by Chomsky's theory of transformational grammar that considered the task of linguistics to be one of identifying the formal properties of language. This view of linguistics was challenged on the grounds that it offered an account of language that was too narrow in scope. In the 1960s Halliday proposed an analysis of language that focussed on the context within which it was used. This came to be known as systemic functional linguistics and its basic premise was that language evolved to fulfil certain functions, with these functions reflected in the grammar. In the 1970s, Halliday shifted his attention from the examination of language used in social contexts to an examination of language within the larger category of society, that is, in relation to social structures. This new perspective on language is examined in a collection of essays called *Language as a social semiotic* (1978), where Halliday introduces a number of concepts that enable him to theorize the social interpretation of language.

In the first section I outline (1) the invaluable contributions of Malinowski and Firth's views on language, followed by (2) a general overview of Halliday's account of the social dimension of language with its emphasis of language functionality. I then proceed to specify (3) the conceptual framework that constitutes Halliday sociolinguistic theory of language and follow this with (4) an account of the development of social semiotics.

Malinowski and Firth on language

There are a number of influences upon Halliday's thinking and these include the Prague school of linguistics, Hjelmslev's glossematics and Whorf's views of linguistic relativity (among others). However, in his study on the social dimension of language there are two names that loom large in his thinking: B. Malinowski (1884–1942) and J. R. Firth (1890–1960).

In 'The problem of meaning in primitive languages' (1923) Malinowski introduces the concept of the context of situation. He derived this concept while studying the life of the Trobriand Islanders in the South Pacific who lived by fishing and gardening and spoke a language known as Kiriwinian. Malinowski was able to learn Kiriwinian conversing with the islanders using it while also taking copious notes. Since the culture of the Trobriand Islanders was obviously very different from that of English language speakers, the problem which faced Malinowski was that of translation: how does one translate a text from one culture into that of another such that it becomes intelligible to the other culture?

Malinowski adopted the practice of commenting on the text (his notes) that he was translating. The goal of this commentary was that of highlighting the background environment within which the text was embedded. He coins the expression 'context of situation' to include both the verbal and the non-verbal situation that generates the text. To illustrate his point Malinowski describes the situation of the islanders when they go out of their lagoon into the open sea on a fishing expedition. Having succeeding in their fishing, the return to the lagoon with their load of fish is hazardous because of the reefs they need to navigate through. To guide them back to the lagoon a number of islanders communicate instructions to the boats from the shore and there is a competitive twist to this, with the canoes vying with each other as to who arrives first. This is a classic example of language in action since it is impossible to understand the meaning of what the islanders were saying unless you could visualize the actions they were performing, their doings. This is what Malinowski did by providing an account of the actions during the fishing expedition. However, he realized that describing the immediate background to the language used was not enough since fishing was part of the way of life of the islanders. It was also important to provide an account of the cultural background of the islanders and this includes their practices and rituals. This is the context of culture and together with the context of situation contributes to the meaning of the texts.

The upshot of Malinowski study of the language used by the Trobriand Islanders is that it was strictly pragmatic in that it could be directly connected to something the people were doing at the time they were using it; language was used to fulfil a specific function or purpose by enabling cooperation between the Islanders. And this pragmatic or functional use of language could also be extended to situations that were not immediately connected to the context as, for example, storytelling. Frequently, Malinowski noticed the islanders would gather round to listen to stories, and the content of these stories was not directly related to their context: they could be narrated at any time of the day and at any location. But the narratives had a function within the community in that they provided a feeling of solidarity between members of the community; during a year of famine when the community felt threatened narratives were told that would recount how the community had been through similar situations but had survived them by uniting together.

As a result of his work with the Trobriand Islanders, Malinowski rejected the correspondence view of meaning as a connection between words and things; instead of words, he argued for sentences that were produced in a context as the basic unit of semantics. Language was 'a mode of action, rather than a countersign of thought' (Malinowski 1923: 296–97). For some time Malinowski thought that the concept of the context of situation was necessary to describe languages of primitive cultures, that is, with no written history, but was not necessary with the languages of civilizations. He came to realize that this opposition was a mistake arguing that all language is pragmatic and therefore understood within a context maintaining that the difference between primitive and civilized languages is a difference in degree, not in kind (1935: vol, 2: 58).

In the 1930s, the linguist J. R. Firth developed Malinowski's account of language and context in such a way as to give it a central position within linguistics. Firth maintained the view that meanings were 'intimately interlocked not only with an environment of particular sights and sounds, but deeply embedded in the living process of persons maintaining themselves in society' (in Palmer 1968: 13).

To achieve his goal, Firth needed to generalize from the insights derived from Malinowski. For a start, he had realized that Malinowski was not interested in a constructing a theory of linguistics; rather his account of the context of situation was narrowly tied down to very specific instances of language use. It was, therefore, incumbent upon Firth to develop a broader account and to this end he constructed a number of abstract categories so as to study 'repetitive events in the social process' (1957: 182). The categories that describe the context of situation are

1. those participating in the situation: this category takes into account the relevant features of the participants (personalities) such as their status and roles and including their verbal and non-verbal actions;
2. the objects and events that are within the situation and have some relevance to what is going on;
3. the effects of verbal actions in so far as what the participants said brought about changes to the situation.[1]

However, the context of situation as articulated in this way was not enough to account for what Firth perceived as the different levels of meaning. These different levels of meaning were the product of other contexts such as the grammatical or lexical or phonological contexts. Within each of these, grammatical or lexical or phonological items functioned as aspects of meaning that Firth described as 'modes' (1957: 19). So too, Firth also proposed that other broader contexts need to be taken into account: social structures (economic, religious), types of discourse (narrative, monologue, etc.), speech acts (orders, flattery) and social techniques (deception, flattery, etc.)

In his linguistics theory, Firth positioned himself against the then prevalent linguistics of Saussure. He was highly critical of Saussurean linguistics in that it theorized a 'macro' theory of language that used one model of language to explain all contexts; Firth argued for a 'micro' view of language in the sense that different contexts entailed different linguistic systems. However, it should be pointed out that Firth's linguistics is modelled along the Saussurean distinction between paradigmatic and syntagmatic relations, even though his account is more detailed.

Firth is one of the most important influences upon the development of Hallidayan linguistics, in particular, the principle of meaning as function of context. It is this principle that is refined and elaborated upon by Halliday.

The social dimension of language

The starting point for Halliday's linguistic theory is 'social man' and his interest lies in the way speaker/listeners and writers/readers interact in social situations. In his early writings, the behavioural potential was the larger framework of meaning within which the sociosemantic system ('can mean') and the lexicogrammatical system ('can say') were realized. An analysis of the behavioural domain remained in the (relative) background. In his work from the mid-1970s Halliday shifts his attention to the behavioural potential ('can do') of the cultural and sub-cultural domains. The behavioural potential is the social semiotic of a culture constituted by its own system of meanings and values in an intricate network of connections. And while language is one of the most important symbolic systems for the communication of meaning, there are others (1975: 121) such as forms of art, social structures and institutions, educational and legal systems.

> The social system, viewed in these terms, is a system of meaning relations; and these meaning relations are realized in many ways, of which one, perhaps the principal one as far as the maintenance and transmission of the system is concerned, is through their encoding in language. The meaning potential of a language, its semantic system, is therefore seen as realizing a higher level system of relations, that of the social semiotics, in just the same way as it is itself realized in the lexico-grammatical and phonological systems. (1975: 121)

In *Language as social semiotic* (1978) Halliday broadens his analysis of language from that of systemic grammar to the relation between language and society. The social dimension of language had already received considerable attention by a number of theorists but Halliday contributes further to the discussion by focussing attention on the way participation in society implies the attribution of roles and these, in turn, are the conditions that make possible the formation of one's personality. Language is central to the entire process of transforming the individual into a person. The point of departure for this transformative process is our membership into a group which (unlike other species) can only be obtained with the use of language. At this stage, the individual is just part of a group of people but further participation within society transforms the individual into a person: while a group is a simple structure with participation entailing the 'minimum' requirement of existing with others, living in a society entails the adoption of social role(s). It is language that enables the attainment of social roles and the performance of which results in the construction of a personality (1978: 14–15).

The study of language from a social dimension views language from what Halliday calls an 'inter-organism perspective' or 'language as behaviour'. This is opposed to the study of language from an 'intra-organism perspective' or 'language as knowledge' which focusses on the processes that take place within the individual makeup (psychological and physiological) of the human organism. It studies the internal biological equipment that enables speakers to use a language; questions typically asked are, what must the structure or the mechanism of the brain be like for an individual to learn, speak and understand a language? On the other hand, the inter-organism perspective is the social perspective inasmuch as it concerns the way individuals interact with each other; it is the behaviour of the individual as a complete person (as opposed to the study of the parts of the individual in the intra-organism perspective) as he/she relates to the social environment. This is where the emphasis on the social takes a different slant from other social theories of language, for Halliday's construction of the social is not framed in opposition to the individual but rather to the 'psychophysiological', that is, to the intra-organism perspective (1978: 12).

The upshot of Halliday's interest in the social dimension of language is that it centres on what the individual does or can do with language. It is the language of action whereby the individual actualizes the meaning potential in language as he/she connects with other members of society. On this account, the functions of language take precedence as it is through its functioning that social relations are established; understanding the nature of language involves understanding its functioning to create meaning between members of a society (1978: 14–16).

The analysis of linguistic function derives considerable insight from the way children learn their mother tongue. In the past, this process of language learning had been called 'language acquisition' but Halliday prefers to use the term 'language development' as the former has misleadingly led to the view that a child can be somehow 'deficient' in language if he/she has not acquired it properly (for example) on account of the child's social background (1978: 16).

There are two main theories that attempt to explain the development of language: the 'nativist' and the 'environmentalist'. According to the nativist position learning a language is different from learning other activities such as walking or swimming, for the child has a special faculty (unlike other animals) that allows him/her to learn the language. Given that the child is exposed to a particular language, the innate structures of language in the child will allow it to learn that particular language. The environmentalist theory maintains that the child has no special faculty for learning a language; on the contrary, any learning activity involves using the same mental processes that the child would use for learning other activities. The emphasis for the environmentalist is that of the context: it is the context within which language is used that enables the child to successfully learn its mother tongue.

Halliday points out that while both of these theories attempt to understand what is essential about language, to discover its nature, they remain theories that are psychologically derived. The fact that the process of learning a language takes place within a particular situation where the child uses language for its specific needs demonstrates the importance of taking into consideration a functional and sociological approach to language. This approach examines the social processes that enable individuals to both interact and transmit their culture. This is not to say that psychologically based theories are redundant; for Halliday the psychological and the sociological approaches go hand in hand as they focus on different aspects of language learning.

Adopting the functionalist approach to understanding how children learn a language entails examining the function of language in their lives. Halliday uses the concept of language in a broad sense to include the sounds children use to communicate their meanings; at times he uses the term 'proto language' to describe the communication of children. This view is opposed to traditional accounts of child linguistic acquisition insofar as children are not said to have a language until they use the formal resources of their mother tongue. For Halliday if the child consistently and regularly uses the same sound and meaning to achieve a specific function, then the child is said to possess a language. The question remains, why should studying the way children develop a language be useful in understanding the nature of language? There are four reasons that justify this approach: (1) the same questions can be asked of adult language; (2) it is easier to answer questions concerning functional meaning of young children than of adults; (3) the explanation of why children develop language is related to their motivation for using it, that is, to satisfy their needs; (4) a developmental approach to language sheds light on the nature of language itself. As Halliday pointedly remarks, 'Language is as it is because of what it has to do' (1978: 19).

Halliday introduces the term 'meaning potential' to express the idea that the early language of the child is there to fulfil certain functions. They do not involve the use of a formal language such as English but use sounds and meanings to obtain what they want (unlike crying or sneezing). At this early stage, the child learns how to mean by using language to fulfil a number of functions, within which an increasing number of choices are possible. These are:

1. The instrumental function, where the child is interested in satisfying material needs. This is the language used to obtain goods and services irrespective of who provides them. ('I want.')
2. The regulatory function, where the child is interested in controlling the behaviour of others. ('Do as I tell you.')
3. The interactional function, where the child is interested in relating to others. Language is used to interact with others, from the mother early in life to other adults and peers. ('Me and you')
4. The personal function, where the child is interested in expressing itself and its identity (emotions, wishes). ('Here I come.')
5. The heuristic function, where the child is interested in exploring the external and internal world. Language is used to learn about the environment that is now perceived as separate from oneself. ('Tell me why.')
6. The imaginative function, where the child is interested in creating a world through stories or games. ('Let's pretend.')

7. The informative (or representational) function, where the child is interested in transmitting new information to others who do not have this information ('I've got something to tell you') (1978: 19–20).

Halliday points to an interesting paradox that characterizes the language development of children. Although all children eventually learn an adult language, during the passage from childhood to adulthood, each child undergoes different experiences in learning the language so that the process of learning the language is unique for each child. The paradox is that while every child learns it differently, every child learns the same language.

However, despite the differences of each child's experiences it must be remembered that the language and environment of the child are framed within a culture. The role of culture is important for Halliday (1978: 23) and he elaborates upon the relationship between language and culture by pointing out that (1) one feature of a culture is its linguistic environment and this influences the child's choice of language, together with any dialects of the child's particular socioregional subculture. (2) It is through language that cultural values are transmitted to the child and just as the child learns the language he/she is also learning the value systems and norms of behaviour of that culture. Its importance is such that Halliday considers educational failure to be the result of the cultural environment not the linguistic one. Drawing upon the empirical work of Bernstein he writes that 'what determines the actual cultural-linguistic configuration is, essentially, the social structure, the system of social relations, in the family and other key social groups, which is characteristic of a particular subculture' (1978: 24).

The development of language follows a trajectory of 'behaviour potential' through which we relate to others, to a 'meaning potential' through which we communicate following the rules of grammar and vocabulary (the 'lexicogrammatical system') what we want to mean (the 'semantic system'). Language is a form of verbal doing through meaning. Halliday's account explains the nature of language: it has evolved in this way because of what it is required to do, requirements that are found in any culture. These include:

1. The possibility of interpreting all our experiences: language must be able to order the internal and external worlds (consciousness, events, actions and classes of objects).
2. The possibility of expressing both logical relations ('and', 'or') and other linguistic relations ('namely', 'means').
3. The possibility of self-expression as speakers, role bearers and subjectivities (wishes, emotions, judgements).
4. The possibility of doing the aforementioned simultaneously by being connected to a context: 'it has to be capable of being organized as relevant discourse, not just as words and sentences in a grammar-book or dictionary' (1978: 22).

A sociosemiotic theory of language

Halliday's sociolinguistic theory of language employs a number of concepts. These are the concepts of text, situation, register, code, linguistic system and social structure.

The concept of text

The concept of the text describes any linguistic interaction (spoken, written) between people within a context. It is defined as 'whatever is said, or written, in an operational context, as distinct from a citational context like that of words listed in a dictionary' (1978: 109). This definition is broad in scope and includes anything from speech acts and events, topic units, episodes, narratives and so on[2] (1978: 60). Halliday uses the term 'supersentence' to describe a text since it is like a sentence but much bigger. However, he is quick to qualify this claim by adding that a text should not be construed merely as a combination or accumulation of sentences, but as 'semantic unit' in itself, as a whole. The important point is that a text represents the choices of meaning that the speaker has selected and manifested with a particular lexicogrammatical structure. While a culture can be defined in terms of a network of meaning potential, with the linguistic system as sub-species of meaning potential, a text itself constitutes actualized meaning potential (1978: 109, 122).

The concept of situation types

A text does not exist in isolation but is firmly connected to a context of situation. The concept of context of situation is important because it is only within a situation that language is alive and dynamic. Language is not a phenomenon that takes place in isolation from specific situations involving by persons, actions and events, each of which contributing to the meaning. The situation is inbuilt within the use of language, but as Firth had already pointed out it is not necessary for the language used to be directly connected to the situation; rather the concept of situation is an abstraction from the environment using general categories that are relevant to the text. Thus, if we try to understand the language use of children the immediate environment is relevant as their language is directly connected to it. However, if we try to understand more technical language, the language being used is related to a problem that is not immediately apparent in the material environment. It is the latter capability of using language in abstraction from the immediate context that distinguishes the language of adults from that of children (1978: 109, 229–30).

For the concept of situation to be a part of a sociolinguistic theory, it will require further abstraction into what Halliday calls the 'situation type' by which he means 'the configuration of environmental factors that typically fashions our ways of speaking and writing' (1978: 230). By refining the concept of situation into that of situation type he is able to outline a theoretical framework that will enable the analysis move from that of situation type to text and vice versa.

The semiotic structure of a situation type is derived from the field, tenor and mode:

> The field is the social action in which the text is embedded; it includes the subject-matter, as one special manifestation. The tenor is the set of role relationships among the relevant participants; it includes the levels of formality as one particular instances. The mode is the channel or wavelength elected, which is essentially the function that is assigned to language in the total structure of the situation; it includes the medium (spoken or written), which is explained as a functional variable. (1978: 110)

1. The field of discourse describes what is happening and this usually includes a number of actions that are usually linked together in some sequence. The field of discourse 'is what the participants in the context of situation are actually engaged in doing' (1978: 222) with the text and its subject matter as one aspect of it (1978: 142–43). Halliday offers an example to illustrate the field of discourse by describing the situation of buying and selling a newspaper: although in the act of buying it we might talk about the weather, the field of discourse remains that of buying the newspaper, not meteorology (1978: 222, 143–44).
2. The concept of tenor describes socially meaningful relationships between participants. Roles are a feature of these relations and while they can be permanent they can also be specific to the situation with various degrees of formality (1978: 110, 144). Other aspects include the duration of the relationship or the emotional relation between participants. Halliday describes a number of contexts within which role-relationships reflect the language used; these range from teacher/pupil, parent/child, doctor/patient to casual acquaintances on a train and so on (1978: 222).
3. The concept of mode describes the function of language, what it is being used for: is it being used to persuade or to sell or to explain? Halliday distinguishes between mode and medium: the mode is the purpose of the linguistic exchange while the medium is the tool being used – spoken or written – to fulfil that purpose. The mode–medium dichotomy is not always clear-cut, as there are times the mode is influenced by the medium such as (for example) the difference between a written advertisement and sales talk. It is a difference, according to Halliday, grounded in the different functions of language (1978: 222–23, 144–45).

The importance of the concepts of field, tenor and mode is that together they constitute the background or context of situation that determines the kind of language that should be used, that is, the register; they are not found segregated from each other but operate together and it is because the speaker knows about the field, tenor and mode that he/she is able to predict what is appropriate to the context and therefore continue the conversation (1978: 223). They are not the way language is used and neither are they just aspects of the total speech situation. This is why he emphasizes that they are not the way language is used, nor are they just aspects of the total speech situation; their function is more constitutive since they provide the conceptual framework with which an analysis of the social context – as the space within which meanings are exchanged – can be conducted (1978: 110).

The concept of register

If the way language is used varies according to the situation, then the concept of register is an important tool in helping us understand the way various situations determine various linguistic features. Within a certain situation (e.g. an office meeting) a formal use of language is required so that one person might consider his/her colleagues' informal use of language as inappropriate, as a case of using the wrong register. Registers are defined as 'configurations of meanings that are typically exchanged – that are 'at risk', so to speak – under given conditions of use' (1978: 185).

While it is an obvious truism that language is activated within a context, and therefore refers to it, Halliday points out that the analysis of the relationship of language to situation is not one of identifying the vocabulary, grammar or pronunciation used within that situation but rather a specification of which situations generate which linguistic selections (1978: 32).

By being able to specify the situation one can predict the language that will be used. Halliday asks: what is it about the social context that one needs to know to make such predictions possible? The difficulty this question raises is that it is not necessarily the case that one is actually using language related to what one is doing at the moment (1978: 32–33). There are three things that one needs to know about the situation in order to predict the language that is most likely to be used. These are the field, tenor and mode, and they constitute what is linguistically significant in a situation; they are, in effect, the register and their function to connect what is said with how it is said. Halliday specifies that this should create a misleading separation of what is said from how it is said, since language is always actualized in some context so that the 'what' is always connected to the 'how'.

Although the concept of register explains language variety, there is another distinctive explanation for this variety. Halliday contrasts registers with dialects and while the former can be described as ways of saying different things the latter are different ways of saying the same thing. Dialects are oriented towards the speaker, on who the person is, and depend largely on region or origin of the person; they involve an understanding of the hierarchies pertaining to social structures. Registers are oriented towards the language used in relation to the situation type and reflect various and ongoing social processes; the variety of social processes mirror the variety of possible registers (1978: 185).

The concept of code

Halliday's analysis of codes is greatly influenced by the sociolinguistic studies of Basil Bernstein (1924–2000), whose research revealed the connection between the social structure and the various linguistic codes found in a culture. Bernstein's empirical research (1971) uncovered the connection between the working class and their use of 'restricted codes' and the middle class and their use of 'elaborated codes'. Typical features of the restricted code are a lesser degree of informality and the use of short phrases in the middle of or at the end of sentences to confirm understanding. The use of elaborated codes involves complicated and complete sentence structures with infrequently used words. It is during the process of socialization that children learn their codes and while children from working-class families only learn the restricted codes, children from middle-class families learn both.

The concept of codes describes the way social structures regulate access to language. Within a culture or subculture, codes function to filter the types of register that can be used. They are 'the principle of semiotic organization governing the choice of meanings by a speaker and their interpretation by a hearer' (1978: 111). Unlike registers (and dialects), they are 'outside' the linguistic system even though they are actualized in language through the register used. Codes are part of the social system (1978: 111).

It is during the process of socialization that the child learns which codes to use, and since it is codes that regulate the meanings of texts these become crucial transmitters of culture. A two-way process takes place, for as the child is transformed into a member of a culture by appropriating its code, the child will, in turn, continue to transmit that culture (1978: 123). The interesting thing is that while the environment of each child is different they share a common social background of social roles and systems. It is these that determine the choices of meaning that the child will adopt and that contribute in an essential way to the socialization of the child. While all children have access to the meaning potential of the linguistic system, the different social groups to which children belong give rise to different interpretations of which are the appropriate linguistic codes to use in particular situations.

The concept of linguistic system

In his discussion of the linguistic system, Halliday points out that from the lexicogrammatical, phonological and semantic systems that constituted a language it is the semantic system that is crucial for an understanding of the sociolinguistic context (1978: 111). An analysis of the semantic system shows that it is functional but, and this is crucial to Hallidayan linguistics, the functionality of language must not be construed as the use of language with the speaker positioned 'externally' to it so as to achieve certain things. Rather, language is functionally organized from an internal perspective and Halliday calls the internal functions of the semantic system 'metafunctions' (1978: 112–13, 128). They are as follows:

1. The ideational function represents the content of linguistic communication or what the communication is about. The content can be about the world, objects, events, persons, oneself and even language itself. Through the ideational function, language encodes the experiences of a culture just as the individual – as a member of that culture who has inherited these linguistic codes – is able to encode his/her own personal experiences. Elsewhere, Halliday distinguishes between the experiential and the logical aspects of the ideational so that while the experiential focusses on the experience and expression of participants in certain processes with qualities and circumstances that these entail, the logical focusses on the linguistic expression of logical connectors such as 'and', 'or' (1978: 48–49, 187).

2. The interpersonal function represents the participation of the speaker in the situation. This is the domain of action where the speaker does something with language by intervening within the context of situation so as to express his/her attitudes, judgements or attempt to influence others. The context of situation gives rise to certain social roles such as those of 'questioner-respondent', 'informer-doubter', and so on.

3. The textual function represents language in context as opposed to language in isolation or abstracted from the context. The textual function weaves together language, whether spoken or written, with the environment whether verbal or non-verbal. The textual function is crucial in that it is only through this function that the ideational or the interpersonal functions can be actualized.

While the three 'metafunctions' have been examined individually, Halliday points out that the three are found together whenever and in whichever social context: '[e]ach functional component contributes a band of structure to the whole' (1978: 112).

The concept of social structure

The social structure is the form or organization of a particular society (1978: 113). It provides the background for a sociolinguistic theory constituting an important tool on account of:

1. The significance it gives to the various social contexts. It is the social structure that determines which of the values of a situation type – field (social activities), tenor (social roles and status) and mode (rhetorical styles) – are to be given central importance.

2. The significance it gives to the patterns of communication within the family and to the monitoring of meanings that are circulated within other social contexts. Through the socialization process the child is inducted into certain codes that allow access to certain registers.

3. The significance it gives to social hierarchy as manifested in class and caste, which in turn explain different social dialects. These are a direct expression of social hierarchy whilst simultaneously functioning to maintain the status quo.

Given the importance of semantics for the understanding of the sociolinguistic context, Halliday elaborates on what a sociological semantics entails. Within a situation type a number of meaning options are available and these are transformed into semantic choices reconfigured into lexicogrammatical combinations. Since the analysis of situation types depends upon the field, tenor and mode, then the situation type influences the selection of meanings that generate the text. There is, therefore, a correspondence between the characteristics of the situation type and the choices made in the semantic system.

> [...] the type of symbolic activity (field) tends to determine the range of meaning as content, language in the observer function (ideational); the role relationships (tenor) tend to determine the range of meaning as participation, language in the intruder function (interpersonal); and the rhetorical channel (mode) tends to determine the range of meaning as texture, language in its relevance to the environment (textual). (1978: 117, 189)

The choices in meaning will, therefore, vary according to whether the texts differ with regard to field, tenor or mode.[3] A sociological semantics will examine the following.

1. The semantics of situation types: Sociological semantics is not a general theory of linguistic semantics but a context-specific account that identifies the semantics of a situation type. This semantics is positioned between the social system and the linguistic system where it realizes social meanings in the lexicogrammatical forms of the text (1978: 114).
2. The structure of the situation and its relation to the semantic system: The semiotic structure of the situation type follows the pattern of the field (a child playing), the tenor (the exchanges between the parent and child) and the mode (variously dialogue and monologue). There is a parallel between the semiotic structure of the situation type and the semantic functions of the linguistic system: in this respect, the field parallels the ideational functions of meaning, the tenor parallels the interpersonal functions of meaning and the mode parallels the textual functions. Halliday (1978: 116–17) argues that such a parallelism is not just a 'coincidence': given that language evolved between people in social contexts, it seems only natural that these functions evolved internally to language. The relationship between situation, text and semantic system is a continuous one since the semiotics of the situation activates the corresponding semantics in a specific register that generates a text that is appropriate to the situation.
3. The sociosemantics of language development. At the early stages of a child's 'proto-linguistic' development, the meaning potential that the child is learning is directly correlated to a small number of social functions, such as (for example) the regulatory function from which the child learns to control the behaviour of others. These social functions configure the world of the child constructing his/her social semiotic (1978: 121).

The difficult question is that of explaining how the child arrives from these basic functions to the complexities of the adult semantic system. The starting point is clearly what Halliday calls 'proto-contexts' inasmuch as they ultimately generate the future social contexts and the semantic system. As the child learns, he/she moves from the six functions of his/her 'proto-language' to a basic classification of language as a form of doing and a form of knowing or learning. At around 18 months, each utterance of the early six functions can be located within either the 'doing' or the 'knowing' category. This localization is performed though the intonation: when an utterance is a 'doing' one it has a rising tone, while when it is a 'learning' one it has a falling tone. At this stage, linguistic interaction is restricted to the 'doing' form as it is in this mode that a response is expected. For the child to engage in true dialogue with others it is necessary for this state to be superseded. What is needed is a semiotic system that enables both the learning and the doing to be actualized simultaneously, that is, in a single utterance. This process takes place in two steps: (1) there is an abstraction of these functions into the semantic system so that the learning form is part of the 'ideational' and the doing form is part of the 'interpersonal'; (2) the development of the lexicogrammar (syntax) whereby two sets of meaning can be simultaneously expressed in one utterance.

The difference between the adult language system and that of the child is that with adult language each utterance is multifunctional such that each has an ideational, interpersonal and textual meaning, while that of the child is mono-functional with each function related specifically to its use. The child's development is a process of learning 'how to mean' where from basic functional uses of language the child develops a more general and abstract system so that by the age of (about) 2 years the child has the basis for an adult language system involving meta-functions. This is the process of the 'sociosemantics of language development' (1978: 121).

Halliday and the development of social semiotics

The ideas of Halliday have influenced a number of theorists and social semiotics now flourishes as a branch of semiotics in its own right. In this section, I will outline the social semiotics of Robert Hodge and Gunther Kress who in *Social Semiotics* (1988) provide a conceptual framework for the analysis of texts that highlights the importance of the social context in the study of signs. Traditional or 'mainstream semiotics' focussed on the structures, codes or systems of signs in isolation as opposed to the processes of interaction by participants within social contexts (1988: 2). Hodge and Kress's analysis of the social context necessitates the introduction of a number of concepts:

1. The ideological complex: the point of departure for the social semiotics of Hodge and Kress is Marxist in the sense that society is theorized as being constituted by a parallel relationship between the social/material world and the kind of sign systems that circulate within that society; although parallel, these sign systems depend upon the social/material world for their continued existence (1988: 2–3). Within any society there are two groups: those who dominate and those who are dominated. Each of these groups has its own

interests at heart but it is the dominating group that represents the world that satisfies its own interests and which it imposes upon the dominated groups as the 'true version' of the world. In addition, for the dominating group to maintain its power it must project an image of solidarity with the dominated as it would be challenged. In turn, while traditional Marxist account portrays the dominated as passive 'victims', resistance can take place in many different forms.

2. Hodge and Kress use the term 'ideological complex' to describe the contradictions that arise in the conflict of visions between the dominant and the dominated. On the one hand, the dominant consider their vision of the world as the true one and attempt to impose it on the dominated; while on the other hand, the dominated have their own vision and therefore attempt to resist the dominant group. The function of the ideological complex is to maintain social order and it is composed of (1) 'relational models' which function to classify social agents, actions and objects, and so on; and (2) 'actional models' which function to regulate the behaviour of social agents (1988: 3).

3. Logonomic systems: the problem is that given the existence of the two opposing groups it would seem that any message communicated by the dominant group would be merely rejected by the dominated group. To explain the functioning of the ideological complex, Hodge and Kress introduce another level of meaning which focusses on the production and reception of messages. They call it the logonomic system and it 'is a set of rules prescribing the conditions for production and reception of meanings; which specify who can claim to initiate (produce, communicate) or know (receive, understand) meanings about what topics under what circumstances and with what modalities (how, when, why)' (1988: 4). The logonomic system serves the ideological complex by making the messages of the dominant groups transparent so as to further their dominance, but even as they attempt to do so, a close observation of the semiotic process reveals the different forms and sites of resistance (1988: 7).

4. Messages, texts and discourses: the basic unit that constitutes the semiotic process is the message. It is produced and exchanged at the 'semiotic plane' and it refers to, or represents something beyond itself, the 'mimetic plane' (1988: 5). Messages are embedded within a social context and are directed at a purpose. Messages do not 'float' around on their own but are transformed into texts. This does not mean that a text is merely the sum total of messages within it but rather that the text is constituted as a text socially by incorporating structured messages and their traces as a unity. A text is a material object representing something in the world and so placing it within the mimetic plane. Texts are generated within discourses so that the latter concerns the system of production and circulation of texts; discourses function at the semiotic plane. Hodge and Kress point out that one should not think of text/messages and discourse as opposed to each other, since discourse belongs to the semiotic plane and text/messages to the mimetic plane. Both sets of concepts are interrelated features of the same social processes, so (for example) the discourse of medicine has a number of meanings that are appropriate to that institution and its members (doctors, surgeons, nurses, researchers) employ those

meanings as messages and texts. It is in the circulation of meanings by the participants that the discourse is validated or challenged (1988: 6).

5. Genres are systems of rules that connect producers with consumers to topics through a medium in a particular manner and on a certain occasion (1988: 7). These rules are a prime example of logonomic rules and function to correlate the behaviour of the producers with the expectations of the consumers. The generation of a genre is a social event and the boundaries of a genre are policed in the sense of specifying which types of actions are permitted by the participants.

In *Social Semiotics*, Hodge and Kress apply their conceptual framework to a number of different areas such as style, the real, time and narrative. However, given the emphasis of social semiotics on the centrality of the context for an understanding of meaning, I want to conclude this section with an overview of their analysis of traffic lights (1988: 37–40). As they rightly point out, it would seem that not much can be said about them if one ignores the context within which they are situated and it is by contextualizing them that their social and ideological implications can be understood. The starting point for the analysis of traffic lights is their location: they are situated at an intersection and their colours inform motorists, who must be included as part of the message, on how to proceed. Within this context, motorists have certain expectations about the way others will behave as they read the colours.

The interesting point made in this analysis is that not everybody reads traffic signs in the same way. Reading such texts depends on class, gender and so on. So (for example) in Sydney some motorists read amber as 'speed up if you are approaching the traffic lights' and red as 'just turned red' and 'red for a few seconds' with the former understood as 'proceed through the intersection'. Green no longer means 'proceed' but 'proceed after checking for the possible presence of users of the other dialect' and this applies not only to the particular group but to everybody. The transformation of the meaning of traffic lights by a particular group has had a ripple effect upon all motorists. To understand why such a transformation took place, Hodge and Kress suggest one would have to examine any number of social factors ranging from the conditions of traffic and commuting times, attitudes related to authority and gender, different ethnicities and so on.

The social and ideological reading of traffic signs is explicitly related to the lack of human subjects in their actual functioning which depends upon (1) an electrical system for the operation and synchronization of traffic lights and (2) the state that guarantees that traffic lights function in an equal, rational and benign way to all its citizens. However, despite this benevolent picture the state deploys a police force to ensure that infractions are punished. The ideological vision communicated by traffic lights is that of a state that is good to everybody and it is because citizens buy into this belief that they diligently obey the traffic lights day in day out. Hodge and Kress highlight the importance of power and solidarity both in their analysis of traffic lights but also in their other analyses throughout the text. The power dimension the case of traffic lights has already been alluded to in the way traffic lights command obedience, with violations resulting in penalties. Solidarity is the flip side of power in that motorists are 'formed' into two groups, those driving without hitting each other and those who are stationary. As Hodge and Kress point out,

> The traditional illustration of traffic lights should be stripped of its implicit ideology of the communication process. Semiosis is never simple, clear and rational, even when it is operated by electricity. We assume that it always involves conflict, disagreement, a lack of clarity and consensus, even in the seemingly simple instance of the traffic lights. (1988: 39–40)

Critical remarks

There is a growing and widespread interest in Halliday's work, and his views on language are so innovative that Butler suggests one 'suspend certain pre-conceptions' about language if one wants to understand his approach (1985: 1). There are, however, some features of his work that Berry (1982: 64–94) has pointed out require some attention: (1) Halliday's definitions of the categories of field, tenor and mode – all fundamental for the analysis of the situation type – are not specific enough. The result has been that other linguists have placed other features under each of these categories such that Gregory (for example) places rhetoric under the category of tenor while Halliday places it within the category of mode. (2) Halliday's work, and in particular *Language as a Social Semiotic*, presents an 'outline' of a theory of language but not a complete one, and neither Halliday nor any other systemic linguist has filled in the outline. The problem, she argues, is of Halliday's own doing in that he rules out the methods typically used by linguists to check their theories and in so doing excluding himself and others from providing an alternative.

There is no doubt that the foundation of Halliday's theory of language lies with its emphasis on the context of situation. This is evident in the early empirical studies on language that focussed on the way children used language to fulfil their needs and in the later Halliday who considered the context of situation as a basic theoretical requirement for an understanding of language use within society.

His point of departure for the analysis of language and society is the social system, since it is within the larger category of society that one finds a network of interrelated meanings. These meanings are behavioural in the sense that a person's behaviour is itself meaningful and this constitutes the domain of action that Halliday calls the 'can do'. However, within any human society there is another set of (linguistic) meaning where what we 'can do' is translated into what we 'can mean' through the process of what we 'can say'. In his analysis of the relationship between language and society, language is a form of action that enables meaningful interaction to take place between members of that society.

In this chapter, I have highlighted (1) the contributions by Malinowski and Firth towards the understanding of language and proceeded with (2) a detailed description of what the concept of social semiotics entails for Halliday. This is followed (3) by his elaboration of the components – the text, situation, register, code, social structure and linguistic system – that constitute a sociolinguistic theory of language. The final section examines (4) the way Hodge and Kress have developed Halliday's social semiotics.

Notes

1. An example of the application of Firth's categories to the text and the context of situation can be seen in the work of T. F. Mitchell, who studied the 'language of buying and selling' in North Africa.
2. Butler (1985: 63) writes, 'A text could be as short as a one-sentence public notice, or as long as a whole committee meeting or a novel.'
3. See Halliday for an analysis of child play (1978: 115) or for the analysis of a literary text (1978: 145).

Conclusion

The purpose of this text has been to demonstrate the theoretical background to communication studies. These studies are frequently associated with matters related to film, television, Web design, advertising, photography and journalism. However, such practical activities are organized within a theoretical framework: theory and practice are not divorced but symbiotically interrelated. It is, therefore, fruitful to provide an account of this theoretical framework, and the *Philosophical Approaches to Communication* offers an initial overview of the various aspects entailed by the concept of communication.

In dealing with the production of communication, I have examined the role of the context of production as it features in the work of Ferdinand de Saussure, Charles Sanders Peirce and Michel Foucault. Saussure inaugurated the study of signs as an internally regulated system that can be explained without reference to the world. Peirce also studied sign-systems, but his account is broader, in that it is not limited to an examination of the conventional signs of a language but seeks to explain the way everything – perception, nature, the universe – can be understood as signs. Foucault's early writings show the way knowledge is produced and transmitted by employing a number of concepts – episteme and discourse – to describe this process. In his later writings, he shifts emphasis to the relationship between discourse and power as they percolate from within institutional sites to society in general.

From the context of production I then proceeded to examine the context of reception. Chapters 4–7 focussed on the way messages are received and interpreted. I started with an overview of Umberto Eco's theory of codes, which explains how messages are interpreted keeping in mind the 'encyclopaedia' that conditions the competence of the addressee in the act of interpretation. While the theory of codes allows Eco to study the interpretation of signs in general, he is also interested in applying his insights to the narrower domain of textual interpretation. After Eco, I turned to Derrida, whose view on the nature of language as a disseminating 'force' has influenced his account of the interpretation of texts. This account is considered radical in that it allows language to escape from the control of the author. Gadamer highlights the importance of language in the interpretation of messages while articulating interpretation in terms of a dialogical relationship between the interpreter and the text.

In chapters 7–12, I examined the relationship between communication and the context within which actions take place. The starting point is the work of L. Wittgenstein, whose fundamental contribution to the idea of language as an activity entailed an examination of language from the context in which it is used. In the next chapter I turn to the writings of J. L. Austin, who elaborated upon the idea that through the process of communicating one is doing something, performing an action. Traditionally, the study of language had focussed on descriptive statements, while Austin introduced the notion of performative utterances as playing an important role in the communicative exercise. This account segregates language into two groups – constatives and performatives, a segregation that Austin later goes on to reconfigure in his theory of speech acts. P. Grice and J. Searle both develop Austin's ideas. Grice's analysis of conversational interactions led to the development of the idea of conversation implicature, a discussion of the maxims that govern conversations, and an outline of the ways in which such rules or maxims may be flouted, possibly, leading to the breakdown of the process of communication. Searle extends the analysis of speech acts to elaborate the necessary conditions for the generation of speech acts while also providing a classification that accounts for their various types. The work of Habermas combines the insights of speech act theory with social theory. His theory of communicative action attempts to explain the way a society can evolve rationally – despite conflicts – through the process of communication. The final chapter examines the social semiotics of Halliday that aims to highlight the social dimension of language together with the constituent conceptual framework needed for a sociolinguistic theory of language.

The philosophy of communication is a growing branch within both philosophy and communication studies, and although it has been traditionally studied as part of the philosophy of language, it is rapidly achieving an identity of its own. This text hopes to make a small contribution in that direction.

Bibliography

Abhik, Roy and Starosta, William J (2001), 'Hans-Georg Gadamer, language, and intercultural communication', *Language and Intercultural Communication*, 1: 1, pp. 6–20.

Austin, J. L. (1975), *How to Do Things with Words*, Cambridge: Harvard University Press.

—— (1979), *Philosophical Papers*, Oxford: Oxford University Press.

Barthes, Roland (1993), *Mythologies*, London: Vintage.

Bernstein, Basil (1971), *Theoretical Studies Towards a Sociology of Language*, London: Routledge and Kegan Paul.

Berry, M. (1982), 'Review of Halliday 1978', *Nottingham Linguistic Circular*, 11, pp. 64–94.

Best, Steven and Kellner, Douglas (1991), *Postmodern Theory: Critical Interrogations*, London: Macmillan Press.

Bondella, Peter (2005), *Umberto Eco and the Open Text*, Cambridge: Cambridge University Press.

Botz-Bornstein, Thorsten (2003), 'Nishida and Wittgenstein: From 'pure experience' to *Lebensform* or new perspectives for a philosophy of intercultural communication', *Asian Philosophy*, 13: 1, pp. 53–70.

Branigan, Edward (2005), 'Wittgenstein, Language-Games, Film Theory', http: //www.filmandmedia. ucsb.edu/people/faculty/professors/branigan/SCMStalkWitt05.pdf. Accessed 11 November 2010.

—— (2006), *Projecting a Camera*, London: Routledge and Kegan Paul.

Brunette, Peter (1986), 'Toward a deconstructive theory of film', *Studies in the Literary Imagination*, 19: 1, pp. 55–71.

Brunette, Peter and Wills, David (1989), *Screen/Play: Derrida and Film Theory*, Princeton, NJ: Princeton University Press.

Butler, Christopher S. (1985), *Systemic Linguistics*, London: Batsford Academic.

Butler, Judith (1997), *Excitable Speech*, London: Routledge and Kegan Paul.

Caesar, Michael (1999), *Umberto Eco*, Cambridge: Polity Press.

Cassar, Mary Ann (2006), *Logic, laughter and laughter-provocation*, Unpublished doctoral dissertation, University of Malta.

Chapman, Siobhan (2005), *Paul Grice: Philosopher and Linguist*, Hampshire: Palgrave Macmillan.

Cosenza, Giovanna (ed.) (2001), *Paul Grice's Heritage*, Bologna: Brepols Publishers.

Culler, Jonathan (1982), *On Deconstruction: Theory and Criticism After Structuralism*, Ithaca, NY: Cornell University Press.

—— (1985), *Saussure*, London: Fontana.

Derrida, Jacques (1976), *Of Grammatology* (trans. Gayatari Spivak), Baltimore, MD: John Hopkins University Press.

—— (1978), *Writing and Difference*, London: Routledge.

—— (1981), *Dissemination* (trans. Barbara Johnson), Chicago: The University of Chicago Press.

—— (1982), *Margins of Philosophy* (trans. Alan Bass), Chicago: The University of Chicago Press.

—— (1983), 'Letter to a Japanese friend', http: //hydra.humanities.uci.edu/derrida/letter.html. Accessed 15 January 2009.

—— (1988), *Limited Inc.*, Evanston, IL: Northwestern University Press.

—— (2002), *Positions*, London: Continuum.

De Saussure, Ferdinand (1983), *Course in General Linguistics* (trans. Roy Harris), London: Duckworth.

De Waal, Cornelius (2001), *On Peirce*, Belmont, CA: Wadsworth.

Dooley Mark, and Kavanagh, Liam (2007), *The Philosophy of Derrida*, Durham, NC: Acumen Publishers.

Eco, Umberto (1976), *A Theory of Semiotics*, Bloomington and Indianapolis, IN: Indiana University Press.

—— (1979), *The Role of the Reader*, Bloomington and Indianapolis, IN: Indiana University Press.

—— (1984), *Semiotics and the Philosophy of Language*, Bloomington and Indianapolis, IN: Indiana University Press.

—— (1990), *The Limits of Interpretation*, Indianapolis, IN: Indiana University Press.

—— (1992), *Interpretation and Overinterpretation*, Cambridge: Cambridge University Press.

—— (1995), *Six Walks in the Fictional Woods*, Cambridge, MA: Harvard University Press.

Edgar, Andrew (2005), *The Philosophy of Habermas*, Durham: Acumen Publishers.

—— (2006), *Habermas*, London: Routledge.

Fann, K. T. (1969), *Wittgenstein's Conception of Philosophy*, Oxford: Basil Blackwell.

Finlayson, James Gordon (2005), *Habermas: A Very Short Introduction*, Oxford: Oxford University Press.

Firth, R. John (1957), *Papers in Linguistics 1934–1951*, London: Oxford University Press.

Fiske, John (1990), *Introduction to Communication Studies*, London: Routledge.

Fotion, Nick (2000), John Searle, Teddington: Acumen Publishing Limited.

Foucault, Michel (1970), *The Order of Things*, London: Tavistock Pulications.

—— (1972), *The Archeology of Knowledge and The Discourse of Language*, New York: Pantheon Books.

—— (1978), *The History of Sexuality*, vol. 1 (trans. R. Hurley), New York: Pantheon Books.

—— (1991), *Discipline and Punish* (trans. A. Sheridan), Harmondsworth: Penguin Books Ltd.

—— (1993), *Madness and Civilisation*, London: Routledge.

Friggieri, Joe (1991), *Actions and Speech Actions in the Philosophy of J. L. Austin*, Malta: Gutenberg Press.

Gadamer, Hans-Georg (1977), *Philosophical Hermeneutics*, Berkeley, CA: University of California Press.

—— (1989), *Truth and Method*, New York: The Continuum Publishing Company.

Gary, Richmond (2008), 'Cultural pragmatism and *The Life of the Sign*', *Critical Arts*, 22: 2, pp. 155–65.

Gasche, Rudolphe (1988), *The Tain of the Mirror*, Cambridge, MA: Harvard University Press.

Gorner, Paul (2000), *Twentieth Century German Philosophy*, Oxford: Oxford University Press.

Graham, Keith (1977), *J. L. Austin: A Critique of Ordinary Language Philosophy*, Atlantic Highlands, NJ: Humanities Press, Inc.

Grayling, C. Anthony (1988), *Wittgenstein*, Oxford: Oxford University Press.

Grice, Paul (1989), *Studies in the Way of Words*, Cambridge, MA: Harvard University Press.

Gutting, Gary (2001), *French Philosophy in the Twentieth Century*, Cambridge, Cambridge University Press.

Habermas, Jurgen (1987a), *The Theory of Communicative Action*, vol. 1 (trans. Thomas McCarthy), Cambridge: Polity Press.

—— (1987b), *The Theory of Communicative Action*, vol. 2 (trans. Thomas McCarthy), Cambridge: Polity Press.

—— (1987c), *The Philosophical Discourse of Modernity*, Cambridge: Polity in association with Blackwell.

—— (1988), *Legitimation Crisis*, Cambridge: Polity Press.

—— (1990), *Moral Consciousness and Communicative Action* (trans. Christian Lenhardt and Shierry Weber Nicholson), Cambridge, MA: MIT Press.

—— (2001), *On the Pragmatics of Social Interaction* (trans. Barbara Fultner), Cambridge: Polity.

—— (2002), *On the Pragmatics of Communication*, Maeve Cooke (ed.), Cambridge: Polity Press.

—— (2006), 'Political communication in media society: Does democracy still enjoy an epistemic dimension? The impact of normative theory on empirical research', *Communication Theory*, 16, pp. 411–26.

—— (1986), 'A Review of Gadamer's *Truth and Method*', in Brain Watchterhauser (ed.), *Hermeneutics and Modern Philosophy* (trans. Fred Dallmayr and Thomas McCarthy), Albany: State University of New York, pp. 213–44.

—— (1995), 'Peirce and communication', in Kenneth Ketner Laine (ed.), *Peirce and Contemporary Thought: Philosophical Inquiries*, New York: Fordham University Press, pp. 243–66.

Hahn, Stephen (2002), *On Derrida*, Belmont, CA: Wadsworth/Thomson Learning.

Halliday, A. K. Michael (1975), *Learning how to mean: explorations in the development of language*, London: Edward Arnold.

—— (1978), *Language as social semiotic: the social interpretation of language and meaning*, London: Edwards Arnold.

Hamilton, Paul (1996), *Historicism*, London: Routledge.

Hanfling, Oswald (2000), *Philosophy and Ordinary Language*, London: Routledge.

Heidegger, Martin (1962), *Being and Time*, Oxford: Blackwell.

Held, David (1980), *Introduction to Critical Theory*, Cambridge: Polity Press.

Hillis Miller, J. (2001), *Speech Acts in Literature*, Stanford, CA: Stanford University Press.

Hodge, Robert and Kress, Gunther (1988), *Social Semiotics*, Cambridge: Polity Press.

Holdcroft, David (1991), *Saussure: Signs, System and Arbitrariness*, Cambridge: Cambridge University Press.

Horster, Detlef (1992), *Habermas: An Introduction*, Stuttgart: Metzler.

Houser, Nathan and Kloeel, Christian (eds) (1992–1998a), *The Essential Peirce, Volume 1 (1867–1893)*, Bloomington and Indianapolis, IN: Indiana University Press.

—— (eds) (1992–1998b), *The Essential Peirce, Volume 2 (1893–1913)*, Bloomington and Indianapolis, IN: Indiana University Press.

Ketner Laine, Kenneth (ed.) (1995), *Peirce and Contemporary Thought: Philosophical Inquiries*, New York: Fordham University Press.

Lawn, Chris (2006), *Gadamer: A Guide for the Perplexed*, London: Continuum.

Levinson, Stephen (1983), *Pragmatics*, Cambridge: Cambridge University Press.

Lin-qiong, Yan (2007), 'Pragmatic interpretation of humour production and comprehension', *US-China Foreign Language*, 5: 4, pp. 17–20.

Lyotard, J. F. (1979), *The Postmodern Condition: A Report on Knowledge*, Manchester: Manchester University Press.

Malinowski, B. (1923), 'The problem of meaning in primitive languages', Supplement to Ogden, C. K. and Richards, I. A. (1952), *The Meaning of Meaning: A Study of the Influence of Language upon Thought and the Science of Symbolism*, London: Routledge and Kegan Paul, pp. 296–336.

McHoul, Alec and Grace, Wendy (1995), *A Foucault Primer*, London: UCL Press.

Merquior, J. G. (1985), *Foucault*, London: Fontana.

Merrell, Floyd (1995), *Peirce's Semiotics Now: A Primer*, Toronto, ON: Canadian Scholars Press Inc.

Michelfelder, Diane P. and Palmer, Richard E. (1989), *Dialogue and Deconstruction: The Gadamer-Derrida Encounter*, Albany: State University of New York Press.

Mills, Sarah (2003), *Michel Foucault*, London: Routledge.

Norris, Christopher (1987), *Derrida*, London: Fontana Modern Masters.

Oehler, Klaus (1995), 'A response to Habermas', in Kenneth Ketner Laine (ed.), *Peirce and Contemporary Thought: Philosophical Inquiries*, New York: Fordham University Press, pp. 267–71.

Palmer, F. R. (ed.) (1968), *Selected Papers of J. R. Firth 1952–1959*, London: Longman.

Poster, Mark (1990), *The Mode of Information*, Cambridge: Polity Press.

Radford, P. Gary (2003), *On Eco*, California: Wadsworth.

Ramsey, Eric Ramsey and Miller, David James (2003), *Experiences Between Philosophy and Communication: Engaging the Philosophical Contributions of Calvin O. Schrag*, Albany: State University of New York Press.

Read, Rupert and Goodenough, Jerry (eds) (2005), *Film as Philosophy: Essays on Cinema after Wittgenstein and Cavell*, Basingstoke, England; New York: Palgrave Macmillan

Ropars-Wuilleumier, Marie-Claire (1981), *Le Texte divisé*, Paris: Presses Univérsitaires de France.

Salih, Sarah (2002), *Butler*, London: Routledge.

Schirato, Tony and Yell, Susan (2000), *Communication and Culture: An Introduction*, London: Sage Publications.

Schmidt, Lawrence K. (2006), *Understanding Hermeneutics*, Stocksfield: Acumen Publishing Limited.

Searle, John (1969), *Speech Acts: An Essay in the Philosophy of Language*, Cambridge: Cambridge University Press.

—— (1977), 'Re-iterating the differences: A reply to Derrida', *Glyph 2. John Hopkins Textual Studies 7*, pp. 198–208.

—— (1983), *Intentionality*, Cambridge: Cambridge University Press.

—— (1984), *Minds, Brains and Science*, London: British Broadcasting Corporation.

—— (1985), *Expression and Meaning*, Cambridge: Cambridge University Press.

—— (1995), *The Construction of Social Reality*, London: Penguin Books.

Sebeok, Thomas (1995), 'Indexicality', in Kenneth Ketner Laine (ed.), *Peirce and Contemporary Thought: Philosophical Inquiries*, New York: Fordham University Press.

Serracino Inglott, Peter (1995), *Peopled Silence*, Malta: Malta University Publishers Ltd.

Shepperson, Arnold (2008), 'Realism, logic, and social communication: C.S. Peirce's classification of science in communication studies and journalism', *Critical Arts*, 22: 2, pp. 242–94.

Stevenson, Charles (1944), *Ethics and Language*, New Haven, CT: Yale University Press.

Strinati, Dominic (1995), *An Introduction to Theories of Popular Culture*, London: Routledge.

Stroll, Avrum (2002), *Wittgenstein*, Oxford: Oneworld Publications.

Sutton, John (2003), *Habermas and Contemporary Society*, Hampshire: Palgrave Macmillan.

Talisse, B. Robert and Aikin, F. Scott (2008), *Pragmatism*, Cornwall, ON: Continuum.

Warnke, Georgia (1987), *Gadamer: Hermeneutics, Tradition and Reason*, Cambridge: Polity Press.

West, David (1996), *An Introduction to Continental Philosophy*, Cambridge: Polity Press.

Wittgenstein, Ludwig (1921), *Tractatus Logico-Philosophicus*, London: Routledge and Kegan Paul.

—— (1953), *Philosophical Investigations*, Oxford: Blackwell.